Walt Disney World® *& Orlando*
FOR
DUMMIES®
9TH EDITION

by Laura Lea Miller

D0026885

WILEY

Wiley Publishing, Inc.

Walt Disney World® & Orlando For Dummies,® 9th Edition
Published by
Wiley Publishing, Inc.
111 River St.
Hoboken, NJ 07030-5774
www.wiley.com

For general information on our other products and services, please contact our Customer Care Department within the U.S. at 800-762-2974, outside the U.S. at 317-572-3993, or fax 317-572-4002.

For technical support, please visit www.wiley.com/techsupport.

Wiley also publishes its books in a variety of electronic formats. Some content that appears in print may not be available in electronic books.

ISBN: 978-0-470-38224-0

Manufactured in the United States of America

10 9 8 7 6 5 4 3 2 1

WILEY

About the Author

Laura Lea Miller is a freelance writer based in Orchard Park, New York, though she's spent countless hours scouring Central Florida's theme parks, resorts, and restaurants over the years — both with and without her five kids. A family-travel expert who religiously makes an annual pilgrimage (or two or three or more) to the Land the Mouse Built, and who summers in nearby St. Augustine, she's the author of *Frommer's Walt Disney World & Orlando 2009* and *Frommer's Walt Disney World & Orlando with Kids,* as well as a contributor to *Frommer's Florida.* She has even created a comprehensive Web site dedicated to family travel throughout Central Florida.

Author's Acknowledgments

Thanks to Amy Voss at the Orlando/Orange County Convention & Visitors Bureau, Gary Buchanan at Walt Disney World, Rhonda Murphy at Universal Orlando, and Jacquelyn Wilson at SeaWorld. Thanks also to all those who took the time out of their schedules to help me with this endeavor. A special thanks goes out to my family, most especially my five children — Ryan, Austin, Nicolas, Hailey, and Davis — for all of their assistance in helping to research and write this book.

Thanks as well to my agent, Julie Hill, whose constant encouragement, support, and enthusiasm keep me going.

And, of course, a very special thanks to my editor, Naomi Kraus, whose continued support and encouragement as well as her extensive knowledge of all things Disney have made this book more than just a Mickey Mouse affair.

Publisher's Acknowledgments

We're proud of this book; please send us your comments through our Dummies online registration form located at www.dummies.com/register/.

Some of the people who helped bring this book to market include the following:

Editorial

Editors: Katie Robinson, Production Editor; Leslie Shen, Development Editor; Naomi Kraus, Project Editor

Copy Editor: Anne Owen

Cartographer: Elizabeth Puhl

Editorial Assistant: Jessica Langan-Peck

Senior Photo Editor: Richard Fox

Cover Photos:

Front: Kali River Rapids, Animal Kingdom (© Disney)

Back: Incredible Hulk Coaster, Islands of Adventure (© ICIMAGE/Alamy Images)

Cartoons: Rich Tennant (www.the5thwave.com)

Composition Services

Project Coordinator: Kristie Rees

Layout and Graphics: Carrie A. Cesavice, Stephanie D. Jumper, Julie Trippetti

Proofreader: Debbye Butler

Indexer: Broccoli Information Management

Publishing and Editorial for Consumer Dummies

Diane Graves Steele, Vice President and Publisher, Consumer Dummies

Kristin Ferguson-Wagstaffe, Product Development Director, Consumer Dummies

Kelly Regan, Editorial Director, Travel

Publishing for Technology Dummies

Andy Cummings, Vice President and Publisher, Dummies Technology/General User

Composition Services

Debbie Stailey, Director of Composition Services

Contents at a Glance

Maps at a Glance

Table of Contents

Introduction

● ●

*W*elcome to **Walt Disney World** and **Orlando, Florida,** a land ruled by a mouse who thinks nothing of sporting bright red shorts, gigantic white gloves, and big yellow shoes — a place that, for some, including the young and young-at-heart, is absolutely magical. Walt Disney World has continued to evolve, bringing back its faithful followers and enticing future fans. Though the wear and tear of a weakened economy is beginning to show elsewhere in Orlando, Walt Disney World has remained somewhat resilient; it continues to add attractions throughout its parks and regularly announces plans for future projects. Millions of people make the pilgrimage each year — a group that includes Olympic medal winners, a prince or two, pop-star personalities, and of course us regular folks. To some, WDW is a national shrine; to others, a right of passage, albeit a crowded one.

For some folks, charting a successful course through the Mouse's house can seem like a lot of work. For you, it won't be. All you need to ensure an enjoyable trip to Orlando is patience, planning, and a little childlike wonder — now how hard is that?

About This Book

Pay full price? Read the fine print? Do it their way?

Excuse me. There's no need for any of that.

You picked this book because you know the *For Dummies* series, and you want to go to Walt Disney World. You also probably know how much you want to spend, the pace you want to keep, and the amount of planning you can handle. You may not want to tend to every little detail, yet you don't trust just anyone to make your plans for you.

In this book, I boil down what has become a world unto itself — Walt Disney World — and the surrounding Orlando area. Walt Disney's Florida legacy is still growing a full four decades after his death in 1966. At current count, WDW includes four theme parks and a dozen lesser attractions, an entertainment district, tens of thousands of hotel rooms, scores of restaurants, and twin cruise ships.

Universal Orlando and **SeaWorld** add another five theme parks, three resorts, and an entertainment district to the mix. Nearby are 80 or so additional smaller attractions, as well as an avalanche of restaurants and more than 114,000 lodging rooms in Orlando.

Dummies Post-it® Flags

As you're reading this book, you'll find information that you'll want to reference as you plan or enjoy your trip — whether it be a new hotel, a must-see attraction, or a must-try walking tour. Mark these pages with the handy Post-it® Flags included in this book to help make your trip planning easier!

How can anyone sort through all these choices, you ask? It takes experience.

After decades of stomping through the House of the Mouse, I know where to find the best deals (deals that are not rip-offs). In this book, I guide you through Walt Disney World and Orlando in a clear, easy-to-understand way so that you can find the best hotels, restaurants, and attractions without having to read this book like a novel — cover to cover. Although you can read this book from front to back if you choose, you can also flip to only those sections that interest you. I also promise not to overwhelm you with choices. I simply deliver the best, most essential ingredients for a great vacation.

Please be advised that travel information is subject to change at any time — and this disclaimer is especially true of prices (the theme parks like to raise theirs on a whim). Therefore, I suggest that you call ahead for confirmation or check the Internet when making your travel plans. Doing so is especially important when you have your heart set on visiting a particular attraction, because theme parks are constantly making changes to their lineups, including shortening hours, closing shows on certain days, and boarding up restaurants in poor economic times.

The author, editors, and publisher cannot be held responsible for the experiences of readers while traveling. Your safety is important to us, however, so we encourage you to stay alert and be aware of your surroundings. Keep a close eye on cameras, purses, and wallets, all favorite targets of thieves and pickpockets.

Conventions Used in This Book

To make this book an easier reference guide for you, I use some handy abbreviations when I review hotels, restaurants, and attractions.

You'll probably notice first that I often substitute *WDW* or *Disney World* for *Walt Disney World* to spare you from having to read those three words again and again. Another common abbreviation that you'll find is the use of *Universal* in place of *Universal Orlando*. Also, because almost everything in Orlando revolves around its theme parks, I often refer to the section of Central Florida that encompasses the theme parks as simply *the parks.*

And because Orlando does its best to make you max them out, I use the following abbreviations for commonly accepted credit cards:

AE: American Express

DC: Diners Club

DISC: Discover

MC: MasterCard

V: Visa

I also include general pricing information to help you decide where to unpack your bags or dine on the local cuisine. I use a system of dollar signs to show a range of costs for one night in a double-occupancy room or a meal at a restaurant. For detailed discussions of this pricing information, see Chapter 9 (for hotel costs) and Chapter 10 (for restaurants).

Foolish Assumptions

As I wrote this book, I made some assumptions about you and what your needs might be as a traveler. Here's what I assumed:

- ✔ You may be an experienced traveler who hasn't had much time to explore Orlando and wants expert advice on how to maximize your time and enjoy a hassle-free trip.

- ✔ You may be an inexperienced traveler looking for guidance when determining whether to take a trip to Walt Disney World and Orlando and how to plan for it.

- ✔ You're not looking for a book that provides all the information available about Orlando or that lists every hotel, restaurant, or attraction available to you. Instead, you're looking for a book that focuses on the places that will give you the best experience in Orlando.

If you fit any of these criteria, then *Walt Disney World & Orlando For Dummies,* 9th Edition, gives you the information you're looking for!

How This Book Is Organized

Walt Disney World & Orlando For Dummies, 9th Edition, is divided into seven parts. The chapters in each part lay out the specifics on each section's topic. Likewise, each chapter is written so that you don't have to read what came before or after, although I sometimes refer you to other areas of the book for more information.

Here's a brief look at the parts.

Part I: Introducing Walt Disney World and Orlando

Think of this part as the hors d'oeuvres. In this part, I tempt you with the best experiences, hotels, eateries, and attractions at Disney and in the rest of Orlando. I give you a little history lesson (but not to worry — no quiz will follow), suggest a few movies and books to get you in the Mickey mood, and then tip you off to Orlando's best special events. Because the city has some pretty distinct seasons, I also delve into the pros and cons of visiting during different times of the year and even throw in a weather forecast.

Part II: Planning Your Trip to Walt Disney World and Orlando

This part covers the nitty-gritty of trip planning. Orlando has been known to take a chunk of change out of unsuspecting visitors' wallets, so I suggest some ways to save money so that you don't feel like you have to take out a second mortgage to do this trip. I delve into the various ways to get here and give you the lowdown on vacation package options; they're a very popular method of traveling to Orlando — and you'll find a whole lot of them out there. And because I'd like everyone to have fun on their vacation, I provide tips for those who could use some more specialized trip information: families, seniors, travelers with disabilities, and gay and lesbian travelers.

Part III: Settling into Orlando

After I get you to Orlando, I introduce you to the neighborhoods and explore some of the *modus transporto* (local buses, trolleys, taxis, shuttles, and other vehicles to get from hither to yonder). I also give you the lowdown on Disney's special transportation system. From there, it's on to a discussion of the city's plethora of accommodations options and in-depth reviews of the best places to sleep. And because it takes lots of fuel to keep you going inside the theme parks, I discuss the city's best places to eat and introduce you to that most Orlando of dining experiences: the character meal. (Because what says Disney more than having dinner with Donald Duck and Goofy? Or Cinderella? Or Simba? Well, you get the idea.)

Part IV: Exploring Walt Disney World

You're now checked in and fueled up. Great. Welcome to Walt Disney World, the number-one tourist destination in the country. You could easily spend months exploring this mammoth resort, but if you're like most visitors to the House of the Mouse, you have only a week or less to get it all in. No worries. In this part, I explain Disney's ticket system and tell you about the best options in each of Disney's major parks. And if you don't think a visit to WDW would be complete without a set of

Mickey ears or some other souvenir, I also fill you in on Disney's best shopping opportunities.

Part V: Exploring the Rest of Orlando

Can't face all Mickey, all the time? No problem. There is, in fact, a lot more to Orlando than Disney World. If theme parks are your thing, Universal Orlando, SeaWorld, Discovery Cove, and Aquatica await you, and I fill you in on their highlights. The city is also home to a plethora of smaller attractions and rides, and I provide in-depth information on the best of them. If you prefer exercising your credit card to walking the parks, I let you know the best places for shopaholics to indulge. And if you need a break from the city itself, I give you two great day-trip options. One thing is for certain: You won't get bored.

Part VI: Living It Up After Dark: Orlando Nightlife

Kids may rule this town, but Disney and the rest of Orlando have discovered that many people want to party into the night. In Part VI, I explore Pleasure Island, CityWalk, and other thriving Orlando hotspots. Then I give you details on Orlando's popular dinner shows and the city's performing arts. (Yes, Orlando does have a respected cultural scene.)

Part VII: The Part of Tens

Every *For Dummies* book offers the Part of Tens. Finding this part in a *For Dummies* book is as certain as annual price hikes at Disney and Universal. In Part VII, I give you parting knowledge about cheap attractions and places to stay fit as a fiddle.

I've also included an appendix — your Quick Concierge — containing plenty of handy information you may need when traveling to, in, and around Orlando, such as phone numbers and addresses of emergency personnel or area hospitals and pharmacies, contact information for baby sitters, and lists of local newspapers and magazines. Check out this appendix when searching for answers to the many little questions that may come up as you travel.

If you want even more detailed or specialized information, I also include a list of the best sources of Orlando and Disney information, from official tourist offices to Web sites to newspapers and magazines.

You can easily find the Quick Concierge because it's printed on yellow paper.

Icons Used in This Book

You find six icons throughout this guide:

Keep an eye out for the Bargain Alert icon as you seek out money-saving tips or great deals.

Best of the Best highlights the best that Orlando has to offer in all categories — hotels, restaurants, attractions, activities, shopping, and nightlife.

Watch for the Heads Up icon to identify annoying or potentially dangerous situations such as tourist traps, unsafe neighborhoods, budgetary rip-offs, and other things to beware.

Find out useful advice on things to do and ways to schedule your time when you see the Tip icon.

You encounter the first of these two similar icons — this one showcasing the good — when I start barnstorming through the big parks. Because you may very well be toting kids when you visit Orlando, I decided to get some kids' input (namely, my five children, ages 7 to 15) on many of the popular rides and attractions in the city.

And, of course, this icon points to some negative reviews from my critics. Keep in mind that not all rides and attractions garner unanimous praise or dissatisfaction, so many reviews include both icons.

Where to Go from Here

I've briefed you on what to expect from this book and told you how to use it to plan a magical vacation to Walt Disney World — no pixie dust necessary. So start reading; you have a lot to do before you arrive, from arranging a place where you'll rest your weary feet each night to exploring the best that Orlando's theme parks have to offer. Like the Boy Scouts' creed, the successful Orlando traveler needs to "be prepared"; follow the advice in this book, and you will be. So put on your Mouse ears and smile — you're going to Disney World!

Part I

Introducing Walt Disney World and Orlando

The 5th Wave   By Rich Tennant

"The hotel said they were giving us the 'Indiana Jones' suite."

In this part . . .

To get the most enjoyment out of a vacation — with the least amount of hassle — it helps to know what awaits you in your chosen paradise before the landing gear lowers. In this part, I highlight the joys of a trip to Orlando and give you the lowdown on the city's best bets, from rides and attractions to hotels and restaurants. I also tell you a bit about the city's history, fill you in on some of the local lingo, and guide you to the best times of the year to visit Mickey.

Chapter 1

Discovering the Best of Walt Disney World and Orlando

In This Chapter
▶ Experiencing the best that Orlando has to offer
▶ Finding the city's best hotels
▶ Getting a taste of the best dining in Orlando
▶ Boarding the coolest theme-park rides
▶ Discovering the greatest shows and attractions

*V*acationing in Orlando is like escaping to another time and place, a world of fantasy, a world filled with fun. The city attracts the young and the young at heart from all over the world, all of whom come to experience the theme parks, the world-class resorts, and the area's spectacular natural beauty. It should come as no surprise to you that Orlando is the number-one family vacation destination in the United States, not to mention one of the top vacation destinations in the world. Yes, it gets crowded, and in the summer it's hot and sticky, but one thing you definitely won't ever be is bored. And in this chapter, I offer the best of the best that Orlando and Walt Disney World have to offer.

Note: With the exception of the items listed in "The Best Orlando Experiences," I highlight all the hotels, restaurants, and attractions in this chapter with a Best of the Best icon when reviewed in this book.

The Best Orlando Experiences

If images of Cinderella Castle pop into your head at the mention of Orlando, you're not alone. The **Magic Kingdom**'s iconic castle and the lovable mouse who started it all are, by far, the most famous of all Disney icons and the reason most folks venture to the Sunshine State in the first place. Keep in mind that although a visit to the Magic Kingdom

Walt Disney World and Orlando

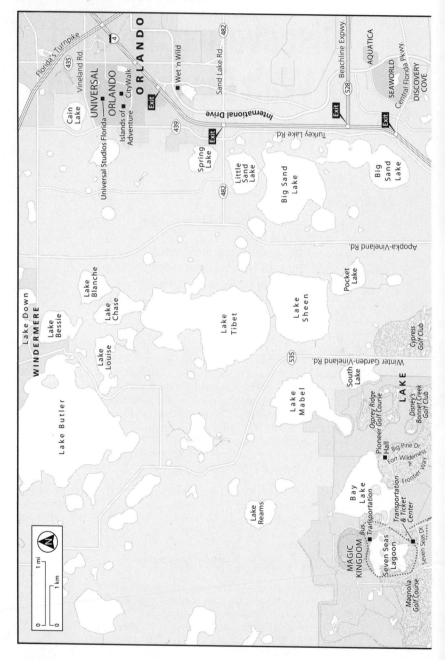

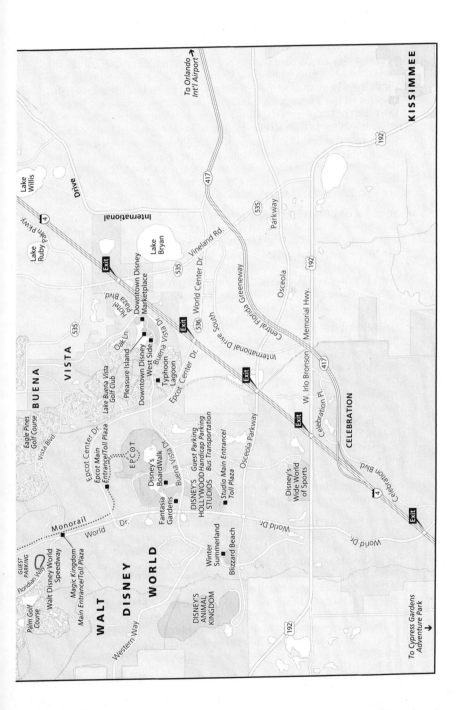

is one of the biggest highlights of the Orlando experience, especially for kids, plenty more attractions and experiences await:

- ✓ **Spend a day exploring Disney's Animal Kingdom.** Embark on an undersea adventure at **Finding Nemo–The Musical,** trek through the Himalayas in search of the legendary Yeti on **Expedition Everest– Legend of the Forbidden Mountain,** or make your way by foot through the jungles of Asia for a glimpse of the exotic wildlife that inhabit the park. **Kali River Rapids** will leave you soaked, but that's half the fun. Head out on **Kilimanjaro Safaris** for an expedition through the African savanna or travel back to the time when dinosaurs ruled the Earth. Be sure to catch **Mickey's Jammin' Jungle Parade,** one of the liveliest parades in all of Disney. (Check out Chapter 15 for details about the park.)

- ✓ **Spend a day traveling the world at Epcot.** At Epcot, you can find high-speed thrills aboard **Mission: SPACE** and **Test Track,** a breathtaking experience **Soarin'** over the California landscape, and undersea adventure exploring **The Seas with Nemo & Friends.** Then it's off to tour some of the world's most fascinating countries along the World Showcase. Dance with the **oompah band** in Germany or try to **belly-dance** with the natives in Morocco. (For more details about things to do at Epcot, see Chapter 13.)

- ✓ **Go behind the scenes at Disney's Hollywood Studios.** You can find some of the most intense thrills in all of Disney World here, with both the **Twilight Zone Tower of Terror** and **Rock 'n' Roller Coaster Starring Aerosmith** taking center stage. **Toy Story Mania!,** the park's newest attraction, will test your skill as you play your way through the re-imagined midway. Be sure to take in the spectacular shows, too — this is a studio, after all. Top billing goes to **Lights, Motors, Action! Extreme Stunt Show** and the **Indiana Jones Epic Stunt Spectacular!** Debuting in 2009, the **American Idol Experience** will allow park-goers a chance to sing their way to stardom. Close out the night with the incredible **Fantasmic!,** an after-dark show that combines a love for all things Disney with the most amazing combination of water and fireworks. (See Chapter 14 for the lowdown on all the park has to offer.)

- ✓ **Test your physical limits at Islands of Adventure.** You can spin; you can fly upside down; you can get wet. And that's all just in the first few minutes in this park. Don't miss the **Amazing Adventures of Spider-Man; Dueling Dragons** twin roller coasters; **Jurassic Park River Adventure;** and the big, green **Incredible Hulk Coaster.** If it's really hot out, a good soak on **Popeye & Bluto's Bilge-Rat Barges** is just the thing to refresh you. In late 2009, look for the **Wizarding World of Harry Potter** — including Hogwarts Castle, the village of Hogsmeade, and the Forbidden Forest — to apparate (that's debut, for those not familiar with wizarding lingo). (For information on other adventures awaiting you in the park, see Chapter 19.)

✔ **Explore the ocean depths at SeaWorld, Discovery Cove,** and **Aquatica.** SeaWorld has a few thrill rides — namely, **Journey to Atlantis, Kraken,** and **Wild Arctic** (with **Manta** on its way later in 2009) — but the real reason to visit these parks is the chance to observe and interact with a wide variety of marine life. Discovery Cove even allows you to swim with a dolphin. If you'd rather slide, ride, and splash the day away, head to Aquatica, the eco-themed water park. (For details on all three parks, see Chapter 20.)

✔ **Experience Universal Studios Florida (USF).** Once just a diversion, Universal has turned itself into a true destination. Not-to-be-missed attractions include **Revenge of the Mummy, Terminator 2: 3D Battle Across Time, Men in Black Alien Attack, Fear Factor Live, Shrek 4-D, Disaster!–A Major Motion Picture Ride . . . Starring YOU,** and the new **Simpsons Ride.** In 2009, add **Hollywood Rip, Ride, Rockit** to your to-do list. Call it a night after taking in the **Universal 360–A Cinesphere Spectacular,** when the entire lagoon lights up with pyrotechnics, lasers, and four 360-degree projection cinespheres. (Chapter 18 has info on other cool things to see and do at USF.)

✔ **Top off the day with a spectacular nighttime show.** Many of the parks love to close out the day with fireworks or a show-stopping performance. Check out the Magic Kingdom's **Wishes Nighttime Spectacular** or **"SpectroMagic" Parade,** Epcot's **IllumiNations: Reflections of Earth,** Disney's Hollywood Studios' **Fantasmic!,** Universal Studios' **Universal 360,** or SeaWorld's **Odyssea, Fusion,** or **Mistify** (with select shows offered only seasonally). For a truly magical performance, see **Cirque du Soleil's** *La Nouba;* it's expensive, but unforgettable. (For information on all these spectacles, see Chapters 12–14, 18, 20, and 25.)

✔ **Wrestle a gator at Gatorland.** An Orlando original, Gatorland was astounding visitors with its crocodiles and alligators long before the Mouse moved in. Catch one of the amazing shows, such as **Gator Wrestlin'** and **Gator Jumparoo,** or just take a leisurely stroll through swamp and marsh on the boardwalks — no one's in a hurry here. (For more information on Gatorland, see Chapter 21.)

The Best Hotels

One of the cool things about a trip to Orlando is the chance to stay at one of its great resorts or themed hotels. Check out Chapter 9 for more in-depth information about all the accommodations listed in this section:

✔ **Best for Families:** Both **Disney's Animal Kingdom Lodge** and **Disney's Wilderness Lodge** offer spectacular surroundings, kid-friendly eateries, and rooms with bunk beds. At nearby Lake Buena Vista, the **Nickelodeon Family Suites** features themed KidSuites (separate sleeping areas with bunk beds, game stations, and TVs for the kids), water-park-like pools, and Nick-style entertainment. In

Kissimmee, **Seralago Hotel & Suites Main Gate East** features tons of on-site activities and kid suites, too.

✔ **Best Inexpensive Hotels:** Several good choices offer basic amenities in convenient locations for a low price. On Disney property, choose **Disney's Pop Century Resort,** which offers themed motel-style rooms for the lowest prices in Mickeyville. **Disney's All-Star Resorts** recently revamped several of its rooms, making them into suites — and they're some of the least expensive in town. The **Masters Inn Maingate** offers a good location and moderate amenities for less than $50 a night, as does **Americas Best Value Inn & Suites.**

✔ **Best Moderate Hotel: Disney's Coronado Springs Resort** edges out the other two WDW moderate resorts with slightly larger rooms and a cool Mayan temple pool.

✔ **Best for a Romantic Getaway:** The **Portofino Bay Hotel** at Universal is *molto* romantic with its quaint Italian-village theme. If money is no object, sweep your significant other off to a getaway at the lushly tropical **Ritz-Carlton Orlando, Grande Lakes,** or the Mediterranean-inspired **Villas of Grand Cypress.**

✔ **Best Hotels for Business Travelers:** The **Orlando World Center Marriott Resort** in Lake Buena Vista and the **Peabody Orlando** both offer an extensive array of business services and amenities.

✔ **Best Location:** All three Universal resorts are within walking distance of Universal's parks and CityWalk, and all offer boat transportation to the theme parks as well. For location and value, the **Royal Pacific Resort** is the best of the bunch. At WDW, **Disney's Grand Floridian Resort & Spa** offers the best accommodations in the World and is right on the monorail. For those who must be in the thick of it all, **Disney's Yacht Club Resort, Disney's Beach Club Resort,** and **Disney's BoardWalk Inn** (all close to Epcot) also get my vote.

✔ **Best Pools:** The **Hard Rock Hotel** boasts a sandy beach and an underwater sound system that brings out the lounging rock star in you. Stormalong Bay is the 3-acre mini water park that calls itself a pool at **Disney's Yacht Club Resort** and **Disney's Beach Club Resort.** Away from the theme parks, the **Hyatt Regency Grand Cypress** has an amazing lagoon-like pool with rock grottoes and 12 waterfalls, while the **JW Marriott Orlando, Grande Lakes,** boasts an incredible lazy river surrounded by lush landscaping. The **Nickelodeon Family Suites** wins the kids' vote with its water-park-style pools sporting flumes, climbing nets, and slides.

The Best Restaurants

Fast food may rule in Orlando, but the city doesn't lack good places to dine. Find more information about all these restaurants in Chapter 10:

- ✔ **Best for Kids:** It's hard to go wrong with any of the Disney **character breakfasts.** Among Disney's resorts, the **Whispering Canyon Café** (Disney's Wilderness Lodge) ensures a stompin' good time. Kids also love the jungle-themed **Rainforest Café** (Downtown Disney and Animal Kingdom).

- ✔ **Best Seafood:** The **Oceanaire Seafood Room** (Pointe Orlando), a recent addition to Orlando's dining scene, features a menu filled with fresh seafood, an upscale atmosphere reminiscent of a 1930s supper club, and service that's simply unparalleled. **Todd English's bluezoo** (inside the Dolphin) consistently draws raves for its flavorful food and unique décor. **Fulton's Crab House** (Pleasure Island) is a longstanding favorite with a great wine list.

- ✔ **Best Steakhouse:** The highly regarded **Yachtsman Steakhouse** (Disney's Yacht Club Resort) offers wood-fire grilled steaks.

- ✔ **Best Dining with a View:** This one's a toss-up between **Manuel's on the 28th,** which offers a stunning after-dark view of the city and food to match, and the **California Grill,** which boasts spectacular views of Disney's fireworks and a winning wine list.

- ✔ **Best Buffet: Boma–Flavors of Africa,** inside Disney's Animal Kingdom Lodge, offers the most eclectic buffet in Orlando, mingling traditional items with exotic African fare.

- ✔ **Best Margarita:** Head to **Jimmy Buffett's Margaritaville,** of course. The mango margarita's the best of the bunch.

- ✔ **Best Spot for a Romantic Meal: Victoria & Albert's,** in Disney's Grand Floridian Resort & Spa, is the runaway leader.

- ✔ **Best Value: Kim Wu,** a local favorite for over 20 years, features fabulous food and friendly service. **Café Tu Tu Tango** offers inexpensive tapas dishes that are perfect for sharing.

The Best Thrill Rides

If you're a speed freak who lives for the ups and downs of a good ride, here are the top stomach churners and G-force generators in Orlando:

- ✔ **Expedition Everest–Legend of the Forbidden Mountain** (Disney's Animal Kingdom): This hair-raising expedition through the Himalayas ends in a face-to-face encounter with the legendary Yeti. (See Chapter 15.)

- ✔ **Mission: SPACE** (Epcot): Disney folks used NASA technology to create an astronaut simulator so effective that they've installed "lunch bags" for all the motion sickness it causes. (See Chapter 13.)

- ✔ **Rock 'n' Roller Coaster Starring Aerosmith** (Disney's Hollywood Studios): You launch from 0 to 60 mph in 2.8 seconds and go right into the first inversion as 120 speakers in your "stretch limo" mainline Aerosmith at (yeeeow!) 32,000 watts right into your ears. (See Chapter 14.)

✔ **Twilight Zone Tower of Terror** (Disney's Hollywood Studios): The free-fall experiences are more than thrilling — they're scary. After your legs stop shaking, you *may* want to ride again. (See Chapter 14.)

✔ **Summit Plummet** (Disney's Blizzard Beach): This one starts slow, with a lift ride to a 120-foot mountain summit. But it finishes with the world's fastest body slide, a test of your courage and swimsuit as it goes virtually straight down and has you moving sans vehicle at 60 mph by the end. (See Chapter 16.)

✔ **Revenge of the Mummy the Ride** (Universal Studios Florida): This thrill ride combines a coaster run with the best special-effects technology (flame ceilings, scarabs pouring out of the walls) for a ride that touches on your worst phobias. (See Chapter 18.)

✔ **The Amazing Adventures of Spider-Man** (Islands of Adventure): 3-D doesn't get any better than this ride where you twist, spin, and soar before a simulated 400-foot drop. It's sure to get your Spidey senses tingling. (See Chapter 19.)

✔ **Dueling Dragons** (Islands of Adventure): Your legs dangle as you do five inversions at 55 to 60 mph and — get this! — three times come within 12 inches of the other roller coaster. (See Chapter 19.)

✔ **The Incredible Hulk Coaster** (Islands of Adventure): You blast from 0 to 40 mph in two seconds, spin upside down more than 100 feet from the ground, and execute seven rollovers and two deep drops on this coaster. You may find this hard to believe, but it's the smoothest ride around. (See Chapter 19.)

✔ **Jurassic Park River Adventure** (Islands of Adventure): Riders travel through a prehistoric land inhabited by fierce dinosaurs that growl and bare their teeth, some within inches of your face. After being threatened by a Tyrannosaurus rex, you plunge 85 feet almost straight down into water below. (See Chapter 19.)

✔ **Kraken** (SeaWorld): This floorless, open-sided coaster uses speed, steep climbs, deep drops, and seven loops to create a stomach-churning ride that lasts far too long for some folks. (See Chapter 20.)

The Best of the Rest

For those who can't stomach the thought of boarding anything that pulls the same G-forces as a fighter jet or induces adrenaline rushes of any sort of magnitude, the theme parks have several exceptional (and tamer) rides and shows that nobody should overlook:

✔ **The Haunted Mansion** (Magic Kingdom): Forget the unfortunate Eddie Murphy film and be sure to visit this cult favorite, which shows off Disney's knack for details as 999 ghosts offer up more delights than frights. (See Chapter 12.)

✔ **Pirates of the Caribbean** (Magic Kingdom): This oldie but goodie features randy pirates and lots of yo-ho-ho music. Recent refurbishments have spiced it up even further, with improved special effects and such famous faces as Captain Jack Sparrow, Barbossa, and Davy Jones. (See Chapter 12.)

✔ **Test Track** (Epcot): Fasten your seat belts. This collaboration with GM allows riders to take a "car" through a series of standard motor vehicle test sequences that include a near-crash, a speed run, and some rather interesting weather. It's not a thriller, but it's definitely a cool ride. (See Chapter 13.)

✔ **The Seas with Nemo & Friends** (Epcot): Aboard slow-moving "Clamobiles," you'll join in the search for Nemo alongside a slew of familiar finned friends as they swim right along with the aquarium's live inhabitants. (See Chapter 13.)

✔ **Soarin'** (Epcot): After boarding the multiseat gliders, you'll find yourself flying high over some of California's most spectacular landscapes with realistic multisensory effects. (See Chapter 13.)

✔ **Indiana Jones Epic Stunt Spectacular!** (Disney's Hollywood Studios): Special effects, razzle-dazzle stunts, and pyrotechnics make this stunt show worth the (incredibly long) wait. Wear a brightly colored shirt, wave your arms spastically, and you may be called up on stage as an extra. (See Chapter 14.)

✔ **Lights, Motors, Action! Extreme Stunt Show** (Disney's Hollywood Studios): A high-speed car chase, pyrotechnics, special effects, and some amazing stunt driving add up to a thrill-packed show for the whole family. (See Chapter 14.)

✔ **Toy Story Mania!** (Disney's Hollywood Studios): This all-new interactive 3-D ride immerses guests in a whimsical world of midway-style games with a high-tech *Toy Story* twist. No matter your age, this one's an absolute winner. (See Chapter 14.)

✔ **Mickey's PhilharMagic** (Magic Kingdom): This amusing show combines a comedic cast of Disney characters, a delightful score, and an array of 3-D effects that will tickle your senses as Mickey, Donald, Lumiere, and Ariel, to name a few, seemingly spring right off the screen. This one's not to be missed. (See Chapter 12.)

✔ **Muppet Vision 3-D** (Disney's Hollywood Studios): The action takes place in a re-creation of the Muppets' theater (complete with the blessedly crotchety Statler and Waldorf critiquing the action from the balcony) and is a zany mix of 3-D film, animatronics, live action, and special effects. (See Chapter 14.)

✔ **Finding Nemo–The Musical** (Disney's Animal Kingdom): Film favorites including Nemo, Marlin, Dory, and Bruce jump from the big screen into the "big blue," live and on stage. Coming to life before your eyes, actors combine with creatively designed puppet-like costumes to re-create the original undersea adventure in this spectacular and entrancing production. (See Chapter 15.)

✔ **Festival of the Lion King** (Disney's Animal Kingdom): One of the best shows in town, this is a don't-miss Broadway-esque version of the famous Circle of Life. (See Chapter 15.)

✔ **Kilimanjaro Safaris** (Disney's Animal Kingdom): At this must-see attraction, the special safari trucks bump you about as you head out into Disney's version of the African wilderness. You'll enjoy the thrill of seeing giraffes and zebras up close. (See Chapter 15.)

✔ **Men in Black Alien Attack** (Universal Studios Florida): Zap icky aliens with ray guns as you ride through the streets of New York. At the conclusion, you tackle the Big Roach himself and then get rated by Will Smith for your shooting prowess. (See Chapter 18.)

✔ **Shrek 4-D** (Universal Studios Florida): This one uses 3-D effects and seats that move and bounce to continue the story of Shrek and Fiona. It's fun for all ages and *very* popular! (See Chapter 18.)

✔ **The Simpsons Ride** (Universal Studios Florida): Homer, Marge, Bart, Lisa, and Maggie come along for the ride on this wildly wacky action-packed adventure through a Krusty-the-Clown-created carnival. (See Chapter 18.)

✔ **Terminator 2: 3D Battle Across Time** (Universal Studios Florida): This production features the creepy-steely T-1,000,000 and live-action doubles of Arnold Schwarzenegger and Edward Furlong, who roar onto the stage on Harleys and then into a giant movie screen, a very cool trick you absolutely must see. This show is an absolute winner. (See Chapter 18.)

✔ **Popeye & Bluto's Bilge-Rat Barges** (Islands of Adventure): A bit too tame to be considered a thrill ride, this white-water raft experience can have you soaked in no time at all. (See Chapter 19.)

✔ **Believe** (SeaWorld): This Shamu extravaganza will have you "oohing" and "ahhing" as the sleek black-and-white killer whale shows off his skill on a splashy souped-up set. (See Chapter 20.)

✔ **Shark Encounter** (SeaWorld): At this aquatic exhibit, you find a walk-through tunnel populated with the scarier denizens of the deep, such as moray eels, barracudas, rays, scorpion fish, and (of course) sharks. It's the coolest aquarium in town. (See Chapter 20.)

Chapter 2

Digging Deeper into Orlando

*T*his chapter offers a bit of perspective on how Orlando evolved from a sleepy little Southern town to the theme-park capital of the world. After a quick trip back in time, I give you an overview of Florida's cuisine and offer a tutorial on the local lingo. If you want even more background on Orlando and WDW, I recommend a handful of books and films at the end of this chapter.

History 101: The Main Events

Believe it or not, there was life in Orlando before Mickey. The city's transformation into theme-park mecca didn't happen overnight — and may never have happened if Walt Disney hadn't run out of real estate in California.

Orlando B.D. (before Disney)

Before Disney, Universal, SeaWorld, and the wealth of other tourist attractions that exist today, Central Florida was ruled by the economics of the three *C* industries: cotton, cattle, and citrus.

Originally named Jernigan, the town now known as Orlando had its genesis in the remnants of an Army post that was abandoned in 1849. The name was officially changed to Orlando in 1857, though the origin of the moniker is somewhat unclear. (Depending on whom you ask, the city was named for a plantation owner, the friend of a city commissioner, or a character from Shakespeare's *As You Like It.*) The cattle and cotton industries thrived here until the Civil War, when area homesteaders realized that citrus trees were far easier to grow than cotton. By the 1950s, more than 80,000 acres of citrus trees were thriving throughout Central Florida. The '50s also saw two major developments that would bring even more people and industry to the area: the building of the space center at nearby Cape Canaveral and (most important of all) the invention of air-conditioning.

Around this time — July 17, 1955, to be precise — Walt Disney opened Disneyland in Anaheim, California, and it was an instant hit. Soon, the overwhelming demand made it obvious to Walt that he needed to expand. However, his 27 acres in Southern California didn't give him room for his next endeavor. So he turned his eyes eastward, to Florida.

Orlando A.D. (after Disney)

In a top-secret operation that would have impressed even the CIA, Walt Disney began a search for the site of his next theme park, and, having decided on the location, started secretly buying up land through dummy corporations. On November 11, 1965 — after acquiring more than 28,000 acres for a mere $5.5 million — Disney came clean and announced that a new park would be built in Orlando. Unfortunately, he passed away a mere year after his plans were unveiled. His brother, Roy O. Disney, decided to carry on in Walt's name.

Construction began on the **Magic Kingdom** (see Chapter 12) and its first two resorts in 1969. The **Walt Disney World Resort** officially opened to the public in 1971.

SeaWorld (see Chapter 20) splashed onto the scene in 1973. Meanwhile, Disney continued to break attendance records each year and continued expanding. In 1982, **Epcot** (see Chapter 13) was christened the second WDW theme park. In 1989, **Disney–MGM Studios** (renamed **Disney's Hollywood Studios** in 2008; see Chapter 14), a behind-the-scenes look at Tinseltown, became the third jewel in the WDW park crown. At the same time, WDW added **Typhoon Lagoon** (a 56-acre water theme park; see Chapter 16) and **Pleasure Island** (a nightclub district for adults; see Chapter 25).

In 1990, **Universal Studios Florida** (see Chapter 18) brought the world of movies to life in Orlando. Direct competition spurred Disney to create its fourth theme park in Orlando, **Disney's Animal Kingdom** (see Chapter 15), in 1998. Universal countered with **CityWalk,** a vast nighttime entertainment district (see Chapter 25). Not to be outdone, Disney stormed back by consolidating its three major after-park-hours entertainment, dining, and shopping venues — Disney's West Side, Pleasure Island, and the Disney Village Marketplace — into an all-encompassing zone called **Downtown Disney.** Disney also started its own cruise line for good measure.

Universal didn't follow out to sea, but it upped the ante when it opened its second park in 1999. **Islands of Adventure** (see Chapter 19) was all about the thrills of the theme-park experience. Islands, when combined with CityWalk, Universal Studios Florida, and several on-property resorts, helped Universal complete its transformation into the resort destination of **Universal Orlando,** as it's now known. And to ensure that you keep coming back for more, the **Simpsons Ride** moved into Universal Studios in 2008; **Hollywood Rip, Ride, Rockit,** the park's newest mega-coaster, is scheduled to rock your world in 2009. Also in 2009, look for the **Wizarding World of Harry Potter** at Islands of Adventure. No longer just a day trip, Universal now offers the total vacation experience, just as Disney does.

SeaWorld decided to keep doing what it does best and opened **Discovery Cove** (see Chapter 20) in 2000. More than just a theme park, this is an all-inclusive, interactive marine experience, offering snorkeling and dolphin swims. Even more surprising, SeaWorld added its first roller coaster, the thrilling **Kraken.** And in 2007, to keep the kid set content, SeaWorld added several new sea-themed rides that appeal to tots and kids under age 10. Without stopping to come up for air, SeaWorld continued its expansion efforts with the 2008 debut of **Aquatica,** an all-new eco-themed water park — and the latest theme park to splash onto the Orlando scene in almost a decade. Construction of **Manta,** an all-new undersea-themed thriller at SeaWorld, is currently underway (slated to open in 2009).

Disney isn't remaining idle: Recent announcements include plans that will double the capacity of its cruise line by 2012, adding two new ships. Back on land, an unprecedented partnership with the **Four Seasons** hotel and resort chain has also been announced, adding an entirely new dimension to Disney's resort collection by 2010. In addition, an all-new tourist district that will include value-priced resorts, dining, and shopping venues is currently on the books and scheduled for development along the western edge of Disney property.

Things may have quieted down a bit in the expansion department, but the theme parks are hardly sitting still — they're constantly revising and building new attractions. Orlando currently offers more than 100 attractions, 115,000 hotel rooms (and counting), and 5,300-plus restaurants, as well as the second-largest convention center in the nation. The city continues to show signs of growth, even in this downtrodden economy. But while the travel landscape remains bright as visitor-turnout closes in on the sky-high levels reported prior to the terrorist attacks, increases have begun to slow down. Tourism, of course, is the leading industry for Central Florida, with more than 50 million visitors annually and an economic impact of close to $30 billion. And it all started because of a mouse named Mickey.

Taste of Orlando: Local Cuisine

Offerings have greatly improved in recent years, but the Orlando dining scene can't compete with the likes of foodie cities such as San Francisco or New York. And if there's a predominant cuisine, it's fast food, with

casual chain eateries coming in a very close second. The biggest decision that most theme-park-goers have to make is whether to opt for a
burger, a taco, or a hot dog along with the ubiquitous french fries. And
don't worry about finding a branch of your favorite chain; should the
urge strike you, the odds are that you can find not just one but several
outlets of it within reach of your hotel.

Though the city caters to a diverse clientele, don't expect to find an
equitable number of ethnic eateries. The most famous spots in town for
ethnic cuisine are **Epcot's World Showcase** restaurants. Although theme-
park food is not exactly first class, some of it can be surprisingly good.
On the healthy front, you'll find plenty of fresh fruit — Orlando is still a
major citrus town — and even the theme parks now offer a few healthier
and vegetarian options beyond the usual fast food.

The biggest news on the city's dining front has been the increasing
number of gourmet spots. Famous culinary magicians, such as Wolfgang
Puck, Emeril Lagasse, and Todd English, have opened restaurants here.
A few first-class steakhouses will please carnivores. And Universal has
stepped up theme-park dining a few notches with the addition of its
Islands of Adventure eateries.

Given the importance that the city places on entertainment value, it
probably shouldn't surprise you that Orlando's most famous dining
experience — the **character meal** — doesn't really revolve around the
cuisine. The name says it all: You and the kids get to chow down on
buffet food with Mickey or Goofy, SpongeBob SquarePants, or even
Shamu. The fare at these ubiquitous events, staged at most of the theme
parks in some form or another, and even at select hotels, won't often
tickle your taste buds, but the food's not really the point. Who cares
what pancakes taste like when Cinderella is smiling beatifically at your
enthralled 3-year-old or Mickey is posing with you for that all-important
Kodak moment? Disney has turned its character meals into something of
an art form, and Universal and SeaWorld have recently followed suit. For
a rundown of the best character meals in town, see Chapter 10.

Word to the Wise: The Local Lingo

Though good old-fashioned English is all you need to know in order to
have a blast in Orlando, the theme parks do have a language all their
own. Knowing the right word or phrase may help ease your way as you
navigate the maze of the city's rides and attractions. Here's a rundown of
common terms you'll likely come across while in Orlando:

> ✔ **FASTPASS:** FASTPASS is Disney's legal line-jumping pass, and it's
> available at most of WDW's primo park rides. You insert your park
> ticket into a machine, which spits out a pass with a time window
> (usually of about an hour) stamped on it. You come back within the
> window indicated, and you can access the ride via a special line that
> offers little or no wait. For more about FASTPASS, see Chapter 11.

- ✔ **Universal Express Plus Pass:** Universal's answer to Disney's FAST-PASS, but you have to pay extra for the privilege of skipping the lines here. For more information, see Chapter 18.

- ✔ **Ride-share:** Most theme parks operate a ride-share program (also known as a *parent-swap* or *child-swap*) at major attractions for parents with small kids. With this option, one parent can ride an attraction with the kids who are able to ride, while the other parent stays with the kids too young to partake; then the adults can switch places without the second one having to stand in line again. Notify one of the ride staff when you get in line if you want to participate.

- ✔ **Cast member:** In its ever-present attempt to keep up the illusion that WDW is some kind of giant ongoing production, Disney refers to its staff as *cast members.* Whatever you call them, they are almost always knowledgeable and well trained.

- ✔ **Advanced Dining Reservations:** This is the Disney version of a restaurant reservation (and it's being used increasingly at other Orlando restaurants as well). Instead of reserving an exact time at a restaurant, you reserve the right to arrive at a specific time and get the next available table (which can sometimes — though not often — take up to 30 minutes). For more on this system, see Chapter 10.

Many locals commonly shorten or abbreviate the major theme-park names, as do a number of the region's highway signs. Universal Orlando is often just referred to as *Universal,* while Universal Studios Florida is shortened to *Universal Studios* or abbreviated *USF,* and Islands of Adventure is either *Islands* or *IOA.* Walt Disney World is usually known merely as *Disney World, Disney,* or *WDW.*

Background Check: Recommended Books and Movies

The best Walt Disney World and Orlando guidebook on the planet (yes, this one) covers almost everything most travelers need and want to know. But, to be fair, here are a few others that can get you into Mickey mode before you arrive:

- ✔ *The Walt Disney World Trivia Book, Volume 2,* by Louis A. Mongello (The Intrepid Traveler), is loaded with fun facts and minutiae about Disney World. Hundreds of multiple-choice questions keep you and your kids entertained even as they enlighten.

- ✔ *Hidden Mickeys: A Field Guide to Walt Disney World's Best Kept Secrets,* 3rd Edition, by Steven M. Barrett (The Intrepid Traveler), will have you looking here, there, and everywhere to find these famous hidden icons. The guide is filled with pages of the best places to find them, but you're likely to find even more after you've gotten the hang of how to look.

✔ *Married to the Mouse: Walt Disney World and Orlando,* by Richard E. Foglesong (Yale University Press), is a serious and not always flattering look at the relationship between the Disney corporation and the city of Orlando. It's a trifle didactic in tone, but its in-depth details make it fascinating reading nonetheless.

✔ *Since the World Began,* by Jeff Kurtti (Disney Editions), is a history of WDW's first 25 years. It offers interesting information and insight into the creation of all Disney's parks and resorts.

✔ *Spinning Disney's World: Memories of a Magic Kingdom Press Agent,* by Charles Ridgway (The Intrepid Traveler), allows readers a peek into the inner workings behind Walt's World. Filled with insider and, at times, amusing accounts, Charles Ridgway, a Disney legend, fondly recalls over four decades of service to the Mouse. From the years he spent working directly with Walt to his retirement, *Spinning Disney's World* chronicles the events and recalls the people (some famous, others not so) that helped to create the empire — it's a memoir of sorts from Mickey's most famous publicist.

✔ *Orlando: City of Dreams,* by Joy Wallace Dickinson (Arcadia), is a meticulously researched history of Orlando before it became the city of the Mouse.

✔ *How It Feels to Be Colored Me, Mules and Men, Their Eyes Were Watching God, The Florida Negro,* and other books by Zora Neale Hurston chronicle life and racism in Florida, including Eatonville, the town just north of Orlando where she grew up. If you're a Hurston fan, don't miss the listing in Chapter 3 for the January festival in her honor.

If your tastes run more toward the visual, there's no shortage of films that can get you in the mood for your Orlando vacation. Here are a few viewing suggestions before you set out on your trip:

✔ Disney's plethora of animated films will introduce kids to the characters and ride themes they'll be running into inside WDW. A few recent goodies include *Finding Nemo; The Lion King; Toy Story* and *Toy Story 2; Cars; Monsters, Inc.; Aladdin; Lilo & Stitch; 101 Dalmatians; The Little Mermaid;* and *Beauty and the Beast.* For an introduction to Disney's classic characters, I suggest *Cinderella, Alice in Wonderland, Peter Pan, Sleeping Beauty, Dumbo, Pinocchio,* and *Fantasia* (though this last film may be a tad too sophisticated for very young kids).

✔ If you prefer live action, break out the popcorn and put on any of these pictures, all of which are represented in some form or another inside the Disney parks: *Mary Poppins; Honey, I Shrunk the Kids;* and *Swiss Family Robinson.* More recent entries to this category include *Disney's High School Musical 2: School's Out; The Haunted Mansion;* and the *Pirates of the Caribbean* trilogy *(The Curse of the Black Pearl, Dead Man's Chest,* and *At World's End).*

- It's known as the place to "Ride the Movies," so it should come as no surprise that Universal Studios Florida is filled with rides and attractions that seemingly put you smack in the middle of some of Universal's most famous films. Some of the best previews include *The Mummy, Twister, Jaws, Men in Black, Shrek* and *Shrek 2, E.T.,* and *Terminator 2: Judgment Day.* If you're heading to Islands of Adventure, then *Jurassic Park, X-Men,* and *Spider-Man* should be on your movie list. Pick up a copy of *The Cat in the Hat* (or any of Dr. Seuss's classic books) for the younger kids.

  Universal caters more to teens and adults than Disney does, and these films (like the rides they inspired) are definitely aimed more at that audience, so take your child's age into consideration before popping that movie in.

- Before heading off to SeaWorld, you may want to watch a few marine-related *National Geographic* specials to get some background on some of the animals you can see in that park.

Chapter 3

Deciding When to Go

● ●

In This Chapter

▶ Considering the pros and cons of traveling in each season

▶ Checking out Orlando's weather patterns

▶ Consulting a calendar of special occasions

● ●

*A*lthough Orlando bustles with activity throughout the year, some seasons are definitely busier than others. When you go may very well affect what you see, how much you pay, and how long you stand in line. In this chapter, I explain the advantages and disadvantages of visiting during the spring, summer, fall, and winter months so that you can decide the best time for your big vacation.

The Secrets of the Seasons

Although Orlando has something for all ages, the city is primarily a destination for families. So any time children are out of school, whether for spring break or a three-day holiday, the theme parks are a tangle of pushy, sweaty little bodies.

 By far the busiest times to visit are during spring break (Feb to mid-Apr), the summer (Memorial Day weekend to Labor Day weekend), and the winter holidays (Thanksgiving week and mid-Dec to early Jan). Keep in mind that any holidays that fall during those peak-season weeks bring with them exponential increases in crowd levels.

Obviously, your vacation experience would be the best when crowds are thin and the weather is mild. In most destinations, such times would normally describe the off season; however, Orlando really has no off season. As the tourists begin their homeward journey, business clients and the convention trade start pouring in. International visitors also keep things busy year-round. This year-round popularity means that many hotels don't offer a traditional high- and low-season rate scale — and it also means that you need to book your trip as early as possible.

 My favorite time of year to head to Orlando is between September and mid-November. The crowds tend to be thinnest following the Labor Day weekend and through the first weeks of November because school is once again back in session. Florida residents often scoot to the parks during this time for a day trip or a long weekend. But most out-of-state guests don't have that luxury. If you have younger children, consider pulling them out of school for a few days during the slower months to avoid the horrendous lines. Ask their teachers for schoolwork to take with you. You can also suggest that your kids write a report on an educational element of the vacation. (And yes, they'll actually learn something while they're traipsing around places like **Innoventions: The Road to Tomorrow** and the **World Showcase,** both at Epcot; the various marine-life exhibits at SeaWorld; and the Orlando Science Center in downtown Orlando, among other venues.)

Even if you come during the slower season, the parks run close to full tilt, although operating hours are generally markedly shorter. No matter what time of year you find yourself heading to Orlando, you'll want to be aware of that season's perks and pitfalls.

Spring: Excitement blooms in Orlando

Spring is sensational in Orlando because

- ✔ The weather is mild. Sunny days are followed by cool breezy nights. By early spring, the flowers are beginning to bloom; they're bursting with color later in the season. If your hometown is still blanketed by snow, you'll be in heaven.

- ✔ Accommodations often offer spring discounts (with the exception of the weeks surrounding the Easter holiday, when rates can be at their highest).

- ✔ The lines inside the theme parks are relatively short. Visit on a weekday and your wait for a ride is likely to be less than 30 minutes (again, the exception being the two, sometimes three, weeks on either side of the Easter holiday).

But keep in mind that

- ✔ In a region that has no winter to speak of, spring is fleeting. The daytime hours can be hot and humid by late April, although the really sticky weather doesn't usually arrive until mid- to late May.

- ✔ The high pollen count can drive allergy sufferers crazy.

- ✔ April is, by far, one of the busiest months to visit, especially around Easter. College students head down for their share of fun, while families take advantage of the time off for travel. Hotels are booked well in advance; the lines are, at times, unbearable; and the crowds border on intolerable. Everything is jam-packed.

Summer: Have fun in the Orlando sun

Summer is superb in Orlando because

- ✔ Daylight is plentiful, most parks take full advantage by remaining open until 9 p.m. or often later (10 p.m., 11 p.m., or even midnight closings are not out of the question), and long days are usually capped off by spectacular nighttime fireworks displays.

✔ Crowds are manageable. Even though summer is one of the most popular seasons, it pales in comparison to spring break and the winter holidays. The weekends are busier than at almost any other time of the year, but the weekdays bring a bit of relief.

✔ August offers back-to-school sales at Orlando's malls and outlets.

✔ All hotels, major restaurants, and indoor tourist attractions in Central Florida have air-conditioning.

✔ Orlando has some cool pools and unique water parks. Splashing around in any one of them makes for a fun way to beat the heat.

However, keep in mind that

✔ Outside, the heat and humidity can be downright oppressive. Those with respiratory problems may feel as if they're trying to breathe in a steam room.

✔ Crowds and sweat create a sometimes-unpleasant perfume in the air. And with the UV index at its extreme, you'll burn in less than 20 minutes without a good sunscreen.

✔ There's not much of a chance of getting discounts. Why should anyone cut prices when everything is running at capacity?

Fall: Harvest good times in Orlando

Fall is fabulous in Orlando because

✔ With schools back in session, crowds are at their thinnest.

✔ Accommodations may offer discounts in the fall.

✔ With smaller crowds, wait times for lines can be 30 minutes or less.

But keep in mind that

✔ Although the weather is cooler, the temperature doesn't get as mild as it is in the spring until Thanksgiving or later.

✔ Smaller crowds mean shorter park hours. Closing times of 6 or 7 p.m. (sometimes even earlier) are not uncommon.

✔ When mid-December arrives, so do the higher prices.

Winter: You'll be warm and welcome in Orlando

Winter is wonderful in Orlando because

✔ Orlando doesn't have a true winter. Some nights approach freezing temperatures, but the days are still relatively mild and sunny.

January and February have the biggest temperature swings. One day it can reach 80°F, the next it may only get into the 40s.

✔ With the exception of the holiday period from mid-December to just after New Year's — the busiest season of all — lines at the parks don't get much shorter than they do during this time of year.

However, remember that

✔ The many conventions held in Orlando throughout the year keep room rates from plunging completely, and conventioneers can take over entire hotels, sometimes making rooms hard to find.

✔ During the Thanksgiving and mid-December to early January holidays, the parks are just as crowded as on summer weekends (if not more so).

Weather warnings

You don't need to worry too much, but knowing a little about Florida's weather-related temper tantrums is a good idea. Here's a list of weather events that you may experience during your stay:

✔ **Hurricanes:** The Gulf and Atlantic hurricane seasons run from June 1 to November 30. In an average year, the Atlantic churns out ten of these storms, and on average one or two touch Florida. The Gulf adds three to five. The good news: Orlando's inland location generally means the worst a hurricane can do is ruin a couple days of vacation with heavy rains. (That said, in Aug and Sept of 2004, hurricanes Charley, Frances, and Jeanne swept through Orlando, causing massive shutdowns and evacuations. Although this was an extremely rare occurrence, it's something to keep in mind.)

✔ **Lightning:** This scary but beautiful show, courtesy of Mother Nature, makes regular appearances during Orlando's frequent summer thunderstorms. Don't let lightning ruin your trip, however. Unless you go out of your way to attract it, lightning's wrath likely won't bother you. Use common sense and you should be fine.

✔ **Sun:** Florida isn't called the Sunshine State without good reason. Make sure that you use plenty of sunscreen (SPF 30 or higher). You won't enjoy your vacation much if you're laid up with a painful sunburn or, even worse, sun poisoning.

Go to www.weather.com just before your trip and enter the zip code 32830 to get an extended forecast for the area.

Table 3-1 lists, by month, average high and low temperatures recorded in Central Florida.

Table 3-1			Central Florida Average Temperatures								
	Jan	*Feb*	*Mar*	*Apr*	*May*	*June*	*July*	*Aug*	*Sept*	*Oct*	*Nov*	*Dec*
High (°F/°C)	72/ 22	73/ 23	78/ 26	84/ 29	88/ 31	91/ 33	92/ 33	92/ 33	90/ 32	84/ 29	78/ 26	73/ 23
Low (°F/°C)	49/ 10	50/ 10	55/ 13	60/ 16	66/ 19	71/ 22	73/ 23	73/ 23	73/ 23	65/ 19	57/ 14	51/ 11

Keeping cool, hydrated, and burn-free

Take frequent breaks in the shade or in the comfort of air-conditioning, especially if you have kids in tow. Wearing lightweight, light-colored clothing will help alleviate the effects of the searing sunshine.

Sunburns can really ruin a fun day at the parks. Slather yourself and your kids (even the ones in covered strollers) with a sunblock that has an SPF of at least 30 (SPF 50 is even better for the kids). Pick a formula that's both waterproof and sweatproof. And don't forget sunglasses.

To avoid dehydration, drink more fluids than you think you need. By the time you're thirsty and cranky from walking around in the heat, you're already dehydrated. Ignoring these signs could lead to heat exhaustion or worse. Avoid caffeinated or carbonated beverages, as well as alcoholic drinks and those high in sugar. Sports drinks can supplement fluids in your body, but water should be your first choice.

Freeze a couple of water bottles to bring along — they stay cold far longer and save you a few dollars in the end (especially because you can refill them throughout the day at a drinking fountain for free).

Orlando's Calendar: Attractions in Review

In this section, I list a few of Orlando's many exciting festivals and special events. Double-check with the festivals' respective governing organizations before planning your vacation around any of them. Event dates, as with everything else, are subject to change.

The Orlando/Orange County Convention & Visitors Bureau Web site at www.orlandoinfo.com has information about other upcoming events.

January

The second-ranked teams from the Southeastern and Big Ten college football conferences square off at the annual **Capital One Florida Citrus Bowl.** Tickets are $65 before November 1 and $75 up until the day of the game. Call ☎ **407-423-2476** for information, or **Ticketmaster** at ☎ **866-448-7849** or 407-839-3900 (or go to www.fcsports.com). January 1.

Why walk through the WDW parks when you can run the **Walt Disney World Marathon** (☎ 407-939-7810; www.disneysports.com)? The course starts and ends at Epcot, winding through each of the other Disney parks. Spots fill up fast, so sign up as early as possible. The entrance fee will run you $125. A half-marathon ($115) is an option for those not quite ready for all 26.2 miles. If you're up for the challenge of running both races, sign up for **Goofy's Race and a Half Challenge** ($235), which fills up especially quickly. Those with children won't be left behind: The **Family Fun Run** ($40–$45) winds around Disney's Hollywood Studios. Shorter kiddie races ($10–$25) take place at the Wide World of Sports Complex. January 9, 10, and 11.

Pint-size pirates and pretty princesses reign at the **Magic Kingdom** during **Mickey's Pirate & Princess Party** (☎ 407-934-7639; www.disneyworld.com), a new after-hours event. Set out on a quest for treasure, filling your booty bag with beads and chocolate doubloons. Party the night away at pirate coves and princess courts where live entertainment includes Captain Jack's Pirate Tutorial and Sebastian's Undersea Dance Party. Be sure to catch the Enchanted Adventures Parade and the fireworks spectacular. A separate admission ticket is required. Advance-purchase tickets run $46 for adults and $40 for kids ages 3 to 9; add $6 per ticket if purchased the day of the event. Select nights from mid-January through mid-June and again in August.

The multiday **Zora Neale Hurston Festival** (☎ 407-647-3307; www.zorafestival.com) is celebrated in Eatonville, the first incorporated African-American town in America. The festival highlights the life and works of author Zora Neale Hurston. Eatonville is 25 miles north of the parks. Admission ranges from $5 to $15 adults, $3 kids ages 4 to 17. Lectures, seminars, and special events are extra. Late January.

February

Authentic parade floats from New Orleans, stilt walkers, and traditional doubloons and beads add to the fun at **Mardi Gras at Universal Studios Florida** (☎ 800-837-2273 or 407-363-8000; www.universalorlando.com). This party flows with plenty of alcohol, making it more of an adult-oriented event. Nationally known bands and artists ranging from KC and the Sunshine Band to Kid Rock play the stage inside the park. Mardi Gras events are included in the regular price of admission to the park, with discounted admission available after 5 p.m. Select Saturday nights from February to mid-April.

The **Atlanta Braves** head south to **Disney's Wide World of Sports Complex** for spring training. The Braves play a 15-game spring season that begins in early March. Tickets range from $14 to $24. For information, call ☎ 407-939-4263 or go to www.disneysports.com or www.atlantabraves.com. For tickets, call Ticketmaster at ☎ 866-448-7849 or 407-839-3900. Late February to March.

The **Silver Spurs Rodeo** features real cowboys in calf roping, bull riding, and more. It's held at the Silver Spurs Arena, 1875 E. Irlo Bronson Memorial Hwy. (U.S. 192), Kissimmee. Tickets cost $15. Call ☎ **407-677-6336** or go to www.silverspursrodeo.com. It runs for three days in February and again for three days in June.

March

The **SeaWorld BBQ Fest** (☎ **800-327-2424** or 407-351-3600; www.seaworld orlando.com) features a great barbecue and performances by popular country artists. The concerts are included with regular park admission, but if you're hankering after a mouth-watering meal, you'll have to pay extra to eat. Two weekends in mid-March.

The **Winter Park Sidewalk Art Festival** (☎ **407-672-6390**; www.wpsaf. org) is one of the nation's most prestigious fine-arts festivals. This free three-day event is filled with art, food, kids' activities, and jazz performances. March 20, 21, and 22.

April

The ten-day **Florida Film Festival** (☎ **407-644-6579** or 407-629-1088; www.floridafilmfestival.com or www.enzian.org) showcases the year's best independent and foreign films. Single-film tickets are $10, with special ticket packages also available. Early April.

SeaWorld offers four weekends of sensational music, dance, food, and crafts to celebrate Hispanic culture in Florida at its **Viva La Musica** (☎ **800-327-2424**; www.seaworldorlando.com). The festivities are included with regular park admission. Four weekends in April.

From garden beds in the form of those famous Mickey ears to whimsical topiaries in the shape of Disney characters, the six-week **Epcot International Flower & Garden Festival** (☎ **407-934-7639**; www.disneyworld. com) shows what Disney can do to Mother Nature's finest foliage. Themed weekends, workshops, and concerts are all part of the fun. Included with regular admission. Late April to early June.

May

More than 100 acts from around the world participate in the eclectic ten-day **Orlando International Fringe Festival** (☎ **407-648-0077**; www. orlandofringe.org), which takes place at various locations in downtown Orlando. Outdoor concerts and Kids Fringe round out the offerings. Fringe buttons cost $6 — you'll need one to enter the shows. Ticket prices vary by performance, with most under $10. Mid-May.

June

Gay Days (www.gayday.com or www.gaydays.com) draws tens of thousands of gay and lesbian travelers to Central Florida. This event began in 1991 at **Disney World;** it has since expanded to a weeklong celebration, during which **Universal Orlando** and **SeaWorld** also host events. Saturday is when they descend en masse on the **Magic Kingdom.** First weekend in June.

The Force will be with you during the four *Star Wars* Weekends at **Disney's Hollywood Studios** (☎ **407-934-7639;** www.disneyworld. com). In addition to various themed shows and parades, each weekend features meet-and-greets with actual actors from the movies. Included with regular Disney's Hollywood Studios admission. Five weekends from late May through June.

July

Independence Day is celebrated with bands, singers, dancers, and fireworks at **Disney** (☎ **407-824-4321;** www.disneyworld.com). The parks stay open late for the occasion. **SeaWorld** (☎ **407-351-3600;** www. seaworld.com) puts on a dazzling laser/fireworks spectacular, as does **Universal Orlando** (☎ **407-363-8000;** www.universalorlando.com). Orlando's **Lake Eola Park** (☎ **407-246-2827;** www.cityoforlando.net) features activities and entertainment throughout the late afternoon, as well as free nighttime fireworks.

The NFL's **Tampa Bay Buccaneers** run their training camp at **Disney's Wide World of Sports.** Call ☎ **407-939-GAME (4236)** or go to www. buccaneers.com for details. Late July through August.

September

The **Magic Kingdom** plays host to a contemporary Christian and gospel music festival, **Night of Joy** (☎ **407-824-4321;** www.disneyworld.com/ nightofjoy). Get tickets far in advance. Concert admission is ticketed separately from regular admission; park attractions are included. Prices are $45 (one night) if purchased in advance, $50 at the gate, and $76 (two nights). Early September.

Universal goes head-to-head with Disney, scheduling its **Rock the Universe** Christian music concert the very same weekend (☎ **800-837-2273;** www.rocktheuniverse.com). Tickets purchased in advance run $37 for one night or $60 for both nights; tickets purchased the day of the event run $6 extra. Admission includes entrance to **Universal Studios** after 4 p.m., the concerts, and full use of the park's rides and attractions until 1 a.m. Combination tickets that include all-day park admission are also available. Early September.

October

At the **Epcot International Food & Wine Festival** (☎ **407-824-4321;** www.disneyworld.com), you can savor the food and beverages of 25 countries for under $6 per sample. Events include wine tastings, seminars, concerts, and cooking demonstrations by celebrity chefs. Some specially ticketed dinners or wine tastings are available at prices ranging from $35 to $200. Late September to mid-November.

Islands of Adventure transforms its grounds with haunted attractions for 20 or so nights in honor of Universal Orlando's **Halloween Horror Nights** (☎ **800-837-2273** or 407-363-8000; www.halloweenhorrornights. com). Complete with live bands, special shows, a psychopath's maze, and hundreds of ghouls and goblins, the studio closes at dusk and then reopens in a new, chilling form at 7 p.m. The park charges full adult admission ($71) for this event (children under 10 aren't permitted), which lasts until about midnight. Guests aren't allowed to wear costumes so that Universal employees can spot their peers. This event tends to sell out. Select nights in October.

If your young ones are more into treats than tricks, try **Mickey's Not-So-Scary Halloween Party** (☎ **407-824-4321;** www.disneyworld. com) at the **Magic Kingdom,** complete with Mickey's "Boo-to-You" Halloween Parade and the Happy HalloWishes fireworks display. Cast members hand out treats throughout the park. This is a separately ticketed event held after regular park closing, but most attractions remain open. Tickets are $49 to $56 for adults and $43 to $46 for children 9 or younger. This event tends to sell out; tickets go on sale in May. Select nights in September and October.

Family-friendly festivities at **SeaWorld's Halloween Spooktacular** (☎ **800-327-2424** or 407-351-3600; www.seaworld.com) include parades, not-so-spooky shows, and trick-or-treating throughout the park. Included with regular park admission. Select weekends in October.

Top PGA tour players compete at WDW golf courses during the month of October at **The Disney Golf Classic.** Many tour professionals, including Tiger Woods, call Orlando home, so there's usually plenty of first-rate talent on display. Daily ticket prices range from $15 to $35. Tickets for the 4-day event run about $50. For information, contact Walt Disney World Golf Sales, P.O. Box 10000, Lake Buena Vista, FL 32830 (☎ **407-824-2250;** www.disneyworld.com). You also can get tickets through the Children's Miracle Network at www.childrensmiraclenetworkclassic.com.

November

Soap-opera fanatics descend upon **Disney's Hollywood Studios** during the **ABC Super Soap Weekend** (☎ **407-824-4321;** www.disneyworld. com) to get up-close-and-personal with their favorite stars from *All My Children, One Life to Live,* and *General Hospital.* Included with regular park admission. First weekend of November.

Downtown Disney Marketplace is home to the free **Festival of the Masters** (☎ **407-824-4321;** www.disneyworld.com), one of the largest art shows in the South. Second weekend in November.

December

During the **Disney Christmas festivities,** Main Street in the **Magic Kingdom** is lavishly decked out with lights and holly. **Epcot** and **Disney's**

Animal Kingdom offer special entertainment throughout the season, as do all Disney resorts. **Disney's Hollywood Studios** offers the world-famous **Osborne Family Spectacle of Lights. Mickey's Very Merry Christmas Party,** an after-hours specially ticketed event, takes place on select evenings at the Magic Kingdom. Admission ($49 –$56 adults, $43–$46 kids 3–9) includes cookies, cocoa, and a souvenir photo. The best part? Shorter lines for rides. The **Candlelight Procession** at **Epcot** has hundreds of candle-holding carolers, a celebrity narrator telling the Christmas story, and a 450-voice choir that's very moving. Regular park admission is required, but special dinner packages include special seating for the event ($34–$54 adults; $13–$15 kids 3–9, depending on the restaurant and the tier of seating chosen). Call ☎ **407-824-4321** for details on these events or visit www.disneyworld.com. Dates vary by event, but most take place from late November to late December.

Part II

Planning Your Trip to Walt Disney World and Orlando

"Good news! I got us a great theme park inspired flight to Orlando. The 'Bumpity Flubbity Flight to Adventure.'"

In this part . . .

Okay, it's nitty-gritty time. In this part, I suggest some ways you can save money on your vacation, and I lay out the different ways you can get to Disney World and Orlando. I also sort out the various travel packages available to the city and offer suggestions on buying travel insurance, staying healthy, and staying in contact with those who didn't get to make the trip. And so everyone has a good time, I offer dedicated advice to those people who have special travel needs or interests — families, seniors, and gays and lesbians.

Chapter 4

Managing Your Money

● ●

In This Chapter

▶ Managing your dollars and cents
▶ Cutting your vacation costs
▶ Paying for it all

● ●

*D*eveloping a realistic budget is an important key to enjoying your vacation. The last thing you want to experience when you get to Orlando is sticker shock — Central Florida is famous for its ability to exact a pound of flesh from even the most cost-conscious traveler. From hotel rooms to meal tabs to admission fees, you can easily break the bank if you don't do some homework and set some limits in advance. The good news is that there are ways to avoid blowing your bankroll, and I show them to you in this chapter.

Planning Your Budget

When it comes to your Orlando vacation, working out a budget may be the single most important thing you do. The hard part is sticking to it after you've been swept up in all the excitement. Mickey and his pals are masters when it comes to separating you from your money. But by using the tips I give you, you can come up with a pretty accurate estimate of what a trip to Mickey's place may cost you.

 When making your budget, be sure to include every possible expense, especially hidden charges that, unless you specifically ask, are almost never quoted when you inquire about hotel or rental-car rates, attraction admissions, and restaurant prices. Florida sales taxes, which run from 6.5 percent on merchandise to almost 25 percent on rental cars, are chief on the list of these hidden charges. For more information, see "Taxes" in the Quick Concierge appendix.

Another hidden expense many travelers fail to budget for is tips. Orlando is a tip-happy place. A 15 percent tip is the general rule for restaurant service and cab rides. The hotel housekeeper deserves $1 to $2 a day for cleaning up your mess, making your beds, and keeping you stocked with towels and toilet paper. Baggage handlers usually receive at least $1 per bag. And don't forget about a $1 to $2 tip for valet parking.

Most of your Orlando vacation expenses fall into six categories:

- ✔ **Lodging:** The average rack rate for a three-star hotel in Orlando is about $106 per night (see Chapter 9). In most cases, those rates include any children younger than 12, and usually younger than 18, staying in your room. The lowest standard room rates at WDW are those at the All-Star and Pop Century resorts, which, depending on the season, run from $82 to $151. They're pricier than comparable rooms in the outside world; they're tiny, basic, and heavily themed; but they're on Disney soil.

- ✔ **Transportation:** Some hotels offer free shuttles to the parks; others take you for a fee (see Chapter 8 for more information). If you stay at Disney, you can access its free Disney Transportation system (though it's plodding). Rental-car rates start at about $35 a day after you've tossed in Florida's various taxes and surcharges (which can total 20 percent to 25 percent above the quoted rate). And don't forget to add the $11 ($12 for some) daily charge to park your car at the theme parks — though you won't have to pay this at the Disney parks if you're a guest at one of Mickey's resorts. If you're a fan of valet parking, add at least $7 to $25 per day (and possibly a whole lot more) for fees and tips. And an increasing number of hotels charge to park your car yourself — at times as much as $12 (though I've seen rates as high as $18) per day. If you're flying into Orlando, don't forget to add the cost of getting to the airport, air-port parking (if you're driving yourself), airline tickets (you can find tips for getting the best airfare in Chapter 5), and transporta-tion from the Orlando airport to your room (unless you're staying with Mickey and take Disney's Magical Express — see Chapter 9 for details). If you're driving to Orlando, be sure to include your fuel costs and tolls.

- ✔ **Dining:** Satisfying your stomach in Orlando is the biggest variable in your budget, and outside of admissions, tickets, and accommo-dations it can easily end up being your biggest expense. If you're happy with a diet of nothing but fast food, expect an average of $35 to $45 per person, per day, including tax and tip. Adding one or two restaurant meals jumps the average up to $50 to $65 per person, per day; expect to spend $65 or more per person if you dine mostly in the theme parks or at Disney's and Universal's resorts, where prices are almost 25 percent higher than those in the outside world. (See Chapter 10 for more information on dining.) Keep in mind that food in the parks and resorts is overpriced and is average at best (though there are exceptions). Outside the parks, you can find delis and pizzerias for takeout as well as assorted budget-minded eateries.

- ✔ **Attractions:** Your expenses for attractions depend on which parks you plan to visit and how many days you spend at each. Before you throw in sales tax, Disney and Universal charge $75 per adult and $63 per child ages 3 to 9, per day. SeaWorld tickets come in slightly lower. (See Chapters 12–16 and Chapters 18–20 for information about the individual parks.) If you're planning to visit any of these parks more than once, buying a multiday and, in some cases, multipark pass is by far the best — and most cost-effective — way to go. Chapter 21 includes some less expensive and even free attractions that you can visit if you want to cut your costs and broaden your experiences.

✔ **Shopping:** Orlando is a shopper's paradise, with several large malls and outlets (see Chapter 22) and an array of souvenir shops to choose from. The amusement-park gift shops are notorious for inflating prices on souvenirs; although I don't recommend picking up more than a couple of souvenirs at the parks, be prepared for their ability to lure you in. Budget accordingly.

✔ **Nightlife:** If you stick to the theme-park options, plan on dropping anywhere from $5 to $22 for admission to the various nightspots, but after including a few $5 beers (or $9 cocktails), your total can easily reach $30, $40, $50, or more for a night on the town. (See Chapter 25 for information about the various park nightlife options.) If you have a car (a rental or your own), you can take advantage of downtown options, which can be slightly less expensive, at around $20 to $30 for cover charges and a few beers (but because I don't recommend you drink and drive, the theme parks, entertainment districts, and hotel lounges may well be a better option).

After estimating your expenses, be sure to tack on another 15 percent to 20 percent to your budget as a safety net — a pair of fuzzy light-up Mickey ears are bound to be calling the name of someone in your group.

Table 4-1 outlines various vacationing costs in Orlando.

Table 4-1	What Things Cost in Orlando	
	U.S. $	*U.K. £ **
Taxi from airport to WDW (4–5 people)	50	26
Shuttle (round-trip) from airport to WDW (two adults, two kids)	65–92	33–47
Double room at Masters Inn Maingate, Kissimmee	31–150	16–77
Double room at Disney's All-Star Resorts	82–151	42–77
Double room at Disney's Coronado Springs Resort	149–240	76–122
Double room at Hard Rock Hotel Universal Orlando	244–369	124–187
Double room at Disney's Grand Floridian	385–990	198–508
Coca-Cola (restaurant)	2.25	1.15
Bottle of beer (restaurant)	3.75	1.90

(continued)

Table 4-1 *(continued)*

	U.S. $	U.K. £ *
All-you-can-eat buffet dinner at Akershus Royal Banquet Hall in Epcot, not including tip or wine	30	15
Six-course fixed-price dinner for one at Victoria & Albert's, not including tip or wine	115–205	59–105
Child 1-day, 1-park admission to Walt Disney World	63	32
Adult 1-day, 1-park admission to Walt Disney World	75	38
Child 2-day, 2-park Universal Orlando ticket (purchased at gate)	110	56
Adult 2-day, 2-park Universal Orlando ticket (purchased at gate)	120	61
Child 4-day Magic Your Way ticket with Park Hopper Option to Walt Disney World	234	119
Adult 4-day Magic Your Way ticket with Park Hopper Option to Walt Disney World	269	137

* As of this writing, 1£ = $1.97

Cutting Costs — But Not the Fun

You can conserve your cash in a variety of ways when you vacation in Orlando. Using these tips can keep your costs manageable:

- **Visit during non-peak times.** Hotel prices from September to November or from late April to early June can be substantially lower, depending on the property.

- **Travel midweek.** If you can travel on a Tuesday, Wednesday, or Thursday, you may find cheaper flights to your destination. When you ask about airfares, find out whether you can get a cheaper rate by flying on a different day. For more tips on getting a good fare, see Chapter 5.

- **Try a package tour.** For many Orlando destinations, you can book airfare, hotel, ground transportation, and even some additional perks just by making one call to a travel agent or packager, often for a price much less than if you put the trip together yourself. (See Chapter 5 for more about package tours.)

- **Ask whether your kids can stay in the room with you.** A room with two double beds usually doesn't cost any more than one with a queen-size bed. And many hotels don't charge you the additional-person rate if the additional person is pint-size and related to you.

Many Orlando hotels offer "suites" with bunk beds or separate sleeping areas for kids. They may cost more than a regular room, but even if you have to pay extra for the additional space or a roll-away bed, you can save hundreds by not having to book two rooms.

✔ **Reserve a room with a refrigerator and coffeemaker.** You don't have to slave over a hot stove to cut costs; several hotels have minifridges, coffeemakers, and even microwaves. Buying supplies for breakfast saves you money — and probably calories.

✔ **Don't bunk with Mickey.** This one may be hard to swallow for those who want to immerse themselves in all things Disney. And if your vacation can't be complete without a stay on Walt Disney World property, then by all means splurge. But if you're on a tight budget, you can stay in some wonderful, at times themed (albeit non-Mickey) properties for less than you would pay for the cheapest Disney hotels.

✔ **Take advantage of your in-and-out privileges if you have a multi-day pass to a theme park.** Go back to your hotel for a picnic lunch and a swim or a nap. You can eat economically, avoid the midday sun, and refuel for an afternoon or, in some cases, an evening at the park without having to pay admission fees again.

✔ **Avoid splurging — pace yourself.** Your money goes fastest when you overexert yourself exploring the parks, and you end up too hungry, thirsty, or tired to care about how much you spend. Be sure to schedule rest breaks throughout the day and begin each day with a big breakfast (several hotels offer spreads that are included in their room rates). You can find several breakfast buffets outside the parks for around $5 to $7 — and kids can often dine for free (see Chapter 10).

✔ **Brown-bag it.** Bringing your own food is extremely cost-effective. The parks are wise to this scheme and many don't allow coolers, but they generally ignore it when you aren't obvious about it, so make your operation covert — hide food in a fanny pack or backpack. If you don't want to schlep food, do bring drinks or stop often at drinking fountains — the bottled water and soda prices in the parks can have you wondering if the theme parks are selling liquid gold instead of Coke.

✔ **Try expensive restaurants at lunch instead of dinner.** Lunch tabs are usually a fraction of what dinner costs at a top restaurant, and the menu often boasts many of the same specialties.

✔ **Don't rent a gas guzzler.** Renting a smaller car is generally cheaper, and you save on gas to boot. For more about car rentals, see Chapter 7.

✔ **Don't spend every day at a theme park.** Discover your hotel's pool, playground, workout room, and other freebies, or head out of town to a state park, beach, or one of the lower-priced attractions away from theme-park central. Check out Chapters 21 and 26 for some suggestions.

✔ **Skip (or at least skimp on) the souvenirs.** Your photographs and your memories could be the best mementos of your trip. If you're worried that you'll blow your budget, you can do without the T-shirts and other trinkets.

✔ **Surf the Web.** The Web site MouseSavers.com keeps track of almost all available discounts for Disney-related vacations (from room discount codes to special packages and promotions). If you want to stay at a Disney resort, MouseSavers.com will likely help you save money doing it.

✔ **Receive instant discounts with an Orlando Preferred Visitor Magicard.** The Orlando Magicard is good for up to $500 in discounts on accommodations, car rentals, attractions, and more. Better yet, the card is free. You can get a Magicard from the Orlando/Orange County Convention & Visitors Bureau, 8723 International Dr., Ste. 101, Orlando, FL 32819 (☎ **800-643-9492** or 407-363-5872; www.orlando info.com/magicard/index.cfm). You may also be eligible for other discounts if you're a member of AARP, AAA, the military, or service clubs, so don't be bashful — just ask.

Handling Money

You're the best judge of how much cash you feel comfortable carrying or what alternative form of currency is your favorite. That's not going to change much on your vacation. True, you'll probably be moving around more and incurring more expenses than you generally do (unless you happen to eat out every meal when you're at home), and you may let your mind slip into vacation gear and not be as vigilant about your safety as when you're in work mode. But, those factors aside, the only type of payment that won't be quite as available to you away from home is your personal checkbook.

Using ATMs and carrying cash

The easiest and best way to get cash away from home is from an automated teller machine (ATM). The **Cirrus** (☎ **800-424-7787**; www. mastercard.com) and **PLUS** (☎ **800-843-7587**; www.visa.com) ATM networks span the globe; look at the back of your bank card to find out which network you're on, and then call or check online for ATM locations at your destination. You can find ATMs at all of Orlando's major theme parks; check the guide map you get upon entering each park for locations.

Keep in mind that many banks impose a fee every time you use your card at a different bank's ATM. In Florida, you're assessed an average charge of $2.75 when you use an ATM that isn't affiliated with your bank. (That's on top of any fees your own bank may charge.)

Disney-style dollars

Walt Disney World theme parks and some resorts offer their own way of paying: You can use your electronic room key as a debit card in Disney's shops and restaurants — and the items are charged directly to your room.

Although I don't recommend doing so, you can also buy Disney Dollars (currency with cute little pictures of Mickey, Goofy, Minnie, or even a familiar pirate or two printed on it) at the resorts or the Guest Services desk in each of the parks. The bills come in $1, $5, and $10 denominations, and they're good at shops, restaurants, and resorts throughout Walt Disney World and in Disney Stores elsewhere on the planet. This currency provides no real benefit other than its negligible souvenir value. If you want to trade Disney Dollars for real currency upon leaving, you end up facing — you guessed it! — one more line in the theme parks.

Be advised that refunds for deposits on wheelchairs, strollers, and such in the theme parks are often paid in Disney Dollars. But if you're persistent, you can get your refunds in Uncle Sam's currency, instead of Mickey's.

Be extremely careful when using ATMs, especially at night and in areas that are heavily traveled but not well lighted. Don't let the land of Mickey lull you into a false sense of security. Minnie and Goofy won't mug you — but thieves working the theme-park zones may.

Charging ahead with credit cards

Credit cards are a safe way to carry money. They also provide a convenient record of all your expenses and generally offer relatively good exchange rates. You can also withdraw cash advances from your credit cards at banks or ATMs, provided you know your PIN. If you forgot yours, or didn't even know you had one, call the number on the back of your credit card, and ask the bank to send it to you. It usually takes five to seven business days, though some banks provide the number over the phone if you tell them your mother's maiden name or some other personal information.

Keep in mind that you start paying interest on credit card cash advances the minute you get them — and it's generally much higher than the rate for charging your purchases. If you use a debit card that carries a Visa or MasterCard logo to make a purchase, choosing to use it as a credit card rather than a debit card will usually save you from paying additional fees (while still simply debiting your account).

Toting traveler's checks

These days, traveler's checks are less necessary because most cities have 24-hour ATMs that allow you to withdraw small amounts of cash as needed. However, keep in mind that you will likely be charged an ATM withdrawal fee if the bank is not your own. So if you're withdrawing money every day, you may be better off with traveler's checks — provided that you don't mind showing identification every time you want to cash one. All the major theme parks and resorts accept traveler's checks from major banks.

 If you choose to carry traveler's checks, be sure to keep a record of their serial numbers separate from your checks in case they're stolen or lost. You'll get a refund faster if you know the numbers.

Dealing with a Lost or Stolen Wallet

Be sure to contact all your credit card companies the minute you discover your wallet has been lost or stolen, and file a report at the nearest police precinct. Your credit card company or insurer may require a police report number or record of the loss. Most credit card companies have an emergency toll-free number to call if your card is lost or stolen; they may be able to wire you a cash advance immediately or deliver an emergency credit card in a day or two. Call the following emergency numbers in the United States:

- **American Express:** ☎ 800-992-3404 (for cardholders and traveler's check holders)
- **MasterCard:** ☎ 800-627-8372 or 636-722-7111
- **Visa:** ☎ 800-847-2911 or 410-581-9994

For other credit cards, call the toll-free number directory at ☎ 800-555-1212.

If you need emergency cash over the weekend, when all banks and American Express offices are closed, you can have money wired to you via **Western Union** (☎ 800-325-6000; www.westernunion.com).

Identity theft or fraud is a potential complication of losing your wallet, especially if you've lost your driver's license along with your credit cards. Notify the major credit-reporting bureaus immediately; placing a fraud alert on your records may protect you against liability for criminal activity. The three major U.S. credit-reporting agencies are **Equifax** (☎ 800-766-0008; www.equifax.com), **Experian** (☎ 888-397-3742; www.experian.com), and **TransUnion** (☎ 800-680-7289; www.transunion.com). Finally, if you lose all forms of photo ID, call your airline and explain the situation; it may allow you to board your plane if you have a copy of your passport or birth certificate and a copy of the police report you've filed.

Chapter 5

Getting to Orlando

* *

In This Chapter

▶ Getting a good airline fare
▶ Arriving in Orlando by car
▶ Taking the train to Orlando
▶ Checking out package tours

* *

*G*etting to your destination isn't always half the fun of your trip, but you can choose ways to get from point A to point B without too much hassle or expense. In this chapter, I eliminate the travel double talk, shed the useless options, and make sure that you have a fun and easy time planning your getaway.

Flying to Orlando

Even as many airlines are cutting their service, getting to Orlando by plane is still a relative breeze. Almost every major domestic airline offers direct service to Mickeyville from most major cities in the United States and Canada. A number of international carriers also fly direct from several major European and South American cities.

Finding Out which airlines fly there

If you're flying to Orlando, the best place to land is **Orlando International Airport** (☎ **407-825-2001;** www.orlandoairports.net). The airport, which locals refer to as OIA (confusingly, the official airport code is MCO), offers direct or nonstop service from approximately 60 U.S. and 25 international cities. About 50 scheduled airlines and several charters feed nearly 37 million people through its gates annually. For a list of all the major airlines that fly into the city, see "Toll-Free Numbers and Web Sites" in the Quick Concierge appendix.

The sheer number of flights in and out of its gates makes OIA the top dog as far as local airports go, and its location reinforces that even more. The airport connects to highways, Interstate 4, and toll roads that get you (whether you're driving or being driven) into the heart of it all within 30 or 40 minutes (fewer if you're headed into downtown Orlando).

If a proposed train running from the airport to the theme-park zones ever gets built, OIA will become that much more convenient.

Orlando Sanford International Airport (SFB; ☎ **407-585-4500;** www. orlandosanfordairport.com) is much smaller than OIA, but it has grown a bit in recent years, thanks mainly to a small fleet of international carriers including **Thomsonfly** and **Thomas Cook Airlines,** as well as regional airlines such as **Allegiant Air.** Although you may save money flying into Sanford International, it has some drawbacks: The flight schedules aren't always convenient, and you definitely need a rental car — the airport is on the northern side of Orlando, well over 45 minutes from Walt Disney World.

Getting the best deal on your airfare

Competition among the major U.S. airlines is unlike that of any other industry. Every airline offers virtually the same product, yet prices can vary by hundreds of dollars.

Business travelers who need the flexibility to buy their tickets at the last minute and change their itineraries at a moment's notice — and who want to get home before the weekend — pay the premium rate, otherwise known as the *full fare.* But if you can book your ticket far in advance, can stay over Saturday night, and are willing to travel midweek (Tues, Wed, or Thurs), you can take advantage of far less expensive tickets — usually a fraction of the full fare. Most flights, even the shortest hops within the United States, can cost upward of $1,000 or more, but a 7- or 14-day advance-purchase ticket may cost half that amount, possibly even less. Obviously, planning ahead pays off.

Search the Internet for cheap fares. The most popular online travel agencies are **Travelocity.com** (www.travelocity.co.uk); **Expedia.com** (www. expedia.co.uk and www.expedia.ca); and **Orbitz.com.** In the U.K., go to **Travelsupermarket** (☎ **0845/345-5708;** www.travelsupermarket. com), a search engine that offers flight comparisons for the budget airlines whose seats often end up in bucket-shop sales. Other Web sites for booking airline tickets include **Cheapflights.com, SmarterTravel.com, Priceline.com,** and **Opodo** (www.opodo.co.uk). Meta search sites (which find and then direct you to airline and hotel Web sites for booking) include **Sidestep.com** and **Kayak.com** — the latter includes fares for budget carriers like JetBlue and Spirit as well as the major airlines.

Site59.com is a good source for last-minute flights and getaways. Great last-minute deals are also available directly from the airlines themselves. Sign up for weekly e-mail alerts at individual airline Web sites or go to **Smarter Travel** (www.smartertravel.com), which compiles comprehensive lists of last-minute specials.

Don't forget to compare fares on the no-frills airlines (though it's difficult to tell the difference between these and the so-called full-service airlines these days) that service Orlando. The biggest of these is **Southwest**

Airlines (☎ 800-435-9792; www.southwest.com). **Spirit Airlines** (☎ 800-772-7117; www.spiritair.com) offers a good selection of flights to Orlando from several U.S. cities. **JetBlue Airways** (☎ 800-538-2583; www.jetblue.com) operates mostly on the East Coast but offers a number of routes from the West Coast. **AirTran Airways** (☎ 800-247-8726; www.airtran.com) regularly has sales on routes to Orlando from around the country; it also offers the option to upgrade to business class on most flights, right at the gate for between $35 and $120 per segment (depending on the length of your flight or whether you have a connection). Most of these no-frills airlines actually offer more in the way of extras than many of the larger carriers, given all the cutbacks and reductions in service of late. Given the numerous policy changes recently, I suggest checking the airlines' individual Web sites for up-to-date information regarding current baggage allowances (including fees) and in-flight services (including which are still being offered and at what cost).

Watch local newspapers for **promotional specials** or **fare wars,** when airlines lower prices on their most popular routes. These sales tend to take place in seasons of low travel volume — September to November and April to early June. Also keep an eye on price fluctuations and deals at websites such as **Airfarewatchdog.com** and **Farecast.com.**

Driving to Orlando

Driving to Orlando is sometimes a less expensive and potentially more scenic option, unless the distance is so great that making the road trip eats up too much of your vacation (and, thanks to rising gas prices, your budget as well).

Table 5-1 lists how far several cities are from Orlando.

Table 5-1	Driving to Orlando
City	*Distance to Orlando*
Atlanta	436 miles
Boston	1,312 miles
Chicago	1,120 miles
Cleveland	1,009 miles
Dallas	1,170 miles
Detroit	1,114 miles
New York	1,088 miles
Toronto	1,282 miles

Need directions? No problem.

- ✔ **From Atlanta,** take I-75 South to the Florida Turnpike to I-4 West.

- ✔ **From Boston and New York,** take I-95 South to I-4 West.

- ✔ **From Chicago,** take I-65 South to Nashville, and then I-24 South to I-75 South to the Florida Turnpike to I-4 West.

- ✔ **From Cleveland,** take I-77 South to Columbia, South Carolina, and then I-26 East to I-95 South to I-4 West.

- ✔ **From Dallas,** take I-20 East to I-49 South to I-10 East to I-75 South to the Florida Turnpike to I-4 West.

- ✔ **From Detroit,** take I-75 South to the Florida Turnpike to I-4 West.

- ✔ **From Toronto,** take Canadian Route 401 South to Queen Elizabeth Way South to I-90 (New York State Thruway) East to I-87 (New York State Thruway) South to I-95 over the George Washington Bridge, and continue south on I-95 to I-4 West.

AAA (☎ **800-222-1134;** www.aaa.com) offers free maps and driving directions to its members. In addition, several Web sites offer door-to-door driving directions — try **Google Maps** (http://maps.google.com), **MapQuest** (www.mapquest.com), and **Yahoo! Maps** (http://maps.yahoo.com).

Arriving by Train

Amtrak (☎ **800-872-7245;** www.amtrak.com) trains pull into two central stations: 1400 Sligh Blvd., in downtown Orlando (about 23 miles from WDW), and 111 E. Dakin Ave., in Kissimmee (about 15 miles from WDW).

Amtrak's **Auto Train** allows you to bring your car to Florida without having to drive it all the way. The service begins in Lorton, Virginia, and ends at Sanford, Florida, about 23 miles northeast of Orlando. Fares begin just under $800 for two passengers and one auto.

As with airfares, you can sometimes get discounts if you book train rides far in advance or travel in the off season. Amtrak also offers money-saving packages, including accommodations (some at WDW resorts), car rentals, tours, and so on. For package information, call ☎ **800-268-7252** or go to www.amtrakvacations.com.

Choosing a Package Tour

For popular destinations, such as Walt Disney World, package tours can be a smart way to go. In many cases, a package that includes airfare, hotel, and airport transportation costs less than the hotel alone on a tour you book yourself. That's because packages are sold in bulk to tour operators, who then resell them to the public. It's kind of like buying your vacation at a buy-in-bulk store — except the tour operator is the one who buys the 1,000-count box of candy bars and resells them 10 at a time at a cost that undercuts the local supermarket.

Package tours can vary: Some offer a better class of hotel than others; others provide the same hotels for lower prices. Some book flights on scheduled airlines; others sell charters. Some packages limit your choice of accommodations and travel days.

If you choose to buy a package, think strongly about purchasing travel insurance, especially when the tour operator asks you to pay upfront. But don't buy insurance from the tour operator! If it doesn't fulfill its obligation to provide you with the vacation you've paid for, you have no reason to think it'll fulfill its insurance obligations, either. Obtain travel insurance through an independent agency. See Chapter 7 for more information about buying travel insurance.

To find package tours, check out the travel section of your local Sunday newspaper or the ads in the back of travel magazines such as *Travel + Leisure, National Geographic Traveler,* and *Condé Nast Traveler.* **Liberty Travel** (☎ 888-271-1584; www.libertytravel.com) is one of the biggest packagers in the Northeast.

Another good source of package deals is the airlines themselves. Most major airlines offer air/land packages, including **American Airlines Vacations** (☎ 800-321-2121; www.aavacations.com), **Continental Airlines Vacations** (☎ 800-301-3800; www.covacations.com), **Delta Vacations** (☎ 800-221-6666; www.deltavacations.com), **NWA WorldVacations** (☎ 800-800-1504; www.nwaworldvacations.com), and **United Vacations** (☎ 888-854-3899; www.unitedvacations.com). Several online travel agencies — Expedia, Travelocity, Orbitz, Site59, and LastMinute.com — also do a brisk business in packages.

If you're unsure about the pedigree of a smaller packager, check with the Better Business Bureau in the city where the company is based, or go to www.bbb.org. If a packager won't tell you where it's based, don't fly with that company.

Theme-park offerings

Disney offers a dizzying array of packages that can include airfare, accommodations on or off Disney property, theme-park passes, a rental car, meals, and a Disney cruise. There are seasonal packages as well as special themed vacations, including, but not limited to, golf, honeymoons, spa makeovers, little ones' travel time, and so on.

Here are some of the plusses of booking a Disney package tour:

  ✔ Disney's Web site (www.disneyworld.com) offers planning tools that help visitors design and price their own packages. There's even a Magical Gatherings option that offers special tips and features for families and groups traveling together.

✔ Nobody knows the Diz better than its own staffers.

✔ Disney reps can offer rooms in all price ranges ($82 and up).

✔ New ticketing options allow far more flexibility than ever before, so you don't end up with all that extra stuff you really don't want.

However, be aware of the following drawbacks to Disney package deals:

✔ Resort guests receive the same perks, whether you buy your Disney package from Disney or somewhere else (and sometimes other places, such as AAA, offer additional perks to people who book with them instead of directly with Disney).

✔ You have to prod Disney reservations agents for details. If you don't ask about deals to begin with, the agents frequently don't volunteer suggestions, such as the possibility that you can save money if you start your Disney vacation a day earlier or later.

✔ Some WDW package perks aren't always worth the extra money. For example, if they say you get your picture taken with Mickey as part of the deal, expect that you can find a better deal elsewhere and pay for your own photo. What you're really paying for is the convenience of having Disney plan the details.

✔ If you want to see more of Orlando than WDW (and most people do), you need to compare the offerings of a Disney agent with those of a regular travel agent. A motivated travel agent can put together a package of Disney and non-Disney accommodations and attractions for less than the amount WDW charges.

For detailed information on Disney packages, order a Walt Disney World Vacations brochure or DVD by contacting Walt Disney World, Box 10000, Lake Buena Vista, FL 32830-1000 (☎ **407-939-7675;** www. disneyworld.com).

Although not on the same scale as Disney, the packages at **Universal Orlando** have improved greatly since the addition of the **Islands of Adventure** theme park (see Chapter 19), the **CityWalk** entertainment district (see Chapters 10 and 25), and the **Portofino Bay, Hard Rock,** and **Royal Pacific hotels** (see Chapter 9). Package choices include resort stays (which include an array of off-property options, though the perks vary slightly from those staying at on-site hotels); VIP access to the parks, rides, and, often, restaurants; and discounts to other non-Disney attractions. Universal also offers packages that include travel and transportation. Contact Universal Vacations at ☎ **877-801-9720** or go to www.universalorlando.com.

SeaWorld offers packages that include a handful of Orlando hotels, including the **Renaissance Orlando Resort at SeaWorld** (see Chapter 9) and the **Orlando World Center Marriott** (see Chapter 9), car rental, tickets to SeaWorld (see Chapter 20), and, in some cases, tickets to other area theme parks. You can get information at ☎ **800-557-4268** or online at www.seaworldvacations.com.

Area hotels often join forces with the parks by offering special ticket deals or stay-and-play packages, so be sure to ask when making your reservations. The **Orlando World Center Marriott** often offers SeaWorld and Aquatica packages, while the **JW Marriott Orlando, Grande Lakes,** and **Ritz-Carlton Orlando, Grande Lakes** (see Chapter 9), often offer holiday packages and themed getaways.

Other places to find packages

You can also find packages elsewhere than the airlines and theme parks. The **United States Tour Operators Association**'s Web site (www.ustoa.com) has a search engine that enables you to look for operators that offer packages to specific destinations. **Touraine Travel** (☎ **800-967-5583;** www.tourainetravel.com) offers a wide variety of packages to Disney and Disney properties, Universal Orlando, and SeaWorld. **Golfpac Vacations** (☎ **800-486-0948;** www.golfpacorlando.com) offers a slate of play-and-stay packages — from basic to comprehensive.

Chapter 6

Catering to Special Travel Needs or Interests

*W*orried that your kids are too young or that you're too old to enjoy Disney and beyond? Afraid you may experience barriers blocking your access or lifestyle? In this chapter, I dispense a little advice for travelers with specific needs.

Traveling with the Brood: Advice for Families

If you have enough trouble getting your kids out of the house in the morning, dragging them thousands of miles away may seem like an insurmountable challenge. But family travel can be immensely rewarding, letting you see the world through smaller pairs of wondrous and curious eyes. Orlando loves kids and welcomes them like no other city in the world. In addition to its theme parks, Orlando has plenty of smaller kid-friendly attractions. All but a few restaurants offer lower-priced children's menus (see Chapter 10 for more info on kids and dining), and most hotels love their younger guests, providing pint-size pools and, in some cases, special gifts and programs. (Look to Chapter 9 to find kid-friendly hotels.)

Despite Orlando's reputation as one of the kid-friendliest places around, you may find some of its attractions a bit too edgy, sophisticated, or intense for younger kids, including a handful of Epcot's exhibits (see Chapter 13) and many of the primo thrill rides at Islands of Adventure (see Chapter 19). Likewise, you may find other attractions, such as Discovery Cove (see Chapter 20), somewhat cost-prohibitive, even for adults.

Traveling with tots

Traveling with young children can often bring you more stress than relaxation on your vacation. Consider that younger children have special needs. They require frequent bathroom breaks and have very short attention spans. (Does the question, "Are we there yet?" ring a bell?) Here are a few general suggestions for making travel plans for you and your youngsters:

- **Consider age — are your kids old enough?** Do you really want to bring an infant or a toddler to an overcrowded, usually overheated world that he or she may not be old enough to appreciate? The large number of stroller-pushing, toddler-toting parents in the parks suggests that many people think the experience isn't too terrible, but I'm warning you anyway. If your child or grandchild is 4 years old or younger, he may be able to appreciate only *some* of the parks' offerings, though a good deal of Disney's Magic Kingdom is geared toward youngsters (see Chapter 12). However, some of the costume-wearing characters may intimidate very young kids. And no matter how organized you are, little ones are going to slow you down. Ask yourself whether your kids are the right ages to make the most out of a trip that costs the equivalent of a developing nation's gross national product.

- **Find the right accommodations for the little ones.** Kids younger than 12 (and at times up to 17) can usually stay for free in their parent's room at most hotels. Look for places that have pools and other recreational facilities so that you have the option to spend a day or two away from the parks without incurring too many additional expenses. If you want to skip a rental car and you aren't staying at Disney, **International Drive** is the next-best place for centralized rooms, restaurants, and attractions. The I-Ride Trolley makes frequent runs up and down the thoroughfare, hotels often offer family discounts (see Chapter 9), and many hotels provide free or moderate-cost shuttles to Walt Disney World, SeaWorld, Aquatica, and Universal Orlando.

- **Take advantage of sitter services.** Most Orlando hotels, including all of Disney's, offer some form of baby-sitting services (usually from an outside service), and several hotels feature counselor-supervised activity programs for children who've been toilet-trained. Baby-sitting rates usually run $10 to $15 per hour for the first child; a discounted rate for additional children is often available.

- **Plan ahead for character dining.** If you'd like to eat a meal with a cast of Disney characters while at Walt Disney World, make **Advanced Dining Reservations** when you reserve your hotel room (or even earlier — these meal events fill up quickly; see Chapter 10 for more details about character dining).

- **Prepare your kids to meet Mickey.** Once inside WDW, check the daily schedule for character meet-and-greets (all the major parks post the information on their guide maps or on boards near the park's entrance) and make sure that the kids know when they're going to meet their heroes because doing so is often the highlight of their day. A little planning can help you avoid running after every character you see, which only tires your little ones and gives you sore feet. And remember — the "in" thing is getting character auto-graphs, so take my advice: If price is no object, buy an autograph book at the parks (it doubles as a good souvenir) — or buy one at home and bring it along.

✔ **Keep tabs on the little ones in the parks.** Getting lost inside a theme park is easy no matter what your age. For adults and older kids, make sure that you arrange a lost-and-found meeting place as soon as you arrive in the park. Attach a name tag to younger kids (on the inside of their clothes) and find a park employee as soon as you've been separated from your party. I list lost-and-found loca-tions in my descriptions of the major theme parks in Chapters 12 to 16 and Chapters 18 to 20.

Consider carrying along a pair of two-way walkie-talkies or cell-phones to help keep in touch with everyone.

✔ **Pack to toddler-proof your hotel room.** Although your home may be toddler-proof, hotel rooms aren't. Bring outlet covers and other necessary safety items to prevent an accident from occurring in your room.

✔ **Stay safe in the sun.** Don't forget to bring sunscreen for the entire family. If you forget, buy sunscreen with a rating of SPF 30 or higher before you go out in the sun. Slather your young children — even if they're in a stroller — and make sure that you pack a hat for infants and toddlers. Likewise, make sure that everyone traveling with you drinks plenty of water to avoid dehydration.

✔ **Remember ride restrictions.** Most parks explain their height restrictions for certain attractions or identify those that may unset-tle young children. (I also list these restrictions in my discussions of the major theme parks in Chapters 12–16 and Chapters 18–20.) Save yourself and your kids some grief before getting in line and experiencing disappointment. Remember that a bad trip down a darkened tunnel or a scary loop-de-loop can upset your youngster for the rest of the day (sometimes longer).

✔ **Take time out for a show.** Catching an indoor, air-conditioned show two or three times a day provides a nice break for everyone, espe-cially on hot and steamy summer afternoons. You may even get your littlest tykes to nap in the darkened theater. Be sure to arrive at least 20 minutes early if you want good seats, but not so early that the kids go berserk waiting. (Most of the waiting areas are out-side, even if the show is inside.)

✔ **Pack a snack.** When dreaming of your vacation, you probably don't envision hours spent waiting in lines. Unfortunately, doing so is inevitable. Store some lightweight snacks in an easy-to-carry backpack, especially when traveling with small kids. You'll save yourself headaches and money.

✔ **Bring your own stroller.** Although you have to haul it to and from the car and on and off trams, trains, and monorails at Disney, having your own stroller can be a tremendous help. It's with you when you need it — say, in your hotel room or in a restaurant as a high chair. And it's an absolute lifesaver at Universal Studios Florida and Islands of Adventure, where you face long walks from the parking lot to the ticket booths. Your stroller should be lightweight, be easy to fold and unfold with one hand, have a canopy, be able to recline for naps, and have plenty of storage space. The parks offer rental strollers for between $13 and $31, but they're often hard and uncomfortable. They don't recline and have little or no storage space for kid gear. And they are absolutely inappropriate for infants and toddlers (some parks rent infant-appropriate strollers, but availability is extremely limited). Park strollers will do, however, if you have older kids who just need an occasional break from all the walking.

For infants and small toddlers, you may want to bring a Snugli-type sling or backpack-type carrier for use in traveling to and from parking lots and while you're standing in line for attractions.

✔ **Take a break.** The Disney, Universal, and SeaWorld parks all feature some rather unique play areas that offer parents a rest and the kids a place to continue to have fun. Depending on your stamina, you may want to schedule two or three visits to these spots a day.

✔ **Bring a change of clothes.** During summer months, the Florida humidity can keep you feeling soggy all day, so bring fresh clothing to change into, especially if you're headed out for dinner afterward. And you'll really feel soggy if you take a spin on any of the parks' water-related rides, so packing changes of clothes or even swimsuits for the whole family is a good idea. Rent a locker ($5–$10) and store your spare duds until you need them.

✔ **Plan playtime for parents.** Walt Disney World and Universal Orlando offer a ride-share program for parents traveling with small children. On many "big-kid" rides, one parent can ride the attraction while the other stays with the kids, and then the adults can switch places and the second parent can ride without having to stand in line again. Notify a staff member that you want to take advantage of this program when you get in line.

Finding kid-friendly tours

Many theme parks design tours for the younger set that include great sources of age-appropriate entertainment.

More fun options for kids

Many of Disney's resorts offer special options for the young set. Here's just a sampling of the best programs for kids:

✔ **Disney's Grand Floridian Resort** offers a **Pirate Cruise Adventure,** where children ages 4 to 10 depart from the Grand Floridian marina to visit exotic "ports of call" to follow clues and collect "buried treasure." Most kids will have a jolly good time. It's offered Monday, Wednesday, Thursday, and Saturday from 9:30 to 11:30 a.m.; the $30 price tag includes lunch. **Grand Adventures in Cooking** invites up to 12 youngsters, 4 to 10 years old, to make dessert, paint an apron, and decorate a chef hat ($30 per child, Tues and Fri 10–11:45 a.m.). The **Wonderland Tea Party** gives kids a one-hour primer in cupcake decorating — with their fingers! They also feast on heart-shaped PB&Js and sip apple-juice "tea" while they listen to stories and play with Alice and the Mad Hatter ($30 per child, Mon–Fri at 1:30 p.m.).

✔ **Disney's Animal Kingdom Lodge** features daily **Junior Researcher** (animal familiarization) and **Junior Chef** (cookie decorating) enrichment programs that are free for children staying at the lodge, as is the nightly African storytelling (among various other unique activities). Both programs are geared to potty-trained children ages 4 to 10; if you're interested, ask about them at check-in. A three-hour **Bush Camp,** available to guests ages 6 to 14 (no matter which resort they're staying at), exposes kids to African culture by engaging them in a variety of activities. It's offered Saturdays at 1 p.m. and costs $70 per child.

✔ At **Disney's Wilderness Lodge,** both kids and adults enjoy taking part in the **Flag Family program.** If you're selected, the entire family can traipse up to the Wilderness Lodge's roof in the morning (times seem to vary, so ask) and raise the American flag that flies over the resort. You get a picture, a certificate, and a fabulous view. If you're interested, ask at the front desk upon check-in.

For information on these and other family programs, call ☎ **407-827-4321** or go to www.disneyworld.com.

SeaWorld has justifiably earned its reputation as a park that makes education fun with a variety of tours. One of the most interesting is the **Polar Expedition guided tour.** This hour-long journey gives kids a chance to come face to face with a penguin and get a behind-the-scenes look at polar bears and beluga whales. **Saving a Species,** another hour-long tour, allows you to see some of the park's rescue and rehabilitation work with several species, including manatees and rare sea turtles. And shark fans will enjoy the **Predators tour.** All tours are kid-friendly, although the latter two may appeal more to older children. SeaWorld tours are offered on a first-come, first-served basis, so reserve a place at the guided-tour information desk when you enter the park. They cost $12 to $18 per adult, $8 to $12 ages 3 to 9, in addition to park admission ($70 adults, $60 kids). Call ☎ **800-406-2244** or go to www.seaworld.com for more information.

At Walt Disney World, **Disney's Family Magic Tour** features an interactive scavenger hunt and costs $27 per person, plus park admission ($75 adults, $63 kids 3–9). Call ☎ **407-939-8687** or go to www.disneyworld. com for info.

Making Age Work for You: Tips for Seniors

Although Orlando is kid and family oriented, many of its hotels, restaurants, and attractions also roll out the red carpet for older travelers, especially those coming with grandkids. The theme parks don't offer discounted admission to seniors, but several attractions do, as does the city's public-transport system. You can find other discounts from several sources listed in this section.

Members of **AARP** (formerly known as the American Association of Retired Persons), 601 E St. NW, Washington, DC 20049 (☎ **888-687-2277** or 202-434-2277; www.aarp.org), get discounts on hotels, airfares, and car rentals. AARP offers members a wide range of benefits, including *AARP The Magazine* and a monthly newsletter. Anyone over 50 can join.

Many reliable agencies and organizations target the 50-plus market. **Elderhostel** (☎ **877-426-8056**; www.elderhostel.org) arranges study programs for those ages 55 and over (as well as for a spouse or companion of any age) in the United States and in more than 80 countries around the world. Most courses last five to seven days in the United States (two to four weeks abroad), and many include airfare, accommodations in university dormitories or modest inns, meals, and tuition. Several study programs — some specific to Walt Disney World, others highlighting Orlando's cultural offerings — are available throughout the Orlando area.

Recommended publications offering travel resources and discounts for seniors include: the quarterly magazine *Travel 50 & Beyond* (www. travel50andbeyond.com); *Travel Unlimited: Uncommon Adventures for the Mature Traveler,* by Alison Gardner (Avalon); *101 Tips for Mature Travelers,* available from Grand Circle Travel (☎ **800-221-2610** or 617-350-7500; www.gct.com); and *Unbelievably Good Deals and Great Adventures That You Absolutely Can't Get Unless You're Over 50,* by Joan Rattner Heilman (McGraw-Hill).

Accessing Orlando: Advice for Travelers with Disabilities

A disability doesn't have to prevent you from savoring the magic of Orlando and Walt Disney World. Many of the city's attractions and hotels are designed to accommodate the needs of individuals with disabilities, ranging from specially equipped guest rooms to audio aids for the sight impaired. A little advance research and planning, however, is a smart idea.

Finding accommodating lodgings

Every hotel and motel in Florida is required by law to maintain a special room (or rooms) equipped for wheelchairs, but keep in mind that the law is being phased in over time, so some hotels may not yet have rooms for those with disabilities. A few have wheel-in showers. **Disney's Coronado Springs Resort** (☎ **407-934-1000**), which opened in 1997, maintains 99 rooms that are designed to accommodate guests with disabilities, so make your special needs known when booking reservations. For information on other special Disney rooms, call ☎ **407-939-7807**.

If you don't mind staying 15 minutes or so from Disney, check out one of the area's various vacation homes. **All Star Vacation Homes** (☎ **800-592-5568** or 407-997-0733; www.allstarvacationhomes.com) is one of the best around, with some handicapped-accessible homes that have multiple bedrooms, multiple bathrooms (including accessible showers), full kitchens, and pools. Most cost less than $300 a night and are located in Kissimmee (though you'll find a handful of villas and town homes near I-Drive as well).

Getting around

Public buses in Orlando have hydraulic lifts and restraining belts for wheelchairs, and they serve Universal Orlando, SeaWorld, shopping areas, and downtown Orlando. When staying on Disney property, you can use shuttle buses that accommodate wheelchairs.

If you need to rent a wheelchair or an electric scooter for your visit, **Walker Medical & Mobility Products** (☎ **888-726-6837** or 407-518-6000; www.walkermobility.com) will deliver one to your room. It offers a model that accommodates guests weighing up to 375 pounds, and it fits into Disney's transports and monorails as well as into rental cars. You can also rent conventional and electric chairs daily at the theme parks (see Chapters 12–16 and Chapters 18–20).

Many of the major car-rental companies now offer hand-controlled cars for drivers with disabilities. See the Quick Concierge appendix in the back of this book for the major rental companies' toll-free numbers and Web sites. **Avis Rent A Car** has an **Avis Access** program that offers such services as a dedicated 24-hour toll-free number (☎ **888-879-4273**) for customers with special travel needs; special car features such as swivel seats, spinner knobs, and hand controls; and accessible bus service.

Amtrak (☎ **800-872-7245**; www.amtrak.com) can provide you with redcap service, wheelchair assistance, and special seats if you give 72 hours' notice. Travelers with disabilities are also entitled to a 15 percent discount off the lowest available adult coach fare. You're required to show documentation from a doctor or an ID card proving your disability, however. Amtrak also provides wheelchair-accessible sleeping accommodations on its long-distance trains. Service dogs travel for free. TTY service is available at ☎ **800-523-6590** or by writing to P.O. Box 7717, Itasca, IL 60143.

Greyhound (☎ **800-752-4841;** www.greyhound.com) allows a physically challenged passenger to travel with a companion for a single fare. When you call 48 hours in advance, the bus line also arranges assistance along the route of your trip. It also permits service dogs aboard.

Maneuvering through the theme parks

All the parks offer parking as close as possible to the entrance for people with disabilities. Tell the parking attendant about your special needs, and he can direct you to the appropriate spot.

Each park's guide map tells you what to expect when you arrive. Most theme-park rides and shows, especially the newer ones, are designed to be accessible to a wide variety of guests. Likewise, theme parks often give people in wheelchairs (and their parties) preferential treatment so that they can avoid long lines. If you use crutches or suffer from some other medical problem that may restrict your mobility in any way, you're probably better off renting a wheelchair; the amount of walking you need to do in the parks may wear you down quickly. You can rent wheelchairs at most major Orlando attractions, but you'll probably be more comfortable in your chair from home (and it will save some money, too).

Keep in mind that wheelchairs wider than 24½ inches may make navigating through some attractions difficult. And crowds can make getting around tough for any guest.

Walt Disney World

The Magic Mickster offers a *Guidebook for Guests with Disabilities* that details many services. Disney no longer mails this prior to visits, but you can pick one up at Guest Relations near the entrances of the four parks; they're also available at some resorts. You can also call ☎ **407-824-4321** or 407-824-2222 for answers to questions about special needs. For accessibility issues relating to the WDW resorts, call ☎ **407-939-7807.** A special link at the bottom of Disney's Web site at www.disneyworld.com leads to a host of information for those with disabilities. Examples of Disney services include the following:

- ✔ Almost all Disney resort hotels have rooms for people with disabilities.

- ✔ You can find Braille directories inside the Magic Kingdom in front of City Hall, and at Guest Relations in the other parks (a $25 refundable deposit is required). Visually impaired guests can also pick up complimentary guided-tour audiocassette tapes and recorders (a $25 refundable deposit is required) at Guest Relations.

✔ Assisted-listening devices are available to amplify the audio at selected attractions at WDW parks. At some attractions, guests can also get handheld wireless receivers that display captions about those attractions. (Both services are free, but require a $25 refundable deposit.) Inquire at Guest Relations inside each park.

✔ Sign translation is available for most of Disney's live shows on a rotating schedule: Mondays and Thursdays at the Magic Kingdom, Tuesdays and Fridays at Epcot, Sundays and Wednesdays at Disney's Hollywood Studios, and Saturdays at Disney's Animal Kingdom. Guests who want sign translation should call Disney at ☎ 407-824-4321 (voice) or 407-827-5141 (TTY) at least two weeks in advance.

✔ Several attractions inside the major parks offer special closed-captioned LED screens for the hearing-impaired. Inquire at Guest Relations inside each park for the list of attractions currently offering this option.

✔ Service animals are allowed in all parks and on some rides.

Universal Orlando

If you're physically challenged, go to Guest Services, located just inside the main entrances of Universal Studios Florida and Islands of Adventure, to get a *Rider's Guide,* a TTY, or other special assistance. You can rent wheelchairs from the concourse area of the parking garage and just inside each park. Wheelchairs can navigate the entry lines at all attractions with the exception of the new Simpsons Ride, which has a special-access entrance. Universal also provides audio descriptions on cassette for visually impaired guests and has sign-language guides and scripts for its shows. (Advance notice is required; call ☎ 800-837-2273 or 407-363-8000, or check each park's Web site at www.universalorlando.com for details.) Sign-language services are available at no charge at Universal Studios Florida and Islands of Adventure. Appointments with an interpreter should be made one to two weeks in advance by contacting the **Sign Language Services Department** at ☎ 888-519-4899 (toll-free TTY), 407-224-4414 (local TTY), or 407-224-5929 (voice).

SeaWorld

SeaWorld provides a guide booklet for guests with disabilities, although most of its attractions are accessible to people in wheelchairs. You can pick one up at Guest Services inside the park or download it at www.seaworldorlando.com. SeaWorld also provides a Braille guide for the visually impaired and a very brief synopsis of its shows for the hearing impaired. Sign-language services are available at no charge, but must be reserved by calling ☎ 407-363-2414 at least a week in advance of your visit. Assisted-listening devices are available at select attractions for a $20 refundable deposit. For a complete rundown on all your options, head to Guest Services when you enter the park; you can also call ☎ 407-351-3600 for more information.

Advice for Gay and Lesbian Travelers

The popularity of Orlando as a destination for gay and lesbian travelers is apparent in the development of the Gay Day Celebration at Disney World into **Gay Days** weekend festivities. Gay- and lesbian-related events also take place at Universal and SeaWorld. These festivals are scheduled the first weekend in June and draw tens of thousands of gay and lesbian travelers to Central Florida. Find information at www.gayday.com or www.gaydays.com.

You can also get information about Gay Days and events that occur throughout the year from **Gay, Lesbian & Bisexual Community Center of Central Florida,** 946 N. Mills Ave., Orlando, FL 32803 (☎ **407-228-8272;** www.glbcc.org). Welcome packets usually include the latest issue of *Triangle,* dedicated to gay and lesbian issues; a calendar of events pertaining to Florida's gay and lesbian community; and information and ads for the area's clubs. **Gay Orlando Network** (www.gayorlando.com) is another good resource.

The entertainment industry and theme parks have helped build a strong gay and lesbian community in Orlando. Same-sex dancing is acceptable at most clubs at **WDW's Pleasure Island,** especially the large and very popular **Mannequins Dance Palace.** Many of **Universal's CityWalk** establishments are similarly gender blind. The tenor of crowds can change, however, depending on what tour is in town, so respect your own intuition.

If you're interested in sampling some of the other local gay and lesbian hotspots, check out the following places:

- **Full Moon Saloon,** 500 N. Orange Blossom Trail, just west of downtown (☎ **407-648-8725;** www.fullmoonsaloon.com): This club stakes a rightful claim to being Orlando's oldest gay bar. DJs keep things hopping most nights, though the Moon sometimes offers live entertainment. Expect a lot of leather and cowboy duds. The interior is big, but much of the fun happens on the patio and in the expanding backyard. The club is open daily from noon to 2 a.m.; showtimes vary. There is no cover. Parking is free.

- **Parliament House,** 410 N. Orange Blossom Trail, just west of downtown (☎ **407-425-7571;** www.parliamenthouse.com): Now under new management, this is still one of Orlando's wilder, and most popular, gay spots. Not a fancy place, the Parliament House has had years of hard partying and shows it. This is a place to drink, dance, and watch shows that include female impersonators and male revues. There are six bars and clubs. Its disco opens daily at 9 p.m., except on Sunday when things start up at 3 p.m.; showtimes vary. Cover charges vary, but usually don't rise above $10. Parking is free.

✔ **Southern Nights,** 375 S. Bumby Ave., between Anderson Street and Colonial Drive (☎ **407-898-0424;** www.southern-nights.com): This perennial award-winner for Orlando's "Best Gay Bar" (according to the readers of a local alternative weekly paper) reopened in spring 2005 after undergoing a top-to-bottom makeover that added a new sound system, lighting, special effects, and a second lounge. It offers theme nights throughout the week, from Latin Night to College Night to Drag Night. Southern Nights opens at 10 p.m. Monday through Saturday; Rendezvous opens at 5 p.m. Closing hours vary according to event. Cover charges vary, but usually don't rise above $10. Self-parking in the club lot is free; valet parking costs $5.

The **International Gay and Lesbian Travel Association (IGLTA)** (☎ **800-448-8550** or 954-776-2626; www.iglta.org) is the trade association for the gay and lesbian travel industry and offers an online directory of gay- and lesbian-friendly travel businesses; go to its Web site and click on "Members."

Many agencies offer tours and travel itineraries specific to gay and lesbian travelers. **Above and Beyond Tours** (☎ **800-397-2681;** www.above beyondtours.com) is the exclusive gay and lesbian tour operator for United Airlines. **Now, Voyager** (☎ **800-255-6951;** www.nowvoyager.com) is a well-known San Francisco–based gay-owned and -operated travel service. **Olivia Travel** (☎ **800-631-6277** or 510-655-0364; www.olivia.com) charters entire resorts and cruise ships for exclusive lesbian vacations and offers smaller group experiences for both gay and lesbian travelers.

The following travel guides are available at most travel bookstores and gay and lesbian bookstores, or you can order them from **Giovanni's Room,** 1145 Pine St., Philadelphia, PA 19107 (☎ **215-923-2960;** www.giovannisroom.com): *Spartacus International Gay Guide* (Bruno Gmünder Verlag; www.spartacusworld.com/gayguide) and *Odysseus* (www.odyusa.com), both good, annual English-language guidebooks focused on gay men; the **Damron** guides (www.damron.com), with separate, annual books for gay men and lesbians; and *Gay Travel A to Z: The World of Gay & Lesbian Travel Options at Your Fingertips,* by Marianne Ferrari (Ferrari International), a very good gay and lesbian guidebook series.

Chapter 7

Taking Care of the Remaining Details

. . . .

In This Chapter

▶ Sorting out your rental-car options

▶ Buying travel and medical insurance

▶ Dealing with illness away from home

▶ Staying in touch using the Web and cellphones

▶ Getting through airport security

. . . .

*Y*ou're almost ready to leave for Orlando. All you need to do is take care of a few last-minute details, plan an itinerary, put the dog in the kennel, stuff your bags with everything that's clean, water the geraniums, pay the mortgage, have your mail held, and finish 50 other eleventh-hour musts.

The information in this chapter gives you planning tips and saves you from wasting precious vacation hours after you're in Magic Mickeyville. You can discover whether it's worth your while to rent a car, get advice about buying travel insurance, check out your options if you get sick on your trip, find out how to keep in touch with your relatives back home, and figure out how to navigate your way through today's airline security procedures.

Renting a Car — Or Not

First off, you have to decide whether you need a rental car for your Orlando vacation. If you're going to spend most of your time at a resort, especially Walt Disney World, you may not need a car. Disney has its own free transportation system: Buses, ferries, trams, and monorails run throughout the property, connecting all its resorts, parks, and entertainment venues. (See Chapter 8 for more information about the Disney Transportation system.)

The Disney system does have some drawbacks: You're a prisoner of WDW's often slow and indirect schedule. Depending on your starting point and your destination, it can take up to an hour to get where you're going. During peak hours in the busiest seasons, you may have trouble getting a seat on the bus, so keep that in mind if you're traveling with kids, seniors, or companions with disabilities. Also, if you're bringing along children and strollers, consider the frustration factor of loading strollers and all their paraphernalia on and off buses, ferries, and trams.

If you plan to spend most of your time at Universal Orlando and stay at one of its resorts, a rental car may also be unnecessary. Universal's resorts all offer boat transportation to its theme parks and CityWalk. (See Chapters 18 and 19 for more about Universal's theme parks.)

 If you aren't spending all your time solely at either WDW or Universal, and you want to visit SeaWorld and other attractions or areas of Central Florida, you need to either rent a car or choose an alternate form of transportation, such as a hotel shuttle (some are free; others charge an average of $12–$16 per person each way). **Mears Transportation** (☎ **407-423-5566;** www.mearstransportation.com), a popular local shuttle service, and taxis (though horridly expensive) are other options. (See Chapter 8 for more information on transportation options in Orlando, including the I-Ride Trolley.) Getting several people to the parks on a daily basis can be expensive if you choose these routes, but you can save on car-rental fees, gas, and the $11- or $12-per-day parking fees at the major attractions if you take advantage of Orlando's transit system. You need to decide whether the added convenience and mobility of a rental car are worth the extra expense; if you plan to be in Orlando only for a short while or are traveling with kids, I definitely recommend you rent a car in order to maximize your vacation mobility.

WDW has an **Alamo** car-rental desk (☎ **800-327-2996**) on property, so if you need to rent for only a day or two instead of for your entire vacation, this may be a good option (though be aware that rental prices are generally higher if you rent anywhere other than the airport).

Getting a good rate

Car-rental rates vary even more than airline fares. The price depends on the size of the car, the length of time you keep it, where and when you pick it up and drop it off, where you take it, and when you actually book your reservation, along with a host of other factors. Doing a little research can often save you hundreds of dollars. Here are some tips to get you started:

✔ **Ask whether the rate is the same for pickup Friday morning as it is for Thursday night.** Weekend rates may be lower than weekday rates. If you're keeping the car five or more days, a weekly rate may be cheaper than the daily rate.

✔ **Find out whether the company you're renting from assesses a drop-off charge if you don't return the car to the same rental location.** Some do, some don't. National and Thrifty are two of the companies that *don't* charge in this situation.

✔ **Check whether the rate is cheaper if you pick up the car at a location in the tourist district rather than at the airport.**

✔ **Find out whether age is an issue.** For drivers under 25, many car-rental companies add on a fee, and some don't rent to them at all. Under-age rental fees are common in Orlando and can add as much as $15 or more a day to your total rate.

✔ **If you see an advertised price in your local newspaper, be sure to ask for that specific rate; otherwise you may be charged the standard (higher) rate.** Don't forget to mention membership in AAA, AARP, and trade unions. These memberships usually entitle you to discounts ranging from 5 percent to 30 percent.

✔ **Check your frequent-flier accounts.** Not only are your favorite (or at least most-used) airlines likely to offer discounts on rentals, but most car rentals also add at least 500 miles to your airline account.

✔ **Comparison-shop on the Internet.** As with other aspects of planning your trip, the Web can make comparison shopping for a car rental much easier. You can check rates at most of the major agencies' Web sites. Plus, all the major travel sites — **Travelocity** (www. travelocity.com), **Expedia** (www.expedia.com), **Orbitz** (www. orbitz.com), and **Smarter Travel** (www.smartertravel.com), for example — can dig up discounted car-rental rates.

Most car-rental companies charge on a 24-hour basis. That means if you pick up the car at 3 p.m., you need to return it by 3 p.m. on the specified end date of your rental. Often, if your flight arrival and departure times in Orlando are far apart (say you arrive at 10 a.m. and don't fly out until 8 p.m.), you need to rent the car for a day longer than your stay. However, if the inbound and outbound flight times are within an hour or two of each other, inquire about hourly rates — they may be less than the cost of another full day. In addition, weekly rentals often cost less than (or the same as) a three-, four-, or five-day rental, so be sure to check which option is least expensive in the end. If you want information about specific rental-car companies serving Orlando, see the Quick Concierge appendix in the back of this book.

Adding up extra rental costs

In addition to the standard rental prices, other optional charges apply to most car rentals (and some not-so-optional charges, such as taxes). The **Collision Damage Waiver (CDW),** which requires you to pay for damage to the car in a collision, is covered by many credit card companies. Check with your credit card company before you go so you can avoid paying this hefty fee (as much as $20 a day or more).

The car-rental companies also offer additional **liability insurance** (if you harm others in an accident), **personal accident insurance** (if you harm yourself or your passengers), and **personal effects insurance** (if your luggage is stolen from your car). Your insurance policy on your car at home probably covers most of these unlikely occurrences. However, if your own insurance doesn't cover you for rentals or if you don't have auto insurance, definitely consider the additional coverage (ask your car-rental agent for more information). Unless you're toting around the Hope diamond, and you don't want to leave that in your car trunk anyway, you can probably skip the personal effects insurance, but driving around without liability or personal accident coverage is never a good idea. Even if you're a good driver, other people may not be, and liability claims can be complicated.

Some companies also offer **refueling packages,** in which you pay for your initial full tank of gas upfront and can return the car with an empty gas tank. The prices can be competitive with local gas prices, but you don't get credit for any gas remaining in the tank. If you reject this option, you pay only for the gas you use, but you have to return the car with a full tank or face hefty per-gallon refueling charges for any shortfall (and the station nearest the airport won't offer much relief — prices run $1 to $2 per gallon higher than what you'll pay back in Mickeyville). If you usually run late and a fueling stop may make you miss your plane, you're a perfect candidate for the fuel-purchase option.

Playing It Safe with Travel and Medical Insurance

Three kinds of travel insurance are available: trip cancellation insurance, medical insurance, and lost luggage insurance. The cost of travel insurance varies widely, depending on the cost and length of your trip, your age and health, and the type of trip you're taking, but expect to pay between 5 percent and 8 percent of the vacation itself. Here is my advice on all three:

  ✓ **Trip cancellation insurance** helps you get your money back if you have to back out of a trip, if you have to go home early, or if your travel supplier goes bankrupt. Allowed reasons for cancellation can range from sickness to natural disasters to the State Department declaring your destination unsafe for travel. (Insurers usually won't cover vague fears, though, as many travelers discovered when they tried to cancel trips in Oct 2001 because they were wary of flying.)

  A good resource is **Travel Guard Alerts,** a posted list of companies considered high-risk by Travel Guard (www.travelguard.com). Protect yourself further by paying for the insurance with a credit card — by law, consumers can get their money back on goods and services not received if they report the loss within 60 days after the charge is listed on their credit card statement.

  Note: Many tour operators, particularly those offering trips to remote or high-risk areas, include insurance in the cost of the trip or can arrange insurance policies through a partnering provider, a convenient and often cost-effective way for the traveler to obtain insurance. Make sure the tour company is reputable, however, and avoid buying insurance from the tour or cruise company you're traveling with so that you don't put all your money in one place.

✔ Buying **medical insurance** for your trip doesn't make sense for most domestic travelers. Most existing health policies cover you if you get sick away from home — but check before you go, particularly if you're insured by an HMO.

✔ **Lost luggage insurance** isn't necessary for most travelers. On domestic flights, checked baggage is covered up to $3,000 per ticketed passenger. On international flights (including U.S. portions of international trips), baggage coverage is limited to approximately $9.07 per pound, up to $400 per checked bag. If you plan to check items more valuable than the standard liability, see whether your valuables are covered by your homeowner's policy, get baggage insurance as part of your comprehensive travel insurance package, or buy **Travel Guard's BagTrak** product. Don't buy the overpriced insurance at the airport. Be sure to take any valuables or irreplaceable items with you in your carry-on luggage — many valuables (including books, money, and electronics) aren't covered by airline policies.

If your luggage is lost, immediately file a lost luggage claim at the airport, detailing the luggage contents. For most airlines, you must report delayed, damaged, or lost baggage within four hours of arrival. The airlines are required to deliver luggage, once found, directly to your house or destination free of charge.

For more information, contact one of the following recommended insurers: **Access America** (☎ 866-807-3982; www.accessamerica.com), **Travelex Insurance Services** (☎ 888-457-4602; www.travelex-insurance.com), **Travel Guard** (☎ 800-826-4919; www.travelguard.com), or **Travel Insured International** (☎ 800-243-3174; www.travelinsured.com).

Staying Healthy When You Travel

Getting sick can ruin your vacation, so I *strongly* advise against it. (Of course, last time I checked, the bugs weren't listening to me any more than they probably listen to you.)

If you have a serious or chronic illness, talk to your doctor before leaving on a trip. For conditions such as epilepsy, diabetes, or heart problems, wear a **MedicAlert identification tag** (☎ 888-633-4298; www.medicalert.org), which immediately alerts doctors to your condition and gives them access to your records through MedicAlert's 24-hour hotline.

Preventing the easily preventable

The biggest health obstacle you'll encounter in Orlando will be the strong Florida sun. Limit your exposure, especially during the first few days of your trip and, thereafter, during the hours of 10 a.m. to 2 p.m., when the sun is at its strongest. Use a sunscreen with at least a sun protection factor (SPF) of 30 (especially for children) and apply it liberally and often. If you have children under a year old, check with your pediatrician before applying a sunscreen — some ingredients may not be appropriate for infants. A hat and sunglasses are de rigueur fashion in Florida for a reason — they'll keep you from suffering sun glare or a painful sunburn.

Dehydration is another potential issue when touring Orlando. Be sure to drink plenty of fluids and see that any children traveling with you do so as well. Note that soft drinks loaded with caffeine, a diuretic, can cause or make dehydration worse, so stick to water or decaffeinated drinks.

Finally, the bane of many a theme-park walker who hasn't hoofed it anywhere lately are blisters. If you have problematic feet (and even if you don't), bring comfortable walking shoes and lots of socks, buy some protective moleskin, and, just in case, pack a package of adhesive bandages. A change of socks midday may keep you from hobbling by nightfall.

Knowing what to do if you get sick

All the major theme parks have first aid stations; ask a park employee or consult your park map for its location. Disney offers in-room medical service at its resorts 24 hours a day — call ☎ **407-238-2000.** If you're staying off Disney property, **Doctors on Call Service (☎ 407-399-3627)** is a group that makes house and room calls in most of the Orlando area.

To find a dentist, call **Dental Referral Service (☎ 800-235-4111;** www. dentalreferral.com), which can refer you to the nearest dentist who meets your needs. Phones are staffed weekdays from 10 a.m. to 7 p.m.

If your ailment isn't a life-threatening emergency, visit a walk-in clinic in Orlando. You may not get immediate attention, but you'll probably pay around $75 rather than the $300 minimum for just signing in at an emergency-room counter. **Centra Care** (www.centracare.org) has several walk-in clinics listed in the Yellow Pages, including ones on Vineland Road near Universal (☎ **407-351-6682**) and at Lake Buena Vista near Disney (☎ **407-934-2273**), among others.

You can fill your prescriptions at dozens of pharmacies listed in the Yellow Pages. **Walgreens** operates a 24-hour pharmacy at 12100 S. Apopka-Vineland Rd. (☎ **407-238-0400;** www.walgreens.com), in addition to several other 24-hour locations throughout the area; check the company's Web site for details.

Staying Connected by Cellphone or E-mail

Want to tell the folks back home that you've arrived safe and sound? Or e-mail them that digital snapshot of your meeting with Mickey? Staying in touch with your friends, family, or even the office (unlucky for you), while you're on the road, is easier than ever.

Using a cellphone

Just because your cellphone works at home doesn't mean it'll work elsewhere in the country (thanks to the nation's fragmented cellphone system). It's a good bet that your phone will work in Orlando, however. But take a look at your wireless company's coverage map on its Web site before heading out — T-Mobile, Sprint, and Nextel are particularly weak in rural areas. If your wireless company doesn't have good coverage in the Orlando area, rent a phone that does from **InTouch USA** (☎ 800-872-7626; www.intouchglobal.com) or a rental-car location, but beware that you'll pay $1 a minute or more for airtime.

If you're not from the U.S., you'll be appalled at the poor reach of our **GSM (Global System for Mobile Communications) wireless network,** which is used by much of the rest of the world. Your phone will probably work in most major U.S. cities; it definitely won't work in many rural areas. (To see where GSM phones work in the United States, check out www.t-mobile.com/coverage.) And you may or may not be able to send SMS (text messaging) home. Assume nothing — call your wireless provider and get the full scoop. In a worst-case scenario, you can always rent a phone; InTouch USA delivers to hotels.

Voice-over Internet Protocol (VOIP)

If you have Web access while traveling, consider a broadband-based telephone service (in technical terms, **Voice over Internet protocol,** or **VoIP**) such as **Skype** (www.skype.com) or **Vonage** (www.vonage.com), which allow you to make free international calls from your laptop or in a cybercafe. Neither service requires the people you're calling to also have that service (though there are fees if they do not). Check the Web sites for details.

Accessing the Internet away from home

Travelers have any number of ways to check their e-mail and access the Internet on the road. Of course, using your own laptop — or even a personal digital assistant (PDA) or electronic organizer with a modem — gives you the most flexibility. But even if you don't have a computer, you can still access your e-mail and even your office computer.

Without your own computer

It's hard nowadays to find a city that *doesn't* have a few **cybercafes.** Although there's no definitive directory for cybercafes — these are independent businesses, after all — two places to start looking are at www.cybercaptive.com and www.cybercafe.com.

Inside Walt Disney World, there's an Internet cafe inside **DisneyQuest,** and you can also send e-mail at **Innoventions: The Road to Tomorrow** in Epcot, though you have to pay the park admission fees to use the Web terminals. Pay phones with touch-screen displays offering Internet access have been installed at locations throughout Walt Disney World; you can access your e-mail for 25¢ a minute with a four-minute minimum.

Aside from formal cybercafes, most **public libraries** offer Internet access free or for a small charge. Avoid **hotel business centers** unless you're willing to pay exorbitant rates.

Most major airports have **Internet kiosks.** These kiosks, which you'll also see in shopping malls, hotel lobbies, and tourist information offices, give you basic Web access for a per-minute fee that's usually higher than cybercafe prices. Because of their clunkiness and high price, you should avoid using these kiosks whenever possible.

With your own computer

If you're bringing your own computer, the buzzword in computer access is **Wi-Fi** (short for *wireless fidelity*), which lets you get high-speed connection without cable wires, networking hardware, or a phone line. To find public Wi-Fi hotspots at your destination, go to www.jiwire.com.

At many hotspots, you sign up for wireless-access service much as you do cellphone service, through a plan offered by one of several commercial companies that have made wireless service available in airports, hotel lobbies, and coffee shops. **AT&T** (www.t-mobile.com/hotspot) serves up wireless connections at more than 7,000 **Starbucks** coffee shops nationwide (also accessible to T-Mobile subscribers). **Boingo** (www.boingo.com) and **Wayport** (www.wayport.com) have set up networks in airports and high-class hotel lobbies. Best of all, you don't need to be staying at the Four Seasons to use the hotel's network; just set yourself up on a nice couch in the lobby.

WDW offers high-speed Internet connections to guests at all its resorts, with limited Wi-Fi access at select resorts. All Universal Orlando resorts offer high-speed Internet access. Most business and higher-end hotels in Orlando offer at least an in-room dataport, and several offer Internet connections. You can bring your own cables, but most hotels rent them for around $10 (others at no charge). Connection fees vary, though most hotels charge in 24-hour increments. Be sure you inquire when you check in.

In addition, major ISPs have **local access numbers** in Orlando, allowing you to go online by simply placing a local call. Check your ISP's Web site or call its toll-free number and ask how you can use your current account away from home and how much it will cost.

Keeping Up with Airline Security

With the federalization of airport security, security procedures at U.S. airports are more stable and consistent than ever. Generally, you'll be fine if you arrive at the airport one hour before a domestic flight and two hours before an international flight; if you show up late, tell an airline employee and she'll probably whisk you to the front of the line.

Bring a **current, government-issued photo ID** such as a driver's license or passport. Keep your ID at the ready to show at check-in, the security checkpoint, and sometimes even the gate. (Children under 18 don't need government-issued photo IDs for domestic flights, but they do for international flights to most countries.)

In 2003, the TSA (Transportation Security Administration) phased out **gate check-in** at all U.S. airports. And **E-tickets** have made paper tickets nearly obsolete. Passengers with E-tickets can beat the ticket-counter lines by using airport **electronic kiosks** or even **online check-in** from a home computer. Online check-in involves logging on to your airline's Web site, accessing your reservation, and printing out your boarding pass — and the airline may even offer you bonus miles to do so! If you're using a kiosk at the airport, bring the credit card you used to book the ticket, your frequent-flier card, or your confirmation number. Print out your boarding pass from the kiosk and simply proceed to the security checkpoint with your pass and a photo ID. **Curbside check-in** is also a good way to avoid lines, although a few airlines still ban curbside check-in; call before you go.

Speed up security by **not wearing metal objects** such as big belt buckles. If you've got metallic body parts, a note from your doctor can prevent a long chat with the security screeners. Keep in mind that only **ticketed passengers** are allowed past security, except for folks escorting disabled passengers or children.

Federalization has stabilized **what you can carry on** and **what you can't.** Travelers in the U.S. are allowed one carry-on bag, plus a "personal item" such as a purse, briefcase, or laptop bag. Carry-on hoarders can stuff all sorts of things into a laptop bag; as long as it has a laptop in it, it's still considered a personal item. The TSA has issued a list of restricted items; check its Web site (www.tsa.gov/public/index.jsp) for details.

Airport screeners may decide that your checked luggage needs to be searched by hand. You can now purchase luggage locks that allow screeners to open and re-lock a checked bag if hand-searching is necessary. Look for **Travel Sentry certified locks** at luggage or travel shops and Brookstone stores (you can buy them online at www.brookstone.com). For more information on the locks, visit www.travelsentry.org.

Part III
Settling into Orlando

The 5th Wave   By Rich Tennant

"Oh, that? That's part of our character dining experience. Haven't you ever seen 'A Bug's Life?'"

In this part . . .

Orlando isn't New York or London, but getting around the tourist areas and downtown Orlando can be a little overwhelming, and even intimidating, at first. Don't worry, though — it isn't as complicated as it looks. In this part, I walk you through the city's neighborhoods, tell you where to catch local transportation, and erase any confusion you may have.

After you've gotten your bearings, I review the city's best hotels so that you can zero in on a room that's right for you. Then I detail Orlando's top eateries and give you lists of the city's best restaurants by location, cuisine, and price. And for dessert, you get a thorough rundown of that most quintessential of Orlando experiences — character meals.

Chapter 8

Arriving and Getting Oriented

. . . .

In This Chapter

▶ Landing at the airport

▶ Discovering Orlando's neighborhoods

▶ Getting information when you arrive

▶ Exploring Orlando's transportation options

. . . .

*A*ll roads in Orlando *don't* lead to Disney, although the reverse may seem true to first-time visitors. Yes, you'd be hard-pressed to drive along a street or highway without coming across a sign directing you to Walt Disney World, but this abundance of directions doesn't mean that you won't find other signs pointing you to the rest of the city's highlights. In this chapter, you take the first step, getting from the airport to the parks, and you gain some insight into Orlando's "other" major neighborhoods.

Arriving in Orlando

Unlike many tourist-oriented cities, Orlando's airports do not lie in the heart of the city's action. But fear not — both of the city's airports are relatively user-friendly, and getting to any one of the theme parks is a generally hassle-free experience.

Navigating the airport

While some of your fellow travelers are aimlessly meandering through the halls of the **Orlando International Airport** (☎ **407-825-2001;** www. orlandoairports.net), you'll zip-a-dee-doo-dah to baggage claim and into your chariot of choice. Though the airport itself is generally easy to navigate, it's usually quite busy, there are plenty of distractions, and it can take you a while to get from point A to point B.

Follow the signs carefully to get from the terminal you land in to baggage claim. (You may need to take the tram to the main terminal and then go to Level 2 for your bags.) *Note:* If you're arriving from a foreign country, you have to go through Immigration before baggage claim and then through Customs after picking up your luggage.

 If you need cash, ATMs are located in the arrival and departure terminals near the four pods of gates (1–29, 30–59, 60–99, and 100–129). ATMs are also located where the shuttles deposit you in the main terminal, as well as along the North and South walkways and the West Hall. If you need to convert foreign currency, you can find currency exchanges (open 9:30 a.m.–7 p.m.) in the 100–129 pod of gates and along the South walkway in the main terminal (near the food court).

Most major car-rental companies are located at the airport (on Level 1), with others located a mile or so down the road. Keep in mind that if the company you choose is at a nearby location instead of right on-site, you'll need to take the shuttle to pick up your car. (See the Quick Concierge appendix for the toll-free numbers of the major rental companies.) You can catch hotel shuttles or taxis on the ground level of the main terminal.

If you're arriving on a regional or international budget airline that serves **Orlando Sanford International Airport** (☎ 407-585-4000; www.orlando sanfordairport.com), you'll appreciate the smaller airport layout. Baggage claim is downstairs, ATMs are in the gate areas, and most car-rental companies are located right at the airport.

Making your way to your hotel

The **Orlando International Airport** is a 25- to 40-minute hop, skip, and long jump from Walt Disney World, depending on traffic, and 15 to 25 minutes from Universal Orlando and downtown.

Mears Transportation Group (☎ 407-423-5566; www.mears transportation.com) is the major shuttle player. It runs vans between the airport (board at ground level) and all Disney resorts and official hotels, and most other area properties, every 15 to 25 minutes. The round-trip to downtown Orlando or International Drive is $28 for adults ($21 for kids 4–11); it's $32 for adults ($24 for kids) to Walt Disney World/Lake Buena Vista or Kissimmee/U.S. 192.

Quicksilver Tours and Transportation (☎ 407-299-1434; www. quicksilver-tours.com) is more personal than Mears — you're greeted at baggage claim with a sign bearing your name. The cost is more than Mears, but Quicksilver is coming for you — not other travelers, too — and it's going only to your resort. Included is an array of services, including a quick stop for groceries. Rates run $110 (up to four, round-trip) to I-Drive/Universal Orlando and between $115 to $125 to Disney. If you have a larger group (five to ten passengers, round-trip) and require a van, the rates run $125 to $130 to Universal and I-Drive and $130 to $135 to Disney.

Selective Limousine (☎ **888-784-2522** or 407-354-2456; www.selective limo.com) also offers a high level of service. For $210, you get round-trip stretch-limo service from the airport to your hotel for up to eight people; the price includes a free stop at a supermarket for food supplies, and safety seats for any children in your party. Cheaper shuttle rates are also available; check its Web site for specials.

Taxis are another option for groups. The standard rates for **Ace Metro** (☎ **407-855-0564**) and **Yellow Cab** (☎ **407-699-9999**) run as high as $3.25 for the first mile and $1.75 per mile thereafter, although you can sometimes get a flat rate. A one-way trip to the I-Drive area could cost upwards of $30, to Disney closer to $60, and to the U.S. 192 area around $50. Vans and taxis load on the ground level of the airport.

 If you're bunking at the Mouse's house, **Disney's Magical Express** will transport you and your luggage (which the Mouse will magically retrieve from baggage claim, allowing you to head straight to the shuttle) from the airport (Orlando International only) to your WDW resort — and it's free (saving a family of four about $110 or more). See Chapter 9 for details.

 A few hotels offer **free shuttle service** to and from the airport, so be sure to ask when booking your room. Hotel shuttles load on the ground level.

If you're driving a **rental car** from OIA to your hotel, you have two options. You can take the north exit out of the airport to Hwy. 528 West (a toll road, also known as the Beachline Expwy.). Follow the signs to I-4, then go west to exits marked for Disney (you'll find three), and follow the signs to the appropriate area. Your drive should take about 30 to 40 minutes if traffic isn't too heavy. Disney exits are clearly marked on big green signs. This route is also best if you're heading to Universal Orlando, SeaWorld, or the International Drive area. If your destination is solely Disney, you can also take the south exit from the airport, which leads you down Boggy Creek Road to S.R. 417 West (another toll road known as the Greeneway). Exit onto 536 and follow the signs straight to Disney. This route has less traffic but costs an extra few dollars in tolls.

If you're traveling from **Orlando Sanford International Airport,** a **rental car** is really your best bet — even if you only rent it for the days you arrive and depart Orlando (if this is the case, choose a company with locations in or near your hotel for pickups and drop-offs). Taxi or shuttle service from the airport is expensive; expect minimum one-way fares of $60 to the Universal Orlando and International Drive areas and $100 to the Disney and Kissimmee areas.

Upon leaving Sanford airport, exit onto Lake Mary Boulevard. From here, you can take the 417/Greeneway exit and follow that to Disney. Or you can go past that exit and take the one for I-4 West, which leads you past downtown to all the major theme-park attractions. Again, the Greeneway is the less-traveled, faster route, but it's a toll road. For either route, expect about 45 minutes to the Universal Orlando and International Drive areas and about 60 minutes to Disney (even longer if you're driving I-4 between 3 and 6 p.m.).

Figuring Out the Neighborhoods

Though the area encompassing the various theme parks and their accompanying paraphernalia (hotels, restaurants, and so on) is almost always referred to as *Orlando,* the region has some very distinct sections, several of which are not actually in Orlando proper at all.

Walt Disney World

The empire — parks, resorts, restaurants, shops, and assorted trimmings — is scattered across 30,500 acres, or about 47 square miles. What you may find most surprising is that WDW isn't really located in Orlando at all — it's just southwest of the city, off I-4 between West U.S. 192 and S.R. 535. If you choose to stay with Mickey, you'll find that convenience has its price. Accommodations at the Mouse's house can run as much as double the price of nearby Kissimmee hotels and resorts. On the plus side, you get access to the free Disney Transportation system (though at times that may not be that big of a plus) and a handful of perks and privileges (such as early park entry and extra evening hours) that are offered only to Disney resort guests.

Also on Disney property is **Downtown Disney,** an area off to itself encompassing three very distinct zones: **Downtown Disney West Side, Pleasure Island,** and **Downtown Disney Marketplace.** They're filled with restaurants, shops, entertainment venues, and clubs; each zone is quite unique in its offerings, atmosphere, and price. Downtown Disney is closest to the Lake Buena Vista zone described in the next section.

Lake Buena Vista

Lake Buena Vista is Disney's next-door neighborhood. It's where you find "official" (yet not Disney-owned) hotels, and it's close to Downtown Disney and all its offerings. This charming area has manicured lawns, tree-lined thoroughfares, and free transportation throughout the realm, but it may take a while to get from point A to point B because of a combination of slow shuttle service and heavy traffic. A plethora of shops, services, and restaurants is practically at your doorstep, and all within minutes from the Mouse. Although this area is not nearly as costly as Walt Disney World itself, it's generally more expensive than International Drive and Kissimmee.

Celebration

Imagine an entire town designed by Disney, with perfect white picket fences, tree-lined walkways, and gingerbread-trimmed houses. In

Orlando Neighborhoods

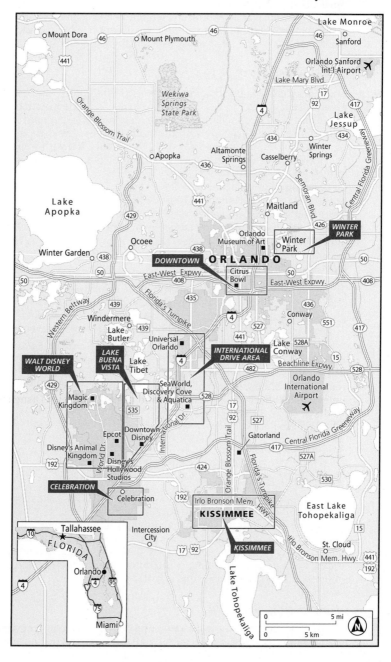

Celebration, Disney redesigned reality to reflect an idealized version of Small Town, U.S.A. Residents of the 4,900-acre town live in beautiful old Florida–, Colonial-, and Victorian-inspired homes. Celebration's charming downtown is designed for tourists, with upscale boutiques, restaurants, coffee shops, and even its own small yet elegant hotel.

Kissimmee

Way back before Mickey moved to town, Kissimmee was the hotspot. Overlooked, in recent years, with the expansion of the International Drive and Lake Buena Vista districts, Kissimmee is being revived and made more tourist-friendly with the addition of wide walkways, landscaping, and improved roadways. Although still filled with some of the tackier T-shirt shops and tourist traps in the area, some moderately priced hotels and even a few luxury resorts have begun to spring up just to the south. Kissimmee is only a short drive (roughly 10–15 miles) southeast from the House of Mouse. With plenty of modest motels and resorts, it's a great choice for travelers on a budget. The town centers on U.S. 192/Irlo Bronson Memorial Highway, which, alas, is perennially under construction.

International Drive

Known locally as I-Drive, the tourist mecca of International Drive extends 7 to 10 miles north of the Disney kingdom between Highway 535 and the Florida Turnpike. With bungee jumping, skateboarding, surfing, shopping, themed restaurants, more than a hundred hotels, and a slew of shops, this stretch of road is *the* tourist strip in Central Florida. It's home to **Orlando's Official Visitor Center** and offers easy access to SeaWorld and Universal Orlando. The northern half of I-Drive beyond Sand Lake Road is already packed, and developers continue to eat up space in the southern half, especially near the Orange County Convention Center; south of the Beachline Expressway (Hwy. 528), the resorts become far more spread out than in the north. Traffic along this route is perennially problematic, so be sure to allot plenty of extra time if you're traveling on it during the morning or evening rush hours.

Dr. Phillips

Once a nondescript residential area dotted with a few odd shops and doctors' offices, the Sand Lake strip of Dr. Phillips, just west of I-4, has been developed into an upscale shopping and dining mecca. The new mall complexes at the intersection of West Sand Lake Road and Dr. Phillips Boulevard now host no fewer than a dozen fine-dining restaurants. For a quiet and sophisticated dining experience, outside the commotion of the theme parks, this is by far your best bet.

Downtown Orlando

Right off I-4 East, downtown Orlando lies north of the theme-park areas and is home to clubs, shops, cultural attractions, and restaurants — a great place for a night on the town. Dozens of antiques shops line **Antique Row,** on Orange Avenue near Lake Ivanhoe. Hotels in this area are aimed mostly at business travelers — it's also the commercial center of the city and not at all a convenient place to stay if visiting the theme parks is the major point of your trip to Orlando — though a few B&Bs draw couples seeking more sophisticated surroundings.

Winter Park

Just north of downtown Orlando, the quiet town of Winter Park is where many of Central Florida's old-money families call home (and where the newly moneyed come to shop and dine). It's noteworthy for **Park Avenue,** a collection of upscale shops and restaurants along a tree-lined, cobblestone street. Winter Park's appeal comes from its sophisticated yet charming offerings; it has little, if any, kid appeal. It's definitely too far north to use as a home base if you plan on spending much of your time at the Disney parks. If you want some quiet time away from the theme-park madness, though, it's a nice place to spend an afternoon (but leave the kids behind).

Finding Information After You Arrive

After you've landed, your best and most immediate source for up-to-date information is the concierge or the front desk at your hotel (especially if you're staying at Disney or Universal, where they're more knowledgeable than most).

At **Orlando International Airport,** arriving passengers can find assistance at the **Magic of Disney** (third level, behind the Northwest Airlines ticket counter) and **Disney Earport** (across from the Hyatt Regency), two shops located in the main terminal. They sell Disney multiday park tickets; make dinner, show, and hotel reservations; and provide brochures and information. The stores open daily at 7 a.m., with Disney Earport closing at 9 p.m. and the Magic of Disney at 10 p.m.

Also in the main terminal at the airport, you'll find two locations each of the **Universal Studios Store** and the **SeaWorld Store,** as well as a **Kennedy Space Center Store.** All provide similar services with ticketing and are open daily from 6 or 7 a.m. to 9 or 10 p.m.

If you're in the International Drive area, stop for information at **Orlando's Official Visitor Center,** 8723 International Dr. (☎ **407-363-5872;** www. orlandoinfo.com), 4 blocks south of Sand Lake Road.

Both the *Orlando Weekly,* distributed every Thursday, and Friday's calendar section in the *Orlando Sentinel* include plenty of tourist-friendly information about dining and entertainment.

Getting Around Orlando

Your major decision regarding Orlando transportation will be whether to use Walt Disney World's Disney Transportation system (which is truly useful only to those staying at a WDW resort), drive a car (yours or a rental), or stick to other means. The system that works best for you depends on what you want to see, where you're staying, and how much time (and money) you want to spend getting around the city.

By the Disney Transportation system

If you plan to stay at a Disney resort or an official hotel (see Chapter 9 for more information about Disney hotels) and spend the majority of your time visiting Disney parks, you can probably skip a rental car — at least for most of your stay. A free transportation network runs through Walt Disney World, with buses, ferries, water taxis, and monorails operating from two hours prior to the parks' opening until two hours after closing. Likewise, Disney offers service to Downtown Disney, Typhoon Lagoon, Blizzard Beach, Pleasure Island, Fort Wilderness Resort & Campground, and all the Disney resorts.

Here are the advantages of using the Disney Transportation system:

- ✔ It's free.

- ✔ You save on car-rental and gasoline charges.

- ✔ You don't have to pay $12 a day to park in the theme-park lots. (*Note:* Disney resort guests are exempt from parking fees at the theme parks.)

- ✔ If your party wants to split up, you can easily head elsewhere while others remain behind without being stranded.

- ✔ During busy periods when Disney's parking lots may close (and this does happen), those riding Disney Transportation will still get to the parks.

Disadvantages include the following:

- ✔ You're at the mercy of Disney's schedule.

- ✔ The shortest distance between two points is not always a straight line. You may very well have to take a ferry to catch a bus to get on the monorail to reach your hotel. The system makes a complete circuit but doesn't necessarily travel the most direct route for *you*. It can take an hour or more to get somewhere that's right across a lagoon from you.

- ✔ You must endure multiple stops, particularly on buses and at peak periods, with crowds that may well force you to wait for the next bus.

- ✔ Parents may find herding young children and their accompanying paraphernalia off and on buses exhausting.

If you plan to travel on Disney Transportation, first verify with the driver, the bell staff, or someone at your hotel's Guest Relations desk that you're taking the most direct route. Keep asking questions along the way. Unlike missing a highway exit, missing a stop on the bus route means you have to take another ride on the Mickey-go-round.

By car

Most visitors to Orlando — especially those staying a week or more — choose to rent a car for at least a day or two in order to venture beyond the parks. (Yes, there *is* far more to Florida than its thrills and theme parks.) See Chapter 7 for more information on renting a car in Orlando; check out the Quick Concierge appendix for toll-free numbers of various car-rental agencies.

Orlando's major artery is Interstate 4. Locals call it I-4 or that #@$*%^#!! road, because it's often horridly congested, especially during weekday rush hours (7–9 a.m. and 4–6 p.m.), when it more likely resembles a parking lot. I-4 runs diagonally across the state from Tampa to Daytona Beach. Exits from I-4 lead to all WDW properties, Universal Orlando, SeaWorld, International Drive, U.S. 192, Kissimmee, Lake Buena Vista, downtown Orlando, and Winter Park. Most of the exits are well marked, but construction is common and exit numbers occasionally change. If you get directions by exit number, always ask for the name of the road as well, to avoid getting lost. (Cellphone users can call ☎ 511 to get a report of I-4 delays.)

Despite the fact that, when you look at any map of the area, it will seem that I-4 runs north to south, on road signs it's always listed as east and west. To avoid getting lost, remember that I-4 West takes you toward Disney World (and Tampa) from Universal Orlando, I-Drive, and down-town Orlando; I-4 East heads from Disney and Kissimmee toward Universal Orlando (and Daytona).

The Florida Turnpike crosses I-4 near Universal Orlando and links with I-75 to the north. U.S. 192, a major east–west artery that's also called the Irlo Bronson Memorial Highway, reaches from Kissimmee to U.S. 27, crossing I-4 near the WDW entrance road. Farther north, the Beachline Expressway toll road (or Hwy. 528) goes east from I-4 past Orlando International Airport to Cape Canaveral and the Kennedy Space Center. The East-West Expressway (also known as Hwy. 408) is another toll road that runs from I-4 near downtown east to S.R. 50 by the University of Central Florida. The final major toll road, S.R. 417 (also known as the Greeneway), partially encircles the eastern edge of Orlando starting at I-4 just south of Disney and winds past the southern edge of Orlando International Airport before ending up near the northern edge of Orlando by the Orlando Sanford Airport.

One of the area's lesser known roads, Turkey Lake Road, runs parallel to I-4 and is often used by locals to avoid the heavy traffic of I-4 from WDW to Universal Orlando. It starts as the Palm Parkway near Disney and turns into Turkey Lake Road just past the hotel area, eventually running right up to Universal. It intersects with both Central Florida Parkway, which takes you right to SeaWorld, and Sand Lake Road, which takes you to both Dr. Phillips and the I-Drive areas.

Here are a few (in some cases, redundant) tips for driving in Orlando:

- ✔ Remember to allow for rush-hour traffic from 7 to 9 a.m. and 4 to 6 p.m. daily.

- ✔ In Florida, you can turn right on red after coming to a full stop and making sure that the coast is clear (unless signs say otherwise). Consider yourself warned: If you're sitting at a red light with your blinker on and not turning right, you'll probably hear horns blaring. Make sure that your path is clear and then *move it.*

- ✔ Posted speed limits are enforced vigorously. Fines for speeding begin at more than $150. Pay particular attention to road construction and school zones, where speed limits are reduced and speeding fines are doubled — they're not kidding.

- ✔ You must have a handicap permit to park in handicap parking places. Handicap permits from other states are honored, but a disabled license plate alone won't do.

- ✔ Buckle up: Florida law says front- and rear-seat passengers alike must wear a seat belt. This includes children, who, if younger than age 5, must be restrained in an approved safety seat (seat belt or booster seat) and, if younger than age 3, in an approved car seat. If you don't want to bring your own from home, most car-rental agencies can provide one for about $10 a day.

- ✔ In an emergency, dial ☎ **911,** or you can reach the Florida Highway Patrol on a cellphone by dialing ☎ ***FHP.**

By taxi

Yellow Cab (☎ **407-699-9999**) and **Ace Metro** (☎ **407-855-0564**) are among the taxi companies serving the Orlando area. But for day-to-day travel to and from attractions or restaurants, cabs are expensive unless your group has five or more people. Rates can run as high as $3.25 for the first mile and $1.75 per mile thereafter, though sometimes you can get a flat rate.

By shuttle

Mears Transportation Group (☎ **407-423-5566**; www.mears transportation.com) operates shuttle buses to all major attractions, including Universal Orlando, SeaWorld, and Disney. Shuttles also run to Kennedy Space Center at Cape Canaveral and Busch Gardens in Tampa. This is one of the most cost effective of all the shuttle services available. (For more about great attractions just outside Orlando, see Chapter 23.) Rates vary by destination.

By trolley

The **I-Ride Trolley,** on International Drive (☎ 407-248-9590; www.iride trolley.com), runs every 20 to 30 minutes, from 8 a.m. to 10:30 p.m. ($1 for adults, 25¢ for seniors, kids younger than 12 ride free; exact change is required). An unlimited one-day pass is available for $3 per person. The main route runs from the Prime Outlets International center to SeaWorld, with an additional route that runs along Universal Boulevard from Sea World Road to Kirkman Road. Because of I-Drive's heavy traffic, the trolley is usually the best way to get around whenever you're in this area.

By motorcycle

If you have a valid motorcycle license, you can rent bikes at **Orlando Harley-Davidson,** 3770 37th St. (☎ 877-740-3770 or 407-423-0346; www. orlandoharley.com), and **American V Twin,** 5135 International Dr. (☎ 800-268-8946 or 407-903-0058; www.amvtwin.com). Their inventories can be in short supply, so call in advance. You must be at least 21 (and sometimes 25) years of age, have a motorcycle license, and have a major credit card.

Reserve months in advance if you're visiting during **Bike Week,** in late February and early March, or **Biketober Fest,** in mid-October. (Both events are held in Daytona Beach, but many bikers stay in Orlando.)

By bus

LYNX (☎ 407-841-5969; www.golynx.com) public bus stops are marked with a paw print. Some routes serve Disney, Universal, I-Drive, and the downtown area ($1.75 for adults, 85¢ for kids grades K–12), but they're slow-going and not very visitor-friendly.

On foot

I don't recommend traveling on foot anywhere in Orlando, but it is occasionally necessary to walk across a parking lot or street. Be extremely careful. With rare exceptions, this city isn't conducive to strolling. Within the safe confines of the theme parks, you'll have no problems hoofing it (in fact, you'll be on your feet quite a bit), but walking anywhere outside the theme parks is a thrills-and-chills experience most people would prefer to avoid. Orlando is among the most dangerous cities in the country for pedestrians, according to a Washington, D.C.–based research group. Wide roads designed to move traffic quickly and a shortage of sidewalks, streetlights, and crosswalks are to blame.

Chapter 9

Checking In at Orlando's Best Hotels

*W*here you plant yourself during your Orlando vacation determines many things about your trip, including your itineraries, the amount of money you'll spend, and your need, if any, for a car rental. Deciding where to stay in the city isn't easy because its 114,000 rooms come in many different flavors: hotels, motels, bed-and-breakfasts (B&Bs), and so on. In this chapter I help you narrow your choices.

Getting to Know Your Options

Something you can take to the bank: Unlike the less competitive areas of Florida, almost all hotels in Orlando — at least the ones listed in this guide — have been either built or renovated in the past 10 or 12 years (though it's likely renovations have been closer to within the last 1–4 years), so you can expect reasonably modern trimmings. The city sometimes seems like Chain Central, and you'll find branches of pretty much every major hotel and motel chain in the major tourist zones, especially on International Drive and in Kissimmee. Note that even the high-end properties tend to have a more relaxed feel than counterparts in other cities, thanks to the theme parks; you're more likely to see Goofy hats than Gucci ones here. (See the Quick Concierge appendix for a list of the major hotel chains' toll-free numbers.)

Every hotel that I list in this chapter has air-conditioning and at least one pool (or I tell you otherwise). Most have cable TV, and some offer in-room movies, Internet connections, and Nintendo for a fee. Likewise, many have hair dryers, coffeemakers, and in-room safes. Almost all hotels in the city (with a few exceptions that I alert you to) offer free parking, but few hotels these days throw in breakfast with your room rate (most that do tend to fall on the lower end of the price scale). Most places in Orlando try to make kids feel as if they're Mickey's favorite relatives and offer lots of little extras and amenities for families. Although that's great for parents, Orlando (believe it or not) is the top honeymoon destination in the United States, so there are plenty of places that cater to adults, too.

 Avoiding children for almost any length of time during your visit is next to impossible, but if you're childfree and don't relish the thought of screaming kids in the room next door, there are ways to improve your odds. The bad news is that the quiet definitely costs you. As a general rule — Disney and Universal Orlando properties not included — the more expensive a hotel is, the less likely you are to run into children (but keep in mind that even business hotels here still cater to the family market in some form or another). Some of Orlando's B&Bs don't allow children under 16, and these often feature luxurious rooms that rival those of the big resorts. If you don't want to spend the extra money, remember that few people spend much time in their rooms anyway.

Price and location, when all is said and done, are the factors that really decide where you rest your head for the night. Although you pay more for the best locations, you may find these hotels well worth the conveniences they offer. The closer your hotel is to the things you want to do and see, the less time and money you waste getting to your destination. And that's why the two major players in town are deserving of a closer look.

Walt Disney World

Disney has the corner on the Orlando hotel market, with high occupancy rates even during slow times. Located on WDW property are 23 (soon to be 24) Disney-owned and -operated resorts and nine *official* hotels (privately owned hotels that have earned Disney's seal of approval).

Disney's accommodations run the gamut from motel-style rooms to grand villas with full kitchens. The decision to bunk (or not to bunk) with the Mouse is probably the most important one you make regarding your accommodations. To decide whether an on-property stay is right for you, consider its pros and cons.

The benefits of lodging in Mickey's backyard include the following:

✔ You get unlimited free transportation via the **Disney Transportation** system of buses, monorails, ferries, and water taxis to and from the four theme parks, resorts, and smaller attractions. This also means you're guaranteed admission to all the parks, even during peak times when parking lots fill to capacity and many folks not staying with Mickey are left in the cold.

✔ You can take advantage of free parking inside theme-park lots if you choose to chauffeur yourself. Other visitors pay $12 a day.

✔ Kids younger than 17 stay free in their parent's room, and reduced-price children's menus are available in most restaurants.

✔ You have access to some of the best hotel pools in all of Orlando.

✔ Resort guests can charge most purchases (including meals) made anywhere inside WDW to their rooms. You can also usually have your purchases delivered to your resort at no extra charge, so you don't have to lug them around the park with you all day.

✔ You can purchase WDW park and attraction tickets right at your hotel's Guest Relations or concierge desk, avoiding the often long lines at the parks themselves. (See Chapter 11 for more details on WDW admission options.) You can also make reservations for dining and preferred tee times at Disney's golf courses through Guest Relations or the concierge.

✔ No resorts are more convenient to the Disney parks and attractions.

✔ The **Extra Magic Hours** allows resort guests before- and after-hours admission to one of the four theme parks or two water parks. Disney distributes a schedule that lists which parks are open extra hours on what days and at what times. (See Chapter 11.)

✔ **Disney's Magical Express Service** transports you and your luggage from the airport to your resort if you fly via participating airlines (currently AirTran Airways, Alaska Airlines, American, Continental, Delta, JetBlue, Northwest, United and US Airways) to Orlando International Airport (and have arranged to use the service prior to departure). Thanks to special luggage tags (sent to you via mail) and some of Mickey's magic, your luggage appears in your resort room without your having to retrieve it from baggage claim in Orlando (though it may take up to three hours, so bring along a carry-on with any items you'll need immediately). Keep in mind that the individual airlines retain control over their baggage policies — so while the transportation to and from the airport is free, baggage charges levied by the airline, if applicable, will have to be paid for in advance through Baggage Airline Guest Services (☎ 407-284-1231; credit cards only). Other perks include the ability to check in and print your boarding pass (domestic flights on participating airlines only) prior to departing from your resort, thereby avoiding at least one line at the airport. (Note that certain restrictions, such as when this service is available, apply.) Be sure to keep your Magical Express documents handy — you need your vouchers to ride the shuttle each way. Also note that your shuttle back to the airport is determined by your flight departure time and will be at least three hours prior to your flight. If you revise your plans or have questions, call **Magical Express Guest Services** (☎ 866-599-0951). This free service is currently scheduled to be available through 2011.

The drawbacks of staying with the Mouse include the following:

✔ **Disney Transportation** can be excruciatingly time-consuming (even with improvements currently in the works) and at times difficult to maneuver with young children and all their paraphernalia.

✔ Resort rates are about 20 percent to 30 percent higher than prices at comparable hotels and motels beyond the parks' boundaries.

✔ You may wind up a prisoner of Disney, unable to avoid the stiff pricing for meals, trinkets, and so on.

✔ Without your own vehicle, it's difficult and expensive to leave Disney property to experience the rest of what Orlando has to offer (which is quite a bit).

Don't plan on lighting up in the comfort of your room if you're staying at the Mouse's house. As of June 2007, all Disney-owned and -operated resorts became officially nonsmoking. Smoking is now prohibited in all guest rooms, indoor public areas, and on balconies. Only in designated outdoor areas will smoking be allowed (similar to the theme parks).

Universal Orlando

Universal Orlando is a relatively new player on the Orlando hotel scene and has only three properties (though future plans to tack on at least two more have been drawn up). The Universal resorts are all operated by the luxury Loews Hotel group, and the standard of accommodations is actually a bit better than the majority of those at Disney. If your itinerary favors Universal Orlando, staying at one of its three properties affords you some rather meaningful perks at the Universal parks.

The benefits of staying at one of Universal's three resorts include the following:

✔ You get unlimited free transportation via water taxi or bus from the resorts to CityWalk and both Universal parks.

✔ Unlike Disney, Universal Orlando's smaller number of resorts means everything really is within walking distance of the parks.

✔ Resort guests enjoy special privileges at the Universal Orlando theme parks, including **Universal Express** (unlimited express-line access to rides) and preferred seating at shows and at many of the restaurants from the day of check-in to the day of check-out. This is a huge benefit, especially during the more crowded months when lines can be excruciatingly long. Just show your room key and you'll get to the fun that much faster. Additionally, guests are allowed early entry to the parks on scheduled days.

✔ Universal's resorts all accept pets, so Fido or Fluffy can live the luxurious lifestyle right along with you instead of having to be relegated to a kennel. The resorts even offer a special pet program that includes food, supplies, and walking services.

The drawbacks of staying at the Universal resorts are as follows:

✔ Although there is shuttle service to SeaWorld and Wet 'n Wild from the resorts, you'll have to arrange your own transportation if you want to set foot on Disney property.

✔ Resort rates are at least 30 percent higher than at comparable hotels and motels located even a block from the parks (though, honestly, few are really comparable). You won't find anything for under $100 (usually higher) a night.

✔ As when staying at a Disney resort, you're subjected to higher prices for dining and other vacation necessities.

✔ Universal resorts don't offer free self-parking (it costs a whopping $15 a night, $20 if you're just there for the day), which is a perk of staying at Disney hotels.

Finding the Best Room at the Best Rate

The **rack rate** is the maximum rate a hotel charges for a room. It's the rate you get if you walk in off the street and ask for a room for the night. You sometimes see these rates printed on the fire/emergency-exit diagrams posted on the back of your door.

Hotels are happy to charge you the rack rate, but you can almost always do better. Perhaps the best way to avoid paying the rack rate is surprisingly simple: Just ask for a cheaper or discounted rate. You may be pleasantly surprised.

Reserving a room through the hotel's toll-free number may also result in a lower rate than calling the hotel directly. On the other hand, the central reservations number may not know about discount rates at specific locations. Your best bet is to call both the local number and the toll-free number and see which one gives you a better deal. Whatever you do, don't ever come to town without a reservation. Orlando is a year-round destination; it has a heavy convention and business trade, and school lets out during varying times of the year in other nations. If you come without a reservation, you may find yourself extremely disappointed — or even completely out of luck.

If you're a student, a senior, a military or government employee (or retiree), or a member of AAA or AARP, ask about discounts. The Orlando/Orange County Convention & Visitors Bureau's free **Magicard** (☎ 800-643-9492; www.orlandoinfo.com) is good for a family of six and offers hundreds of dollars in discounts on accommodations, car rentals, attractions, and restaurants. The **Entertainment Book** (www.entertainmentbook.com) is another good source for discounts on hotels, car rentals, restaurants, and attractions. It costs $32 for the Orlando version, but you'll recoup your investment after using just a few coupons.

As a rule, Disney resorts, villas, and official hotels don't offer regular discounts other than for slight seasonal variations. WDW's 2008 value seasons or lowest rates were available from January 1 to February 13, August 3 to October 1 (value resorts, moderate resorts, and deluxe resorts), July 20 to October 1 (deluxe villa resorts and campsites), August 3 to November 20 (campsites only), and November 30 to December 18 (value resorts, moderate resorts, deluxe resorts, deluxe villa resorts, and cabins). Regular season rates were available from March 30 to May 21 (value resorts and moderate resorts), March 30 to July 19 (deluxe resorts, deluxe villa resorts, and cabins), March 30 to August 2 (campsites only), and October 2 to November 29 (all resorts). Summer season rates applied from May 22 to August 2 (value resorts and moderate resorts). Peak rates applied from February 14 to March 29 (all resorts), pre-holiday rates applied from November 21 to December 18 (campsites only), and holiday rates took effect from December 19 to December 31 (all resorts). Although the actual dates will shift a little, the same periods should apply in 2009. The following list outlines what you can expect to find at each of the four designations of resorts (value, moderate, deluxe, and deluxe villa):

- ✔ **Value:** The least expensive and most basic of all the Disney resorts have very few, if any, of the bells and whistles found elsewhere.

- ✔ **Moderate:** These mid-priced resorts feature larger rooms, upgraded amenities (including in-room minifridge and microwave), additional guest services, and recreational facilities.

- ✔ **Deluxe:** Disney's best of the best, these full-service resorts feature spacious rooms along with extensive guest services and recreational facilities.

- ✔ **Deluxe Villa** (previously known as — and sometimes still referred to as — **Vacation Club Resorts**): Disney's deluxe villa resorts, in addition to the extensive guest services and recreational facilities, feature all the comforts of home. Rooms range from studios to grand villas with room to sleep 12 (villas sport full kitchens and laundry facilities).

Similarly, discounts (again, other than slight seasonal variations) are just as rare at the Universal resorts. Universal's 2008 value or lowest rates were available from January 2 to February 13, August 17 to October 2, and November 30 to December 18. Regular season rates were available from April 13 to June 4 and October 3 to November 25. Summer rates applied from June 5 to August 16. Peak rates applied from February 14 to March 13, March 30 to April 12, and November 26 to November 29, while holiday rates took effect from March 14 to March 29 and December 19 to January 3. Again, the actual dates will shift slightly, but the same periods should apply in 2009.

One of the best ways to catch a break from Mickey's prices is through a travel package (see Chapter 5). Disney offers vacation plans that can include meals, tickets, recreation, airfare, rentals, dinner shows, and other features. Call the **Walt Disney Travel Company** (☎ **407-939-7675**) to book a package, call the **Central Reservations Office** (☎ **407-939-7429**) to book a room, or go online to www.disneyworld.com, where you can get the lowdown on WDW and order vacation brochures and DVDs.

Before calling Disney to make reservations, take a moment to visit **MouseSavers.com** (www.mousesavers.com). This unofficial Disney discount site is extremely diligent about keeping up-to-date listings on all discounts offered by Disney, whether it be room discount codes or details on special package deals. A few minutes looking over the listings can save you hundreds of dollars when booking direct with Disney.

When booking your room, don't forget to allow for the area's combined sales and resort taxes. In Orange County (Orlando, Lake Buena Vista, Winter Park, and Maitland), the tax is 11 percent. In Osceola County (Kissimmee/St. Cloud), the taxes add 12 percent to your bill.

Surfing the Web for hotel deals

Shopping online for hotels is generally done one of two ways: by booking through the hotel's own Web site or through an independent booking agency (or a fare-service agency like Priceline). These Internet agencies have multiplied in mind-boggling numbers of late, competing for the business of millions of consumers. This competitiveness can be a boon to consumers who have the patience and time to shop and compare the online sites for good deals — but shop they must, because prices can vary considerably from site to site. And keep in mind that hotels at the top of a site's listing may be there for no other reason than that they paid money to get the placement.

You almost never find a WDW resort on any discounter's Web site (however, Disney's All-Star Resorts were recently spotted on Priceline). If you want to book a Disney hotel online, you have to go through a packager or Disney's own Web site (www.disneyworld.com). Each individual resort is listed on the site, with information on rooms, rates, floor plans, restaurants, recreation, and so on. Generally, the only hotels on Disney property that you can book through a discounter are the "official" hotels.

In addition to the online travel booking sites **Travelocity, Expedia, Orbitz, Priceline,** and **Hotwire,** you can book hotels through **Hotels.com, Quikbook** (www.quikbook.com), and **Travelweb** (www.travelweb.com), which is partly owned by the hotels it represents (including the Hilton, Hyatt, and Starwood chains), so it's plugged directly into the hotels' reservations systems. An excellent Web site called **Travelaxe** (www.travel axe.net) can help you search multiple hotel sites at once, even ones you may never have heard of — and conveniently lists the total price of the room, including the taxes and service charges. It covers a large number of Orlando's best hotels, and I heartily recommend giving it a try.

HotelChatter.com is a daily webzine offering smart coverage and critiques of hotels worldwide. Go to **TripAdvisor.com** or **HotelShark.com** for helpful independent consumer reviews of hotels and resort properties.

It's a good idea to **get a confirmation number** and **make a printout** of any online booking transaction.

Reserving the best room

 After you make your reservation, asking one or two more questions can go a long way toward making sure you get the best room in the house. Always ask for a corner room. They're usually larger, quieter, and have more windows than standard rooms, and they don't always cost more. If the hotel is renovating, request a room away from the work. Inquire, too, about the location of the restaurants, bars, and discos in the hotel — all sources of annoying noise. And if you aren't happy with your room when you arrive, talk to the front desk. If they have another room, they should be happy to accommodate you, within reason.

Arriving without a Reservation

My first bit of advice: Don't come to Orlando without a reservation. If you do, you're more likely to end up feeling like Grumpy than Happy. This advice is especially true during the high travel season, when rooms are both pricey and scarce. If you do decide, however, to head for Orlando on the spur of the moment, you'll want to pursue a few options before setting up camp in your car.

 Orlando's Official Visitor Center is related to the Orlando/Orange County Convention & Visitors Bureau. These folks find last-minute rooms for non-planners. Room rates, depending on the season, can be a bargain. However, you can get a room only for the night you visit the center, and you have to come in person to find out what's available. The Visitor Center is located in Orlando at 8723 International Dr., a mile west of Sand Lake Road (☎ **407-363-5872** for information only).

Orlando's Best Hotels

All the rates in this section are per-night double occupancy, but many accommodations, including all Disney resorts, allow kids younger than 17 to stay free with their parents or grandparents (as long as the number of guests doesn't exceed the maximum occupancy). However, always ask about rates for kids when booking your room. Also, unless otherwise noted, all the hotels in this section offer free self-parking.

 To make it easy for you to recognize expensive versus moderately priced hotels, each of the following entries includes one or more $ symbols (see Table 9-1 for the meaning behind the symbols). In general, expect higher hotel prices on the more upscale digs as well as those in

Walt Disney World and Lake Buena Vista Accommodations

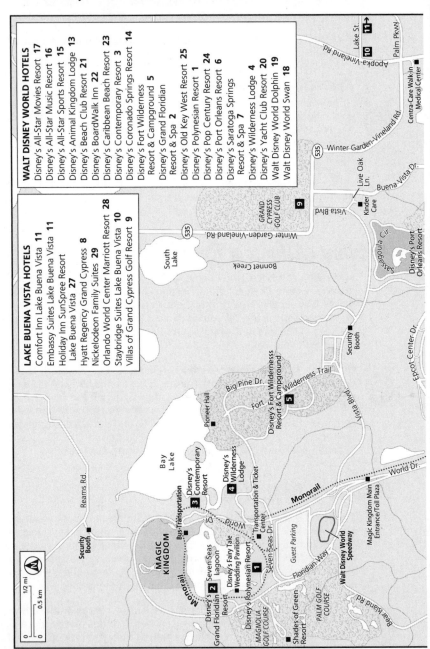

WALT DISNEY WORLD HOTELS
Disney's All-Star Movies Resort **17**
Disney's All-Star Music Resort **16**
Disney's All-Star Sports Resort **15**
Disney's Animal Kingdom Lodge **13**
Disney's Beach Club Resort **21**
Disney's BoardWalk Inn **22**
Disney's Caribbean Beach Resort **23**
Disney's Contemporary Resort **3**
Disney's Coronado Springs Resort **14**
Disney's Fort Wilderness
Resort & Campground **5**
Disney's Grand Floridian
Resort & Spa **2**
Disney's Old Key West Resort **25**
Disney's Polynesian Resort **1**
Disney's Pop Century Resort **24**
Disney's Port Orleans Resort **6**
Disney's Saratoga Springs
Resort & Spa **7**
Disney's Wilderness Lodge **4**
Disney's Yacht Club Resort **20**
Walt Disney World Dolphin **19**
Walt Disney World Swan **18**

LAKE BUENA VISTA HOTELS
Comfort Inn Lake Buena Vista **11**
Embassy Suites Lake Buena Vista **11**
Holiday Inn SunSpree Resort
Lake Buena Vista **27**
Hyatt Regency Grand Cypress **8**
Nickelodeon Family Suites **29**
Orlando World Center Marriott Resort **28**
Staybridge Suites Lake Buena Vista **10**
Villas of Grand Cypress Golf Resort **9**

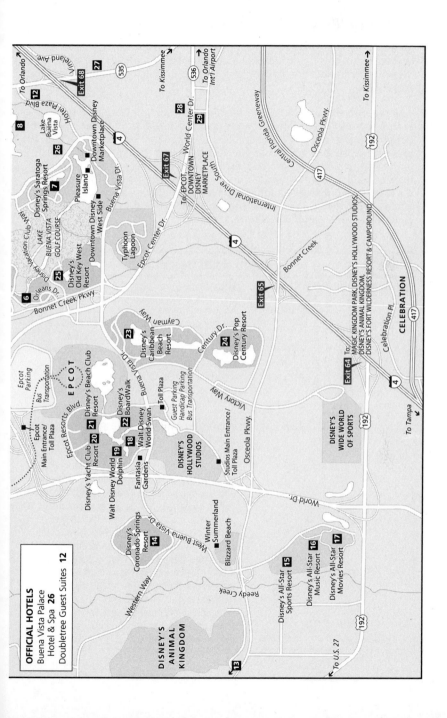

OFFICIAL HOTELS
Buena Vista Palace
Hotel & Spa **26**
Doubletree Guest Suites **12**

or near the attractions. Almost every hotel in Orlando caters to families with children, but I list hotels, resorts, and inns that are especially good for adults on the "Good for Grown-Ups" list on the tear-out Cheat Sheet at the front of this book. I also include some handy indexes at the end of this chapter to help you narrow your choices by neighborhood or price category.

 Several properties in this chapter add resort fees that can range from $5 to upwards of $15 to their daily room rates. That's part of an unfortunate but growing hotel trend of charging for services that used to be included in the rates, such as use of the pool, admission to the health club, or use of the in-room coffeemaker, safe, or phone (each hotel varies greatly). If it's a concern, ask whether your hotel charges such a fee (and just what it's for) when booking so that you don't get blindsided at check-out. At some hotels, the fee is optional and you don't pay it if you don't use the amenities or recreational facilities it covers.

Table 9-1	Key to Hotel Dollar Signs	
Dollar Sign(s)	**Price Range**	**What to Expect**
$	Less than $100	Accommodations at this level generally include basic trimmings and limited space. They also lean toward the no-frills side. Those at the higher end may offer amenities such as hair dryers, coffeemakers, cable TV, a midsize pool, a kids' play area, and continental breakfast. If they're multistory, they also usually have an elevator.
$$	$101–$200	Lodgings in this price range probably offer a choice of king-size or double beds, possibly suites if they fall in the higher end, a full range of amenities (hair dryer; coffeemaker; two TVs in the two-room models; multiline phones and, possibly, a dataport; VCR; free daily newspaper; and designer shampoos), and room service. Rooms are slightly larger, and a Jacuzzi and fitness center may accompany the pool. The continental breakfast probably includes fresh fruit, granola, and muffins rather than day-old doughnuts and little boxes of cereal. The hotel may also have at least one palatable on-site restaurant. Some may have a Guest Services desk for purchasing attraction tickets and making dinner arrangements.

Dollar Sign(s)	Price Range	What to Expect
$$$	$201–$300	Hotels at this level are sure to have a Guest Services desk, possibly a concierge. They usually include a large resort-style pool, possibly a second smaller or toddler pool, and multiple Jacuzzi tubs (some of the higher-end rooms have their own), a fitness center, and occasionally a small spa. Rooms generally have multiple phones, minibars, and a bathtub *and* separate shower. Many rooms are larger — some with small sitting areas, a pull-out sofa, and large work desks. Some hotels in this category offer supervised children's programs and activities.
$$$$	$301 and up	Nothing in this price range is impossible. In addition to the amenities in the previous categories, many of these hotels offer concierge levels, extra-large rooms, spacious suites, 24-hour room service, gorgeous pool bars, and live entertainment in their lounges. Some also include full-service spas, gourmet restaurants, shopping arcades, and tight security. Recreational facilities are usually extensive and lavish. Many offer supervised children's programs and activities.

Americas Best Value Inn & Suites
$ **Kissimmee**

Formerly the Hawaiian Maingate, this newly revitalized budget hotel offers clean, comfortable accommodations close to Disney's gates. You'll find the basics — including a large pool, a casual restaurant, a rental-car desk, and reasonably comfortable rooms with a TV, Internet access, and either two double or two queen beds (though not a lot of extra space) — but fewer frills mean you won't break the bank. Shuttle service to WDW, Universal, and SeaWorld parks is free.

See map p. 113. 7514 W. Irlo Bronson Memorial Hwy. (From I-4, take Exit 64B, follow for 1 mile, and then turn left on Old Lake Wilson Rd.) ☎ **888-315-2378** *or 407-396-2000. Fax: 407-396-1295.* www.bestvalueinn.com. *444 units. Rack rates: $49–$99 double. AE, DC, DISC, MC, V.*

Best Western Lakeside
$–$$ **Kissimmee**

Relatively recent renovations ensure that this Best Western (formerly the La Quinta Inn Lakeside) remains in tip-top shape. Just up the road from

A home away from home

If you want all the comforts of home or you are traveling in a group of five or more, you might consider bypassing hotels and motels in favor of a rental condo or home. Rates vary widely depending on quality and location, and some may require a two- or three-night minimum stay. Many of these properties are 5 to 15 miles from the theme parks and offer no transportation, so having a car is a necessity.

On the upside, most have two to six bedrooms and a convertible couch, two or more bathrooms, a full kitchen, multiple TVs and phones, and an iron. Some have a washer and dryer. Homes often have their own private, screen-enclosed pool, while condos have a common recreation area.

On the downside, rentals can be lacking in services. Most don't have daily maid service, and restaurants can be as far away as the parks (another reason you'll need a car). Be sure to ask whether the rentals include useful items such as dinnerware, utensils, or salt and pepper shakers — it generally depends on the level of the home.

Rates generally range from about $125 to $600 per night ($875–$4,200 per week), but can vary depending on the season and type of home you choose.

All Star Vacation Homes (☎ 800-592-5586 or 407-997-0733; www.allstar vacationhomes.com) offers an array of homes and condos, many of which are within 4 miles of Disney (its newest town-home community, Vista Cay, is located near SeaWorld) and close to all area restaurants and attractions. Homes fall into a wide range of luxury levels and size. Many have private, screened-in pools. A variety of guest services are available (some cost extra).

the Disney entrance, this 24-acre resort looks deceptively small when you arrive (most of the accommodations are hidden behind the lobby area), but amenities include numerous recreational options (pools, playgrounds, and so on), a food court, a good-size convenience store, and a bountiful free breakfast. Rooms are standard in size and offerings, but are nicely decorated and comfortably sleep four. Other pluses include an evening child-care facility (for a fee), free transportation to *all* major theme parks, free high-speed or Wi-Fi Internet in select rooms, free Wi-Fi in the lobby and eateries, a general store, and three casual on-site dining options.

See map p. 113. 7769 W. Irlo Bronson Memorial Hwy./U.S. 192. (Take I-4 to Exit 64B/U.S. 192 West. The hotel is approximately 3 miles on the right.) ☎ *800-848-0801 or 407-396-2222. Fax: 407-997-1171.* www.bestwesternlakeside.com. *651 units. Rack rates: $59–$139 double. AE, DC, DISC, MC, V.*

Buena Vista Palace Hotel & Spa
$$–$$$$ Lake Buena Vista/Official WDW Hotel

Thanks to a $45-million makeover, this hotel's spacious accommodations now feature 32-inch flatscreen TVs, wired and wireless Internet access, and all-new very comfy bedding (though I can't say the same for the furnishings elsewhere in the rooms). Literally across the road from Downtown Disney, this former Wyndham resort, though suitable for families, is an ideal spot for honeymooners, those looking for a romantic weekend getaway, and the business set. Many of the rooms have lakeview balconies or patios; ask for one above the fifth floor with a "water view." Because businesspeople make up 75 percent of its guests, the hotel offers some of its best rates in July and August, contrary to the other Orlando mainstream tourist resorts. Amenities include three pools, a fully equipped and newly renovated spa, a sauna, a video arcade, and six restaurants and lounges. Rates include free transportation to Disney; you pay a fee for transportation to the other theme parks.

See map p. 96. 1900 Buena Vista Dr. (Off Hwy. 535; turn in the entrance to Downtown Disney Marketplace; the hotel is on Hotel Plaza Blvd.) ☎ 866-397-6516 or 407-827-2727. Fax: 407-827-6034. www.buenavistapalace.com. *1,012 units. Rack rates: $99–$278 double, $219–$450 suite. Daily resort fee: $12. Valet parking: $16. AE, DC, DISC, MC, V.*

Celebration Hotel
$$$–$$$$ Kissimmee

Located in the Disney-esque town of Celebration, this upscale and charmingly sophisticated hotel has a three-story, wood-frame design straight out of 1920s Florida. A bit off the beaten path, it offers a romantic atmosphere for couples. (Although children are welcome, I wouldn't suggest bringing them here.) All rooms offer dataports, safes, hair dryers, and TVs with Nintendo. Suites and studios have refrigerators and wet bars. Other amenities include a pool, Jacuzzi, and fitness center. Shops, an 18-hole golf course, a movie theater, and several restaurants are within walking distance. A free shuttle to WDW parks and transportation to other parks (for a fee) are available.

See map p. 113. 700 Bloom St. (Take I-4 to the U.S. 192 exit. Go east to the second light, and then right on Celebration Ave.) ☎ 888-499-3800 or 407-566-6000. Fax: 407-566-1844. www.celebrationhotel.com. *115 units. Rack rates: $219–$359 double, $299–$459 suite. Daily resort fee: $10. Valet parking: $14. AE, DC, DISC, MC, V.*

Comfort Inn Lake Buena Vista
$ Lake Buena Vista

Set back from the main drag, yet close to the action of Downtown Disney, this hotel is one of best bargains in the area. The accommodations — 640 standard rooms and a small number of family suites (that sleep up to five) — are clean and comfortable and include extras like a microwave and fridge. Keeping cool is no problem with two pools to choose from. You can stay connected to the real world with free Wi-Fi in the lobby (in-room high-speed access is available for a daily fee). A complimentary continental breakfast ensures you'll start your day off right, and the kids-eat-free program ensures you won't break the bank when dining here. Complimentary shuttle service is available to WDW, Universal, and SeaWorld parks.

See map p. 96. 8442 Palm Pkwy. (Take I-4 to Exit 68, follow S.R. 535, and turn right onto Palm Pkwy. The hotel is on the right.) ☎ *800-999-7300 or 407-996-7300. Fax: 407-996-7300.* www.comfortinnorlando.com. *640 units. Rack rates: $69–$175 double. Rates include continental breakfast. AE, DC, DISC, MC, V.*

Comfort Suites Maingate at Formosa Gardens
$–$$$ **Kissimmee**

Just across the street from the Best Western Lakeside (see listing earlier in this section) and up the road from WDW, this clean, comfortable place has kept itself modern and in good shape. The suites have a small dividing wall slightly separating the living area from the sleeping quarters, creating an illusion of privacy. Accommodations are a bit bigger than most and can squeeze in up to six. Conveniences include a small fridge and microwave. A bit of tropical landscaping gives it an inviting atmosphere and shelters guests from busy U.S. 192. A small shopping plaza and at least ten restaurants are within walking distance, and a miniature golf course is right across the street. Perks include free high-speed Internet access, free breakfast buffet, a 24-hour concierge, on-site car rental, and a complimentary shuttle to the area theme parks.

See map p. 113. 7888 W. Irlo Bronson Memorial Hwy./U.S. 192. (Take I-4 to Exit 64B/W. Hwy. 192. The hotel is 3 miles on the left.) ☎ *888-390-9888 or 407-390-9888. Fax: 407-390-0981.* www.comfortsuiteskissimmee.com. *150 units. Rack rates: $59–$199 suite. Rates include breakfast buffet. AE, DC, DISC, MC, V.*

Comfort Suites Maingate East
$–$$ **Kissimmee**

Set back, hidden from the action that plagues the very busy thoroughfare, this fairly new and welcoming hotel is one of the nicest in the area. The lobby and accommodations — consisting of studios and one-bedroom suites — are bright and inviting. The main pool and the children's pool, with an umbrella fountain to keep everyone cool, are open around the clock. High-speed Internet access is free. For entertainment, Old Town (a small-scale shopping, dining, and entertainment complex) is next door, and a great miniature golf course is located just in front of the property. Complimentary shuttle service is available to all area theme parks.

See map p. 113. 2775 Florida Plaza Blvd. (Take I-4 to the U.S. 192 exit. Go east 1¾ miles, and then right on Florida Plaza Blvd.) ☎ *888-784-8379 or 407-397-7848. Fax: 407-396-7045.* www.comfortsuitesfl.com. *198 units. Rack rates: $79–$175 double. Rates include expanded continental breakfast. AE, DC, DISC, MC, V.*

Comfort Suites Orlando
$–$$ **International Drive Area/Universal Orlando**

This recently updated hotel is closest to Universal Orlando, although getting to Disney is an easy drive south — you don't even have to hop on the highway if you simply follow Turkey Lake Road until it turns into Palm Parkway. Comfortable rooms offer partially separated living and sleeping areas, a sleeper sofa, and a microwave and fridge, among other amenities. Perks include an inviting pool area, a mini convenience store, complimentary shuttle service to Universal and SeaWorld parks, a Guest Services desk that sells tickets to all area theme parks, and a complimentary breakfast buffet.

See map p. 119. 9350 Turkey Lake Rd. (From I-4, take Exit 74A to Sand Lake Rd.; then turn left onto Turkey Lake Rd.) ☎ *800-277-8483 or 407-351-5050. Fax: 407-363-7953.* www.comfortsuitesorlando.com. *213 units. Rack rates: $99–$149 suite. Daily resort fee: $2.50. Rates include breakfast buffet. AE, DISC, MC, V.*

The Courtyard at Lake Lucerne
$–$$$ Downtown Orlando

This charming B&B hideaway is located within walking distance of several of downtown's cultural attractions, upscale eateries, and shops. It is made up of several historic buildings. The Norment-Parry Inn is an 1883 Victorian-style home with six rooms decorated with English and American antiques; four have sitting rooms, and all have private bathrooms. A honeymoon suite has a walnut bed, a fireplace, and a small, glass-enclosed porch. The I. W. Phillips House, built in 1919, is a Southern jewel with three upstairs suites, one with a whirlpool, and all with verandas overlooking the gardens and fountain. The Dr. Phillips House (1893) and the Wellborn Suites (1946) round out the offerings.

See map p. 349. 211 N. Lucerne Circle E. (Take Orange Ave. south. Immediately past City Hall, turn left onto Anderson. After 2 lights, at Delaney Ave., turn right. Take the first right onto Lucerne Circle. Follow the brown HISTORIC INN *signs.)* ☎ *800-444-5289 or 407-648-5188. Fax: 407-246-1368.* www.orlandohistoricinn.com. *30 units. Rack rates: $89–$225 double. Rates include continental breakfast. AE, DC, MC, V.*

Crowne Plaza Orlando-Universal
$$–$$$ International Drive Area/Universal Orlando

Sleek, modern, and upscale, this 15-story hotel is close to Universal Orlando and SeaWorld (about midway between them), although getting to Disney is no problem because the hotel offers free shuttles to all the major parks. It's also close to the I-Ride Trolley, making it easy to get to the many attractions and eateries lining I-Drive. Subdued but well-appointed rooms offer floor-to-ceiling windows. Some of the pricier rooms are in the Atrium Tower, where glass elevators climb to the top. Other perks include a fitness center and a heated pool. This place is geared toward business travelers and adults without kids in tow.

See map p. 119. 7800 Universal Blvd. (From I-4, take Sand Lake Rd./Hwy. 482 east to Universal, and then turn left.) ☎ *877-781-4185 or 407-355-0550. Fax: 407-355-0504.* www.cporlando.com. *400 units. Rack rates: $129–$299 double, $439–$689 suite. Valet parking: $9. AE, DISC, MC, V.*

Disney's All-Star Movies Resort
$–$$ Walt Disney World

Kids aren't the only ones amazed by the, uh, aesthetics of this resort. When did you last see architecture as inspiring as Goliath-size Dalmatians leaping from balconies? If you're not saying, "Oh, brother!" by now, you may enjoy all the larger-than-life versions of a host of other characters from famous Disney movies (*Toy Story, 101 Dalmatians,* and *Fantasia,* among others) that decorate the buildings here, and the low rates (by Mickey standards) will thrill some travelers. The All-Star Resorts that follow this listing are pretty much the same, save the theme — expect tiny (260 sq. ft.) standard rooms, postage-stamp-size bathrooms, few frills, but plenty of families. Either way, you're "on property," and you're enjoying the lowest prices your Mouse money can buy. This All-Star Resort has a family-friendly food court that serves pizza, pasta, sandwiches, salads, burgers, chicken, and family-dinner platters. Room service is very limited. Each of the All-Star Resorts features a main pool, a smaller second pool, a toddler pool, and a very small playground, as well as an arcade.

See map p. 96. 1991 W. Buena Vista Dr. ☎ *407-934-7639 or 407-939-7000. Fax: 407-939-7111.* www.disneyworld.com. *1,920 units. Rack rates: $82–$151 double. AE, DC, DISC, MC, V.*

Disney's All-Star Music Resort
$–$$ Walt Disney World

If you insist on staying on Disney property and you're on a tight budget, the rates at the All-Star Resorts are difficult to beat. But you'd better be prepared for full-time family togetherness, because the mouse-size rooms mean you'll be up close and personal. (They're about the size of what you get on a cruise ship if you choose a midprice cabin.) Fortunately, recent remodeling reduced the number of smaller rooms to create 214 family suites that can sleep up to six and include two bathrooms, a kitchenette, and a separate master bedroom with a flatscreen TV. But if the idea of residing in buildings decorated with immense musical notes and other music-related motifs doesn't appeal, head elsewhere.

See map p. 96. 1801 W. Buena Vista Dr. (at World Dr. and Osceola Pkwy.). ☎ *407-934-7639 or 407-939-6000. Fax: 407-939-7222.* www.disneyworld.com. *1,706 units. Rack rates: $82–$151 double, $184–$315 suite. AE, DC, DISC, MC, V.*

Disney's All-Star Sports Resort
$–$$ Walt Disney World

Adjacent to the All-Star Music Resort, this 82-acre property is an instant replay of its sister All-Star Resorts. It draws sports fans looking for a vacation and visual overload. The buildings feature football (huge helmets protect stairwells from rain), baseball, basketball, tennis, and surfing motifs. Amenities include a brightly decorated food court, very limited room service, baby-sitting (from an outside service), a Guest Services desk (standard at Disney resorts), pools, and a video arcade. Like its two siblings (listed earlier), the All-Star Sports Resort is fairly isolated in WDW's southwest corner. Renting a car is a far better choice than relying on the Disney Transportation system if you want to get anywhere quickly.

See map p. 96. 1701 W. Buena Vista Dr. (at World Dr. and Osceola Pkwy.). ☎ *407-934-7639 or 407-939-5000. Fax: 407-939-7333.* www.disneyworld.com. *1,920 units. Rack rates: $82–$151 double. AE, DC, DISC, MC, V.*

Disney's Animal Kingdom Lodge
$$$–$$$$ **Walt Disney World**

Disney's most remote resort offers the exotic atmosphere of an African game preserve. The rooms follow a *kraal* (semicircular) design, giving guests a hit-or-miss view of 130 species of birds and 75 giraffes, gazelles, and other grazing animals on the 30-acre savanna. The huge picture windows in the lobby offer similar views, while the interior public areas are adorned with authentic African artwork and artifacts. The rooms are quite comfortable, although bathrooms are a bit cramped (a problem with many of Disney's properties). Two of the best and most unique restaurants among Disney resorts (Jiko and Boma) are located here. Not surprisingly, this resort is the closest one to Animal Kingdom, but almost everything else on WDW property is quite a distance away. And although families appreciate the animals and wide array of activities for kids (not to mention the bunk beds available in some rooms and the supervised kids' club), the more relaxed and sedate nature of the resort also makes it a good spot for couples. A concierge level is available.

Disney's Animal Kingdom Villas, the latest addition to the **Disney Vacation Club,** are currently under construction. Rooms on the fifth and sixth floors of the main lodge were converted to villas in 2007; subsequent phases, including a new restaurant, recreational facilities, and a separate themed pool area, are slated for completion in 2009.

See map p. 96. 2901 Osceola Pkwy. (west of Buena Vista Dr.). ☎ *407-934-7639 or 407-938-3000. Fax: 407-939-4799.* www.disneyworld.com. *1,293 units. Rack rates: $225–$475 double, $335–$2,820 concierge, $705–$2,820 suite, $265–$2,155 villa. AE, DC, DISC, MC, V.*

Disney's Beach Club Resort
$$$$ **Walt Disney World**

It's only a brisk walk to Epcot from the Beach Club, which resembles the grand seaside resorts that once dotted the eastern seaboard around the turn of the 20th century. The Beach Club's atmosphere is a bit more casual than at its sister resort (the Yacht Club, listed later), which shares its many restaurants and recreational facilities. Though still upscale, the brightly colored beach umbrellas, seashells, and a casual Cape Cod feel permeate the resort. Kids love the 3-acre free-form, sand-bottom swimming pool of Stormalong Bay, winding its way along the beachfront. Rooms can sleep up to five, and views range from the pool to the parking lot. Studios have kitchenettes, while **Disney's Beach Club Villas** have one or two bedrooms (which sleep up to eight), full kitchens, washer/dryers, and whirlpool tubs.

All units come with balconies. The BoardWalk, Swan, and Dolphin resorts are just a short walk across the bridge, adding their own entertainment and dining options to the mix. The proximity to the parks (Disney's Hollywood Studios and Epcot especially) and other resorts makes this one of the best upscale destinations at Disney, particularly for families.

See map p. 96. 1800 Epcot Resorts Blvd. (off Buena Vista Dr.). ☎ **407-934-7639** *or 407-934-8000. Fax: 407-934-3850.* www.disneyworld.com. *583 units, 205 villas. Rack rates: $325–$750 double, $445–$730 concierge, $560–$2,400 suite, $325–$1,140 villa. AE, DC, DISC, MC, V.*

Disney's BoardWalk Inn
$$$$ **Walt Disney World**

More than any other Disney property, the BoardWalk Inn appeals to those looking for a sliver of yesterday. The 1940s "seaside" resort overlooks a village green and lake. Some of the Cape Cod–style rooms have balconies (rooms sleep up to five); the corner units offer a bit more space. Center rooms on the upper floors facing the lake have the best view of the nightly fireworks at Epcot. Recreational facilities are extensive, including two pools set in a lavish Coney Island atmosphere, tennis, fishing, boating, bike rentals, and even a moonlight cruise. **Disney's BoardWalk Villas** sleep up to 12, and the one- to three-bedroom villas have full kitchens, washer/dryers, and whirlpool tubs. The resort has a quarter-mile boardwalk, reminiscent of those once made popular along the mid-Atlantic seaboard, featuring shops, restaurants, and street performers, which means you'll find plenty to do after the sun goes down. *Note:* Rooms overlooking the BoardWalk have the best views, but they tend to be noisy due to the action below.

See map p. 96. 2101 N. Epcot Resorts Blvd. (north of Buena Vista Dr.). ☎ **407-934-7639** *or 407-939-5100. Fax: 407-934-5150.* www.disneyworld.com. *378 units, 520 villas. Rack rates: $325–$600 double, $455–$875 concierge, $610–$2,620 suite, $325–$2,155 villa. AE, DC, DISC, MC, V.*

Disney's Caribbean Beach Resort
$$–$$$ **Walt Disney World**

This moderately priced hotel's amenities may not be quite as extensive as those at some of Disney's higher-end properties (or those in the same class outside the World), but the hotel still offers great value for families. Grouped into five Caribbean island–themed villages, many of the rooms offer views out over the beaches and the water. Standard rooms feature two double beds, a small bathroom, and privacy curtains for a vanity area with a double sink. The main swimming pool resembles a Spanish-style fort, and most of the villages have their own basic pool as well. Other pluses are a nature trail, a small aviary, and a picnic area. The hotel also has a restaurant, as well as a lively market-style food court. The closest park is Disney's Hollywood Studios, though it can take up to 45 minutes to get there using Disney Transportation — you're probably better off renting a car if you stay here. *Note:* When booking, ask for a recently refurbished room.

See map p. 96. 900 Cayman Way (off Buena Vista Dr. toward Epcot, on Sea Breeze Dr. and Cayman Way). ☎ **407-934-7639** *or 407-934-3400. Fax: 407-934-3288.* www. disneyworld.com. *2,112 units. Rack rates: $149–$240 double. AE, DC, DISC, MC, V.*

Disney's Contemporary Resort
$$$–$$$$ **Walt Disney World**

If location is a priority, the Contemporary has one of the best in the World because the monorail literally runs through the hotel, allowing you a fast track to Epcot or the Magic Kingdom. The 15-story, A-frame resort — Disney's first in Florida — overlooks the manmade Seven Seas Lagoon and Bay Lake. The original rooms in this tower were built separately and then slid into the framework, an unusual process befitting the futuristic architecture. The separate two-story Garden Wing buildings were added several years later. Standard rooms are among Disney's biggest. The more expensive Tower rooms have the best views, and the higher floors tend to be quieter. Recent room renovations include an upscale décor with an Asian-retro flair that looks amazing. Parents will appreciate the rounded corners and kid-proof locks on the sliding doors (remember how high up you are here). And did I mention the flatscreen TVs? Major renovations throughout the lobby were wrapped up in 2008, as were noticeable changes to the fourth floor, where the shops and most restaurants are located (with the exception of the **Wave,** an all-new eatery on the first floor that focuses on healthy dining). The pool area is a virtual mini water park, and many of Disney's watersports options are headquartered here. The hotel offers three restaurants, including one of WDW's most popular dining spots, the **California Grill,** and a character meal at **Chef Mickey's** (see Chapter 10). Other notable changes include the demolition of the North Garden Wing and the tower (currently under construction) that has begun to rise in its place — word has it that it will be Disney's newest addition to the lineup of Vacation Club villas.

 This is still the least Disney-esque of the expensive WDW resorts, and although the room décor has improved exponentially, and the public areas have seen great improvements (most especially the fourth-floor shopping and dining), other public areas are still somewhat bland by comparison — so if you want an all-Mickey atmosphere, stay elsewhere.

See map p. 96. 4600 N. World Dr. ☎ **407-934-7639** *or 407-824-1000. Fax: 407-824-3539.* www.disneyworld.com. *1,053 units. Rack rates: $270–$600 double, $515–$775 concierge, $885–$2,755 suite. AE, DC, DISC, MC, V.*

Disney's Coronado Springs Resort
$$–$$$ **Walt Disney World**

The spirit of the Southwest permeates this moderately priced resort, which has a slightly more upscale feel than others of its class. Rooms are housed in four- and five-story hacienda-style buildings with terra-cotta tile roofs and palm-shaded courtyards (many of which look quite similar, so make note of your building if you don't want to get lost). Some overlook the 15-acre Golden Lake; the better your view, the higher the price. Rooms feature two double beds (the décor differs in each section, but the layout is the same), with a small bathroom and dual vanities set inside a separate niche. Ninety-nine rooms are specially designed to accommodate travelers with disabilities. If you like to swim, you'll delight in the Mayan temple–inspired main pool. Dining options include a restaurant and a food court. **Rix Lounge,** Disney's newest and trendiest club to date, opened its doors here in late 2007 (see Chapter 25). The nearest park is Disney's Animal Kingdom, but the Coronado is at the southwest corner of WDW and a good distance from most other areas in the park.

See map p. 96. 1000 Buena Vista Dr. ☎ 407-934-7639 or 407-939-1000. Fax: 407-939-1001. www.disneyworld.com. *1,967 units. Rack rates: $149–$240 double, $340–$1,245 suite. AE, DC, DISC, MC, V.*

Disney's Fort Wilderness Resort & Campground
$–$$$　**Walt Disney World**

This woodsy, 780-acre resort delights campers, but it's quite a hike from most of the Disney parks, except the Magic Kingdom (and even that might feel far away if you use Disney Transportation to get there). Even so, you'll have more than enough to keep you busy right here. Guests enjoy extensive recreational facilities, ranging from a riding stable to a video arcade, with fishing, biking, tennis, and swimming among the offerings. Secluded campsites offer 110/220-volt outlets, barbecue grills, picnic tables, and kids' play areas. Wilderness cabins (actually cleverly disguised trailers) can sleep up to six; they have living rooms, fully equipped kitchens, coffeemakers, hair dryers, and barbecue grills. Pioneer Hall plays host to the rambunctious **Hoop-Dee-Doo Musical Revue** (see Chapter 24). The nightly campfire and marshmallow roast, followed by a Disney movie, shown right in the great outdoors, is a big hit with families.

Some sites (the ones with full hookups) are open to pets at an additional cost of $5 per site — not per pet — which is less expensive than using the WDW Pet Care Kennels, where you pay $13 to $20 per pet.

See map p. 96. 3520 N. Fort Wilderness Trail (located off Vista Blvd.). ☎ 407-934-7639 or 407-824-2900. Fax: 407-824-3508. www.disneyworld.com. *784 campsites, 408 wilderness cabins. Rack rates: $42–$111 campsite, $255–$395 cabin. AE, DC, DISC, MC, V.*

Disney's Grand Floridian Resort & Spa
$$$$　**Walt Disney World**

The Grand Floridian is Disney's upper-crust flagship, and it's as pricey as it is plush. You won't find a more luxurious address — in a Victorian sense, anyway — than this 40-acre *Great Gatsby*–era resort on the shores of the Seven Seas Lagoon. It's a great choice for couples seeking a bit of romance. Families will appreciate the extensive recreational facilities, which include a child-friendly pool with waterfalls, organized children's activities, and character dining. The opulent, five-story domed lobby hosts afternoon teas accompanied by piano music. In the evenings, an orchestra plays big-band tunes. Virtually all the inviting Victorian-style rooms overlook a garden, pool, courtyard, or the Seven Seas Lagoon; many have balconies; and the dormer rooms have vaulted ceilings. The hotel is one of three on the Disney monorail line. The resort also has a first-rate health club and spa, plus five restaurants, including the incomparable **Victoria & Albert's** (see Chapter 10).

See map p. 96. 4401 Floridian Way (northwest corner of the WDW property, just north of the Polynesian Resort). ☎ *407-934-7639 or 407-824-3000. Fax: 407-824-3186.* www.disneyworld.com. *900 units. Rack rates: $385–$710 double, $505–$990 concierge, $670–$2,795 suite. AE, DC, DISC, MC, V.*

Disney's Old Key West Resort
$$$–$$$$ **Walt Disney World**

The peace and quiet of a remote locale away from the dizzying Disney theme-park pace is just part of your reward when you stay here. This **Disney Vacation Club** timeshare property (also referred to at times as a deluxe villa resort) mirrors turn-of-the-20th-century Key West, though the theme is tastefully understated. Pastel colors and gingerbread trim adorn the charming buildings, while scattered palm trees provide a bit of shade along the beaches. Tourists can rent rooms here when their owners are not using them, and they're a great choice for large families or long stays. The accommodations include studios, along with one-, two-, and three-bedroom villas that have full kitchens, washer/dryers, Jacuzzis, and balconies. Extensive recreational facilities include beaches, pools, an array of watersports, a playground, a video arcade, and more. There's a restaurant as well as a large grocery store.

See map p. 96. 1510 N. Cove Rd. (off Community Dr.). ☎ *407-934-7639 or 407-827-7700. Fax: 407-827-7710.* www.disneyworld.com. *761 units. Rack rates: $285–$405 studio, $385–$1,645 villa. AE, DC, DISC, MC, V.*

Disney's Polynesian Resort
$$$$ **Walt Disney World**

This 25-acre Polynesian Resort, built to resemble the South Pacific, is an original, open from the time Disney first opened its doors. Its popularity is due in part to its location — one of the best in all of WDW — just across from the Magic Kingdom and right on the monorail line. Extensive renovations have rejuvenated the entire resort, its age no longer apparent. The guest rooms, most with balconies or patios, are reasonably large and sport an all-new décor, with muted earth-tone color schemes that create an island feel, and added amenities that include flatscreen TVs and refrigerators. The Tahiti and Rapa Nui buildings have rooms that are slightly larger, but they're also the farthest from the main building, dining, and volcano-pool area. Numerous recreational activities are available, including fishing and boat rentals. The **Spirit of Aloha Show** (see Chapter 24) is the big nighttime activity here, and **'Ohana** is a favorite restaurant for families because it features kid-friendly activities during the dinner hour and a lively character meal at breakfast.

Though the South Pacific theme may bring on visions of romance, many honeymooners who stay here are dismayed to discover the resort is over-flowing with kids. Adults looking for privacy, beware.

See map p. 96. 1600 Seven Seas Dr. (off Floridian Way, across from Magnolia Palm Dr.). ☎ *407-934-7639 or 407-824-2000. Fax: 407-824-3174.* www.disneyworld.com. *853 units. Rack rates: $340–$860 double, $480–$2,810 concierge and suite. AE, DC, DISC, MC, V.*

Disney's Pop Century Resort
$-$$ **Walt Disney World**

Flower power, the Rubik's Cube, and Play-Doh still rule supreme at the Pop Century Resort. Nestled behind the Caribbean Resort, near Disney's Wide World of Sports, this newest Disney value property is still a work in progress; only one section of the resort was open at press time. The remaining sections, while scheduled to open in phases, remain unfinished — with no clear timetable for completion. This value (Disney's word for *budget*) resort is perhaps the most fun for adults, who will enjoy the many reminders of their past, including a bowling alley–shaped pool and a three-story-tall Big Wheel. The all-too-small rooms are in buildings decorated with pop-culture references from the last four decades and mirror those at the All-Star Resorts in most every way. Forget frills — there aren't any. But it is new, so there's little wear and tear. Amenities include a brightly decorated food court, three pools, and a video arcade.

See map p. 96. 1050 Century Dr. (midway between Buena Vista Dr. and Osceola Pkwy.). ☎ *407-934-7639 or 407-938-4000. Fax: 407-938-4040.* www.disneyworld. com. *2,880 units. Rack rates: $82–$151 double. AE, DC, DISC, MC, V.*

Disney's Port Orleans Resort
$$-$$$ **Walt Disney World**

Port Orleans has the best location, the best landscaping, and the coziest atmosphere of the resorts in this class. This Southern-style property is really a combination of two distinct resorts: the French Quarter and Riverside. Overall, this resort offers some romantic spots and is relatively quiet, making it popular with couples; but the pools, playgrounds, and array of activities make it a favorite for families as well. The Doubloon Lagoon pool in the French Quarter has a water slide that curves out of a sea serpent's mouth before entering the recently refurbished pool. The rooms and bathrooms (equivalent to all rooms at Disney's moderate resorts) are somewhat of a tight fit for four (the Alligator Bayou rooms have a trundle bed, allowing for an extra person), but the vanity areas now have privacy curtains. **Boatwright's Dining Hall** (see Chapter 10) serves New Orleans–style cuisine; there's also a lively food court. Port Orleans is just east of Epcot and Disney's Hollywood Studios. *Note:* All rooms on the French Quarter side had a top-to-bottom refurbishment in 2004, while the rooms in Riverside were renovated in 2005.

See map p. 96. 2201 Orleans Dr. (off Bonnet Creek Pkwy.). ☎ *407-934-7639 or 407-934-5000 (French Quarter) or 407-934-6000 (Riverside). Fax: 407-934-5353 (French*

Quarter) or 407-934-5777 (Riverside). www.disneyworld.com. *3,056 units. Rack rates: $149–$240 double. AE, DC, DISC, MC, V.*

Disney's Saratoga Springs Resort & Spa
$$$–$$$$ **Walt Disney World**

Saratoga Springs, the newest **Disney Vacation Club** timeshare property (also referred to as a deluxe villa resort), opened in phases — the first opening in 2004, the third completed in 2007. Rooms and villas are rented out to tourists when owners aren't using them — a good choice for large families or long stays. The place is modeled after the luxurious upstate New York country retreats of the late 1800s. The small resort town of Saratoga Springs is evoked through lavish gardens, Victorian architecture, a pool designed to look like natural springs, and a country setting. The renowned spa offers a chance for relaxation and rejuvenation after a day at the parks. Accommodations include one-, two-, and three-bedroom villas that have full kitchens or kitchenettes, coffeemakers, hair dryers, and all the comforts of home. Studios are also available. Extensive recreational facilities include a playground, a video arcade, tennis courts, shuffleboard, and four pools. The water taxi can transport you to Downtown Disney for more dining and evening entertainment options.

See map p. 96. 1960 Broadway (off Buena Vista Dr., next to Downtown Disney Marketplace). ☎ **407-934-7639** *or 407-827-7700. Fax: 407-827-7710.* www.disney world.com. *828 units. Rack rates: $285–$405 studio, $385–$1,645 villa. AE, DC, DISC, MC, V.*

Disney's Wilderness Lodge
$$$–$$$$ **Walt Disney World**

Here's an option for those who like the great outdoors but prefer the comforts of an indoor luxury resort. The geyser out back, the mammoth stone hearth in the lobby, and bunk beds for the kids are just a few reasons this resort is a favorite of families, though couples will find the surroundings to their liking as well. The theme of the Great American Northwest is felt throughout the property; its rustic architecture is patterned after a lodge at Yellowstone National Park. The immense and winding swimming area cuts through the rocky landscaping. The nearest park is the Magic Kingdom, but because the resort is in a remote area, it can take some time to get there. The main drawback is the difficulty in accessing other areas via the Disney Transportation system.

The adjacent **Villas at Disney's Wilderness Lodge** were added in 2000. This is another **Disney Vacation Club** timeshare property (also referred to as a deluxe villa resort) that rents vacant rooms to tourists. It offers a more upscale mountain retreat experience, and more space than the accommodations at the Wilderness Lodge, though the properties share a grand lobby, amenities, and activities. Two notable restaurants, **Artist Point** (better for adults) and the **Whispering Canyon Café** (great for families), are on-site.

See map p. 96. 901 W. Timberline Dr. (on Seven Seas Dr., south of the Contemporary Resort on the southwest shore of Bay Lake). ☎ **407-934-7639** *or 407-938-4300. Fax: 407-824-3232.* www.disneyworld.com. *909 units. Rack rates: $225–$730 double, $385–$1,330 concierge and suite, $325–$1,120 villa. AE, DC, DISC, MC, V.*

Disney's Yacht Club Resort
$$$$ Walt Disney World

This posh resort resembles a turn-of-the-20th-century New England yacht club and is located on the 25-acre lake it shares with the Beach Club (reviewed earlier in this chapter), which is a notch below the Yacht Club in sophistication and atmosphere. This property is geared more toward adults and families with older children, although young kids are still catered to (you're in Disney World, after all). The relatively large rooms sleep up to five, and most units have patios or balconies, although some views are of the asphalt parking lots. The resort has two restaurants, an extensive swimming area that it shares with the Beach Club, a marina, and two tennis courts. Epcot is a 10- to 15-minute walk from the front door.

See map p. 96. 1700 Epcot Resorts Blvd. (off Buena Vista Dr.). ☎ **407-934-7639** *or 407-934-7000. Fax: 407-924-3450.* www.disneyworld.com. *621 units. Rack rates: $325–$750 double, $445–$2,600 concierge and suite. AE, DC, DISC, MC, V.*

Doubletree Guest Suites
$$–$$$$ Lake Buena Vista/Official WDW Hotel

Among the "official" hotels, this seven-story, all-suite hotel is the best for large families. Young patrons get their own check-in desk and theater. All accommodations are two-room suites that offer 643 square feet and plenty of space for up to six to catch some *zzzz*s. You'll also find an array of recreational facilities, including a pool, two lighted tennis courts, and a playground. Bus service to WDW parks is free; it's available, for a fee, to other parks. Downtown Disney is only minutes away.

See map p. 96. 2305 Hotel Plaza Blvd. (just west of Apopka-Vineland Rd./Hwy. 535; turn into the entrance to Downtown Disney Marketplace). ☎ **800-222-8733** *or 407-934-1000. Fax: 407-934-1015.* www.doubletreeguestsuites.com. *229 units. Rack rates: $99–$309 double. AE, DC, DISC, MC, V.*

Embassy Suites Lake Buena Vista
$$–$$$ Lake Buena Vista

Set near the end of Palm Parkway, just off Apopka-Vineland, this fun and welcoming all-suite resort is close to the action of Downtown Disney and the surrounding area, yet remains a quiet retreat. Each suite sleeps five and includes a separate living area (with a pull-out sofa) and sleeping quarters. The roomy accommodations make it a great choice for families. Some of the other perks here include a complimentary cooked-to-order breakfast and a daily manager's reception.

U.S. 192/Kissimmee Accommodations

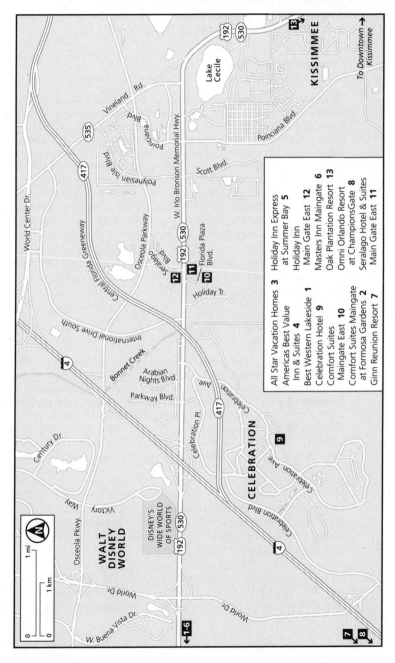

KISSIMMEE

To Downtown Kissimmee →

Lake Cecile

Vineland Rd.

Poinciana Blvd.

W. Irlo Bronson Memorial Hwy.

Scott Blvd.

Florida Plaza Blvd.

Holiday Tr.

International Drive South

Bonnet Creek

Arabian Nights Blvd.

Parkway Blvd.

Century Dr.

Celebration Pl.

Celebration Ave.

Celebration Ave.

CELEBRATION

Celebration Blvd.

Victory Way

Osceola Pkwy.

WALT DISNEY WORLD

DISNEY'S WIDE WORLD OF SPORTS

World Dr.

W. Buena Vista Dr.

World Center Dr.

Central Florida Greeneway

Polynesian Isle Blvd.

Poinciana Blvd.

Osceola Parkway

Seralago Blvd.

All Star Vacation Homes **3**
Americas Best Value Inn & Suites **4**
Best Western Lakeside **1**
Celebration Hotel **9**
Comfort Suites Maingate East **10**
Comfort Suites Maingate at Formosa Gardens **2**
Ginn Reunion Resort **7**
Holiday Inn Express at Summer Bay **5**
Holiday Inn
Main Gate East **12**
Masters Inn Maingate **6**
Oak Plantation Resort **13**
Omni Orlando Resort at ChampionsGate **8**
Seralago Hotel & Suites Main Gate East **11**

1 mi

1 km

N

See map p. 96. 8100 Lake Ave. (From I-4, take the Hwy. 535/Apopka-Vineland Rd. exit east to Palm Pkwy. Follow ½ mile to Lake Ave. on the right.) ☎ **800-257-8483** or 407-239-1144. Fax: 407-239-1718. www.embassysuiteslbv.com. 333 units. Rack rates: $109–$249 suite. Valet parking: $7. AE, DC, DISC, MC, V.

Floridays Resort Orlando
$$–$$$ **International Drive Area/Universal Orlando**

This new Mediterranean-inspired, all-suite resort features a nicely land-scaped pool and play area, an on-site cafe and marketplace (albeit a small one), and a game room, all in an inviting village-like setting. Among the newest (and the nicest) to pop up in recent months, Floridays offers spacious, tastefully decorated two- and three-bedroom suites (both with two bathrooms). Each is well appointed with upscale amenities such as flatscreen TVs, a full-size stocked kitchen, a washer/dryer, and a private patio or balcony. Coming later in 2009 is a water-park-style pool. The combination of apartment-like accommodations, inviting grounds, and a location that's close to the many shops, restaurants, and attractions that line I-Drive makes this a great choice — especially for families.

See map p. 119. 12550 International Dr. S. (Take I-4 to 528 W. to I-Drive S. Turn left at the end of the exit and follow I-Drive. The hotel is on the right.) ☎ **866-797-0022** or 407-238-7700. Fax 321-329-4000. www.floridaysresort.com. 360 units. Rack rates: $200–$400 suite. AE, DC, DISC, MC, V.

Ginn Reunion Resort
$$$$ **Kissimmee**

One of the first luxury resorts south of U.S. 192, the Ginn Reunion is a resort community still in its mid-phase of development (with a completion date some eight years into the future). Currently operational are several villas and vacation homes, a new 11-story luxury condo-hotel that includes a handful of upscale dining options, an extensive on-site water park (in addition to other resort pools located throughout the property), a tennis complex, stables, retailers, restaurants, and a spa. Three championship golf courses and a golf academy are open as well. A kids' program with a variety of supervised activities allows parents time to tee off at the golf course. Future plans call for some 8,000 units, including additional luxury hotels, villas, resort homes, condominiums, town homes, restaurants, and more. Top-notch personal service is just one of the attributes distinguishing the Ginn Reunion from others in its class. Just down the way (at ChampionsGate) is a small shopping plaza with a grocery store, pharmacy, and some shops and very casual eateries.

See map p. 113. 1000 Reunion Way. (Take I-4 to Exit 58; turn left onto Hwy. 532, and go approximately ¾ mile. Hotel entrance is on left.) ☎ **888-418-9611** or 407-662-1000. Fax: 407-662-1111. www.reunionresort.com. Rack rates: $295–$535 villa, $425–$945 house. A 9.6 percent gratuity is added to total bill. AE, DC, DISC, MC, V.

Grand Bohemian Hotel
$$$–$$$$ Downtown Orlando

The Grand Bohemian has an early-20th-century Euro-Bohemian look. Formerly a Westin property, the hotel still caters almost exclusively to the business and romance crowds, which means you'll find few children on the premises. New ownership has also introduced a slew of personalized themed packages for romantics, shoppers, golfers, and more. Its rooms feature an Art Deco motif, with plenty of chrome, mirrors, reds, and purples. The custom pillow-top beds (with firm mattresses, down comforters, and five pillows) are among the best in town. The upper floors on the east side overlook the pool; the north side faces downtown. The hotel, which is smoke-free, is filled with 19th- and 20th-century American fine art. This isn't the most convenient choice if your vacation is solely centered on the parks, but it's far enough away if you need a break from all the manic energy of screaming kids and adults in costume. The wonderful downtown nightlife is right outside the front door.

See map p. 349. 325 S. Orlando Ave. (across from City Hall). ☎ **866-663-0024** *or 407-313-9000. Fax: 407-313-6001.* www.grandbohemianhotel.com. *250 units. Rack rates: $199–$599 for up to 4, from $599 suite. Valet parking: $18. AE, DC, DISC, MC, V.*

Hard Rock Hotel
$$$–$$$$ International Drive Area/Universal Orlando

You can't get rooms closer to CityWalk, Islands of Adventure, or Universal Studios Florida than those at this California mission–style hotel. This Loews resort is on par with Disney's Animal Kingdom Lodge, although its rooms are 15 percent larger. Recently renovated accommodations, now with an urban-chic décor, come with two queens or one king bed and extras such as 32-inch flatscreen TVs and MP3 docking stations. The giant outdoor pool with sand beach and underwater sound system may bring out the lounging rocker in you. Unfortunately, although the rooms are relatively soundproof, a few notes seep through the walls — ask for a room away from the lobby area if quiet is important to you. **Camp Li'l Rock** keeps the kids entertained while offering Mom and Dad some time off. Free transportation is available to the Universal and SeaWorld parks; as for Disney, you're on your own. The biggest perk: Guests get Universal Express access to almost all rides and restaurants at Universal's theme parks.

See map p. 119. 5800 Universal Blvd. (Take I-4 to the Kirkman Rd./Hwy. 435 exit and follow the signs to Universal Orlando.) ☎ **800-232-7827** *or 407-503-2000. Fax: 407-503-2010.* www.hardrock.com *or* www.universalorlando.com. *654 units. Rack rates: $214–$479 double, $479–$2,020 suite. Self-parking: $15. Valet parking: $22. AE, DC, DISC, MC, V.*

Holiday Inn Express at Summer Bay
$–$$ Kissimmee

Without having to break the bank, guests here are treated to all the amenities of the Summer Bay Resort (which houses additional hotels, villas, and vacation homes), including an array of recreational options (five pools, an aqua park, two playgrounds, tennis courts, basketball courts, and miniature golf), a grocery-shopping service, scheduled activities, and more. Typical of the chain, this inexpensive option offers clean and comfortable rooms with kitchenettes, complimentary continental breakfast, and even an on-site rental-car service. Shuttle service is free to WDW parks and available, for a fee, to other parks.

See map p. 113. 105 Summer Bay Blvd., just off W. Irlo Bronson Memorial Hwy. (From I-4, take Exit 64B, go 7 miles, and look for hotel on the right.) ☎ *800-654-6102 or 407-239-8315. Fax: 407-239-8297.* www.summerbayresort.com. *192 units. Rack rates: $99–$109 double. Rates include continental breakfast. AE, DC, DISC, MC, V.*

Holiday Inn Main Gate East
$–$$ Kissimmee

This newly re-created Holiday Inn, formerly the Travelodge Main Gate, has been given the Mouse's "Good Neighbor" stamp of approval. An extensive redesign brought with it an all-new contemporary look inside and out, an inviting pool with a water slide and rocky waterfall, and the hallmark amenities associated with this family-friendly chain. Younger guests will appreciate the children's theater, playground, and roomy KidSuites; parents will appreciate the kids-eat-free program and complimentary high-speed Internet access throughout the hotel. You can even bring Fido for a small fee. Shuttle service is free to WDW parks and available, for a fee, to other parks.

See map p. 113. 5711 W. Irlo Bronson Memorial Hwy. (From I-4, take Exit 64A, go 5 miles, and look for hotel on the left.) ☎ *800-327-1128 or 407-396-4222. Fax: 407-396-0570.* www.holidayinnmge.com. *444 units. Rack rates: $79–$149 double, $159–$239 KidSuite. AE, DC, DISC, MC, V.*

Holiday Inn SunSpree Resort Lake Buena Vista
$–$$ Lake Buena Vista

Close to the Disney parks, this resort caters to kids in a big way. They get their own check-in desk, movies to watch at the theater in the lobby area, and **Camp Holiday,** the supervised activity center (one of the best around). The hotel's spacious KidSuites accommodate up to six and have themes such as a space capsule, igloo, jail, and more. Standard rooms are somewhat smaller and sleep four. All units feature refrigerators and microwaves. If you like sleeping in, ask for a room that doesn't face the pool area. Kids 12 and younger eat free at the restaurants. The hotel provides complimentary shuttle service to WDW.

See map p. 96. 13351 Lake Buena Vista (located off Hwy. 535 near the Crossroads Shopping Center). ☎ *800-366-6299 or 407-239-4500. Fax: 407-239-7713.* www.kidsuites.com. *507 units. Rack rates: $89–$129 for up to 4, $139–$219 KidSuite. AE, DISC, MC, V.*

Hyatt Place Orlando/Universal
$$–$$$ International Drive Area/Universal Orlando

Major renovations have transformed this former AmeriSuites into a modern and stylish property. A newly redesigned lobby now sports a cafe, TV den, and Internet room, all amidst a chic and upscale décor. Self-service check-in and check-out kiosks offer an efficient alternative to standing in line at the front desk. Modern, spacious rooms, with all-new comfy bedding, sleeper sofas, and 42-inch flatscreen TVs, allow you to stretch out. Complimentary Wi-Fi, available throughout the hotel, keeps you connected without costing you a bundle, and there's free shuttle service to Universal Orlando and SeaWorld. Continental breakfast is part of the package, but for those with a heartier appetite, hot breakfast entrees are available (they'll cost you extra). Made-to-order entrees and snacks are available 24 hours. If your goal is to be very close to the Universal parks without having to pay the heftier rates that come with staying on park property, this is the place for you. For those who prefer a more centralized location (close to the convention center), try the Hyatt Place at 8741 International Dr.

See map p. 119. 5895 Caravan Court. (Take I-4 to Exit 75B/Kirkman Rd. Turn right at the first light, Major Blvd., and take the next right, Caravan Court. Hotel is on the right.) ☎ *800-993-6506 or 407-351-0627. Fax: 407-331-3317.* http://orlandouniversal. place.hyatt.com. *151 units. Rack rates: $125–$249 double. Rates include continental breakfast buffet. AE, DC, DISC, MC, V.*

Hyatt Regency Grand Cypress
$$$–$$$$ Lake Buena Vista

A resort destination in and of itself, this hotel is a great place to get away from the Disney frenzy while still remaining close to the action. You need deep pockets to stay here, but the reward is a palatial resort with lush foliage. The hotel's 18-story atrium (which is slated to undergo renovations in 2009, including the expansion of the open-concept sushi bar and a refit of the check-in area) has inner and outer glass elevators, which provide a unique thrill. The beautifully decorated rooms (currently undergoing a transformation of their own) offer the usual amenities expected in a high-end luxury resort. The extensive recreational facilities include championship golf courses (45 holes), 12 tennis courts (5 lighted), two racquetball courts, a spa (which will be expanded), an adjoining equestrian center, and more. The property's half-acre, 800,000-gallon pool is one of the best in town, with caves, grottoes, and waterfalls. Some of the area's top dining experiences are here, including Hemingway's and La Coquina Chef's Table. Transportation to WDW, Universal Orlando, and SeaWorld is covered in the resort fee. If you're in need of a break, the younger kids can play at the supervised child-care facility (one of the nicest ones around) while the older ones can sign up for Camp Hyatt (a supervised activity program for kids ages 5–12).

See map p. 96. 1 N. Jacaranda (Hwy. 535 north of Disney's Lake Buena Vista entrance or Hotel Plaza Blvd.). ☎ 800-233-1234 or 407-239-1234. Fax: 407-239-3800. www.grandcypress.hyatt.com. *750 units. Rack rates: $219–$529 double, $695–$5,750 suite. Daily resort fee: $15. Valet parking: $19. AE, DC, DISC, MC, V.*

JW Marriott Orlando, Grande Lakes
$$$–$$$$ International Drive Area/Universal Orlando

Opened in 2004, this Moorish-themed resort is situated on 500 acres of lush, tropical landscaping at the new Grande Lakes development, just east of SeaWorld. The guest rooms are on par with those in Disney's moderate class. Ask for a west-facing room for the best views. The smoke-free resort is home to six restaurants and lounges and shares its recreational facilities with the neighboring Ritz-Carlton (listed later), including a Greg Norman–designed, par-72 golf course and a 40,000-square-foot spa. The best feature is the fabulous landscaped 24,000-square-foot Lazy River pool, which winds through rock formations and small waterfalls. I could do without the $12-per-day self-parking fee, however.

See map p. 119. 4040 Central Florida Pkwy. (at the intersection of John Young Pkwy., 2 miles east of SeaWorld). ☎ *800-576-5750 or 407-206-2300. Fax: 407-206-2301.* www.grandelakes.com. *1,000 units. Rack rates: $197–$439 double, $339–$4,500 suite. Self-parking: $12. Valet parking: $20. AE, DC, DISC, MC, V.*

Masters Inn Maingate
$ Kissimmee

Clean rooms, a heated outdoor pool, free continental breakfast, and free shuttles to the Disney parks — all for under $50 a night — have made this basic property a favorite with the budget-conscious. Two-room suites (though limited in number) are available at terrific prices as well.

See map p. 113. 2945 Entry Point Blvd. (on U.S. 192, 2 miles west of the Walt Disney World main gate entrance and I-4). ☎ *800-633-3434 or 407-396-7743. Fax: 407-396-6307.* www.mastersinnorlando.com. *106 units. Rack rates: $45–$71 double, $88–$150 suite. Rates include continental breakfast. AE, DISC, MC, V.*

Nickelodeon Family Suites
$$–$$$$ Lake Buena Vista

This all-suite property opened in 1999 as the Holiday Inn Family Suites Resort and does a fantastic job catering to families. A $20-million transformation into an official Nickelodeon property in 2004 made it even more kid-friendly. The suites feature Nick-decorated bedrooms for the kids, complete with bunk or twin beds and a TV and video-game system. The resort's two pool areas are veritable water parks, with multilevel water slides, flumes, climbing nets, and water jets. Poolside activities and recreational options — including a small mini-golf course, playgrounds, and sand play areas — are a hit with kids and parents alike. **Nick After Dark,** an evening supervised activity program for kids ages 5 to 12, allows parents to take a night off. Other kid-friendly amenities include wake-up calls from Nickelodeon stars, daily Nick-character breakfasts, live entertainment featuring the only Orlando appearance of popular Nick characters outside of Universal Orlando, and an all-new 4-D Nic-flick experience (added in 2008). Most suites come with kitchenettes, but the three-bedroom units have full kitchens (not to mention tons of space and a trendy décor). High-speed

International Drive Area Accommodations

Comfort Suites Orlando **6**

Crowne Plaza Orlando–Universal **5**

Floridays Resort Orlando **11**

Hard Rock Hotel **2**

Hyatt Place Orlando/Universal **3**

JW Marriott Orlando, Grande Lakes **10**

Peabody Orlando **7**

Portofino Bay Hotel **1**

Renaissance Orlando Resort at SeaWorld **9**

Ritz-Carlton Orlando, Grande Lakes **10**

Rosen Shingle Creek **8**

Royal Pacific Resort **4**

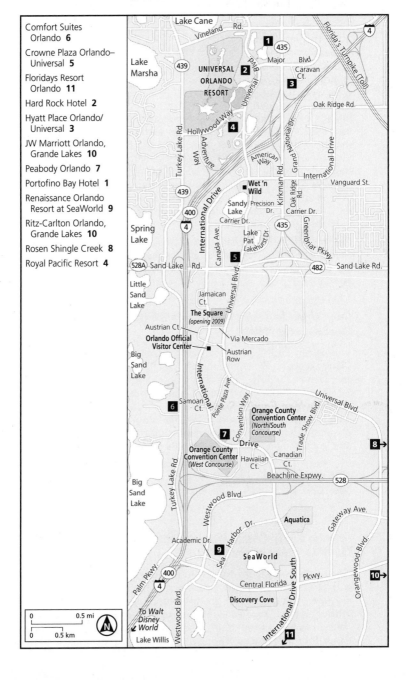

Internet access is free. The location — only a mile away from Walt Disney World — is another plus.

See map p. 96. 14500 Continental Gateway. (From I-4, take the Hwy. 536/International Dr. exit east 1 mile to the resort.) ☎ *877-387-5437 or 407-387-5437. Fax: 407-387-1489.* www.nickhotel.com. *800 units. Rack rates: $179–$1,050 suite. AE, DC, DISC, MC, V.*

Oak Plantation Resort
$–$$ Kissimmee

Slightly off the beaten path, in a remote wooded setting, this quiet retreat offers one- and two-bedroom villas with full kitchens, removed from the hustle and bustle of the main thoroughfare. Recreational facilities — including two pools, a children's pool with fountains, tennis and basketball courts, and an array of scheduled activities — ensure there's plenty to do when you're not touring the theme parks. Snacks and sundries are sold at the general store, where you'll also find a Starbucks. Breakfast is served daily (at a very reasonable price) and complimentary shuttle service is available to all area parks.

See map p. 113. 4090 Enchanted Oaks Circle. (Take I-4 to Exit 64, follow U.S. 192 East 8 miles, turn left on Hogland Rd., and the resort is on your left.) ☎ *800-881-1155 or 407-847-8200. Fax: 407-857-3022.* www.oakplantationresort.com. *242 units. Rack rates: $79–$199 suite. AE, DC, DISC, MC, V.*

Omni Orlando Resort at ChampionsGate
$$–$$$$ Kissimmee

This is one of the newest luxury resorts to spring up just south of the Disney district. Extensive meeting facilities are coupled with comprehensive leisure facilities, including two championship golf courses designed by Greg Norman, a vast Mediterranean-influenced pool area with its very own lazy river, a 10,000-square-foot European spa, and much more. The beautifully appointed rooms feature 9-foot ceilings and a complete roster of amenities. The perks are equally impressive, with a lengthy list of services, including a program especially for youngsters.

See map p. 113. 1500 Masters Blvd. (Take I-4 to Exit 58 and bear right.) ☎ *888-444-6664 or 407-390-6664. Fax: 407-390-6660.* www.omnihotels.com. *730 units. Rack rates: $249–$329 double, $450–$2,500 suite. Daily resort fee: $15. Valet parking: $12. AE, DC, DISC, MC, V.*

Orlando World Center Marriott Resort
$$$–$$$$ Lake Buena Vista

One of the top places to stay in Orlando, this 230-acre resort is popular with the business crowd, couples, and families alike. The sports facilities are first class, and the grotto swimming pool features waterfalls and hidden spas. A recent $6-million renovation enhanced the 200-acre golf course, as well as the dining and lobby areas. The large, comfortable, and beautifully decorated rooms sleep four, with options for larger parties available. The upper floors facing Disney have great views of nightly fire-works. The location, only minutes to Disney via a much-less-congested road, can't be beat. Numerous themed packages and promotional rates are offered throughout the year, making it surprisingly affordable to stay and play here.

See map p. 96. 8701 World Center Dr. (on Hwy. 536 between I-4 and Hwy. 535). ☎ *800-380-7931 or 407-239-4200. Fax: 407-238-8777.* www.marriottworldcenter.com. *2,111 units. Rack rates: $340–$406 double, $750–$1,600 suite. Self-parking: $11. Valet parking: $20. AE, DC, DISC, MC, V.*

Peabody Orlando
$$–$$$$ International Drive Area/Universal Orlando

Welcome to the home of the famous — drum roll, maestro, *s'il vous plaît* — **Marching Mallards.** These real ducks march through the lobby into their luxury pool each morning at 11 a.m. (no kidding!), accompanied by — what else? — John Philip Sousa's marching music and a red-coated duck master, and then back out at 5 p.m.

The Peabody is located across from the convention center, in the thick of all the action that I-Drive has to offer, including attractions, restaurants, and shopping. Guest rooms, even standard ones, are lavishly furnished and come with numerous amenities. The Peabody offers not only the best serv-ice in town but also some of the best hotel dining — look for its signature restaurant, **Dux,** in Chapter 10. You'll have to pay for transportation to all the theme parks, so a rental car is a good idea if you want to stay here.

The Peabody is in the midst of a major expansion, adding 750 rooms, a full-service spa, additional meeting space, family-friendly elements (which are lacking), and a parking garage. Completion is scheduled for late 2009.

See map p. 119. 9801 International Dr. (between the Beachline Expwy. and Sand Lake Rd.). ☎ *800-732-2639 or 407-352-4000. Fax: 407-354-1424.* www.peabodyorlando. com. *891 units. Rack rates: $360–$395 double, $450–$1,775 suite. Valet parking: $18. AE, DC, DISC, MC, V.*

Portofino Bay Hotel
$$$–$$$$ International Drive Area/Universal Orlando

This Loews property really delivers for those with deep pockets. Inspired by a comment from director Steven Spielberg, who at the time was work-ing on a ride at Islands of Adventure, it offers six restaurants/lounges, a spa, a beach pool with a fort and water slide, and a fitness center in a pack-age that's convincingly designed to look like the Mediterranean seaside village of Portofino, Italy. The accommodations offer four-poster beds with cloud-soft pillows, plus bathrooms outfitted with marble tubs and tiled foyers. These state-of-the-art "smart rooms" also provide security, adjust room temperature, and report malfunctions as they occur. The hotel offers free transportation to Universal and SeaWorld parks, but (they're not stupid!) forget the free ride to the Disney ones. Best feature: Guests get Universal Express access to almost all rides at Universal's theme parks.

Note: Getting around this sizeable resort involves having to maneuver numerous stairs.

See map p. 119. 5601 Universal Blvd. (From I-4, take Kirkman Rd./Hwy. 435 and follow the signs to Universal.) ☎ ***888-273-1311*** *or 407-503-1000. Fax: 407-503-1010.* www. loewshotels.com. *750 units. Rack rates: $214–$499 double, $519–$2,500 suite and villa. Self-parking: $15. Valet parking: $22. AE, DC, DISC, MC, V.*

Renaissance Orlando Resort at SeaWorld
$$–$$$$ International Drive Area/Universal Orlando

Oversized guest rooms (now trendier and beautifully decorated), good service, and a thoroughly chic interior (gone are the gardens, waterfalls, koi pond, and aviary) are this hotel's calling cards. Its most valuable feature, however, is a location that's perfect if you're going to Universal, SeaWorld (right across the street), and, to a lesser degree, the second-tier I-Drive attractions. The hotel has four lighted tennis courts; a health club, spa, and sauna (recently expanded); and a completely renovated pool area. It also boasts a full-service restaurant, sports bar, lounge, poolside grill, and sushi bar. Transportation to the parks is available for a fee, though most guests can easily walk to SeaWorld.

See map p. 119. 6677 Sea Harbour Dr. (From I-4, follow signs to SeaWorld. Hotel is across from attraction.) ☎ ***800-327-6677*** *or 407-351-5555. Fax: 407-351-9991.* www. renaissancehotels.com. *778 units. Rack rates: $252–$369 double, $279–$1,999 suite. Self-parking: $12. Valet parking: $16. AE, DC, DISC, MC, V.*

Ritz-Carlton Orlando, Grande Lakes
$$$–$$$$ International Drive Area/Universal Orlando

Part of the lush 500-acre Grande Lakes Resort complex, this luxury resort — styled like an Italian *palazzo* — opened in 2004. All the spacious guest rooms feature dual private balconies, flatscreen TVs, and oversized marble bathrooms with separate tub and shower. For the ultimate experience, upgrade to the Club Level to receive butler service, Bulgari bath amenities, an in-room DVD/VCR/CD player, and free snacks. Seven restaurants and lounges are on-site, and the Ritz shares some recreational amenities with the neighboring JW Marriott (see the review earlier in this chapter), including a Greg Norman–designed golf course and a 40,000-square-foot spa. The **Ritz Kids** program includes a children's pool and playground, separate check-in area, and on-site nanny service (for a fee). Kid suites offer equally lavish accommodations especially designed for younger guests. Transportation to Universal and SeaWorld parks is complimentary; however, you'll need your own transportation if you want to visit Disney's parks and attractions.

See map p. 119. 4012 Central Florida Pkwy. (at the intersection of John Young Pkwy., 2 miles east of SeaWorld). ☎ ***800-576-5760*** *or 407-206-2400. Fax: 407-206-2401.* www.grandelakes.com. *584 units. Rack rates: $219–$406 double, $599–$6,500 Club Level and suite. Valet parking: $18. AE, DC, DISC, MC, V.*

Rosen Shingle Creek
$$$–$$$$ International Drive Area/Universal Orlando

This magnificent Mediterranean-inspired resort evokes thoughts of a bygone era when Florida's legendary grand hotels were the epitome of high style. Striking architecture (both inside and out), lavishly appointed rooms, and exceptional service are signatures of this exceptional resort. Although luxurious by design, the lush natural grounds have been preserved, and references throughout the property recall both the historical and natural significance of the area with rooms named for Florida's lakes, rivers, and historical landmarks — even the resort itself (Shingle Creek) is named for the waterway that winds alongside the property, the headwater to the Florida Everglades. You'll find an array of recreational facilities, including a championship golf course and golf academy, a full-service spa, two pools (one for families), lighted tennis courts, nature trails, and a playground. Dining options are just as varied, ranging from elegant to on-the-go. Even with its old-world style, the hotel's modern conveniences, including on-site airline check-in and bag-check service, cater to guests' needs. Shuttle service to Universal Orlando is complimentary and available, for a fee, to other parks.

See map p. 119. 9939 Universal Blvd. (just east of International Dr., beyond the Convention Center). ☎ *866-996-9939 or 407-996-9939. Fax: 407-996-9938.* www.rosenshinglecreek.com. *1,500 units. Rack rates: $150–$425 double. AE, DC, DISC, MC, V.*

Royal Pacific Resort
$$$–$$$$ International Drive Area/Universal Orlando

The newest Universal resort sports an attractive Polynesian theme that's the best of the bunch. Highlights of the property include an exquisite orchid garden, five restaurants and lounges (one run by famed chef Emeril Lagasse), and a lagoon-style pool — the largest in Orlando. The guest rooms' furnishings were updated and enhanced in 2007, and although the rooms are smaller than those at Universal's other hotels, they're comfortable for four. Eight *Jurassic Park*–themed kid suites were added, too. The Royal Pacific isn't cheap, but it offers good value for the money, especially when you factor in the hotel's free transport to Universal's theme parks, where guests get Universal Express access to almost all rides. One thing I could do without: The outrageous $12 self-parking charge, especially because the parking lot is a hike from the hotel.

See map p. 119. 6300 Hollywood Way. (Take I-4 to the Kirkman Rd./Hwy. 435 exit and follow signs to Universal Orlando.) ☎ *888-273-1311 or 407-503-3000. Fax: 407-503-3010.* www.loewshotels.com. *1,000 units. Rack rates: $214–$429 double, $339–$1,950 suite. Self-parking: $15. Valet parking: $22. AE, DC, DISC, MC, V.*

Seralago Hotel & Suites Main Gate East
$ Kissimmee

Location (just down the road from Disney) and price are just some of the perks here. This recently revamped hotel (formerly the Holiday Inn) sports a bright new look, but it still features themed kid suites with separate sleeping areas for the children, as well as standard rooms and regular suites. The accommodations provide a reasonable amount of space for a family of five, with the two-room unit sleeping up to eight. The place features numerous activities, from swimming to tennis, and the hotel's movie theater shows free family films nightly. There's also a family-friendly food court, and kids 12 and younger eat free (two kids per paying adult) in the hotel's cafe. This hotel has received the ultimate endorsement for a property trying to get in good with Mickey — an official stamp of approval as a Disney "Good Neighbor" hotel.

See map p. 113. 5678 Irlo Bronson Memorial Hwy./U.S. 192. (Take I-4 to Exit 64A to U.S. 192. Hotel is 2 miles on the right.) ☎ *800-366-5437 or 407-396-4488. Fax: 407-396-8915.* www.seralagohotel.com. *614 units. Rack rates: $50–$109. AE, DC, DISC, MC, V.*

Staybridge Suites Lake Buena Vista
$$–$$$ Lake Buena Vista

A Summerfield Suites in a previous life, this recent addition to the Staybridge chain is located just off Apopka-Vineland, close to the action of Downtown Disney and the theme parks, as well as many restaurants. An excellent choice for families, this hotel's room sizes, price, and friendly staff are three more good reasons to stay here. Featured are one- and two-bedroom suites (which can sleep up to eight), all with full kitchens (some two-bedroom suites have two bathrooms, too). The suites here have larger and more comfortable separate living areas when compared to other all-suite hotels. High-speed Internet access is free.

See map p. 96. 8751 Suiteside Dr. (From I-4, take the exit for Hwy. 535 and turn right; follow it to Vinings Way Rd. and turn right. Hotel is on the left.) ☎ *800-866-4549 or 407-238-0777. Fax: 407-238-2640.* www.sborlando.com. *150 units. Rack rates: $139–$299. Rates include continental breakfast. AE, DC, DISC, MC, V.*

The Veranda Bed & Breakfast
$–$$ Downtown Orlando

Located in Thornton Park, this inn near scenic Lake Eola is an option if you want to stay near the downtown museums but not in a motel or hotel. Its four buildings date to the early 1900s. All units (studios to suites) include private bathrooms and entrances; some have garden tubs, balconies, kitchenettes, and four-poster beds. The two-bedroom, two-bathroom Keylime Cottage sleeps four and has a full kitchen. The B&B doesn't offer transportation to the parks, which means a rental car is a necessity for most guests. *Note:* Children are not permitted.

See map p. 349. 115 N. Summerlin Ave. (From I-4, take exit for Hwy. 50 and turn west on Colonial Dr.; follow it to Summerlin Ave. and turn left.) ☎ *800-420-6822 or 407-849-0321. Fax: 407-849-0321, ext. 24.* www.theverandabandb.com. *12 units. Rack rates: $99–$189 double, $169 cottage. Rates include continental breakfast. AE, DC, DISC, MC, V.*

Villas of Grand Cypress Golf Resort
$$$-$$$$ Lake Buena Vista

Meet the sister of the Hyatt Regency Grand Cypress (reviewed earlier in this chapter). These one- to four-bedroom villas, a short drive from the larger hotel, offer privacy not found in most resorts. You can play 45 holes of golf on Jack Nicklaus–designed courses or take lessons at the golf academy. The horse crowd loves the top-of-the-line equestrian center; riding lessons and packages are available (see Chapter 27 for more information about riding). The recently renovated Mediterranean-style villas have Roman tubs, patios or balconies, all-new kitchen appliances, flatscreen TVs, and luxurious beds. Free shuttle service is available to the resort's recreational facilities and to the WDW parks. Unlike its sister Hyatt property, this resort caters primarily to adults, but Villa guests with kids can use the Hyatt's child-care and recreational facilities.

See map p. 96. 1 N. Jacaranda St. (off Hwy. 535, past the Disney entrance on Hotel Plaza Blvd., about a mile on the right). ☎ **877-330-7377** *or 407-239-4700. Fax: 407-239-7219.* www.grandcypress.com. *146 villas. Rack rates: $225–$2,000 villa. Daily resort fee: $15. AE, DC, DISC, MC, V.*

Walt Disney World Dolphin
$$$$ Walt Disney World/Official WDW Hotel

What a wonderful place for folks a) not on a budget, b) wanting to be close to Epcot and Disney's Hollywood Studios, and c) desperate to stay in a place that answers the question: What kind of gingerbread house would Dalí have created if he were an architect? You can't miss the massive, 56-foot twin dolphin statues on the roof of this resort. When you're inside the lobby, you'll encounter prints from the likes of Matisse and Picasso. Rooms offer views of the grounds and parts of WDW; they were upgraded in 2004. The lobby, now more contemporary, was redesigned in 2006. The resort shares with its sister hotel (the Walt Disney World Swan, reviewed next) its extensive recreational facilities, including a grotto pool with waterfalls, water slide, and whirlpools, as well as a Body by Jake health club and the luxurious Mandara Spa. The hotel offers free transportation to WDW parks, but you have to pay for a ride to the others. A mandatory $10 (plus tax) daily resort fee includes Internet access, health-club access, two bottles of water, and a portion of your phone charges (60 min. local, 20 min. long distance).

Though it's essentially treated as a Disney hotel, and guests here get many of the same privileges as Disney resort guests, this one is actually owned and operated by Starwood Hotels & Resorts as a Sheraton. As a result, you may find discounts for this property that wouldn't otherwise be available at Disney-owned hotels.

See map p. 96. 1500 Epcot Resorts Blvd. (off Buena Vista Dr., next to the Walt Disney World Swan). ☎ **800-227-1500** *or 407-934-4000. Fax: 407-934-4884.* www.swandolphin.com. *1,509 units. Rack rates: $369–$529 double, $785–$1,525 suite. Daily resort fee: $10. Self-parking: $9. Valet parking: $12. AE, DC, DISC, MC, V.*

Walt Disney World Swan
$$$$ Walt Disney World/Official WDW Hotel

Located on the same property as the Dolphin (reviewed above), the Swan offers another chance to stay on Mickey's property without being bombarded by Mouse décor. This 12-story Westin is topped with dual 45-foot swan statues and seashell fountains. The Swan and Dolphin hotels are connected by a canopied walkway and share recreational facilities, including four pools and four lighted tennis courts. The luxurious rooms are a shade smaller than those in the Dolphin, but have Nintendo games (for a fee) and Westin's signature Heavenly Bed (firm mattress, down comforter, and five pillows). The rooms underwent a major renovation in 2003 by original architect Michael Graves, who redid the resort in tones of silver-blue and white. The lobby and public areas were upgraded in 2006, resulting in a chic, more contemporary décor. You can get a free ride to the Disney parks and, for a fee, transportation to the other theme parks. A mandatory $10 (plus tax) daily resort fee includes Internet access, health-club access, two bottles of water, and a portion of your phone charges (60 min. local, 20 min. long distance).

See map p. 96. 1200 Epcot Resorts Blvd. (off Buena Vista Dr., next to the Walt Disney World Dolphin). ☎ **800-248-7926**, *800-228-3000, or 407-934-3000. Fax: 407-934-4499.* www.swandolphin.com. *758 units. Rack rates: $369–$529 double, $995–$1,770 suite. Daily resort fee: $10. Self-parking: $9. Valet parking: $12. AE, DC, DISC, MC, V.*

Index of Accommodations by Neighborhood

Downtown Orlando
The Courtyard at Lake Lucerne ($–$$$)
Grand Bohemian Hotel ($$$–$$$$)
The Veranda Bed & Breakfast ($–$$)

International Drive Area/Universal Orlando
Comfort Suites Orlando ($–$$)
Crowne Plaza Orlando-Universal ($$–$$$)
Floridays Resort Orlando ($$–$$$)
Hard Rock Hotel ($$$–$$$$)
Hyatt Place Orlando/Universal ($$–$$$)
JW Marriott Orlando, Grande Lakes ($$$–$$$$)
Peabody Orlando ($$–$$$$)
Portofino Bay Hotel ($$$–$$$$)
Renaissance Orlando Resort at SeaWorld ($$–$$$$)
Ritz-Carlton Orlando, Grande Lakes ($$$–$$$$)

Rosen Shingle Creek ($$$–$$$$)
Royal Pacific Resort ($$$–$$$$)

Kissimmee
All Star Vacation Homes ($–$$$$)
Americas Best Value Inn & Suites ($)
Best Western Lakeside ($–$$)
Celebration Hotel ($$$–$$$$)
Comfort Suites Maingate East ($–$$)
Comfort Suites Maingate at Formosa Gardens ($–$$$)
Ginn Reunion Resort ($$$$)
Holiday Inn Express at Summer Bay ($–$$)
Holiday Inn Main Gate East ($–$$)
Masters Inn Maingate ($)
Oak Plantation Resort ($–$$)
Omni Orlando Resort at ChampionsGate ($$–$$$$)
Seralago Hotel & Suites Main Gate East ($)

Lake Buena Vista (including Official WDW Hotels)

Buena Vista Palace Hotel & Spa ($$-$$$$)

Comfort Inn Lake Buena Vista ($)

Doubletree Guest Suites ($$-$$$$)

Embassy Suites Lake Buena Vista ($$-$$$)

Holiday Inn SunSpree Resort Lake Buena Vista ($-$$)

Hyatt Regency Grand Cypress ($$$-$$$$)

Nickelodeon Family Suites ($$-$$$$)

Orlando World Center Marriott Resort ($$$-$$$$)

Staybridge Suites Lake Buena Vista ($$-$$$)

Villas of Grand Cypress Golf Resort ($$$-$$$$)

Walt Disney World

Disney's All-Star Movies Resort ($-$$)

Disney's All-Star Music Resort ($-$$)

Disney's All-Star Sports Resort ($-$$)

Disney's Animal Kingdom Lodge ($$$-$$$$)

Disney's Beach Club Resort ($$$$)

Disney's BoardWalk Inn ($$$$)

Disney's Caribbean Beach Resort ($$-$$$)

Disney's Contemporary Resort ($$$-$$$$)

Disney's Coronado Springs Resort ($$-$$$)

Disney's Fort Wilderness Resort & Campground ($-$$$)

Disney's Grand Floridian Resort & Spa ($$$$)

Disney's Old Key West Resort ($$$-$$$$)

Disney's Polynesian Resort ($$$$)

Disney's Pop Century Resort ($-$$)

Disney's Port Orleans Resort ($$-$$$)

Disney's Saratoga Springs Resort & Spa ($$$-$$$$)

Disney's Wilderness Lodge ($$$-$$$$)

Disney's Yacht Club Resort ($$$$)

Walt Disney World Dolphin ($$$$)

Walt Disney World Swan ($$$$)

Index of Accommodations by Price

$$$$

All Star Vacation Homes (Kissimmee)

Buena Vista Palace Hotel & Spa (Lake Buena Vista/Official WDW Hotel)

Celebration Hotel (Kissimmee)

Disney's Animal Kingdom Lodge (Walt Disney World)

Disney's Beach Club Resort (Walt Disney World)

Disney's BoardWalk Inn (Walt Disney World)

Disney's Contemporary Resort (Walt Disney World)

Disney's Grand Floridian Resort & Spa (Walt Disney World)

Disney's Old Key West Resort (Walt Disney World)

Disney's Polynesian Resort (Walt Disney World)

Disney's Saratoga Springs Resort & Spa (Walt Disney World)

Disney's Wilderness Lodge (Walt Disney World)

Disney's Yacht Club Resort (Walt Disney World)

Doubletree Guest Suites (Lake Buena Vista/Official WDW Hotel)

Ginn Reunion Resort (Kissimmee)

Grand Bohemian Hotel (Downtown Orlando)

Hard Rock Hotel (International Drive Area/Universal Orlando)

Hyatt Regency Grand Cypress (Lake Buena Vista)

JW Marriott Orlando, Grande Lakes (International Drive Area/Universal Orlando)

Nickelodeon Family Suites (Lake Buena Vista)

Omni Orlando Resort at ChampionsGate (Kissimmee)

Orlando World Center Marriott Resort (Lake Buena Vista)

Peabody Orlando (International Drive Area/Universal Orlando)

Portofino Bay Hotel (International Drive Area/Universal Orlando)

Renaissance Orlando Resort at SeaWorld (International Drive Area/Universal Orlando)

Ritz-Carlton Orlando, Grande Lakes (International Drive Area/Universal Orlando)

Rosen Shingle Creek (International Drive Area/Universal Orlando)

Royal Pacific Resort (International Drive Area/Universal Orlando)

Villas of Grand Cypress Golf Resort (Lake Buena Vista)

Walt Disney World Dolphin (Walt Disney World/Official WDW Hotel)

Walt Disney World Swan (Walt Disney World/Official WDW Hotel)

$$$

Comfort Suites Maingate at Formosa Gardens (Kissimmee)

The Courtyard at Lake Lucerne (Downtown Orlando)

Crowne Plaza Orlando-Universal (International Drive Area/Universal Orlando)

Disney's Caribbean Beach Resort (Walt Disney World)

Disney's Coronado Springs Resort (Walt Disney World)

Disney's Fort Wilderness Resort & Campground (Walt Disney World)

Disney's Port Orleans Resort (Walt Disney World)

Embassy Suites Lake Buena Vista (Lake Buena Vista)

Floridays Resort Orlando (International Drive Area/Universal Orlando)

Hyatt Place Orlando/Universal (International Drive Area/Universal Orlando)

Staybridge Suites Lake Buena Vista (Lake Buena Vista)

$$

Best Western Lakeside (Kissimmee)

Comfort Suites Maingate East (Kissimmee)

Comfort Suites Orlando (International Drive Area/Universal Orlando)

Disney's All-Star Movies Resort (Walt Disney World)

Disney's All-Star Music Resort (Walt Disney World)

Disney's All-Star Sports Resort (Walt Disney World)

Disney's Pop Century Resort (Walt Disney World)

Holiday Inn Express at Summer Bay (Kissimmee)

Holiday Inn Main Gate East (Kissimmee)

Holiday Inn SunSpree Resort Lake Buena Vista (Lake Buena Vista)

Oak Plantation Resort (Kissimmee)

The Veranda Bed & Breakfast (Downtown Orlando)

$

Americas Best Value Inn & Suites (Kissimmee)

Comfort Inn Lake Buena Vista (Lake Buena Vista)

Masters Inn Maingate (Kissimmee)

Seralago Hotel & Suites Maingate East (Kissimmee)

Chapter 10

Dining and Snacking in Orlando

• •

In This Chapter

▶ Sampling Orlando's eateries

▶ Finding dining options for the budget-conscious

▶ Exploring the best dining in Orlando

▶ Sharing a meal with the Mouse and other characters

• •

*W*ith more than 5,000 restaurants in the Orlando area, there's certainly no lack of dining choices. Most are surprisingly decent (Orlando is, after all, a city where food tends to be viewed merely as fuel); some of the more recent entries on the scene are definitely making their mark.

In this chapter, I offer general pointers about dining in the land of Diz, explain the ins and outs of making reservations, provide detailed reviews of the city's best restaurants, and give you the lowdown on Orlando's most famous meal experience: character dining.

Getting the Dish on the Local Scene

Few people come to Orlando with fine dining on the mind, though it's a lot easier to find nowadays than it used to be. The city has its fair share of fancier spots that can compete with the best in the country (Disney's **Victoria & Albert's, Emeril Lagasse**'s two Universal Orlando restaurants, and **Manuel's on the 28th**), but most visitors tend to dine at the chains, which are seemingly everywhere you turn, or inside the theme parks, where the food doesn't often astound, but the atmosphere is right. In this city, the emphasis tends to be more on the experience and the theme than on the food.

With only a very few exceptions, if you want truly first-class cuisine without having to take out a second mortgage, you have to get out of the theme-park zones. Restaurants catering to locals (especially in the Dr. Phillips area and Winter Park, but also in downtown Orlando) usually offer excellent food and a sophisticated atmosphere at prices far less daunting than inside the major tourist zones. I review a number of excellent local restaurants in this chapter.

Most Orlando restaurants go out of their way to cater to kids, offering children's menus, diversions such as crayons at the table, high chairs, and so on. The high kid-quotient generally means a higher volume level and a more jovial atmosphere. Adults seeking a quiet, sophisticated, or romantic night out do have options, however, and I note restaurants that offer some respite from the kids on the "Good for Grown-Ups" list found on this book's tear-out Cheat Sheet.

Orlando's own tend to dine early (as do most visitors with kids). For a more leisurely meal, try to eat after 8:30 p.m., but don't wait too late — except for a few fast-food joints, many restaurants close at 10 or 11 p.m.

For more information on the local Orlando cuisine, see Chapter 2.

Dressing down

Didn't pack the tux this time around, or just not a fan of dressing for dinner? The good news is that the city's casual attitude extends to most of its restaurants. At the theme parks, nobody will look at you twice if you walk into an otherwise formal atmosphere in shorts and a T-shirt. That said, a few high-end restaurants do require semiformal attire; I note this in the relevant restaurant reviews in this chapter.

Lighting up

If you're a smoker, don't plan on lighting up over dinner. Effective July 2003, a state constitutional amendment banned smoking in Florida's public workplaces, including all restaurants and bars that serve food. Stand-alone bars that serve virtually no food are exempt, as are designated smoking rooms in hotels and motels.

Making reservations

Reserving a table is a wise idea for most of Orlando's finest restaurants, but in most cases, you can wait to make same-day reservations. I note the exceptions to this rule in the appropriate restaurant reviews.

Advanced Dining Reservations (previously known as Priority Seating) is the only option available at most Disney properties. This practice is Mickey's way of saying that you get the next available table after you arrive (at your prearranged arrival time). Understand, however, that you'll probably still have to wait 10 to 15 minutes after you get to the restaurant before actually being seated. I recommend that you call ☎ 407-939-3463 as far ahead as possible to make Advanced Dining Reservations (in most cases, you're able to make arrangements 180 days out). If you're staying at a WDW resort, you can make Advanced Dining Reservations at the hotel's Guest Relations desk, with the concierge, or by dialing ☎ 55 from your room phone.

Don't even think of showing up for a **Disney character meal** (see "Dining with Disney Characters," at the end of this chapter) without an Advanced Dining Reservation made far in advance — they're sometimes accepted 180 days ahead of time, and it's essential that you begin calling the moment the phone lines open (7 a.m.).

You can also make Advanced Dining Reservations after you're inside the Disney parks — best done immediately upon arrival. At Epcot, make reservations at the WorldKey interactive terminals at Guest Relations in Innoventions East, at WorldKey Information Service satellites on the main concourse to the World Showcase, at Germany in the World Showcase, or at the restaurants themselves. In the Magic Kingdom, sign up at Guest Relations inside City Hall or at the restaurants. At Disney's Hollywood Studios, reserve a table via Guest Relations just beyond the entrance near Hollywood Junction or at the restaurants. At Disney's Animal Kingdom, reserve at Guest Relations near the entrance.

 Disney can usually handle vegetarian, kosher, and other **special diets** (for people who need sugar-free meals, for example, or for folks who have allergies or are lactose intolerant), as long as guests give advance notice — usually no more than 24 hours. It's a good idea to discuss these requirements when you make your Advanced Dining Reservations. Select counter-service eateries offer specialty items on their menus as well (check your park map for details on which ones and what they offer). If you're not staying at WDW, call ☎ **407-939-3463.**

Trying to eat healthy? Think it's impossible at the theme parks? Well, it's not. In an effort to promote better eating habits, Disney kids' menus have been revised. Healthy items like low-fat milk, 100 percent fruit juice, water, and sides like unsweetened applesauce, veggies, and fresh fruit are now standard on kids' menus. Soda pop and fries are still available, but only upon request.

In addition, all WDW restaurants (in the theme parks and at the resorts) are currently in the midst of transitioning to become entirely trans-fat-free. Universal Orlando has followed suit, also eliminating trans fats in its menu items at parks and resort restaurants. Even SeaWorld now features an eatery with an entire menu dedicated to healthy options.

Tipping and taxes in Orlando

Sales tax on restaurant meals and drinks ranges from 6.5 percent to 7 percent throughout the Orlando area. (These taxes don't apply to groceries.) In addition, the standard tip in full-service restaurants is 15 percent, and a 12 percent tip is usually warranted at a buffet where a server brings your drinks, fetches condiments, and cleans the table. If you have a pre-dinner drink, leave a small tip to reward the server.

 Make sure that you carefully look over your check before coughing up a tip — some restaurants have started automatically tacking a gratuity onto your bill, especially for larger groups.

Trimming the Fat from Your Dining Budget

If you're staying in the parks until closing, you may find it more convenient to eat there, but you'll probably pay an average of 25 percent more than in the outside world. (Dinner for two at a sit-down restaurant in WDW, including tax and tip, can cost $80 or more.) If you don't mind ditching Mickey every now and again, you can substantially decrease your eating expenses.

Here are a few suggestions to get the most out of your dining dollars:

- ✓ I won't list all of them, but if you spend any time on International Drive or U.S. 192/Irlo Bronson Memorial Highway between Kissimmee and Disney, you'll see all sorts of billboards peddling all-you-can-eat breakfast buffets at chain restaurants for $5 to $8. A buffet is a great way to fuel up early for the day and skip, or at least lighten up on, lunch. The drawback: You lose valuable time when the parks are less crowded.

- ✓ Pick up the free magazines and ad books that you see in Orlando hotels, information centers, convenience stores, newspaper racks, highway rest areas, and so on. These publications include coupons good for a free second meal, discounts on entrees, or a free dessert, beverage, or appetizer with a meal. Also watch for ads that offer kids-eat-free specials or discounts for early birds.

- ✓ Inexpensive (by now you know that's a relative term) kids' menus (usually $8 and under with a drink) are common at most of Orlando's moderately priced and family-style restaurants.

Cutting food costs inside WDW

Eating at Disney parks can set you back more than a few bucks. For example, a 20-ounce bottle of cola or water is $2.50 or more. To save money, buy a bottle (or six-pack) of water from a local grocery for far less, freeze it the night before to keep it really cold, and take it with you to the park, refilling it at water fountains throughout the day. At lunchtime, the average price per person is around $10 if you eat at a fast-food area with counter service — much less expensive than at the full-service eateries. One of the best deals at the parks is a smoked turkey drumstick for $5.75 (and they're huge!).

Most of the Disney resorts offer a refillable mug, which is good for refills (with a list of select beverages) for the duration of your WDW visit. (The mugs must be used at the resort in which they were purchased.) The cost for the mug in most of the resorts is $12. The price may seem steep, but if you consider that most sodas cost around $2 or more individually, and you take into account how much you'd drink during your stay, it's actually a good deal. Some of Disney's water parks have refillable glasses, but refills are limited to the day you're in the park. For more information, call Disney at ☎ 407-934-7639.

✔ If you enjoy a cocktail before dinner, don't ignore places with happy-hour specials, including two-for-one drinks — some at bargain rates — usually from 4 to 7 p.m. Again, you can find listings in the free area guides in hotel lobbies and other places throughout Orlando.

✔ If your vacation won't be complete without trying at least one of the sit-down theme-park restaurants, consider eating at lunch instead of dinner, when prices are almost always cheaper.

✔ If you're staying with the Mouse (and have purchased a Magic Your Way vacation package), the Disney Dining Plan (at an additional cost) can save you plenty (almost 40 percent) over dining out at Disney on your own.

✔ If you're on a tight budget and your room has a kitchen, or at least a spot to sit and grab a bite, consider dining in a night or two and saving a few bucks. Area grocers, many with delis that turn out ready-to-eat treats, include **Albertsons,** 7524 Dr. Phillips Blvd. (☎ **407-352-1522;** www.albertsons.com), and **Gooding's,** at the Crossroads shopping center in Lake Buena Vista, 12521 Hwy. 535/ Apopka-Vineland Ave. (☎ **407-827-1200;** www.goodings.com), and at 8255 International Dr. (☎ **407-352-4215**). Gooding's also offers a delivery service — visit its Web site or call for details. In Kissimmee (U.S.192), you'll find a **Winn-Dixie** in the Formosa Gardens Plaza, 7849 W. Irlo Bronson Hwy. (☎ **407-397-2210;** www.winn-dixie.com), and a **Publix** in the Xentury City Center, 2925 International Dr., at U.S. 192 (☎ 407-397-1171). You can find even more options in the Orlando Yellow Pages under "Grocers."

Orlando's Best Restaurants

In this section, I review, in alphabetical order, what I think are some of Orlando's best restaurants. I also throw in some handy indexes at the end of the chapter to help you narrow your choices by category.

Because you may spend a lot of time in the WDW area, I've given special attention to choices there. Don't worry, though. I haven't forgotten to toss in plenty of worthwhile restaurants outside of Disney's domain — including a handful of Universal Orlando's latest entries (you can find in-park dining options for the Universal theme parks in Chapters 18 and 19) and some of the favorites elsewhere around town.

Sit-down restaurants in the WDW *theme parks* (not their resorts) require admission, with one exception: the **Rainforest Café** at Disney's Animal Kingdom. Unless you're a Disney resort guest, all Disney theme-park restaurants also set you back $12 in parking fees. (It's also $12 for Universal Orlando's CityWalk restaurants, unless you arrive after 6 p.m., when parking becomes free; parking fees for Universal Orlando resort restaurants vary.) Keep in mind that alcohol isn't served at Magic Kingdom restaurants, but it is served at Disney's Animal Kingdom,

Walt Disney World and Lake Buena Vista Restaurants

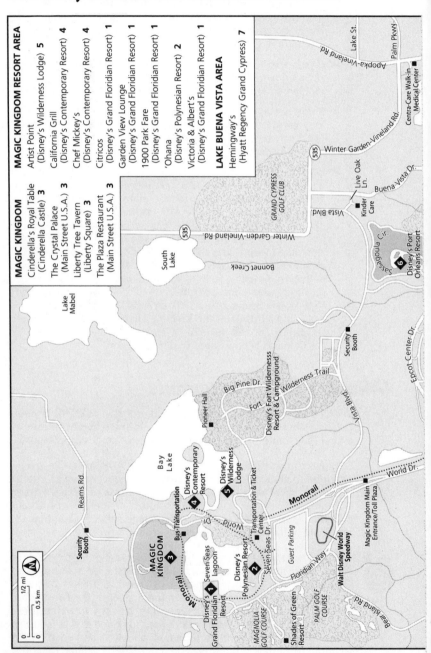

MAGIC KINGDOM

Cinderella's Royal Table
(Cinderella Castle) **3**

The Crystal Palace
(Main Street U.S.A.) **3**

Liberty Tree Tavern
(Liberty Square) **3**

The Plaza Restaurant
(Main Street U.S.A.) **3**

MAGIC KINGDOM RESORT AREA

Artist Point
(Disney's Wilderness Lodge) **5**

California Grill
(Disney's Contemporary Resort) **4**

Chef Mickey's
(Disney's Contemporary Resort) **4**

Citricos
(Disney's Grand Floridian Resort) **1**

Garden View Lounge
(Disney's Grand Floridian Resort) **1**

1900 Park Fare
(Disney's Grand Floridian Resort) **1**

'Ohana
(Disney's Polynesian Resort) **2**

Victoria & Albert's
(Disney's Grand Floridian Resort) **1**

LAKE BUENA VISTA AREA

Hemingway's
(Hyatt Regency Grand Cypress) **7**

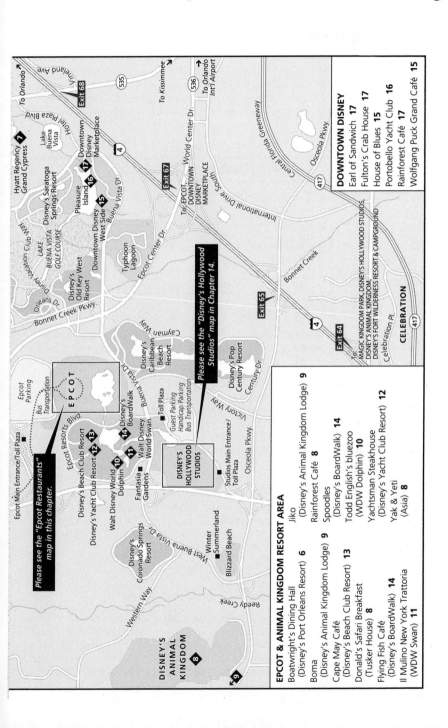

Please see the "Epcot Restaurants" map in this chapter.

Please see the "Disney's Hollywood Studios" map in Chapter 14.

DOWNTOWN DISNEY

Earl of Sandwich **17**
Fulton's Crab House **17**
House of Blues **15**
Portobello Yacht Club **16**
Rainforest Café **17**
Wolfgang Puck Grand Café **15**

EPCOT & ANIMAL KINGDOM RESORT AREA

Boatwright's Dining Hall
(Disney's Port Orleans Resort) **6**
Boma
(Disney's Animal Kingdom Lodge) **9**
Cape May Café
(Disney's Beach Club Resort) **13**
Donald's Safari Breakfast
(Tusker House) **8**
Flying Fish Café
(Disney's BoardWalk) **14**
Il Mulino New York Trattoria
(WDW Swan) **11**

Jiko
(Disney's Animal Kingdom Lodge) **9**
Rainforest Café **8**
Spoodles
(Disney's BoardWalk) **14**
Todd English's bluezoo
(WDW Dolphin) **10**
Yachtsman Steakhouse
(Disney's Yacht Club Resort) **12**
Yak & Yeti
(Asia) **8**

Epcot, and Disney's Hollywood Studios restaurants, and elsewhere in the Disney domain, as well as at the other major theme parks.

 To make it easy for you to recognize expensive versus moderately priced restaurants, each of the following reviews includes one or more $ symbols, based on the average price of an adult dinner entree and one nonalcoholic drink. For the meaning behind the dollar symbols, see Table 10-1.

Table 10-1	Key to Restaurant Dollar Signs
Dollar Sign(s)	Price Range
$	Less than $10
$$	$11–$25
$$$	$26–$50
$$$$	$51 and up

Akershus Royal Banquet Hall
$$–$$$ Epcot   NORWEGIAN

Set inside a Disneyfied 14th-century castle, this eatery now offers character dining at each meal (see Princess Storybook Dining under "Dining with Disney Characters," later in this chapter). Breakfast features American fare (scrambled eggs, French toast, sausage, bacon, potatoes), while lunch and dinner are served up family style, offering a smorgasbord of Norwegian specialties (cured salmon with spicy mustard, poached cod, and venison stew, along with an array of Norwegian breads and cheeses) in addition to traditional American fare for the kids. The food is reasonably good, and the staff is friendly. Sweets and sandwiches are available across the courtyard at the **Kringla Bakeri Og Kafe.**

See map p. 141. In Norway Pavilion, World Showcase, Epcot. ☎ *407-939-3463.* www.disneyworld.com. *Breakfast: $23 adults, $13 children. Lunch: $25 adults, $14 children. Dinner: $29 adults, $14 children. AE, DC, DISC, MC, V. Open: Daily 8:30–10:10 a.m., 11:40 a.m.–2:50 p.m., and 4:20–8:40 p.m.*

Artist Point
$$–$$$ Walt Disney World Resorts   SEAFOOD/STEAKS

Enjoy a grand view of **Disney's Wilderness Lodge** and tasty cuisine at this rustically elegant establishment. Hand-painted murals of Pacific Northwest scenery adorn the impressive two-story ceiling, and ornate iron lanterns hang from tremendous timber columns. Immense windows overlook the grounds. The menu changes seasonally and might offer grilled buffalo sirloin with sweet potato hazelnut gratin and sweet onion jam, but the restaurant's signature is the cedar plank–roasted king salmon. The terrace offers outdoor seating in good weather. Expect a reasonably extensive wine list featuring Pacific Northwest wines.

See map p. 134. 901 W. Timberline Dr., in Disney's Wilderness Lodge. ☎ *407-939-3463.* www.disneyworld.com. *Advanced Dining Reservations recommended. Main courses: $26–$42, fixed-price menu $50. AE, DC, DISC, MC, V. Open: Daily 5:30–10 p.m.*

Bice Ristorante
$$–$$$ Universal Orlando   ITALIAN

Located in the romantic Italian setting of the **Portofino Bay Hotel,** Bice serves creative cuisine in a sophisticated atmosphere. An extensive menu includes items such as a Belgian endive salad with gorgonzola and toasted walnuts; spaghetti with Maine lobster and cherry tomatoes in a tomato bisque; and veal chops with sautéed mushrooms, potatoes, and spinach. The main dining room overlooks the waters along the piazza of the hotel, itself a beautiful setting. A table on the patio, if timed right, may allow you to enjoy the strolling musicians performing just below along the piazza. Disappointingly, some servers and staff are a bit aloof.

See map p. 143. 5601 Universal Studios Blvd., in the Portofino Bay Hotel. ☎ *407-503-3463 or 407-503-1415.* www.universalorlando.com. *Reservations recommended. Main courses: $16–$44. AE, MC, V. Open: Daily 5:30–10:30 p.m.*

B-Line Diner
$–$$ International Drive Area   AMERICAN

Sink into an upholstered booth or belly up to a stool at the counter of this restaurant with décor straight out of the '50s. Gleaming chrome, black-and-white tile, and red leather create a vision of yesterday's roadside diners in this informal and friendly gathering place. Dig into comfort foods such as chicken pot pie or a ham-and-cheese sandwich on a baguette. Health foods and vegetarian specials are also available.

Although this is a diner-style restaurant and there is a kids' menu, it's not a good spot to take young children because it's located at the **Peabody,** a very upscale hotel.

See map p. 143. 9801 International Dr., across from the Orlando Convention Center, in the Peabody Orlando. ☎ *407-345-4460.* www.peabodyorlando.com. *Reservations not accepted. Main courses: Breakfast $4–$16, lunch and dinner $11–$24. AE, DC, DISC, MC, V. Open: Daily 24 hr.*

Boatwright's Dining Hall
$–$$ Walt Disney World Resorts   NEW ORLEANS

A family atmosphere (lively and noisy), good food (by Disney standards), and reasonable prices (ditto) make Boatwright's a hit with **Disney's Port Orleans Resort** guests. Most entrees have a Cajun/Creole spin. The jambalaya is sans seafood, but it's filled with veggies, rice, chicken, and sausage — and it's got a kick. Other entrees include slow-roasted prime rib, penne pasta with shrimp, and pot roast. Boatwright's is modeled after a 19th-century boat factory, complete with the wooden hull of a Louisiana fishing boat suspended from its lofty beamed ceiling. Kids are drawn to the wooden toolboxes on every table; each contains a saltshaker that doubles as a level, a wood-clamp sugar dispenser, a pepper-grinder-cum-ruler, shop rags (to be used as napkins), and a little metal pail of crayons.

See map p. 134. 2201 Orleans Dr., in Disney's Port Orleans Resort French Quarter. ☎ *407-939-3463.* www.disneyworld.com. *Advanced Dining Reservations recommended. Main courses: Breakfast $9–$12, dinner $16–$30. AE, DC, DISC, MC, V. Open: Daily 7–11:30 a.m. and 5–10 p.m.*

Bob Marley–A Tribute to Freedom
$–$$ Universal Orlando   CARIBBEAN

This combination club and restaurant is housed in a replica of the late singer's home in Jamaica, complete with red-tile roof and green shutters. Live reggae plays nightly, but the decibel level doesn't get as high as at Jimmy Buffett's Margaritaville (reviewed later in this chapter). The small menu has modestly priced fare, including a jerk tilapia sandwich on coca bread with yucca fries, or a seafood salad of conch, shrimp, and tilapia, served in a red-tortilla bowl. Of course, most folks don't leave without sipping a Red Stripe — Jamaica's beer of champions.

See map p. 347. 1000 Universal Studios Plaza, in CityWalk. ☎ *407-224-2262.* www.universalorlando.com. *Reservations not accepted. Main courses: $8–$16. AE, DISC, MC, V. Open: Daily 4 p.m.–2 a.m.*

Boma–Flavors of Africa
$$ Walt Disney World Resorts   AFRICAN

Follow your nose to the wood-burning grill and open kitchen at this African-influenced eatery inside **Disney's Animal Kingdom Lodge.** The large wood tables are in the shape of tree trunks; colorful banners hang from the thatched roof. The selection and variety here are vast and often unique. Adventurous diners can expect such treats as Moroccan seafood salad and curried-coconut seafood stew, alongside more familiar favorites at the restaurant's breakfast and dinner buffets. Kids have their own station serving up chicken, pasta, and mac 'n' cheese. Chefs are on hand behind the open buffet to answer questions about the cuisine. The wine list features an array of South African offerings.

See map p. 135. 2901 Osceola Pkwy., in Disney's Animal Kingdom Lodge. ☎ *407-939-3463.* www.disneyworld.com. *Advanced Dining Reservations recommended. Breakfast buffet: $17 adults, $10 ages 3–9. Dinner buffet: $27 adults, $13 kids 3–9. AE, DC, DISC, MC, V. Open: Daily 7–11 a.m. and 5–10 p.m.*

Bubbalou's Bodacious BBQ
$–$$ International Drive Area   AMERICAN

This is, hands down, some of the best barbecue you'll find anywhere. The atmosphere is extremely informal, but you have to watch the sauces. Even the mild may be too hot for tender palates; the killer sauce comes with a three-alarm warning — you may not be able to taste anything else for days. If you can eat the night or day away, go for the Big-Big Pig platter (beef, sliced pork, and turkey with fixin's). And it wouldn't be a barbecue without plenty of brew on hand.

See map p. 143. 5818 Conroy Rd. (a few blocks north of Universal Orlando at the intersection of Kirkman and Conroy). ☎ *407-423-1212.* www.bubbalous.com. *Reservations — you're kidding! Main courses: $4–$15. AE, MC, V. Open: Mon–Thurs 10 a.m.–9:30 p.m., Fri–Sat 10 a.m.–10:30 p.m., Sun 11 a.m.–9 p.m.*

Café Tu Tu Tango
$$–$$$ **International Drive Area INTERNATIONAL**

This colorful eatery with the flair of an artist's loft — and where guests frequently see an artist bringing a canvas to life — features treats from Latin America, the Caribbean, Asia, the Middle East, and the U.S. It's an ideal spot for sampling different dishes, as all come in a miniature size. The roasted pears on pecan crisps, topped with Spanish bleu cheese and a balsamic reduction, are a must. Chocolate fiends will not want to pass up the dessert of handmade truffles. You can also buy wine by the glass or bottle. *Note:* Although individual tapas are relatively inexpensive, a meal of several tapas and drinks can easily make this a $$$ restaurant.

See map p. 143. 8625 International Dr. (just west of the Mercado Shopping Center). ☎ *407-248-2222.* www.cafetututango.com. *Reservations accepted. Main courses: Tapas (small plates) $4–$20 (even those with small appetites will want 2 or 3). AE, DC, DISC, MC, V. Open: Sun–Thurs 11:30 a.m.–11 p.m., Fri–Sat 11:30 a.m.–2 a.m.*

California Grill
$$–$$$ **Walt Disney World Resorts AMERICAN**

The 15th-floor views of the **Magic Kingdom** and environs are stunning, and the food is pretty good, too. The Art Deco dining room at **Disney's Contemporary Resort** features an exhibition kitchen with a wood-burning oven, rotisserie, and sushi station. The constantly changing menu lists fresh market fare, as well as pizzas and pastas. Highlights may include seared day-boat scallops with faro-wheat risotto, braised baby carrots, and crustacean butter sauce. The Grill also has a nice sushi and sashimi menu. The restaurant sports a grand wine list and some excellent vegetarian options. If you time it right, the evening fireworks at the Magic Kingdom make for a spectacular dinner show.

See map p. 134. 4600 World Dr., in Disney's Contemporary Resort. ☎ *407-939-3463 or 407-824-1576.* www.disneyworld.com. *Advanced Dining Reservations require a credit card guarantee. Main courses: $23–$38, sushi $16–$24. AE, DC, DISC, MC, V. Open: Daily 5:30–10 p.m.*

Christini's
$$–$$$ **Dr. Phillips Area ITALIAN**

The numerous awards on the walls attest to restaurateur Chris Christini's high standard of service. The fact that he's been around since 1984 shows he's a survivor. Count on his restaurant for a possible peek at show-biz celebrities from down the road at Disney's Hollywood Studios and Universal. A tender broiled veal chop seasoned with sage and served with applesauce is one of the headliners. Another good choice is the pan-seared Chilean sea bass over shrimp-and-lobster risotto. The food is quite good, and the wine list is definitely a winner. The atmosphere is somewhat formal, making it a good spot for a romantic night out.

See map p. 143. 7600 Dr. Phillips Blvd. ☎ *407-345-8770.* www.christinis.com. *Reservations recommended. Main courses: $18–$48 (many under $28). AE, DC, DISC, MC, V. Open: Daily 6–11 p.m. Jackets for men and dresses for women suggested.*

Citricos
$$$ **Walt Disney World Resorts   FRENCH**

The chef of this bright and airy restaurant at **Disney's Grand Floridian Resort** makes a statement with French, Alsatian, and Provençal cuisine with California and Florida touches (whew!). Depending on when you visit, the menu may include grilled lamb chops with crispy polenta and puttanesca sauce or sautéed salmon with roasted fennel and gold potatoes. The old-world-style dining room, filled with wrought-iron railings, mosaic-tile floors, and flickering lights, features a show kitchen and spectacular views of the **Seven Seas Lagoon** and **Magic Kingdom fireworks.** You can add a three-course wine pairing for around $30.

See map p. 134. 4401 Floridian Way, in Disney's Grand Floridian Resort & Spa. ☎ *407-939-3463.* www.disneyworld.com. *Advanced Dining Reservations recommended. Main courses: $36–$60. AE, DC, DISC, MC, V. Open: Wed–Sat 6–8:30 p.m.*

Coral Reef Restaurant
$$–$$$ **Epcot   SEAFOOD**

Seafood rules at this very popular restaurant, which offers fabulous views of the **Seas with Nemo & Friends aquarium** and a dash of classical music to help set a romantic tone. The menu, unfortunately, is less imaginative than the ambience. Entrees include grilled mahimahi with wasabi-mashed couscous and a honey-soy glaze; seared sterling salmon with mixed greens, roasted potatoes, and pancetta garlic vinaigrette; and a decent selection of landlubber fare as well. The Reef serves wine by the glass. *Note:* You get fish-identifier sheets with labeled pictures so that you can put names on the faces swimming by your table.

See map p. 141. In the Living Seas Pavilion. ☎ *407-939-3463.* www.disneyworld.com. *Advanced Dining Reservations recommended. Main courses: Lunch $12–$22, dinner $16–$32. AE, DC, DISC, MC, V. Open: Daily 11:30 a.m.–3 p.m. and 4:30 p.m. until park closing.*

Dexter's of Thornton Park
$–$$ **Downtown Orlando   INTERNATIONAL**

This popular cafe and neighborhood bar is just a few blocks from Lake Eola in the center of downtown. The creative and ever-changing fare features

Epcot Restaurants

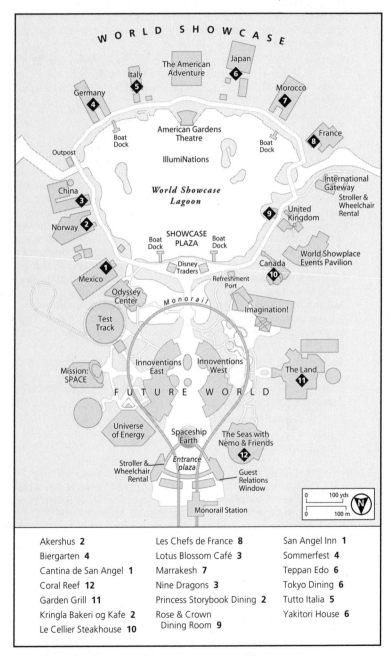

Akershus **2**	Les Chefs de France **8**	San Angel Inn **1**
Biergarten **4**	Lotus Blossom Café **3**	Sommerfest **4**
Cantina de San Angel **1**	Marrakesh **7**	Teppan Edo **6**
Coral Reef **12**	Nine Dragons **3**	Tokyo Dining **6**
Garden Grill **11**	Princess Storybook Dining **2**	Tutto Italia **5**
Kringla Bakeri og Kafe **2**	Rose & Crown	Yakitori House **6**
Le Cellier Steakhouse **10**	Dining Room **9**	

such fun foods as Togarashi seared tuna with sesame greens, shiitakes, and a caramelized miso glaze, and potato-wrapped salmon with shiitakes, caramelized cipollini onions, and a tarragon glacé. Many of the seats are stools at high tables; if that's not for you, you may have a long wait. There's a modest wine list.

See map p. 151. 808 E. Washington St., at the corner of Hyer Ave. ☎ *407-648-2777.* www.dexwine.com. *Reservations not accepted. Main courses: Lunch $9–$14, dinner $17–$27. AE, DC, DISC, MC, V. Open: Mon–Thurs 11 a.m.–10 p.m., Fri–Sat 11 a.m.–11 p.m., Sun 11 a.m.–10p.m.*

Dux
$$$ **International Drive Area   INTERNATIONAL**

Think posh with a capital *P* — that's what comes to mind when you slip inside these walls. The restaurant's name honors the mallards that splash all day in the marble fountains in the **Peabody** hotel's grandly formal lobby. (Staffers assure us that birds of the quacking variety will never appear on the menu.) Candlelit tables surround a large chandelier, and textured gold walls are hung with watercolors of various duck species. The eclectic menu changes with the seasons. Possibilities might include a succulent Alaskan halibut with lobster mashed potatoes and lobster reduction. At other times, hope for a tender veal chop marinated in apple cider and honey; steamed red snapper in tomato fricassee and fennel; or sautéed salmon on a bed of couscous with black olives, tomatoes, and chives. Choose a wine from one of the best wine lists in the city. The service is impeccable; for most people, however, the prices make Dux a choice only for special nights or expense-account meals.

See map p. 143. 9801 International Dr., across from the Orlando Convention Center, in the Peabody Orlando. ☎ *407-345-4550.* www.peabodyorlando.com. *Reservations recommended. Main courses: $30–$50. AE, DC, DISC, MC, V. Open: Mon–Sat 6–10 p.m. Jackets for men and dresses for women suggested.*

Earl of Sandwich
$ **Downtown Disney   AMERICAN**

In 2004, the Earl of Sandwich (the famous edible was invented by said earl in 1762, when he was too busy playing cards to eat a real meal) made its debut in Downtown Disney. It's an alliance between Robert Earl, founder and CEO of Planet Hollywood, and John Montagu, the real 11th Earl of Sandwich. The eatery offers a great selection of hot and cold deli sandwiches, wraps, and salads for those looking for a light meal at a very decent price. It's one of the best dining deals at Disney.

See map p. 134. 1800 E. Buena Vista Dr., in Downtown Disney Marketplace. ☎ *407-827-8500.* www.disneyworld.com. *Reservations not accepted. Main courses: $5–$6. AE, MC, V. Open: Daily 8:30 a.m.–11 p.m.*

International Drive and Dr. Phillips Area Restaurants

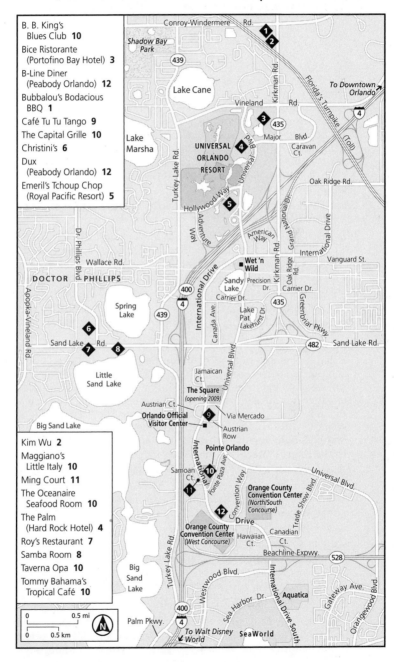

B. B. King's
  Blues Club **10**
Bice Ristorante
  (Portofino Bay Hotel) **3**
B-Line Diner
  (Peabody Orlando) **12**
Bubbalou's Bodacious
  BBQ **1**
Café Tu Tu Tango **9**
The Capital Grille **10**
Christini's **6**
Dux
  (Peabody Orlando) **12**
Emeril's Tchoup Chop
  (Royal Pacific Resort) **5**

Kim Wu **2**
Maggiano's
  Little Italy **10**
Ming Court **11**
The Oceanaire
  Seafood Room **10**
The Palm
  (Hard Rock Hotel) **4**
Roy's Restaurant **7**
Samba Room **8**
Taverna Opa **10**
Tommy Bahama's
  Tropical Café **10**

Emeril's Orlando
$$–$$$ **Universal Orlando** **NEW ORLEANS**

The Florida home of culinary genius Emeril Lagasse, star of *Emeril Live* on cable TV's Food Network (and, therefore, rarely on the premises), offers a feast for both the eyes and mouth. This two-story restaurant resembles an old warehouse, albeit one with pricey art on its walls. The second floor has a 12,000-bottle wine gallery. If you want a show, I highly recommend trying to get one of the eight counter seats, where you can watch the chefs working their Creole-cuisine magic, but to get one, you'll need to make reservations *excruciatingly* early. (Reserve at least six weeks in advance.) Best bets include the andouille-crusted Texas redfish with roasted pecans, a meunière sauce, and shoestring potatoes, and a grilled double-cut pork chop with caramelized sweet potatoes. Though jackets are suggested for gents at dinner, you'll find a lot of diners, fresh out of the Universal theme parks, far less dressy.

Emeril's lunch menu is cheaper than its dinner menu. It's also easier to get a reservation, and the dress code is more casual.

See map p. 347. 6000 Universal Studios Blvd., in CityWalk. ☎ **407-224-2424.** www. emerils.com/restaurants. *Reservations far in advance are a must. Main courses: Lunch $18–$28, dinner $31–$50. AE, DISC, MC, V. Open: Daily 11:30 a.m.– 2 p.m. and 5:30–10 p.m. (until 11 p.m. Fri–Sat). Jackets suggested for men.*

Emeril's Tchoup Chop
$$–$$$ **Universal Orlando** **PACIFIC RIM**

Pronounced "chop chop," this is Emeril Lagasse's second restaurant in Orlando, located in the **Royal Pacific Resort.** Its décor blends flowers, sculpted gardens, and mini waterfalls with batik fabrics, carved-wood grilles, and chandeliers. The exhibition kitchen offers a look at the chefs making your meal in woks or on wood-burning grills. The Polynesian- and Asian-influenced menu offers temptations such as macadamia-crusted salmon with wasabi mashed potatoes and stir-fried vegetables, or Mongolian barbecue marinated filet with vegetable chow mein and yucca shoestrings. The service, matching both the food and décor, is impressive.

See map p. 143. 6300 Hollywood Way, in the Royal Pacific Resort. ☎ **407-503-2467.** www.emerils.com/restaurants. *Reservations strongly recommended. Main courses: $13–$34. AE, DISC, MC, V. Daily 11:30 a.m.–2 p.m., Sun–Thurs 5:30–10 p.m., Fri–Sat 5:30–11 p.m.*

50's Prime Time Café
$$ **Disney's Hollywood Studios** **AMERICAN**

If you yearn to go back to a time when life was simpler, this is the place for you. The décor is right out of the television sitcoms, and servers deliver comfort foods like meatloaf, fried chicken, and pot roast. The food isn't quite the way Mom used to make it, but the place offers enough fun that you might just love it anyway. Black-and-white TVs air shows such as *Topper* and *My Little Margie* as servers zap you back to the days when you had to finish your vegetables if you wanted dessert. Mom (aka your server) may very well scold you if put your elbows on the table or don't clean your plate. Desserts such as s'mores and sundaes top off the menu.

See map p. 248. Near the Indiana Jones Stunt Spectacular. ☎ *407-939-3463.* www. disneyworld.com. *Advanced Dining Reservations recommended. Main courses: $13–$21. AE, DC, DISC, MC, V. Open: 11 a.m. to park closing.*

Flying Fish Café
$$$ Walt Disney World Resorts   SEAFOOD

Welcome to Coney Island, circa 1940, a la Disney. The vibrant décor at this restaurant at **Disney's BoardWalk Inn** is almost as elaborate as the show kitchen, which puts the chefs at center stage. The menu changes frequently, thus the seafood is among the freshest in town. Headliners may include potato-wrapped red snapper, pan-seared Ahi tuna with Moroccan couscous, or oak-grilled salmon. You'll also find beef, poultry, and veggie options. If you can't get a table here, ask about sitting at the counter — you get a great view of the kitchen.

See map p. 134. 2101 N. Epcot Resorts Blvd., in Disney's BoardWalk Inn. ☎ *407-939-3463 or 407-939-2359.* www.disneyworld.com. *Advanced Dining Reservations recommended. Main courses: $28–$38. AE, DC, DISC, MC, V. Open: Daily 5:30–10 p.m.*

Fulton's Crab House
$$–$$$ Downtown Disney   SEAFOOD

Lose yourself in a world of brass, shining mahogany, and river charts as you dine on the city's best seafood while inside a moored Mississippi Delta–style paddle-wheeler. Lobster (Maine and Australian) and crab (stone, king, and Dungeness) dominate the menu. The grilled tuna mignon is served rare, and the Dungeness crab cakes are a real treat. One popular meal for two combines Alaskan king crab, snow crab, and lobster with potatoes and creamed spinach. There's a comprehensive wine list. You can dine on the outdoor deck if the weather's fair.

See map p. 134. Aboard the riverboat at Pleasure Island. ☎ *407-934-2628.* www.levy restaurants.com. *Advanced Dining Reservations recommended. Main courses: Lunch $13–$50, dinner $28–$50. AE, DC, DISC, MC, V. Open: Daily 11:30 a.m.–11 p.m.*

Hemingway's
$$$ Lake Buena Vista   SEAFOOD

If Papa were to eat at his namesake, he might dive into the shrimp ceviche with coconut, curry, and red onion before moving on to the black grouper with tomato and slivered garlic fondue, sautéed spinach, and red potatoes. No doubt, he would skip the wine list (there is a decent one) and opt for a few Papa Dobles, a potent rum concoction he invented. The interior of Hemingway's has a Key West air, and the walls are adorned with sepia photographs of the famous author and his fishing trophies. The eatery has a romantic dining room lighted by hurricane lamps, plus a wooden deck near a waterfall. This establishment in the **Hyatt Regency Grand Cypress** is usually childfree, although there is a kids' menu.

See map p. 134. 1 Grand Cypress Blvd., off Hwy. 535, in the Hyatt Regency Grand Cypress. ☎ *407-239-3854.* www.hyattgrandcypress.com. *Reservations recommended. Main courses: $25–$41. AE, DC, DISC, MC, V. Open: Daily 6–10 p.m.*

Hollywood Brown Derby
$$–$$$ Disney's Hollywood Studios   AMERICAN

A huge derby marks the entrance to this restaurant at Disney's Hollywood Studios. Inside, this re-creation of the restaurant where Hollywood's stars gathered in the '30s and '40s is decorated with caricatures of the regulars on its walls. The food (on the pricey side) won't win an Academy Award, but the restaurant does have a respectable pan-fired grouper with balsamic roasted asparagus; sesame-seared Ahi tuna with honey-gingered spaghetti squash, shiitake broth, and wasabi oil; and roasted pork rib chop with smoked cheese tomato fondue. The two signature dishes are the Cobb salad, invented in the 1930s by Bob Cobb, then-owner of the original Brown Derby, and the grapefruit cake with cream cheese frosting.

See map p. 218. Hollywood Blvd. ☎ *539-939-3463.* www.disneyworld.com. *Advanced Dining Reservations recommended. Main courses: Lunch $14–$22, dinner $18–$30. AE, DC, DISC, MC, V. Open: Daily 11:30 a.m. until park closing.*

House of Blues
$$–$$$ Downtown Disney   AMERICAN

Inside this Louisiana clapboard building, you find hearty portions of down-home Southern fare served in an atmosphere literally pulsing with rhythm and blues. Exceedingly crowded on days of big concerts, the music in the nightclub next door is as much a draw as the food. Funky folk art with a voodooish feel covers the rustic walls from floor to ceiling. The back patio has seating and a nice view of the bay. Foodwise, the spicy Creole jambalaya and pan-seared voodoo shrimp are good bets. Sunday's **Gospel Brunch** is a ton of foot-stomping fun, with plenty of Southern favorites like jambalaya, cornbread, and barbecue chicken alongside breakfast staples such as omelets, sausage, and bacon. Brunch is the only time you can make reservations; make them early.

See map p. 134. 1490 E. Buena Vista Dr., under the old-fashioned water tower in Disney's West Side. ☎ *407-934-2583.* www.hob.com. *Reservations not accepted (except for Gospel Brunch). Main courses: $10–$27, pizza and sandwiches $10–$11; brunch $33 adults, $16 kids 3–9. AE, DISC, MC, V. Open: Mon–Thurs 11:30 a.m.–11 p.m., Fri–Sat 11:30am–midnight, Sun 10:30 a.m.–10 p.m. Sun brunch seatings 10:30 a.m. and 1 p.m.*

Il Mulino New York Trattoria
$$$ Walt Disney World Resorts   ITALIAN

Il Mulino, a chic Italian eatery in the **Walt Disney World Swan** (the original has been a New York City hotspot for over 25 years), features an extensive and tasty menu filled with fresh pastas, meats, and seafood — a sampling of which includes seared red snapper with cherry tomatoes, garlic, pancetta, and white wine served over broccoli rabe; sautéed veal scaloppini and prosciutto with spinach and sage in a white wine sauce; and baby shrimp, clams, mussels, scungilli, and calamari in a spicy red or garlic white wine sauce. The interior, while warm and welcoming, mixes exposed brick, wood, and stainless steel, giving it a trendier upscale feel. Pricier than most, this one is best for a night out without the kids.

See map p. 134. 1200 Epcot Resorts Blvd. (off Buena Vista Dr.), in the Walt Disney World Swan. ☎ *407-934-1609.* www.swandolphin.com. *Reservations recommended. Main courses: $27–$46, pizza and pastas $16–$32. AE, DC, DISC, MC, V. Open: Daily 5–11 p.m.*

Jiko–The Cooking Place
$$–$$$ Walt Disney World Resorts   AFRICAN

The signature restaurant (translation: most expensive) at **Disney's Animal Kingdom Lodge,** Jiko has a show kitchen that turns out a unique menu of international cuisine with African overtones. Dishes, depending on the season, include Durban curry shrimp, maize-crusted and seared Pacific sturgeon, and Chermoula-roasted Tanglewood chicken. The wine list features an extensive number of South African vintages. If you have an adventurous palate, it's well worth the trip.

See map p. 134. 2901 Osceola Pkwy., in Disney's Animal Kingdom Lodge. ☎ *407-939-3463.* www.disneyworld.com. *Advanced Dining Reservations recommended. Main courses: $14–$30. AE, DC, DISC, MC, V. Open: Daily 5:30–10 p.m.*

Jimmy Buffett's Margaritaville
$$ Universal Orlando   CARIBBEAN

The laid-back atmosphere may take you to paradise, but after the Parrotheads have had enough to drink, the noise can make it hard to hear your tablemates. You have your choice of three watering holes: the **Landshark Bar,** the **12-Volt Bar,** and the **Volcano Bar,** which comes complete with a two-story, margarita-spewing mini mountain. Despite the renowned Cheeseburgers in Paradise, the food has Caribbean leanings. And although it isn't contending for a critic's choice award, it is fairly tasty. Best bets include jerk chicken, jambalaya, and a Cuban meat loaf survival sandwich that's a cheeseburger of another kind. The **Porch of Indecision** offers the best spot for those with kids along.

Watch your tab. At up to $9 a pop for margaritas (the mango ones are best), the bill can climb to $50 or more for a routine lunch.

See map p. 347. 1000 Universal Studios Plaza, in CityWalk. ☎ *407-224-2155.* www.margaritavilleorlando.com. *Reservations not accepted. Main courses: $9–$22 (most under $15). AE, DISC, MC, V. Open: Daily 11 a.m.–2 a.m.*

Kim Wu
$–$$ Universal Orlando Area   CHINESE

Tucked away in a shopping center near Universal, you'll find this award-winning favorite. Traditional Chinese dishes are flavorful and excellently presented. Best of all, most entrees are priced in the single digits. It's been around for over 20 years, and for good reason. Most nights, owner Tom Yuen works the floor, greeting guests like family.

See map p. 143. 4904 S. Kirkman Rd. (just a few blocks north of Universal Orlando at the intersection of Kirkman and Conroy roads). ☎ 407-293-0752. Reservations not accepted. Main courses: $4–$16. AE, DISC, MC, V. Open: Mon–Fri 11:30 a.m.–11 p.m., Sat 4–11 p.m., Sun noon to 11 p.m.

Le Cellier Steakhouse
$$–$$$ Epcot   STEAKS

You'll feel welcome in this cozy steakhouse, which tends to be less crowded — and less manic — than some of Epcot's other restaurants. The dining room resembles a wine cellar; you'll sit in tapestry-upholstered chairs under vaulted stone arches and lanterns. Although it doesn't compete with some of the better outside-world steak-and-chop houses, it has a surprisingly good selection of Midwest corn-fed beef in the usual cuts. Options include an herb-crusted prime rib with a veal demi glacé. Wash your meal down with Canadian wine or beer or, for an after-dinner treat, a sweet Canadian ice wine.

See map p. 141. In Canada Pavilion, World Showcase. ☎ 407-939-3463. www.disney world.com. Advanced Dining Reservations recommended. Main courses: Lunch $10–$22, dinner $16–$28. AE, DC, DISC, MC, V. Open: Daily 11:30 a.m.–3 p.m. and 4 p.m. to park closing.

Les Chefs de France
$$–$$$ Epcot   FRENCH

Three famous French chefs — Paul Bocuse, Roger Vergé, and Gaston LeNotre — concocted the menu at this restaurant, which serves respectable fare that's far better than the usual theme-park offerings. The Art Nouveau interior is agleam with mirrors and candelabras, and etched-glass and brass dividers create intimate dining areas. Dinner entrees may include grilled tenderloin of beef with a black pepper sauce, or roasted perch with lobster mousse and a lobster reduction. The sauces tend to be on the lighter side than at most traditional French restaurants. There's also a substantial wine list.

See map p. 141. In France Pavilion, World Showcase. ☎ 407-939-3463 or 407-827-8709. www.disneyworld.com. Advanced Dining Reservations suggested. Main courses: Lunch $10–$20, dinner $17–$30. AE, DC, DISC, MC, V. Open: Daily noon to 3:30 p.m. and 5 p.m. until 1 hr. before park closing.

Liberty Tree Tavern
$$–$$$ **Magic Kingdom   AMERICAN**

This sit-down restaurant's 18th-century colonial-pub atmosphere (the décor features antiques, oak-plank floors, and a huge fireplace filled with copper pots) and good service help make it one of the better places to dine in the Magic Kingdom, but few will be compelled to visit a second or third time. Lunch offers à la carte service with seafood and sandwiches, while dinner gives you basic American favorites, such as roast turkey, carved beef, mashed potatoes, stuffing, and macaroni and cheese.

 Even though it's a tavern of sorts, you won't find alcohol served here. Also, note that the Liberty Tree Tavern's character dinner will not be offered beginning in January 2009.

See map p. 134. In Liberty Square. ☎ **407-939-3463.** www.disneyworld.com. *Advanced Dining Reservations recommended. Main courses: Lunch $11–$16; dinner buffet $28 adults, $13 kids 3–11. AE, DC, DISC, MC, V. Open: Daily 11:30 a.m.–3 p.m. and 4 p.m. until park closing.*

 ### Little Saigon
$ **Downtown Orlando   VIETNAMESE**

Situated in the heart of a tiny Vietnamese neighborhood, this ethnic eatery has been open since 1987 and thrives on regulars from the community. The menu offers everything from appetizers to noodle dishes to stir-fries that mix-and-match pork, beef, seafood, and vegetables. The combo plates are a particularly good deal. Service and attention depend on the traffic. Order food by number; if you need a description of a dish, you may need to ask the manager, whose English is better than that of some of the servers. Don't miss the summer rolls with peanut sauce.

See map p. 151. 1106 E. Colonial Dr., just east of I-4 on Hwy. 50. ☎ **407-423-8539.** *Reservations not accepted. Main courses: Lunch under $5, dinner $5–$10. AE, DISC, MC, V. Open: Daily 10 a.m.–9 p.m.*

 ### Lotus Blossom Café
$ **Epcot   CHINESE**

This recently refurbished open-air cafe offers familiar favorites much like what you find in Chinese restaurants located in mall food courts. Expect veggie stir-fry, beef noodle soup, sesame chicken salad, potstickers, and egg rolls that are slightly above fast-food quality. The outdoor (though covered) seating is refreshing. You can buy Chinese beer and wine as well. Quality aside, it's still a bargain in pricey Epcot.

See map p. 141. In China Pavilion, World Showcase. ☎ **407-939-3463.** www.disney world.com. *Advanced Dining Reservations not accepted. Main courses: $4–$8. AE, DC, DISC, MC, V. Open: Daily 11 a.m. to park closing.*

Manuel's on the 28th
$$$ Downtown Orlando   INTERNATIONAL

Manuel's is, literally, the pinnacle of elegance, situated in a posh, panoramic enclave on the 28th floor of a downtown bank building. Come here for a stunning after-dark vista of the sparkling, sprawling metropolis. The best news: The food matches the scenery. The dozen or more appetizers and entrees hit high notes with duck, lamb, Ahi tuna, lobster, and filet mignon. One popular dish is miso-marinated Chilean sea bass. The service is very professional, and the restaurant has a great wine list.

See map p. 151. 390 N. Orange Ave., in the Bank of America Building. ☎ *407-246-6580.* www.manuelsonthe28th.com. *Reservations required. Main courses: $26–$45; fixed-price menu $55, with wine pairing $75. AE, DC, DISC, MC, V. Open: Tues–Sat 6–10 p.m. Jackets recommended for men.*

Marrakesh
$$–$$$ Epcot   MOROCCAN

For a spot of romance and truly authentic flavor, head for Marrakesh. Of all the **World Showcase** restaurants at Epcot, this venue best typifies the international spirit of the park. Hand-laid mosaics in intricate patterns set the scene for lavish North African dining, complete with belly dancers. Marrakesh uses a long list of spices, including saffron, to enhance flavorful specialties. Most entrees come with the national dish, couscous (steamed semolina), with veggies and sometimes other embellishments. Good bets include the seafood medley and the marinated shish kabob of lamb roasted in its own juices.

See map p. 141. In Morocco Pavilion, World Showcase. ☎ *407-939-3463.* www.disney world.com. *Advanced Dining Reservations recommended. Main courses: Lunch $17–$21, dinner $20–$32, fixed-price menu $25–$40. AE, DC, DISC, MC, V. Open: Daily noon to park closing.*

Ming Court
$$–$$$ International Drive Area   CHINESE

Dine in a romantic setting, graced by lotus ponds filled with colorful koi while you're entertained by — get this — zither music. One of O-Town's favorite Chinese restaurants, and rated one of the country's best, Ming Court lets you rub elbows with more locals than tourists thanks to its innovative twists on traditional cuisine. The flavors are delicate and fresh. Try the grilled filet mignon with Szechuan seasoning or the lightly battered and deep-fried chicken with lemon-tangerine sauce. Portions are sufficient, there's a moderate wine list, and the service is excellent.

See map p. 143. 9188 International Dr. (between Sand Lake Rd. and Beachline Expwy.). ☎ *407-351-9988.* www.ming-court.com. *Reservations recommended. Main courses: Lunch $7–$13, dinner $13–$36. AE, DC, DISC, MC, V. Open: Daily 11 a.m.– 2:30 p.m. and 4:30–11:30 p.m.*

Dining Elsewhere in Orlando

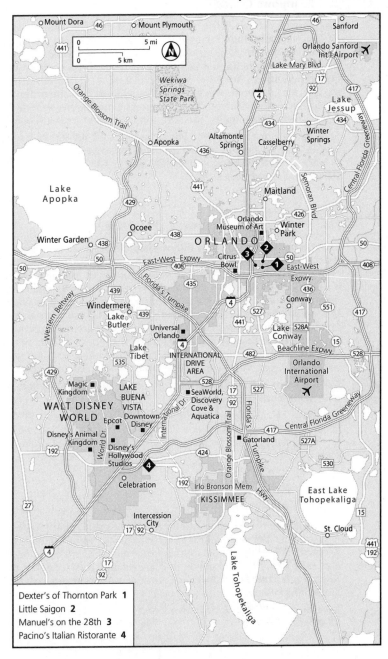

Dexter's of Thornton Park **1**
Little Saigon **2**
Manuel's on the 28th **3**
Pacino's Italian Ristorante **4**

Nine Dragons Restaurant
$$–$$$ Epcot CHINESE

Nine Dragons shines in the décor department, with carved rosewood paneling and an amazing dragon-motif ceiling. But the food doesn't match its surroundings, and portions tend to be smaller than what most expect in a Chinese restaurant. Dishes include spicy beef stir-fried with squash in sha cha sauce, lightly breaded lemon chicken, and a casserole of lobster, shrimp, and scallops with ginger and scallions. You can order Chinese or California wines with your meal. At press time, extensive refurbishments were underway, including the addition of an exhibition kitchen.

See map p. 141. In China Pavilion, World Showcase. ☎ *407-939-3463.* www.disney world.com. *Advanced Dining Reservations recommended. Main courses: Lunch $13–$20, dinner $13–$39; sampler for 2 $29–$44, for 4 $60. AE, DC, DISC, MC, V. Open: Daily 11:30 a.m. until park closing.*

'Ohana
$$$ Walt Disney World Resorts PACIFIC RIM

This restaurant in **Disney's Polynesian Resort** is a hit in the fun department, but the decibel level can climb pretty high. As your luau is prepared over an 18-foot fire pit, the staff keeps your eyes and ears busy. A storyteller is followed by coconut races in the center aisle, and then you can find out how to shake your booty during a hula lesson. After you're seated, the feeding frenzy begins in rapid succession. (Ask your waiter to slow down if the pace is too fast.) Included in the set menu is a variety of skewers (think shish kabob), including turkey, shrimp, steak, and pork with veggies; stir-fried rice; and more. You'll also find lots of trimmings and a full bar with limited wine selections (tropical cocktails cost extra).

Ask for a seat in the main dining room or you won't get a good view of the entertainment.

See map p. 134. 1600 Seven Seas Dr., in Disney's Polynesian Resort. ☎ *407-939-3463 or 407-824-2000.* www.disneyworld.com. *Advanced Dining Reservations strongly recommended. Fixed-price menu: $27 adults, $13 kids 3–9. AE, DC, DISC, MC, V. Open: Daily 5–10 p.m.*

Pacino's Italian Ristorante
$–$$$ Kissimmee ITALIAN

The ceiling of this restaurant contains fiber optics that create an aura of dining under the stars, but try the patio if you want the real thing. Some servers can be a little aloof, but the price and taste make up for it. Pacino's serves thick, juicy veal chops that are usually fork tender, a challenging 32-ounce porterhouse steak, and *frutti di mare* (shrimp, calamari, clams, and scallops) heaped onto a mound of linguine.

See map p. 151. 5795 W. Irlo Bronson Memorial Pkwy./Hwy. 192 (2 miles east of I-4). ☎ *407-396-8022.* www.pacinos.com. *Reservations recommended. Main courses: $8–$32 (most under $20). AE, MC, V. Open: Daily 4 p.m. to midnight.*

The Palm Restaurant
$$–$$$$ Universal Orlando   AMERICAN

This location in the **Hard Rock Hotel** is the 23rd member of a chain started more than 75 years ago in New York, and the food is good, if overpriced. The décor leans toward the upscale supper clubs of the '30s and '40s, and the walls are lined with caricatures of celebrities. Beef and seafood headline a menu that features a 36-ounce New York strip steak for two and a 3-pound Nova Scotia lobster. Smaller appetites and budgets can feast on salmon or veal chops.

See map p. 143. 5800 Universal Blvd., in the Hard Rock Hotel. ☎ *407-503-7256.* www. thepalm.com. *Reservations recommended. Main courses: $20–$52 (many under $30). AE, DC, DISC, MC, V. Open: Mon–Thurs 5–10 p.m., Fri–Sat 5–11 p.m., Sun 5–9 p.m. Validated parking is available.*

Pastamoré Ristorante & Market
$$ Universal Orlando   ITALIAN

This family-style restaurant greets you with display cases brimming with fresh mozzarella and other goodies. The antipasto primo is a meal in itself — it includes bruschetta, melon con prosciutto, olives, tomatoes caprese, fresh mozzarella, a medley of Italian cold cuts, and more. The menu also has traditional offerings such as veal Marsala, chicken parmigiana, fettuccine Alfredo, lasagna, and pizza. There's a basic beer and wine selection. The Marketplace Café, with a lighter menu of breakfast fare and sandwiches, serves from 8 a.m. to 2 a.m.

See map p. 347. 1000 Universal Studios Plaza, in CityWalk. ☎ *407-363-8000.* www. universalorlando.com. *Reservations recommended. Main courses: $11–$19. AE, DISC, MC, V. Open: Daily 5 p.m. to midnight.*

The Plaza Restaurant
$–$$ Magic Kingdom   AMERICAN

This intimate 19th-century-inspired restaurant, located at the end of Main Street, offers a respite from the Magic Kingdom crowds — and the world's best hot-fudge sundae. If you insist on a meal before dessert, the menu offers tasty but pricey burgers, hot and cold sandwiches (try the Reuben or the double-decker hot roast beef), salads, and milkshakes. You can eat inside in an Art Nouveau dining room or on a veranda overlooking Cinderella Castle.

See map p. 134. On Main Street. ☎ *407-939-3463.* www.disneyworld.com. *Advanced Dining Reservations recommended. Main courses: $10–$12, ice cream $4–$6. AE, DC, DISC, MC, V. Open: Daily 11 a.m. until park closing.*

Portobello Yacht Club
$$–$$$$ Downtown Disney   ITALIAN

The pizzas here go beyond the routine to *quattro formaggio* (four cheeses) and *margherita* (basil, plum tomatoes, and mozzarella). But it's the less-casual entrees that pack people into this place. On the menu, you may find wood-roasted Atlantic salmon or pasta with Alaskan king crab, scallops, shrimp, and clams in light wine sauce. Situated in a gabled Bermuda-style house, Portobello's covered patio overlooks Lake Buena Vista. Its cellar is small, but there's a nice selection of wines. *Note:* In late 2008, the Portobello Yacht Club will undergo a transformation, becoming the **Tuscan Country Trattoria.** Along with the name change will come a new menu, a redesigned interior, and an all-new outdoor dining space.

See map p. 134. 1650 Buena Vista Dr., in Pleasure Island. ☎ *407-934-8888.* www. levyrestaurants.com. *Advanced Dining Reservations recommended. Main courses: $18–$56, pizzas $9–$11. AE, DC, DISC, MC, V. Open: Daily 11:30 a.m.–3 p.m. and 5–11 p.m.*

Rainforest Café
$$–$$$ Downtown Disney and Disney's Animal Kingdom AMERICAN

Set amid a jungle with tropical sounds of birds and waterfalls, this place is a hit with kids. The food's pretty respectable (with an extensive menu), but it's really the décor that makes this restaurant. As its name suggests, entering the Rainforest Café is like walking into a jungle — lifelike silk plants, chattering animatronic monkeys and elephants, the occasional rain and thunder rumblings. Fun dishes include Caribbean Coconut Shrimp (with a sweet mango sauce) and Maya's Mixed Grill (ribs, chicken breast, and shrimp), but there are just too many to list. The bar stools resemble zebras, giraffes, and other wild-and-crazy critters.

Don't even think of showing up here without an Advanced Dining Reservation. Also be aware that you have to walk right by the souvenir shop to dine, so keep little heads turned to the left if you can.

See map p. 134. 1800 E. Buena Vista Dr., in Downtown Disney Marketplace. ☎ *407-827-8500. Second location outside the entrance to Disney's Animal Kingdom.* ☎ *407-938-9100.* www.rainforestcafe.com. *Advanced Dining Reservations strongly recommended. Main courses: $11–$40 (most under $25). AE, DISC, MC, V. Open: Downtown Disney Sun–Thurs 10:30 a.m.–11 p.m., Fri–Sat 10:30 a.m. to midnight; Disney's Animal Kingdom daily 8:30 a.m.–6:30 p.m.*

Rose & Crown Dining Room
$$ Epcot BRITISH

The Rose & Crown has dark-oak wainscoting, a beamed Tudor ceiling, English folk music, and spirited servers. Dine on such traditional dishes as fish and chips wrapped in newspaper, bangers and mash, cottage pie, and bread pudding. Bar food includes sausage rolls, a grilled London broil sandwich, and a Stilton cheese and fruit plate. You can order ale, lagers, and stouts by the pint or (designated-driver alert!) half-yard. The pub has an ale warmer to make sure Guinness is served at 55°F, just as its British guests prefer. If you only want to grab a pint or a snack at the bar, you don't need Advanced Dining Reservations.

The restaurant's outdoor seating (weather permitting) offers a fantastic view of **IllumiNations** (see Chapter 13 for details), making this an excellent spot for a late dinner. These seats are first-come, first served, so ask the hostess when you arrive if a patio table is available.

See map p. 141. In United Kingdom Pavilion, World Showcase. ☎ *407-939-3463.* www.disneyworld.com. *Advanced Dining Reservations recommended for dining room. Main courses: Lunch $12–$16, dinner $15–$24. AE, DC, DISC, MC, V. Open: Daily 11 a.m. until 1 hr. before park closing.*

Roy's Restaurant
$$–$$$ **Dr. Phillips Area   PACIFIC RIM**

Part of a small Hawaiian chain, this restaurant has an island theme and an atmosphere that allows for intimate conversation. Menus change often, but entrees may include blackened ahi with spicy soy mustard butter, roasted macadamia nut–crusted mahimahi with a lobster butter sauce, and hibachi-style grilled salmon with Japanese vegetables and citrus ponzu sauce. Roy's also has a reasonably deep wine list.

See map p. 143. 7760 W. Sand Lake Rd. (1 mile west of I-4). ☎ *407-352-4844.* www.roysrestaurant.com. *Reservations recommended. Main courses: $17–$36. AE, DC, DISC, MC, V. Open: Sun–Thurs 5:30–10 p.m., Fri–Sat 5:30–10:30 p.m.*

Samba Room
$$–$$$ **Dr. Phillips Area   CUBAN**

Given the almost ear-splitting decibel level, this place isn't one where you can whisper sweet nothings. But if you like loud salsa and an enterprising menu, Samba Room may be the place for you. The kitchen turns out plantain-crusted mahimahi on coconut rice; paella (chicken, mussels, fish, and sausage over rice); and sugar-cane beef tenderloin with chipotle mashed potatoes and mushroom *sofrito*. A patio offers alfresco dining.

See map p. 143. 7468 W. Sand Lake Rd. (1 mile west of I-4). ☎ *407-226-0550.* www.sambaroom.net. *Reservations recommended. Main courses: $9–$30. AE, DC, DISC, MC, V. Open: Mon–Thurs 11:30 a.m.–10 p.m., Fri–Sat 11:30 a.m. to midnight, Sun 4–10 p.m.*

San Angel Inn
$$–$$$ **Epcot   MEXICAN**

It's always night at the San Angel, where you'll eat at a romantic candlelit table in a hacienda courtyard surrounded by dense foliage. The shadow of a crumbling Yucatán pyramid looms in the distance, and you hear the sound of faraway birds and faint rumblings of the volcano while you dine. The ambience of this restaurant, located inside the Mexico Pavilion, is exotic, and the fare is traditional — that's why you won't find nachos on the menu. Entrees may include *mole poblano* (chicken simmered with more than 20 spices and a hint of chocolate) and *filete motuleño* (grilled beef tenderloin served over black beans, melted cheese, pepper strips, and plantains). Your drinking options include Dos Equis beer and margaritas. A new tequila bar opened right nearby, and an expansion of the restaurant itself, including an all-new menu, was in the works at press time.

See map p. 141. In Mexico Pavilion, World Showcase. ☎ ***407-939-3463.*** www.disney world.com. *Advanced Dining Reservations recommended. Main courses: Lunch $13–$19, dinner $20–$27. AE, DC, DISC, MC, V. Open: Daily 11:30 a.m. until park closing.*

Sci-Fi Dine-In Theater
$$ Disney's Hollywood Studios AMERICAN

Horror flicks too hokey to be scary play on the screen while you dine in a replica of a 1950s drive-in movie emporium, complete with tables ensconced in flashy, chrome-trimmed convertible cars. Fun-loving carhops deliver free popcorn and your meal. This is basic fare such as sandwiches, burgers, chicken, ribs, seafood, pasta, and steaks. The unique atmosphere definitely keeps the crowds and the kids coming.

See map p. 218. Near Indiana Jones Epic Stunt Spectacular! ☎ ***407-939-3463.*** www. disneyworld.com. *Advanced Dining Reservations recommended. Main courses: $11–$20. AE, DC, DISC, MC, V. Open: Daily 11 a.m. until park closing.*

Spoodles
$$ Walt Disney World Resorts MEDITERRANEAN

Tapas, pizza, and pasta are the main items on the menu at this Mediterranean-style restaurant at **Disney's BoardWalk Inn,** which features an exhibition kitchen and a lively atmosphere. The treats include Mediterranean dips with toasted pita, marinated olives, and almonds, followed by entrees such as pan-roasted red snapper with saffron couscous, greens, and a spicy tomato sauce, or lemon garlic shrimp linguini with preserved lemon, parsley, and shaved garlic. A respectable wine list and tableside sangria presentations add something special to the evening.

During the height of summer, Spoodles gets crowded, and the wait can be long, even with Advanced Dining Reservations, so this restaurant isn't a good choice for famished families coming straight from the parks, and it's really not a great choice for families with young kids along either.

See map p. 134. 2101 N. Epcot Resorts Blvd., in Disney's BoardWalk Inn. ☎ ***407-939-3463*** *or 407-939-2380.* www.disneyworld.com. *Advanced Dining Reservations recommended. Main courses: Breakfast $8–$15, dinner $18–$23. AE, DC, DISC, MC, V. Open: Daily 7–11 a.m., noon to 2 p.m., and 5–10 p.m.*

Teppan Edo
$$–$$$ Epcot JAPANESE

Formerly known as the Teppanyaki Dining Room, this popular Epcot eatery reopened as Teppan Edo in 2007. Although the overall dining experience remains the same, the interior has been updated. If you've ever been to a Japanese steakhouse, you know the drill: Diners sit around the large grill-tables while the chefs expertly dice, slice, and stir-fry the chicken, steak, scallops, and lobster, serving your food to your plate with amazing dexterity. Kids especially enjoy watching the chef wield a cleaver and other utensils. Several parties are seated at *teppanyaki* tables, which make for sociable dining, especially for single travelers looking for conversation. Kirin beer, plum wine, and sake are served. *Note:* The neighboring Tempura Kiku and the Matsunoma Lounge have been replaced with an all-new sushi-based eatery named **Tokyo Dining.**

See map p. 141. In Japan Pavilion, World Showcase. ☎ *407-939-3463.* www.disney world.com. *Advanced Dining Reservations recommended. Main courses: Lunch $14–$25, dinner $16–$30. AE, DC, DISC, MC, V. Open: Daily 11 a.m. until 1 hr. before park closing.*

Todd English's bluezoo
$$–$$$$ Walt Disney World Resorts   SEAFOOD

In 2004, celebrity chef Todd English put down roots at the **Walt Disney World Dolphin** with this restaurant, which features innovative seafood in an unusually vibrant and upscale setting. The food is served with an artistic flair almost as impressive as the décor. Try the miso-glazed Chilean sea bass or the rotisserie-roasted catch of the day. Shellfish lovers will enjoy the raw bar (just be sure to bring your wallet!).

See map p. 134. 1500 Epcot Resorts Blvd., in the Walt Disney World Dolphin. ☎ *407-934-1111.* www.thebluezoo.com. *Advanced Dining Reservations recommended. Main courses: $20–$58. AE, DISC, MC, V. Open: Daily 3:30–11 p.m.*

Victoria & Albert's
$$$$ Walt Disney World Resorts   INTERNATIONAL

This restaurant is the most memorable (and memorably expensive) in WDW. But if money's no object, and you're serious about food and romance going hand in hand, head to this intimate Victorian dining room at **Disney's Grand Floridian Resort.** The food is impeccable and presented with a flourish by an attentive and professional staff. (Each table has servers named Victoria and Albert.) The seven-course menu changes nightly. You may begin with roasted duck with candy-striped and golden beets, followed by Monterey abalone with lemon and baby spinach. Shrimp bisque may precede an entree such as Australian Kobe beef tenderloin. English Stilton served with a poached pear sets up desserts such as vanilla-bean crème brûlée and Kona chocolate soufflé. Dinners are 2½- to 3-hour affairs, though the later seating can run longer. If you want to try the chef's table (you actually dine in the kitchen and watch them prepare your meal), be sure to reserve it excruciatingly early (Advanced Dining Reservations are taken up to 180 days in advance). *Note:* I don't recommend this restaurant for children.

See map p. 134. 4401 Floridian Way, in Disney's Grand Floridian Resort & Spa. ☎ *407-939-3463.* www.disneyworld.com. *Advanced Dining Reservations required well in advance, especially for the chef's table. Fixed-price menu: $125 per person, $185 with wine pairing; chef's table $165, $235 with wine. AE, DC, DISC, MC, V. Open:*

Sept–June, 2 dinner seatings daily, 5:45–6:30 p.m. and 9–9:45 p.m.; July–Aug, 1 seating daily, 6:45–8 p.m.; chef's table 6 p.m. only. Jackets required for men.

Wolfgang Puck Grand Café
$$–$$$ Downtown Disney   AMERICAN

This restaurant's sushi bar, an artistic copper-and-terrazzo masterpiece, delivers some of the best sushi in Orlando. Or you can eat gourmet pizza with exotic toppings on the patio or inside. Upstairs, the main dining room presents a seasonally changing menu that may feature braised duck pappardelle with oven-roasted tomatoes, blanched garlic, thyme, and a duck stock reduction, or shrimp garganelli sautéed with garlic, shrimp stock, and tomato sauce. The lower level can be noisy, and the downstairs wait for a table is agonizingly long. Puck's also has a grab-and-go express restaurant that sells sandwiches, pizzas, desserts, and more.

See map p. 134. 1482 Buena Vista Dr., in Disney's West Side. ☎ *407-938-9653.* www. wolfgangpuck.com. *Advanced Dining Reservations recommended for lower-level dining room. Main courses (upstairs): $22–$37, pizzas and sushi $11–$35. AE, DC, DISC, MC, V. Daily 11:30 a.m.–11 p.m.*

Yachtsman Steakhouse
$$–$$$$ Walt Disney World Resorts   STEAKS

Regarded as one of Orlando's top steak-and-chop houses, the Yachtsman Steakhouse at **Disney's Yacht Club Resort** is a good place to come if you love red meat. You can see the cuts age in a glass-enclosed room, and the exhibition kitchen provides a tantalizing glimpse of steaks, chops, and seafood being grilled over oak and hickory. The décor includes knotty-pine beams, plank floors, and leather-and-oak chairs. Steak options range from an 8-ounce filet to a belly-busting 24-ounce T-bone. A filet and warm-water lobster-tail combo tops the price chart. The menu also includes pan-seared sea bass, free-range chicken, and roasted winter squash ravioli, among other choices. The Yachtsman is prone to crowds, but most folks say that it's worth the wait.

See map p. 134. 1700 Epcot Resorts Blvd., in Disney's Yacht Club Resort. ☎ *407-939-3463.* www.disneyworld.com. *Advanced Dining Reservations recommended. Main courses: $21–$80. AE, DC, DISC, MC, V. Open: Daily 5:30–10 p.m.*

Yak & Yeti
$–$$ Disney's Animal Kingdom   ASIAN

Animal Kingdom's newest dining spot opened in Asia (near Expedition Everest) in fall 2007. This Pan-Asian eatery blends into the surrounding Himalayan village thanks to its eclectic and meticulously detailed décor. Specialties include crispy wok-fried green beans (even the kids will love these); lettuce cups filled with minced chicken, chopped veggies, and a yummy maple tamarind sauce; seared miso salmon; and maple tamarind chicken. Leave room for dessert — the mango pie and fried wontons

To the Pointe

Thanks to a recent multimillion-dollar redevelopment, **Pointe Orlando**, 9101 International Dr. (☎ 407-248-2838; www.pointeorlando.com), is brimming with outdoor walkways and inviting courtyards lined with shops and upscale eateries, among the area's newest and trendiest. Here are a handful of noteworthy newcomers (all found at the Pointe):

✔ **B. B. King's Blues Club** (☎ 407-370-4550; http://orlando.bbkingclubs.com) features Southern cuisine ranging from barbecue ribs to Carolina glazed salmon amid live music, four full-service bars, and an inviting patio.

✔ **The Capital Grille** (☎ 407-370-4392; www.capitalgrille.com) offers a menu filled with tempting appetizers, dry-aged steaks, hand-carved chops, fresh seafood, decadent desserts, and an extensive wine list combined with impeccable service and elegant surroundings.

✔ **Maggiano's Little Italy** (☎ 407-241-8650; www.maggianos.com) serves up specialties such as lobster ravioli (basil and saffron pasta stuffed with fresh lobster and served in a light cream sauce) and braised beef cannelloni (with Asiago and Parmesan cheeses). The warm, inviting atmosphere makes you feel as if you're stepping into a neighborhood Italian kitchen.

✔ **The Oceanaire Seafood Room** (☎ 407-363-4801; www.theoceanaire.com) is a sophisticated establishment that combines a menu filled with fresh seafood (flown in daily), an award-wining wine list, and an atmosphere that's reminiscent of a 1930s supper club (albeit it chic and updated). The incredibly knowledgeable and friendly staff round out the exceptional experience.

✔ **Taverna Opa** (☎ 407-351-8660; www.opaorlando.com) diners will appreciate the authentic Greek fare, casual setting, and down-to-earth prices. Later in the evening, a far more festive atmosphere prevails as plate-breaking and napkin-throwing are common occurrences.

✔ **Tommy Bahama's Tropical Café & Emporium** (☎ 321-281-5888; www.tommybahama.com) has an eclectic yet elegant décor that's evocative of the Pacific Rim. The menu is filled with island-inspired entrees such as sautéed jumbo shrimp and scallops in a curry coconut sauce. For those who prefer to dine outdoors, the patio is the place to be.

(served with skewers of pineapple, vanilla ice cream, and a sweet honey vanilla drizzle) are simply delish. Kids will appreciate the mini burgers, veggie lo mein, eggrolls, and chicken bites. For those who prefer to dine outdoors, counter service is available to the right of the main restaurant.

See map p. 134. Asia, near Expedition Everest. ☎ *407-939-3463.* www.disneyworld.com. *Advanced Dining Reservations redcommended. Main courses: $15–$24, under $8 kids ages 3–9. AE, DC, DISC, MC, V. Open: Daily 11 a.m. to park closing.*

Dining with Disney Characters

The opportunity to chow down with Mickey, Donald, Cinderella, and other characters is the major dining experience in Orlando. The eight-and-under crowd usually gets starry-eyed when characters show up to say howdy, sign autographs, pose for photos, and encourage them to eat their broccoli. Character mealtime appearances at Disney parks, attractions, and resorts are incredibly popular. As a result, one-on-one interaction is somewhat brief, so be ready for that Kodak moment — or hope a WDW photographer captures it for you (at a premium price).

You may not find a seat if you show up to a character appearance unannounced, so call ☎ **407-939-3463** to make **Advanced Dining Reservations** as far in advance as possible (these reservations don't lock down a table, but they do give you the next available table after you arrive at your appointed time). To take the guesswork out of figuring out how far in advance (60 days? 90? 180?) you need to make Advanced Dining Reservations, head online to the **PS Planning Guide** (www.ps calculator.net). This unofficial site does a very good job of keeping up to date on all the rules and reservation windows for every restaurant at Disney — but its best feature is a calculator that allows you to punch in your desired reservation date, and then tells you when reservations window for your chosen restaurant will be open.

The cost of catching characters

The prices for character meals are much the same, no matter where you're dining (with one exception — Cinderella's Royal Table). Breakfast (most serve it) runs $19 to $33 for adults and $11 to $23 for kids 3 to 9; those that serve dinner charge $28 to $45 for adults and $13 to $26 for kids. The prices vary a bit from location to location. In general, the character meals listed here score high on the fun front, but are middle-of-the-road when it comes to the food.

Character meals accept American Express, Diners Club, Discover, MasterCard, Visa, and the Disney card. For more information on these meals, check Disney's Web site at www.disneyworld.com.

The most characters money can buy

Although I mention specific characters here, be advised that WDW frequently changes its lineups, so don't promise the kids a specific character or you may get burned. Also, keep in mind that you'll have to *add the price of admission* (and, if you aren't a Disney resort guest, the $12 parking fee) to meals served inside the theme parks. Remember that some very young kids may actually end up scared of — and not delighted with — the larger-than-life characters at these meals.

Character dining at Universal Orlando

Though it's the recognized leader in the category, Disney doesn't have a lock on character dining in Orlando. At **Islands of Adventure,** you can have breakfast with Spider-Man, the Cat in the Hat, and other Marvel and Dr. Seuss characters Thursday through Sunday from park opening to 10:30 a.m. at the Confisco Grille. The cost is $16 for adults and $10 for children 3 to 9, plus tax and tip. Call ☎ **407-224-4012** for the mandatory reservations.

Cape May Café

This delightful New England–themed dining room offers buffet breakfasts (eggs, pancakes, bacon, pastries) hosted by **Admiral Goofy, Chip 'n' Dale,** and **Pluto** (but the characters that show up may vary).

See map p. 134. 1800 Epcot Resorts Blvd., in Disney's Beach Club Resort. Character breakfast: $19 adults, $11 children. Open: Daily 7:30–11:30 a.m.

Chef Mickey's

This whimsical spot welcomes **Mickey** and various pals twice a day: at buffet breakfasts and dinners. Entrees change daily and are joined by a salad bar, soups, vegetables, and ice cream with toppings.

See map p. 134. 4600 N. World Dr., in Disney's Contemporary Resort. Character breakfast: $19 adults, $11 children. Character dinner: $28 adults, $13 children. Open: Daily 7:30–11:30 a.m. and 5–9:30 p.m.

Cinderella's Royal Table

Cinderella Castle — the focal point of the park — is the setting for a character breakfast buffet daily; it recently began serving a character lunch and dinner (with a choice of appetizer, entree, salad, and dessert from a fixed menu) as well. Princess hosts vary, but **Cinderella** always puts in an appearance; the **Fairy Godmother** joins in for dinner.

Advanced Dining Reservations are a must here. I suggest you begin trying as soon as the reservations window opens up 90 days in advance (call exactly at 7 a.m.; if you get through on your first try, don't be picky about seating arrangements and dining times). *Note:* At the time you make your reservations, your credit card will be charged in full.

See map p. 134. In Cinderella Castle, Magic Kingdom. Character breakfast: $33 adults, $23 children. Character lunch: $36 adults, $24 children. Character dinner: $41 adults, $26 children. Open: Daily 8–10:20 a.m., noon to 3 p.m., and 4 p.m. to park closing.

The Crystal Palace

The real treats here are the characters, **Winnie the Pooh** and his pals, who are on location throughout the day. The restaurant serves breakfast (eggs,

French toast, pancakes, bacon), lunch, and dinner (a variety of beef, chicken, veggies, kids' favorites, a sundae bar, and more).

See map p. 134. On Main St., Magic Kingdom. Character breakfast: $19 adults, $11 children. Character lunch: $21 adults, $12 children. Character dinner: $28 adults, $13 children. Open: Daily 8–10:30 a.m., 11:30 a.m.–2:45 p.m., and 4 p.m. until park closing.

Donald's Safari Breakfast

This buffet of eggs, bacon, French toast, and other favorites is held at the newly renovated Tusker House in Africa. **Donald, Daisy, Mickey,** and **Goofy** are on hand to entertain the little ones. *Note:* This is the only place in Disney's Animal Kingdom that offers a character breakfast.

See map p. 134. In Tusker House, Africa, Disney's Animal Kingdom. Character breakfast: $19 adults, $11 children. Open: Daily from park opening until 10:30 a.m.

Garden Grill

There's a Mom's-in-the-kitchen theme at this revolving restaurant with comfortable booths. **Mickey** and **Chip 'n' Dale** play host to family-style meals with a country theme. Lunch and dinner (chicken, fish, steak, vegetables, and potatoes) are served.

See map p. 141. In the Land Pavilion, Epcot. Character lunch: $21 adults, $12 children. Character dinner: $28 adults, $13 children. Open: Daily 11 a.m.–3 p.m. and 4:30 p.m. until park closing.

Garden View Lounge

Every day except Tuesday and Saturday, **Princess Aurora** (aka **Sleeping Beauty**) hosts the **My Disney Girl's Perfectly Princess Tea Party** for all the little princesses in the tea lounge at Disney's Grand Floridian Resort. Girls ages 3 to 11 will receive a My Disney Girl collectible doll dressed in a matching Princess Aurora gown, while boys receive a teddy bear fit for a king.

See map p. 134. 4401 Floridian Way, in Disney's Grand Floridian Resort & Spa. Tea party: $250 for one adult and one child age 3–11; $85 each additional adult, $165 each additional child. Open: Sun, Mon, Wed–Fri 10:30 a.m. to noon.

1900 Park Fare

The elegant Grand Floridian Resort hosts character breakfasts (eggs, French toast, bacon, and pancakes) and dinners (prime rib, pork loin, fish, and more) in the festive, exposition-themed 1900 Park Fare. Big Bertha — a 100-year-old French band organ that plays pipes, drums, bells, cymbals, castanets, and the xylophone — provides music. **Mary Poppins, Alice in Wonderland,** and friends appear at breakfast; **Cinderella** and friends show up for **Cinderella's Gala Feast** at dinner.

See map p. 134. 4401 Floridian Way, in Disney's Grand Floridian Resort & Spa. Character breakfast: $19 adults, $11 children. Character dinner: $30 adults, $15 children. Open: Daily 7:30–11 a.m. and 5–9 p.m.

'Ohana's Best Friends Breakfast with Lilo & Stitch

Traditional breakfast foods (eggs, pancakes, bacon, and more) are pre-pared on an 18-foot fire pit and served family style at this Polynesian-themed restaurant. **Mickey, Pluto, Lilo,** and **Stitch** appear, and children can participate with musical instruments in a special parade.

See map p. 134. 1600 Seven Seas Dr., in Disney's Polynesian Resort. Character break-fast: $19 adults, $11 children. Open: Daily 7:30–11 a.m.

Princess Storybook Dining

Snow White, Mary Poppins, Princess Aurora, Pocahontas, or **Belle** might show up at this character meal. Because of its popularity, the restaurant now offers a lunch (lamb, chicken, salmon, veggies, salads, kids' favorites, and dessert) and dinner (lamb, salmon, venison stew, pasta, veggies, salads, and dessert) in addition to breakfast.

Advanced Dining Reservations are a must here. I suggest you begin trying as soon as the reservations window opens 180 days in advance.

See map p. 141. In Akershus Royal Banquet Hall, Norway Pavilion, World Showcase, Epcot. Character breakfast: $23 adults, $13 children. Character lunch: $25 adults, $14 children. Character dinner: $29 adults, $14 children. Open: Daily 8:30–10:10 a.m., 11:40 a.m.–2:50 p.m., and 4:20–8:40 p.m.

Index of Restaurants by Neighborhood

Disney's Animal Kingdom

Rainforest Café (American, $$–$$$)
Yak & Yeti (Asian, $–$$)

Disney's Hollywood Studios

50's Prime Time Café (American, $$)
Hollywood Brown Derby (American, $$–$$$)
Sci-Fi Dine-In Theater (American, $$)

Downtown Disney

Earl of Sandwich (American, $)
Fulton's Crab House (Seafood, $$–$$$)
House of Blues (American, $$–$$$)
Portobello Yacht Club (Italian, $$–$$$$)
Rainforest Café (American, $$–$$$)
Wolfgang Puck Grand Café (American, $$–$$$)

Downtown Orlando

Dexter's of Thornton Park (International, $–$$)
Little Saigon (Vietnamese, $)
Manuel's on the 28th (International, $$$)

Dr. Phillips Area

Christini's (Italian, $$–$$$)
Roy's Restaurant (Pacific Rim, $$–$$$)
Samba Room (Cuban, $$–$$$)

Epcot

Akershus Royal Banquet Hall (Norwegian, $$–$$$)
Coral Reef Restaurant (Seafood, $$–$$$)
Le Cellier Steakhouse (Steaks, $$–$$$)
Les Chefs de France (French, $$–$$$)
Lotus Blossom Café (Chinese, $)

Marrakesh (Moroccan, $$–$$$)
Nine Dragons Restaurant (Chinese,
$$–$$$)
Rose & Crown Dining Room
(British, $$)
San Angel Inn (Mexican, $$–$$$)
Teppan Edo (Japanese, $$–$$$)

International Drive Area
B-Line Diner (American, $–$$)
Bubbalou's Bodacious BBQ
(American, $–$$)
Café Tu Tu Tango (International,
$$–$$$)
Dux (International, $$$)
Ming Court (Chinese, $$–$$$)

Kissimmee
Pacino's Italian Ristorante (Italian,
$–$$$)

Lake Buena Vista
Hemingway's (Seafood, $$$)

Magic Kingdom
Liberty Tree Tavern (American,
$$–$$$)
The Plaza Restaurant (American, $–$$)

Universal Orlando
Bice Ristorante (Italian, $$–$$$)
Bob Marley–A Tribute to Freedom
(Caribbean, $–$$)

Emeril's Orlando (New Orleans,
$$–$$$)
Emeril's Tchoup Chop (Pacific Rim,
$$–$$$)
Jimmy Buffett's Margaritaville
(Caribbean, $$)
The Palm Restaurant (American,
$$–$$$$)
Pastamoré Ristorante & Market
(Italian, $$)

Universal Orlando Area
Kim Wu (Chinese, $–$$)

Walt Disney World Resorts
Artist Point (Seafood/Steaks, $$–$$$)
Boatwright's Dining Hall (New
Orleans, $–$$)
Boma–Flavors of Africa (African, $$)
California Grill (American, $$–$$$)
Citricos (French, $$$)
Flying Fish Café (Seafood, $$$)
Il Mulino New York Trattoria (Italian,
$$$)
Jiko–The Cooking Place (African,
$$–$$$)
'Ohana (Pacific Rim, $$$)
Spoodles (Mediterranean, $$)
Todd English's bluezoo (Seafood,
$$–$$$$)
Victoria & Albert's (International,
$$$$)
Yachtsman Steakhouse (Steaks,
$$–$$$$)

Index of Restaurants by Cuisine

African
Boma–Flavors of Africa (Walt Disney
World Resorts, $$)
Jiko–The Cooking Place (Walt Disney
World Resorts, $$–$$$)

American
B-Line Diner (International Drive Area,
$–$$)
Bubbalou's Bodacious BBQ
(International Drive Area, $–$$)

California Grill (Walt Disney World
Resorts, $$–$$$)
Earl of Sandwich (Downtown
Disney, $)
50's Prime Time Café (Disney's
Hollywood Studios, $$)
Hollywood Brown Derby (Disney's
Hollywood Studios, $$–$$$)
House of Blues (Downtown Disney,
$$–$$$)

Liberty Tree Tavern (Magic Kingdom, $$–$$$)
The Palm Restaurant (Universal Orlando, $$–$$$$)
The Plaza Restaurant (Magic Kingdom, $–$$)
Rainforest Café (Downtown Disney and Disney's Animal Kingdom, $$–$$$)
Sci-Fi Dine-In Theater (Disney's Hollywood Studios, $$)
Wolfgang Puck Grand Café (Downtown Disney, $$–$$$)

Asian
Yak & Yeti (Disney's Animal Kingdom, $–$$)

British
Rose & Crown Dining Room (Epcot, $$)

Caribbean
Bob Marley–A Tribute to Freedom (Universal Orlando, $–$$)
Jimmy Buffett's Margaritaville (Universal Orlando, $$)

Chinese
Kim Wu (Universal Orlando Area, $–$$)
Lotus Blossom Café (Epcot, $)
Ming Court (International Drive Area, $$–$$$)
Nine Dragons Restaurant (Epcot, $$–$$$)

Cuban
Samba Room (Dr. Phillips Area, $$–$$$)

French
Citricos (Walt Disney World Resorts, $$$)
Les Chefs de France (Epcot, $$–$$$)

International
Café Tu Tu Tango (International Drive Area, $$–$$$)

Dexter's of Thornton Park (Downtown Orlando, $–$$)
Dux (International Drive Area, $$$)
Manuel's on the 28th (Downtown Orlando, $$$)
Victoria & Albert's (Walt Disney World Resorts, $$$$)

Italian
Bice Ristorante (Universal Orlando, $$–$$$)
Christini's (Dr. Phillips Area, $$–$$$)
Il Mulino New York Trattoria (Walt Disney World Resorts, $$$)
Pacino's Italian Ristorante (Kissimmee, $–$$$)
Pastamoré Ristorante & Market (Universal Orlando, $$)
Portobello Yacht Club (Downtown Disney, $$–$$$$)

Japanese
Teppan Edo (Epcot, $$–$$$)

Mediterranean
Spoodles (Walt Disney World Resorts, $$)

Mexican
San Angel Inn (Epcot, $$–$$$)

Moroccan
Marrakesh (Epcot, $$–$$$)

New Orleans
Boatwright's Dining Hall (Walt Disney World Resorts, $–$$)
Emeril's Orlando (Universal Orlando, $$–$$$)

Norwegian
Akershus Royal Banquet Hall (Epcot, $$–$$$)

Pacific Rim
Emeril's Tchoup Chop (Universal Orlando, $$–$$$)

'Ohana (Walt Disney World Resorts, $$$)

Roy's Restaurant (Dr. Phillips Area, $$–$$$)

Seafood

Artist Point (Walt Disney World Resorts, $$–$$$)

Coral Reef Restaurant (Epcot, $$–$$$)

Flying Fish Café (Walt Disney World Resorts, $$$)

Fulton's Crab House (Downtown Disney, $$–$$$)

Hemingway's (Lake Buena Vista, $$$)

Todd English's bluezoo (Walt Disney World Resorts, $$–$$$$)

Steaks

Artist Point (Walt Disney World Resorts, $$–$$$)

Le Cellier Steakhouse (Epcot, $$–$$$)

Yachtsman Steakhouse (Walt Disney World Resorts, $$–$$$$)

Vietnamese

Little Saigon (Downtown Orlando, $)

Index of Restaurants by Price

$$$$

The Palm Restaurant (American, Universal Orlando)

Portobello Yacht Club (Italian, Downtown Disney)

Todd English's bluezoo (Seafood, Walt Disney World Resorts)

Victoria & Albert's (International, Walt Disney World Resorts)

Yachtsman Steakhouse (Steaks, Walt Disney World Resorts)

$$$

Akershus Royal Banquet Hall (Norwegian, Epcot)

Artist Point (Seafood/Steaks, Walt Disney World Resorts)

Bice Ristorante (Italian, Universal Orlando)

Café Tu Tu Tango (International, International Drive Area)

California Grill (American, Walt Disney World Resorts)

Christini's (Italian, Dr. Phillips Area)

Citricos (French, Walt Disney World Resorts)

Coral Reef Restaurant (Seafood, Epcot)

Dux (International, International Drive Area)

Emeril's Orlando (New Orleans, Universal Orlando)

Emeril's Tchoup Chop (Pacific Rim, Universal Orlando)

Flying Fish Café (Seafood, Walt Disney World Resorts)

Fulton's Crab House (Seafood, Downtown Disney)

Hemingway's (Seafood, Lake Buena Vista)

Hollywood Brown Derby (American, Disney's Hollywood Studios)

House of Blues (American, Downtown Disney)

Il Mulino New York Trattoria (Italian, Walt Disney World Resorts)

Jiko–The Cooking Place (African, Walt Disney World Resorts)

Le Cellier Steakhouse (Steaks, Epcot)

Les Chefs de France (French, Epcot)

Liberty Tree Tavern (American, Magic Kingdom)

Manuel's on the 28th (International, Downtown Orlando)

Marrakesh (Moroccan, Epcot)

Ming Court (Chinese, International Drive Area)

Nine Dragons Restaurant (Chinese, Epcot)

'Ohana (Pacific Rim, Walt Disney World Resorts)

Pacino's Italian Ristorante (Italian, Kissimmee)

Rainforest Café (American, Downtown Disney and Disney's Animal Kingdom)

Roy's Restaurant (Pacific Rim, Dr. Phillips Area)

Samba Room (Cuban, Dr. Phillips Area)

San Angel Inn (Mexican, Epcot)

Teppan Edo (Japanese, Epcot)

Wolfgang Puck Grand Café (American, Downtown Disney)

$$

B-Line Diner (American, International Drive Area)

Boatwright's Dining Hall (New Orleans, Walt Disney World Resorts)

Bob Marley–A Tribute to Freedom (Caribbean, Universal Orlando)

Boma–Flavors of Africa (African, Walt Disney World Resorts)

Bubbalou's Bodacious BBQ (American, International Drive Area)

Dexter's of Thornton Park (International, Downtown Orlando)

50's Prime Time Café (American, Disney's Hollywood Studios)

Jimmy Buffett's Margaritaville (Caribbean, Universal Orlando)

Kim Wu (Chinese, Universal Orlando Area)

Pastamoré Ristorante & Market (Italian, Universal Orlando)

The Plaza Restaurant (American, Magic Kingdom)

Rose & Crown Dining Room (British, Epcot)

Sci-Fi Dine-In Theater (American, Disney's Hollywood Studios)

Spoodles (Mediterranean, Walt Disney World Resorts)

Yak & Yeti (Asian, Disney's Animal Kingdom)

$

Earl of Sandwich (American, Downtown Disney)

Little Saigon (Vietnamese, Downtown Orlando)

Lotus Blossom Café (Chinese, Epcot)

Part IV
Exploring Walt Disney World

By Rich Tennant

"I know these are your characters' names, but when you're around guests at the theme park, you're neither sleepy, dopey, nor grumpy."

In this part . . .

1 have some great news for you: You're going to visit the "Happiest Place on Earth." And now for the bad news: If you neglect to plan ahead, you may just be the unhappiest person there.

In an average year, more than 47 million people find their way to Disney's four major theme parks, and all are determined to ride the same rides and eat in the same restaurants as you — sometimes it seems as if all at the same time! You'll have much more fun if you arrive knowing which parks and attractions are best suited to your tastes and which places aren't worth the effort. In this part, I guide you through matching up the parks' features to your liking so that you can decide where you want to spend the majority of your time.

Chapter 11

Getting Acquainted with Walt Disney World

In This Chapter

▶ Familiarizing yourself with the Disney parks
▶ Getting to and around the Disney empire
▶ Pricing the cost of your visit
▶ Getting around the crowds
▶ Maximizing your fun and minimizing your wait

*T*he first time I made a pilgrimage to the Magic Kingdom, I wandered in slack-jawed awe among the many marvels of Mickeyville.

Today, I marvel at a different wonder: growth. Walt Disney's legacy has exploded in the last three decades. It has truly become a world unto itself, with four theme parks, nearly a dozen smaller parks and attractions, clubs, hotels, restaurants, shopping districts, its own transit system, and two cruise ships. It's enough to fog your brain, but that's why I'm here — to defog and demystify the planning process.

In this and the next several chapters, I introduce you to the parks, tantalize you with ride descriptions, and offer you some suggested itineraries. With many thanks to my own children and those of my sisters and friends, I also use a special rating system to give you a kid's view ("Kid Rating") of the rides and shows in the parks. My reviews are based on those of my children: Ryan (15), Austin (13), Nicolas (11), Hailey (9), and Davis (7).

Introducing Walt's World

Disney's four main theme parks line the western half of this 30,500-acre world. The Magic Kingdom is the original attraction; with over 17 million visitors in 2007, it was busier than any other U.S. theme park. Epcot was third busiest with 10.9 million visitors, followed by Disney's Hollywood Studios at 9.5 million, which tied with Disney's Animal Kingdom with just over 9.5 million. (In case you're wondering, Disneyland, in California, holds the number-two slot.) Here's a quick look at what you can find in all four Disney parks:

- ✔ **Magic Kingdom:** Built as Disney's flagship park, the Magic Kingdom is divided into seven themed lands. They're laid out like the spokes of a wheel, with the park's icon — **Cinderella Castle** — at the hub. Anyone with kids, or who is just young at heart, needs to give the Magic Kingdom at least one full day. It offers more for young children than any other Orlando theme park, but it has broad appeal for first-timers and Disney fans, too. If you fall into these categories, I recommend two days or more, provided you have the time and the budget. (See Chapter 12 for more details about the Magic Kingdom.)

- ✔ **Epcot:** Built as an exposition of human achievement and new technology (albeit a somewhat commercialized version), Epcot is symbolized by **Spaceship Earth,** an attraction often described as "that big silver golf ball." **Future World,** the first of Epcot's two sections, has innovative exhibits and rides. This part of the park is also home to three of Disney's newest rides: **The Seas with Nemo & Friends, Soarin',** and **Mission: SPACE.** The far end of the park, **World Showcase,** consists of a lagoon surrounded by pavilions showcasing the cultures of 11 countries. Allowing two days for the shows, rides, shops, and ethnic restaurants in Epcot is a good idea. (See Chapter 13 for more details about Epcot.)

  Even with improvements, this park remains the least attractive for tinier tots, but the best one for inquiring minds and those who appreciate the world's unique cultures (as well as ethnic dining; see Chapter 10).

- ✔ **Disney's Hollywood Studios:** This showbiz-themed park is reminiscent of the Tinseltown of the 1930s and 1940s. It blends working studios with shows such as **Lights, Motors, Action! Extreme Stunt Show** and **Indiana Jones Epic Stunt Spectacular!,** as well as thrill rides such as the **Twilight Zone Tower of Terror** and **Rock 'n' Roller Coaster Starring Aerosmith.** Young kids will find plenty of cool things to occupy their time here; though they won't be able to ride the park's two biggest thrillers, they can definitely hop aboard **Toy Story Mania!,** an all-new interactive midway-style ride (think Buzz Lightyear's Space Ranger Spin with a retro midway twist). And best of all for the foot-weary: You can tackle this part of WDW in only one day, and a more relaxed one at that. (See Chapter 14 for more details about Disney's Hollywood Studios.)

- ✔ **Disney's Animal Kingdom:** The newest Disney kid on the block is symbolized by the 14-story **Tree of Life,** which is to this park what Cinderella Castle is to the Magic Kingdom. At this park, guests explore the mysteries of Asia, the African savanna, and even the age of the dinosaur. Shows include **Finding Nemo–The Musical** (Disney's newest production), the **Festival of the Lion King,** and **It's Tough to be a Bug!** You can also find rides such as **Expedition**

Walt Disney World Parks and Attractions

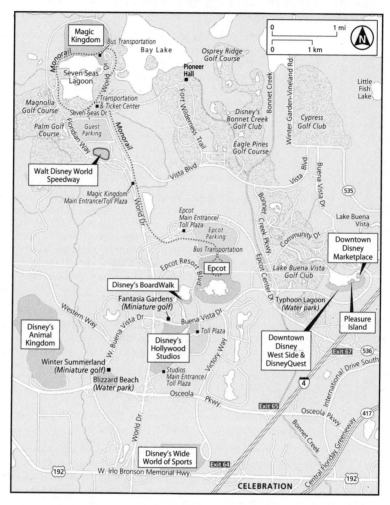

Everest–Legend of the Forbidden Mountain, Kilimanjaro Safaris, and **DINOSAUR.** You won't have trouble touring Animal Kingdom in one day, but keep in mind that this park is best seen early in the day. (See Chapter 15 for more details about Disney's Animal Kingdom.)

Have time for more?

In addition to the big four, a few other parks and attractions round out the Disney empire (I give you more info about these in Chapter 16):

✔ **DisneyQuest** is a whole lot more than just a fancy video arcade. It's a virtual-reality world unto itself, with top-flight games and simulators that put the game consoles you have at home to shame.

✔ **Disney's Wide World of Sports Complex** is a 240-acre complex filled with an array of state-of-the-art facilities for football, soccer, baseball, softball, and other sports and activities. At the interactive **Multi-Sports Experience,** guests can participate in a variety of challenges that put their skills to the test. The complex also has a 7,500-seat baseball stadium that's the spring-training home of the Atlanta Braves.

✔ **Walt Disney World Speedway** has a stock-car racing track that serves as host to the **Richard Petty Driving Experience,** where you can either drive a car or ride shotgun at 145 mph. (If you're from Talladega or Darlington, you probably can do that in your sleep.)

✔ **A pair of themed miniature golf courses** with whimsical décor schemes (think "Santa goes to the beach" and "Disney classic film comes alive") entertain even as they challenge putters with all-too-realistic water hazards and tricky sand traps. To visit Santa in all his sunny glory, head for **Disney's Winter Summerland Miniature Golf Course;** for Mickey's sorcerer's hat and dancing hippos, take your putter to **Fantasia Gardens Miniature Golf Course.**

✔ **Two splashy parks** let you float along lazy streams, scream down gravity-defying water slides, and more. They're especially appealing in summer, when the heat and humidity are above 90°F and 90 percent, respectively. Kids and adults alike will enjoy cooling off at **Blizzard Beach** and **Typhoon Lagoon.**

Planet Disney also has several shopping (see Chapter 17) and nightlife (see Chapter 25) venues. For example:

✔ **Disney's BoardWalk** is a good place to stroll along the waterfront, dine, dance, or catch a game in the sports bar.

✔ **Downtown Disney** comprises **Pleasure Island,** an adult nightclub district; **Downtown Disney Marketplace,** which features dining and shopping; **Downtown Disney West Side,** with shopping, dining, **Cirque du Soleil,** and the **House of Blues;** and **DisneyQuest,** a high-tech, interactive video arcade.

You can get additional information about all WDW properties by calling ☎ 407-934-7639 or visiting www.disneyworld.com.

Want to go behind the scenes?

If you'd like an insider's look at how the Wizards of Diz make magic, **behind-the-scenes tours** are the way to go. So many options are available (14, in fact) that the Disney folks sometimes have trouble remembering them all. Reservations are recommended — and, in many cases, essential — for these tours. Call ☎ 407-939-8687 to make your reservations.

Palling around with Mickey

Pal Mickey is a talking, 10½-inch-tall, stuffed, digital Mickey Mouse who serves as a semi-amusing novelty guide to the Disney parks, telling guests about parades, show-times, and so on when activated. Designed for kids, he nevertheless gets toted around by adults, too. (Pal Mickey comes with an attachable belt clip, and most grown-ups, much to the amusement of their kids, often get confused and go for their pagers when he vibrates to let them know he has a message for them.) His computer chip picks up wireless signals throughout the park and dispenses pertinent fun and facts; after you leave the park, a few corny jokes and silly songs are all that's left of his repertoire. Pal Mickey operates on three AA batteries — they're included! — and dispenses more than 700 bits of wisdom. He's available for purchase ($65) inside all Disney resort gift shops and at select stores inside the theme parks. For that much money, I'd prefer the real Mickey to show me around instead of his little electronic brother, but at least you can take him home.

Note: Unless otherwise noted, you have to pay park admission, currently $75 for adults and $63 for kids 3 to 9, in addition to the price for a behind-the-scenes tour. But ticket prices, times, and tours change often, so check before your trip by calling Disney's tour line at ☎ 407-939-8687. For those up to the task, not to mention the price tag, you can arrange for a custom tour by calling ☎ 407-560-4033. Photo IDs are required at check-in for all tours.

Here's a sampling of the best offerings:

✔ **Backstage Magic:** At the top of the price chain — $199 per person — Backstage Magic is a seven-hour, self- and bus-propelled tour through areas of Epcot, the Magic Kingdom, and Disney's Hollywood Studios that aren't seen by mainstream guests. If you must know how things work, this tour is for you. You may see mechanics repairing and building animatronic beings, and you get to venture into Magic Kingdom tunnels that are not only work areas, but also paths for the cast to get from one place to another without fighting tourist crowds. Tours are offered at 9:45 a.m. weekdays and are limited to 20 adults (age 16 or older), so book as early as possible (Disney recommends at least two months in advance). Lunch is included. *Park admission is not required.*

✔ **Disney's Family Magic Tour:** This two-hour scavenger hunt brings you face to face with Disney characters at the Magic Kingdom. All ages are welcome, the cost is $27, and park admission is required. Tours kick off at 11:30 a.m. daily outside City Hall, but you need to book in advance.

✔ **Disney's Keys to the Kingdom Tour:** Receive a 4½-hour orientation to the Magic Kingdom and a glimpse into the high-tech systems behind Mickey's magic. Tours cost $60 for ages 16 and older; park admission is required. Tours start at 8:30, 9:30, and 10 a.m. daily.

Finding Your Way to the Fun

The Disney exits on Interstate 4 are clearly marked (though the exit numbers periodically change due to construction). You can't miss them unless you close your eyes.

Interstate 4 is woefully crowded, especially during rush hour (7–9 a.m. and 4–6 p.m. daily). In addition to the thousands of people heading for a day at the parks, thousands of locals are heading to work, so remember to factor possible delays into your time schedule.

Parking in the Disney theme-park lots costs $12 per day (unless you're a WDW resort guest, in which case it's free) and is a snap. Just do what the people in the yellow-striped shirts ask you to do. In the size-XXXL Magic Kingdom lot, you'll probably want to ride the tram to the front gate. (The trams are a hoot — the seats are made out of petrified plastic, so if you lack posterior padding, you'll probably remember the ride for a while. And don't forget a jacket if you plan on making a day of it; the ride back to your car at night can make you feel like you're one of those frozen Mickey pops.)

Getting from the parking lot to the action can take up to an hour at the Magic Kingdom, so be patient as you begin the day. The first stop after the tram ride is the **Transportation & Ticket Center,** where you transfer to the monorail or the ferry to get to the park.

At Epcot, Disney's Hollywood Studios, and Disney's Animal Kingdom, trams are available, but walking can be faster — unless you have small children or sore feet — if you're parked in the front half of the lot.

Don't forget to make a note of your parking area, including your row and space number, or you may end up on an unfortunate scavenger hunt when you leave the park. After a day spent standing in lines, listening to screaming kids, and being tapped out by cash registers, you'll have a hard time remembering your name, not to mention where you parked. And the odds are that at least a few of the cars in the lot will be clones of your own, making yours that much harder to spot.

If you don't have a car, or prefer to skip the drive, many area accommodations offer shuttles that are sometimes free but can also carry a fee. (Check the listings in Chapter 9 for hotels that offer shuttle service.)

Traveling within the World

If you're staying at a WDW resort, you can take the **Disney Transportation system** to get to the parks. The system also serves Downtown Disney, Typhoon Lagoon, Blizzard Beach, Pleasure Island, and Disney's Wide World of Sports. It's a thorough network that includes buses, monorails, ferries, and water taxis serving the major parks from two hours prior to opening until two hours after closing. On the downside, it doesn't always offer direct routes, and moving between locations can make for a long and complicated journey. For more about the pros and cons of using the transport system, see Chapter 8. Disney properties also offer transportation to other area attractions, but you have to pay for it.

Ask at the **Guest Relations** desk in your hotel or at the theme parks for a copy of the *Guide to Everything Disney,* which includes a map of the entire WDW Resort that shows you everything in the empire as well as a version of the now out-of-print Disney Transportation Guide Map (which can also be found, sans the tidbits regarding Disney transportation, on the back of Disney's resort hotel maps). With a bit of help from a cast member, you can get an idea of where your hotel is in relation to places that you want to visit. You can also look at the map of WDW's areas in this chapter to help orient yourself.

Preparing for Park Admission Costs

The number of admission options offered at Walt Disney World — from one-day to multiday tickets — is staggering, and they're all expensive. The option that works best for you depends on the number of days you plan to spend in the parks, what parks and attractions you want to see, and whether you're staying at a WDW resort.

Disney's new **Magic Your Way** ticketing system is designed to save you money the longer you stay and play; it also allows you to add on several optional features. Most people get the best value from four- and five-day Magic Your Way passes with the **Park Hopper Option** added on, which, as the name implies, lets you move from park to park on the same day. You can add Park Hopper privileges to a single-day admission pass, but the price tag for a single-day ticket with Park Hopper privileges is staggering.

If you plan on visiting Walt Disney World more than once during the year, inquire about the **No Expiration Option** or money-saving annual passes ($469–$599 adults, $414–$528 children 3–9).

For Magic Your Way ticket prices, see Table 11-1; for other WDW ticket prices, see Table 11-2; and for Magic Your Way ticket options, see Table 11-3.

Here's a brief description of the ticket options you see in Table 11-3:

- ✔ **Park Hopper Option:** This option allows you to visit any combination of the four main theme parks on any given day.

- ✔ **Water Park Fun & More Option:** This option allows you a specific number of visits (anywhere from three to six, depending on what you choose) to your choice of Typhoon Lagoon, Blizzard Beach, DisneyQuest, Pleasure Island, and Disney's Wide World of Sports Complex.

✔ **No Expiration Option:** This option allows you to use any unused portion of your ticket at any time in the future with absolutely no expiration date.

Table 11-1		Magic Your Way Ticket Prices *					
Age Group	**1-Day**	**2-Day**	**3-Day**	**4-Day**	**5-Day**	**6-Day**	**7-Day**
Ages 10+	$75	$149 ($75/ day)	$212 ($71/ day)	$219 ($55/ day)	$222 $44/ (day)	$225 ($38/ day)	$228 ($33/ day)
Ages 3–9	$63	$125 ($63/ day)	$179 ($60/ day)	$184 ($46/ day)	$187 ($37/ day)	$190 ($32/ day)	$193 ($28/ day)

* One theme park per day of your ticket.

Table 11-2	Other Walt Disney World Ticket Prices	
Attraction	**Ages 3–9**	**Ages 10+**
Blizzard Beach	$34	$40
DisneyQuest	$34	$40
Pleasure Island	N/A	$22
Typhoon Lagoon	$34	$40
Wide World of Sports Complex	$8	$11

Table 11-3		Magic Your Way Ticket Options *					
Option	**1-Day**	**2-Day**	**3-Day**	**4-Day**	**5-Day**	**6-Day**	**7-Day**
Park Hopper Option	+$50	+$50	+$50	+$50	+$50	+$50	+$50
Water Park Fun & More Option	+$50 (2 visits)	+$50 (2 visits)	+$50 (3 visits)	+$50 (4 visits)	+$50 (5 visits)	+$50 (6 visits)	+$50 (7 visits)
No Expiration Option	N/A	+$17	+$23	+$50	+$70	+$80	+$110

* Additional cost, on top of the ticket prices in Table 11-1.

WDW considers everyone 10 and older an adult, and the prices that I give you don't include 6.5 percent sales tax. Also, fluctuating attendance figures and new multimillion-dollar rides continue to escalate the single-day admission fee. (It's now $75 for adults, $63 for kids 3–9, but I expect that price to continue rising, so check before your trip for up-to-the-minute costs.) You can save an average of 10 percent off the regular prices of all passes by ordering online in advance at www.disneyworld.com.

As with many of the attractions in the area and across the state, Florida residents can take advantage of additional savings. Inquire about these savings when ordering your tickets.

The average family will spend roughly $120 to $150 per person per day on park admissions, midday food, snacks, and souvenirs alone.

Getting the Most out of Your Trip to the World

The Magic Kingdom, Epcot, and Disney's Hollywood Studios usually open at 9 a.m. (sometimes earlier) throughout the year. They're open at least until 6 or 7 p.m. and often as late as 11 p.m. or midnight during peak periods (holidays and the summer months). Disney's Animal Kingdom usually opens at 8 or 9 a.m. and closes at 5 or 6 p.m. It's a safe bet that the longer a park stays open, the more people will be visiting that day, so planning your schedule before you get to the park is essential. Unfortunately, hours of operation vary greatly, so it's always wise to call ☎ 407-934-7639 ahead of time, or to check the official calendar on Disney's Web site at www.disneyworld.com. When you arrive at the park, pick up a *Times Guide and New Information* brochure to use for the rest of your stay.

Avoiding the crowds

Crowds are a fact of life at Walt Disney World, but that doesn't necessarily mean you'll have to stand in long lines at all the rides and attractions. Forward thinkers can definitely decrease their risk of encountering a major swarm of tourists. In addition to FASTPASS (see the "Beating the lines" section, below), here are some facts to keep in mind as you plan your crowd-avoiding strategy:

- ✔ Mondays, Thursdays, and Saturdays are the busiest days in the Magic Kingdom; Tuesdays and Fridays are the busy days at Epcot; Sundays and Wednesdays are crowded at Disney's Hollywood Studios; and Mondays, Tuesdays and Wednesdays are beastly at Disney's Animal Kingdom.

- ✔ Although it isn't guaranteed, the parks tend to be less crowded from mid-January (save the weeks surrounding the Easter holidays) to late May and from September through November, except for Thanksgiving. You also have a better chance of avoiding crowds if you go in the middle of the week (especially in the summer). Most people steer clear on rainy days, so the parks can be less crowded, and you won't miss much other than parades. (There's plenty of good stuff indoors.) Crowds thin out (though at times only slightly) in the evenings — if you can manage and parks are open late, take a midday break (when crowds are beginning to peak), and head back after dinner.

✔ Finally, if you plan to dine at Disney, make Advanced Dining Reservations early in the day, or before you arrive at the park, to lock in the time you want to eat. (See Chapter 10 for more about Advanced Dining Reservations.)

Beating the lines

Everyone's looking for a shortcut, and no wonder — lines at Disney and the other big parks can be incredibly long and irritating if you come at the wrong time. Twenty or 30 minutes is considered cruising when it comes to line time, and 45 minutes to one hour is common at the primo rides. In peak periods (summer, holidays, weekends, and other times when kids are out of school) it can take an hour, often much longer (sometimes upwards of two hours or more), to reach the front of the line — and in three or four minutes, the ride is over.

Here are the best tips I can give you to beat the long lines:

✔ Arrive as early as possible — the crowds pour in beginning at around 11 a.m. and only get worse from there.

✔ Plan to spend the morning in one section and the afternoon in another, so that you won't waste time and energy running around.

✔ Spend *two* days in the park if time and budget allow.

✔ Ask about or read the health and height restrictions before you get in line to avoid wasting time on a ride that isn't for you.

Don't want to stand in line as long as other guests, yet not flush enough to hire a stand-in? Disney parks have installed a ride-reservation system called **FASTPASS.** Here's the drill: Hang on to your theme-park ticket stub when you enter and head to the hottest ride you want. If it's a FASTPASS attraction (they're noted in the guide map you get when you enter), feed your stub into the waist-level ticket taker. Retrieve your ticket stub and the FASTPASS stub that comes with it. Look at the two times stamped on the latter. You can return during that one-hour window and enter the ride with almost no wait. In the meantime, you can do something else until the appointed time. Keep in mind that you need to get a FASTPASS stub for everyone in your group who wants to ride the ride.

Note: Early in the day, your one-hour window may begin 40 minutes after you feed the FASTPASS machine, but later in the day it may be hours, especially at Epcot's Test Track (see Chapter 13). Initially, Disney allowed you to use this reservation system on only one ride at a time, but now, your FASTPASS ticket has a time when you can get a second

FASTPASS, usually two hours later, even if you haven't yet used the first pass. *And be prepared:* FASTPASS tickets do run out. They're limited in quantity and often run out by noon, so be sure to get yours as soon as you can.

Taking advantage of Extra Magic Hours

Each day, a particular park offers admittance either one hour before opening or up to three hours after closing for guests staying at Disney resorts and select "official" hotels. To take advantage of the **Extra Magic Hours,** your ticket must be good for the participating park or you must have the Park Hopper Option (allowing you to enter any of the four major parks). The Extra Magic Hours vary, so check the online calendar at `http://disneyworld.disney.go.com/wdw/calendar/extra` `MagicHour` or pick up a copy of the *Extra Magic Hours* brochure and the *Times Guide and New Information* brochure when entering the park.

Getting a *Times Guide and New Information* brochure as soon as you enter the park is essential. The guide is filled with useful information including park hours, showtimes, restaurant hours, and more. Spend a few minutes looking it over, noting where you need to be and when. Many of the attractions in Walt Disney World are nonstop, but others, like shows and fireworks, occur only at certain times or once a day. You can find park maps and the *Times Guide* brochures at counters on one side or the other of the turnstiles; sometimes at both. They're also available at Guest Relations and most Disney shops.

Chapter 12

The Magic Kingdom

In This Chapter
▶ Locating resources and services in the Magic Kingdom
▶ Checking out the fun: rides, shows, and attractions

*I*f you have kids or a soft spot for vintage or classic Disney, make your way to this WDW signature park first. The Magic Kingdom is the most popular of Mickey's enterprises, attracting more than 40,000 people a day, with good reason. But be prepared for long lines, and lots of 'em.

Proof of the Magic Kingdom's staying power is that it has changed very little during its nearly 40 years of existence. Most of the park's newer attractions, such as Monsters, Inc. Laugh Floor and Mickey's PhilharMagic, are hardly the adrenaline generators you encounter at other theme parks, but Magic Kingdom remains the fairest of them all.

Managing Magic Kingdom Logistics

Yes, you can find rides, shows, and characters galore, but you also need to be armed with some practical information, too. This section gives you the lowdown on prices, hours, and services at the Magic Kingdom.

Buying tickets and making reservations

Ticket prices (at press time) for a one-day admission are $75 for adults, $63 for kids 3 to 9, but these change frequently, so call ahead. (See Chapter 11 for more information on park admission prices.)

Tickets aren't the only thing you'll spend big bucks on. Disney parks nail you to the tune of $2 or more for a soda or milk, $1.25 to $2 for bottled water, $2.50 for a Mickey ice-cream bar, and $1.70 (and up) for a cup of coffee or cocoa. *Note:* If you're on a tight budget, whenever you can, bring snacks and drinks from the outside world — they'll cost far less and go much further than any you'll find in the parks. You can often get an entire six-pack of bottled water (freeze it the night before so that it's really cold) for less than the cost of two bottles at the parks.

Pick up a guide map upon entering the park — it not only lays out the land but also lists special shows and daily events. In addition, pick up a

Times Guide and New Information brochure for a more thorough schedule of shows, parades, fireworks, special events, and visits from Disney characters. When you're in the park, make Advanced Dining Reservations (if you haven't done so before arriving) if you have any intentions of eating a sit-down meal at a particular restaurant (see Chapter 10 for details).

Arriving early and staying late

Although the Magic Kingdom is usually open daily from 9 a.m. to 6 p.m., there are exceptions. In fact, the gates sometimes open 15 to 30 minutes earlier than the official opening time. I recommend trying to get to the park early, but not just because of the possibility of an early opening. An early arrival helps you beat morning traffic and allows you a more relaxed pace to get from the parking lot to the fun, which can take as long as an hour. At the end of the day, the park often closes later than 6 p.m., sometimes as late as 10 or 11 p.m., especially during the summer and on holidays. The Magic Kingdom may even be open as late as midnight, even 1 a.m., during peak season or for special events. Call ☎ 407-934-7639 for more details.

Locating special services and facilities

In case you forget to bring essential items or need special assistance at the park, here's a list of services and facilities that can help:

- ✔ **ATMs** are located at the main entrance, in Frontierland, and in Tomorrowland. They honor cards from banks using the Cirrus, STAR, and PLUS systems.

- ✔ **Baby-changing facilities,** including rocking chairs and toddler-size toilets, are next to the Crystal Palace at the end of Main Street. Of course, it isn't the most cost-effective place to buy them, but you can purchase disposable diapers, formula, baby food, and pacifiers at the **Baby Care Center.** Changing tables are also located at the center, as well as in all women's restrooms and some of the men's.

- ✔ **Disposable cameras and film** are available throughout the park, and Disney has finally caught on to the popularity of digital cameras, offering limited supplies of rechargeable batteries and storage cards. It also offers CD-burning and picture-printing services at Kodak Picture Kiosks and select stores in all four theme parks.

- ✔ The **First Aid Station,** staffed by registered nurses, is located alongside the Crystal Palace and the Baby Care Center.

- ✔ **Lockers** are available in an arcade underneath the Main Street Railroad Station. They cost $10 per day, including a $5 refundable deposit.

- ✔ **Lost children** are often taken to City Hall or the Baby Care Center, where lost-children logbooks are kept. *Children under 7 should wear name tags inside their clothing.*

The Magic Kingdom

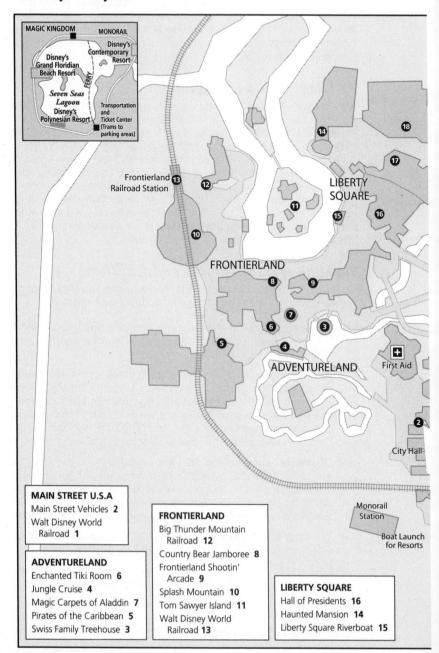

MAIN STREET U.S.A
Main Street Vehicles **2**
Walt Disney World
  Railroad **1**

ADVENTURELAND
Enchanted Tiki Room **6**
Jungle Cruise **4**
Magic Carpets of Aladdin **7**
Pirates of the Caribbean **5**
Swiss Family Treehouse **3**

FRONTIERLAND
Big Thunder Mountain
  Railroad **12**
Country Bear Jamboree **8**
Frontierland Shootin'
  Arcade **9**
Splash Mountain **10**
Tom Sawyer Island **11**
Walt Disney World
  Railroad **13**

LIBERTY SQUARE
Hall of Presidents **16**
Haunted Mansion **14**
Liberty Square Riverboat **15**

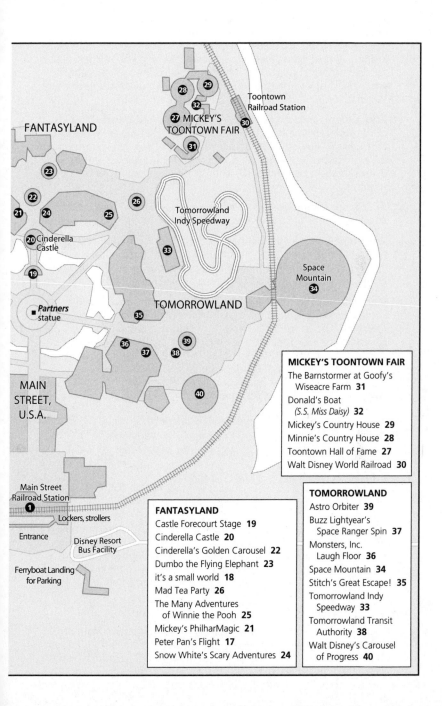

FANTASYLAND

Toontown
Railroad Station

27 MICKEY'S
TOONTOWN FAIR

Tomorrowland
Indy Speedway

20 Cinderella
Castle

Space
Mountain

■ *Partners*
statue

TOMORROWLAND

MAIN
STREET,
U.S.A.

Main Street
Railroad Station

1

Lockers, strollers

Entrance

Disney Resort
Bus Facility

Ferryboat Landing
for Parking

MICKEY'S TOONTOWN FAIR

The Barnstormer at Goofy's
Wiseacre Farm **31**
Donald's Boat
(*S.S. Miss Daisy*) **32**
Mickey's Country House **29**
Minnie's Country House **28**
Toontown Hall of Fame **27**
Walt Disney World Railroad **30**

TOMORROWLAND

Astro Orbiter **39**
Buzz Lightyear's
Space Ranger Spin **37**
Monsters, Inc.
Laugh Floor **36**
Space Mountain **34**
Stitch's Great Escape! **35**
Tomorrowland Indy
Speedway **33**
Tomorrowland Transit
Authority **38**
Walt Disney's Carousel
of Progress **40**

FANTASYLAND

Castle Forecourt Stage **19**
Cinderella Castle **20**
Cinderella's Golden Carousel **22**
Dumbo the Flying Elephant **23**
it's a small world **18**
Mad Tea Party **26**
The Many Adventures
of Winnie the Pooh **25**
Mickey's PhilharMagic **21**
Peter Pan's Flight **17**
Snow White's Scary Adventures **24**

✔ You can send purchases from any store in the park to **Package Pick-Up** (next to City Hall), then readily pick them up at the service desk at day's end instead of having to haul your various souvenirs around all day. Allow three hours for delivery. If you're staying at the Disney resorts, you can have your packages sent straight to your resort at no charge, though it may take a day or two for them to get there.

✔ **Pets,** except service animals, are prohibited in the parks, but you can board yours at the Transportation & Ticket Center's **Pet Care Kennels** (☎ 407-824-6568). Day rates run $10 to $15, depending on the type of pet and whether or not you're a Disney resort guest; overnighters cost extra ($13–$20). Proof of vaccinations is required.

✔ The **Stroller Shop** near the entrance charges $15 to rent a single stroller and $31 for a double.

✔ **Wheelchairs** are available for rent at the gift shop to the left of the ticket booths at the Transportation & Ticket Center or at the Stroller Shop inside the main entrance to your right. Cost is $10. For electric chairs, you pay $45 plus a $5 refundable deposit.

✔ **Find some of your favorite characters at the following spots:** In Fantasyland, look for them in Ariel's Grotto. In Mickey's Toontown Fair, go to the Judge's Tent and the Toontown Hall Of Fame. Characters also appear in Adventureland (by Pirates of the Caribbean) and Main Street (near City Hall), as well as in Liberty Square near the Diamond Horseshoe and occasionally in Tomorrowland behind Buzz Lightyear's Space Ranger Spin. (See the guide map that you get when entering the park.)

You can get more information about WDW properties by calling ☎ 407-934-7639 or visiting Disney's Web site (www.disneyworld.com).

Making the Rounds: The Magic Kingdom's Top Attractions

More than three dozen attractions, an array of shops, and numerous eateries are located within the Magic Kingdom's 107 acres. The following tour, complete with descriptions, begins at the front gates and takes you counterclockwise through the park's seven uniquely themed lands. To find all the listed attractions, see the "Magic Kingdom" map on p. 184.

Main Street U.S.A.

Although it's considered one of the kingdom's seven lands, Main Street is more of a gateway where you can easily lose yourself in the pleasant nostalgia of yesteryear. I recommend passing through it quickly when you arrive (so you can make a beeline for the more popular attractions before the lines get too long), because you have to make a return voyage when you cry "uncle" at the end of the day anyway. At that time, stamina permitting, you can browse through the shops at a more leisurely pace before exiting the park. Here are a few features of Main Street U.S.A.:

- ✔ **Walt Disney World Railroad:** This authentic steam-powered train makes a leisurely 15- to 20-minute loop around the park, with stops in Frontierland and at the far end of Mickey's Toontown Fair. During busy periods and parade times, this is a great way to get around the park without fighting your way through the crowds. It also gives the kids (and you) a well-deserved, albeit brief, break.

- ✔ **Harmony Barber Shop:** This is a real scissor shop where you can get your hair cut. The barbershop quartet may even take a break from entertaining guests along the street to serenade you. Hours are from 9 a.m. to 5 p.m. daily. Adult haircuts are $17; kid cuts are $14; colored gel will run you $5. If it's your child's very first haircut, Disney barbers will throw in a few extras, including a certificate and a set of Mouse ears. The shop is near the firehouse, but it's a bit hidden, so keep your eyes peeled.

- ✔ **Main Street Family Fun Day Parade:** You can join in and march down Main Street right along with floats, marching bands, and your favorite Disney characters. The parade even has a pint-size stroller drill team so that little ones still in strollers — and their parents — can take their place in the parade, too.

- ✔ **Main Street Vehicles:** Ride a horse-drawn trolley, jitney, vintage fire engine, or horseless carriage *only* if you don't mind waiting around. Otherwise, there are far, far better things to see and do throughout the realm.

Tomorrowland

This land looks to the future, but in 1994, the WDW folks realized that Tomorrowland (originally designed in the 1970s) was beginning to look a lot like "Yesteryear." As a result, Disney revamped the entire area to show the future as seen from the past (sometime around the 1920s or '30s) with a galactic, science-fiction-inspired community filled with aliens, robots, and video games.

Here's a sampling of what you can find in Tomorrowland:

- ✔ **Astro Orbiter:** Future astronauts, especially those who are 7 years old and younger, love whirling high (and I mean *high* — you have to take an elevator to get there) into the galaxy in the colorful rockets that circle around while gently rising and falling. Unfortunately, the lines can stretch for lightyears, so if you're on a tight timetable, save it for later.

- ✔ **Buzz Lightyear's Space Ranger Spin:** On this ride, you go to infinity and beyond in an interactive space adventure in which you help Buzz defend the Earth's supply of batteries from the evil Emperor Zurg. You fly an XP-37 space cruiser armed with twin lasers and a joystick that's capable of spinning the craft. (Space Rangers who get motion sickness should sit this attraction out. There's already enough space debris flying around.) While you cruise through space, you collect points by blasting anything that looks or smells remotely like Zurg (just look for all the neon Zs and shoot). Your hits trigger light, sound, and animated effects. This ride is a tamer version of Men in Black Alien Attack at Universal Studios Florida (see Chapter 18). My 7-year-old, 9-year-old, and 11-year-old all adore this ride (and have for years).

✔ **Monsters, Inc. Laugh Floor:** Taking its cue from the hit Disney/Pixar film *Monsters, Inc.,* Monster-of-Ceremonies Mike Wazowski and a few comic recruits tell jokes and poke fun at audience members hoping to generate enough laughs to fill their oversized laugh canister. This new interactive, somewhat amusing show is live and unscripted (a guarantee that you'll never see the same show twice). Behind the scenes, a slew of improvisational comedians stand ready with quirky comebacks and comedic quips while real-time animation and digital projection create the action on-screen. While noticeable time lags detracted from the experience upon its debut, Disney has managed to work out most of the kinks.

If you think you've got a monstrously funny joke (LOL), text it to the show from your cell (but only from right outside the theater, just prior to the show) and you may find yourself cracking up at a joke or two of your own!

✔ **Space Mountain:** Imagine a roller coaster. Then imagine it in the dark. This ride, along with Big Thunder Mountain Railroad and Splash Mountain (both in the "Frontierland" section, later in this chapter), are the three major Magic Kingdom attractions that tweens, teens, and thrill seekers alike head to first, so get here early or use FASTPASS. Space Mountain is a classic roller coaster with plenty of dramatic dips and drops, and the darkness makes it seem like it's going much faster than its top speed of 28 mph. Grab a front seat for the best ride.

This one's a favorite with my 15-year-old (especially because there's not a loop-de-loop in sight). "It was such a rush! In the dark you couldn't tell what was going to happen next." And: "The twists and turns happened really fast — it's definitely the coolest ride at Disney." It's recommended for those ages 10 and older, but because it was one of the first generation of modern, dark-side coasters and is therefore somewhat outdated, it's a bit tamer than some of the more modern thrill rides at Disney's Hollywood Studios.

Note that *you must be 44 inches or taller* to ride, and there's an escape hatch for those who decide at the last minute that they're not quite up to space travel. The seats and lap-bar restraints on Space Mountain may not fit some larger, plus-size riders.

✔ **Stitch's Great Escape!:** Gone is the ultra-scary *ExtraTERRORestrial Alien Encounter,* and in its place is this slightly more family-friendly attraction based on the Disney hit film *Lilo & Stitch*. The story line is a prequel to the movie, showing the mischief caused by rascally Experiment 626 (also known as "Stitch") when he was originally captured. Those who experienced Alien Encounter will notice that not that much has changed other than the characters, who are now far less frightening to look at. The state-of-the-art audio-animatronics are neat, but there are just too many gaps in between. There are long periods of darkness with no sound and really nothing going on — other than the screams of the scared little kids making their way to the door — and the multisensory effects, including an odorous burp belted out by Stitch, are a bit over the top.

You must be 40 inches or taller to experience the great escape, a height restriction that keeps most of Stitch's fans from even entering.

✔ **Tomorrowland Indy Speedway:** Kids, especially those ages 4 to 8, like slipping into these Indy-car knockoffs and taking them for a spin; but older children, teens, and adults (especially those with a need for speed) generally hate them. The long lines and less-than-stellar steering, combined with an ultra-slow top speed of 7 mph, add up to one giant snooze of an experience for those tall enough to reach the pedals on their own. Parents will appreciate the thick iron rail that pretty much keeps their unlicensed drivers on track.

This isn't a ride that will make you go *vroom,* even though *you have to be a minimum of 52 inches tall to drive alone.*

✔ **Tomorrowland Transit Authority:** The small, five-car trains on this elevated people-mover are engineless. They work by electromagnets, create no pollution, and use little power. The environmentally friendly cars wind around Tomorrowland and into Space Mountain (I've even caught a glimpse of the coaster with the lights up on rare occasion) on a lazy ride that encourages you to nod off when it's late in the day, and you begin to realize that you've already covered 4 or 5 miles. There's usually little to no wait, but this ride is another one to skip if you're in a hurry. If you need to rest weary feet or have tired toddlers in tow, however, this one's a real winner. (It's also a good place to wait it out with your little ones when the older kids are riding Space Mountain.)

✔ **Walt Disney's Carousel of Progress:** Open only during busy seasons, this Disney oldie was refurbished to its original state in 1994. The 22-minute show takes you on a quasi-historical trip through time, hosted by an audio-animatronic family who explain how their lives have changed with the introduction of electricity and other technological advances of the past 50 years. Older guests may find it nostalgic; younger ones may wonder how anyone lived before the invention of video games. Although not particularly exciting, and definitely one to be skipped if you're pressed for time, it is nonetheless a good way to spend some downtime waiting for the thrill seekers in the family to get through Space Mountain.

Mickey's Toontown Fair

Head off cries of "Where's Mickey?" by taking young kids (ages 2–8) to this 2-acre site as soon as you arrive. It's by far the best place to meet the characters, including, among others, Mickey, Minnie, Donald Duck, Goofy, and Pluto. The Magic Kingdom's smallest land is filled with a whimsical collection of rides, play areas, and candy-striped tents.

- ✓ **The Barnstormer at Goofy's Wiseacre Farm:** This mini roller coaster is designed to look and feel like a crop duster that flies slightly off-course and right through the Goofmeister's barn. It has a *35-inch height minimum,* and its tight turns and small dips give even some adults a slight rush.

- ✓ **Donald's Boat:** Also known as the S.S. *Miss Daisy,* this interactive play area has fountains and water snakes that win squeals of joy (and relief on hot days). Unless you want to wear wet clothes the rest of the day, bring along a dry change of clothes or a swimsuit.

- ✓ **Mickey's Country House and Minnie's Country House:** These provide a lot of visual fun and some interactive areas for youngsters, though they're usually crowded and the lines flow like molasses. Mickey's place features garden and garage playgrounds. Minnie's lets kids play in her kitchen, where popcorn goes wild in a microwave, a cake billows up in the oven, and the utensils strike up a symphony of their own.

- ✓ **Toontown Hall Of Fame:** This place hosts meet-and-greets with various Disney characters as well as one of the largest souvenir shops in the park. You have to wait in line to meet the characters (each with his or her own separate line, so you'll have to decide which one is most worth the wait), but the payoff is that each family is allowed a few minutes with the character of their choice where hugs are exchanged and photos are snapped.

Fantasyland

Disney classics come to life in Fantasyland, where the rides are based on the movies you grew up with way back when, as well as a few of the more recent additions to the Disney treasure chest of films. The area is dedicated to the younger set, who would happily spend the day here; unfortunately, the seemingly endless lines eat up a good portion of time unless you use FASTPASS. Here's a list of attractions in Fantasyland:

- ✓ **Cinderella Castle:** Modeled on several French châteaux, the fairy-tale Gothic-style castle sits at the end of Main Street in the center of the park. It's hard to miss the 189-foot landmark — its 18 towers reach to the clouds, framed by the picturesque shops of Main Street U.S.A. The castle is a favorite photo op, and if you land at the right time, you can catch the park's latest production, **Dream Along with Mickey,** where dreams of adventure and happily-ever-after are played out on stage. (The cast of characters includes

Mickey, Peter Pan, Captain Hook, and other familiar favorites; the *Times Guide and New Information* brochure lists the daily schedule of shows.) Otherwise, the castle is mainly a visual attraction. The interior corridor is lined with beautiful murals and exquisite mosaics depicting the classic story of Cinderella. The upper level of the castle is home to the **Cinderella's Royal Table** restaurant (see Chapter 10) and the spectacular **Cinderella Suite** (created from a space originally intended as an apartment for Walt and his family, the suite was "re-imagined" for Disney's Year of a Million Dreams celebration in 2007). The castle is also home to the **Bibbidi Bobbidi Boutique** (the original boutique is located in Downtown Disney), where little girls are treated like royalty, magically transformed into pint-sized princesses by fairy godmothers in training (for a price, of course).

✔ **Cinderella's Golden Carousel:** This old beauty was built in 1917 by the Philadelphia Toboggan Company and served tours in Detroit and New Jersey before it was discovered in the late 1960s by Disney Imagineers and brought to the Magic Kingdom. A patriotic red, white, and blue in its first incarnation, it was restored and re-themed in time for the park's opening; now it tells the tale of Cinderella in 18 hand-painted scenes set above magnificent antique horses. It's a delight for kids and carousel lovers of all ages. The organ plays — what else? — Disney classics such as "When You Wish Upon a Star" and "Heigh-Ho."

✔ **Dumbo The Flying Elephant:** This attraction doesn't do much for older adrenaline-addicted kids — or line-hating parents — but it's a favorite of kids ages 2 through 6. Dumbo's ears keep them airborne for a gentle, circular flight with some little dips. Except for the Disney theme, it's not all that different from the kiddie rides at most local carnivals. Most kids older than 6 will be humiliated if you even suggest they ride it. If your little ones are dying to ride Dumbo, get here early — wait times are brutal, and it doesn't have FASTPASS!

This ride is designed for the young ones, so plus-sized parents may have troubles getting their elephant to fly, and the taller among you may feel somewhat cramped.

✔ **"it's a small world":** Young kids and most parents love this attraction; teens and many other adults, however, may find it a real drag. Nevertheless, pay your dues — it's an initiation rite every Disney visitor needs to undergo, and the sun-sheltered line isn't usually too long. You glide around the world in small, slow-moving boats, meeting children (audio-animatronic, of course) from around the world, including Russian dancers, Chinese acrobats, and French cancan girls, and every one of them sings the catchy little tune that eats its way into your brain and refuses to stop playing for months. If you've ridden this attraction in the past, you may notice the recent refurbishments. This attraction, one of the original few that opened with the park in 1971 (and originally built by Walt Disney for the 1964 World's Fair) underwent a major renovation in 2004 that included painting and repairing the animatronics figures, as well as replacing the sound system and lights.

A 13-year-old's take: "It was annoying — the dolls were silly and the song just kept playing over and over . . . it was annoying." A 9-year-old: "It was so pretty with all the fancy costumes and lights in the sky, and nothing was scary." Either way, it's a cool place to rest for a while if you need a break from the summer heat.

✔ **Mad Tea Party:** You make this tea party mild or wild, depending on how much you spin the steering wheel of your gigantic teacup, though the cup does a little spinning of its own as well. This ride is suitable for ages 3 and older. Teens and older kids seem to enjoy this ride's potential for turning unwary passengers green. The woozy mouse who pops out of a big teapot in the center of the platform would no doubt sympathize with those left spinning.

✔ **The Many Adventures of Winnie the Pooh:** Pooh inadvertently created a small storm of protest when Disney used this ride to replace the popular Mr. Toad's Wild Ride in 1999. The Many Adventures of Winnie the Pooh features the cute and cuddly little fellow along with Eeyore, Piglet, and Tigger. You board a golden honey pot and ride through a storybook version of the Hundred-Acre Wood, keeping an eye out for Heffalumps, Woozles, blustery days, and the "floody place." This ride has become a favorite of kids 2 to 6 and their parents, so a FASTPASS is often needed. Just across the way, kids can run about, climb, slide, and explore while parents rest their weary feet at **Pooh's Playful Spot,** a tot-friendly play area themed after the Hundred-Acre Wood.

✔ **Mickey's PhilharMagic:** Mickey, Donald, Ariel, Aladdin, and a handful of other favorites appear in this animated and impressively 3-D–enhanced adventure (it's projected on a 150-foot screen — the largest wraparound screen on the planet), in which a mischievous Donald has not so surprisingly gotten into a spot of trouble. This show is similar to Muppet Vision 3-D at Disney's Hollywood Studios (see Chapter 14), but Mickey's PhilharMagic is far more engaging in its combination of music, animated film, and special effects that tickle several of your senses. Kids love the effects, and if you're a sucker for the classic Disney films, you will absolutely adore it. This one's a must.

✔ **Peter Pan's Flight:** Another popular ride among visitors younger than 8, it begins with a nighttime flight over London (even adults *ooh* and *aah* here) in search of Captain Hook, Tiger Lily, and the Lost Boys. It's one of the old glide rides dating back to the limited technology that was available when the Magic Kingdom was born, but the simplicity is part of what makes it so popular. Terribly long lines are almost a signature of this ride, so plan on using a FAST-PASS to avoid the worst of it. My younger kids wouldn't miss it no matter how long they have to wait.

✔ **Snow White's Scary Adventures:** Your journey takes you to the dwarfs' cottage and the wishing well, ending with the prince's kiss to break the evil spell. This version of the Grimms' fairy tale is much less grim than it was years ago, when the focus was inexplicably on the wicked witch, though she still makes several appearances. Snow White now appears in several friendlier scenes, though kids younger than 5 will likely still get scared.

I can't recommend it if your time schedule is tight. For those young enough to want to ride, it's not worth the tears and screams, and those who won't get frightened are often far beyond the Snow White story line.

Liberty Square

Located between Fantasyland and Frontierland, Liberty Square is a recreation of Revolutionary War–era America that infuses you with colonial spirit. Younger guests may not appreciate the historical touches (such as the 13 lanterns symbolizing the original 13 colonies that hang from the gigantic live oak), but they'll delight in the chance to pose for a picture while locked in the stocks or to march along with the fife-and-drum corps that sometimes makes an appearance on the cobblestone streets. Although it is one of the smallest lands in the park, Liberty Square has an impressive number of attractions, including the following:

✔ **Liberty Square Riverboat:** The steam-powered paddlewheeler *Liberty Belle* departs Liberty Square for scenic cruises along the rivers of America. The passing landscape recalls the Wild West, with an occasional Native village and a large wooden fort peeking through the trees. It makes a restful interlude for foot-weary park-stompers.

✔ **The Hall Of Presidents:** American-history buffs ages 10 and older most appreciate this show, which can be a real squirmer for younger children. The Hall is an inspiring production based on painstaking research, right down to the clothes — each president's costume reflects his period's fashion, fabrics, and tailoring techniques. The show begins with a film on the importance of the Constitution, projected on an immense 180-degree screen, and then the curtain rises on America's leaders, from George Washington through George W. Bush. Pay special attention to the roll call of presidents. The animatronic figures are incredibly lifelike and impressive: They fidget, whisper, and talk to the audience.

✔ **The Haunted Mansion:** This attraction has changed little over the years, though 2007 brought with it a four-month-long refurbishment, enhancing its ghouly special effects and spectral silliness that makes this ride so popular. Long a park favorite, the Mansion even has a cult following. (My editor makes a pilgrimage here every time she hits the park, as do I.) It has detailed special effects (this was one of the last rides Walt Disney actually had a hand in designing) and an atmosphere that's far more fun than creepy. You may chuckle at the corny tombstones lining the entrance before you hop aboard your Doom Buggy and are whisked past a ghostly banquet and ball, a graveyard band, weird flying objects, and more. And don't forget the 999 spirits of the house, one of whom may try to hitch a ride home with you. I always get a kick out of the fact that Disney has to continually add dust and cobwebs to keep up this attraction's old and decrepit appearance.

"The ghosts are really cool, but it's not all that scary — I just wasn't sure what to expect when the lights flickered — that was the scariest part. The neatest part is at the end when you see the ghost right next to you." I wholeheartedly agree with Nicolas and Austin (ages 11 and 13, respectively). The ride doesn't get much scarier than spooky music, eerie howling, and things that go bump in the night. It's best for those ages 6 and older, however. Unfortunately, FASTPASS is no longer an available option when trying to beat the long lines, though you may be able to sneak right in at parade time.

Frontierland

Located beyond Adventureland, Frontierland is where the rough-and-tumble Old West architecture runs to log cabins and rustic saloons, while the landscape is Southwestern scrubby with mesquite, cactus, yucca, and prickly pear. Here are a few of Frontierland's attractions:

✔ **Big Thunder Mountain Railroad:** The lines don't lie: This rocking railroad is a favorite in the Magic Kingdom. Thunder Mountain bounces you around an old mining site, where you dodge floods, a bridge collapse, rock slides, and other mayhem. The ride is something of a low-grade roller coaster with speed and a lot of corkscrew action. It has enough of a reputation that even first-time visitors make a beeline for it. So if you can't get to it as soon as the park opens, FASTPASS is your best bet. Or give it a try late in the day, or when a parade pulls many visitors away. Most Disney coaster veterans maintain the ride is at its best after dark.

"So cool . . . you really whip around the mountain, I loved this ride." "It's really fast and it kind of jerks you around when you're turning — that's so fun." Austin (13) and Nicolas (11), the latter of whom prefers the nighttime version, are both right on the money — the action is fast and a bit jerky, especially compared to some of the newer monster rides.

The ride can be too intense for kids younger than 6 (and for those with neck problems). *Riders must be at least 40 inches tall.*

✔ **Country Bear Jamboree:** The stars of this 15-minute animatronic show are the gigantic bumbling country bears, crooning country-and-western tunes and telling completely corny jokes. The Jamboree is a park standard — a show that's been around since Disney invented dirt — but it's still a huge hit with Disney buffs and little kids. The audience gets caught up in the hand-clapping, knee-slapping, foot-stomping fun as Trixie laments lost love while she sings "Tears Will Be the Chaser for Your Wine." Teddi Beara descends from the ceiling in a swing to perform "Heart, I Did All That I Could," and Big Al moans "Blood in the Saddle." It's a great way to cool off with tired toddlers, so sit back and relax for a spell.

"You can't be serious," were the words uttered by my 15-year-old as he rushed past in search of Splash Mountain. My 7-year-old however, was completely entranced. Unless you have an affinity for all things Disney, or have younger children (6 and under), this show might be best saved for those really hot days when you need a break inside. Even then, most teens, young adults, and repeat visitors won't want to do it.

✔ **Frontierland Shootin' Arcade:** With state-of-the-art electronics in a traditional shooting-gallery format, this arcade offers 97 targets (slow-moving ore cars, buzzards, and gravediggers) in an 1850s boomtown scenario. If you hit a tombstone, it may spin around and mysteriously change its epitaph. Coyotes howl, bridges creak, and skeletal arms reach out from the grave. To keep things authentic, newfangled electronic firing mechanisms with infrared bullets are concealed in genuine buffalo rifles. When you hit a target, you set off sound and motion gags. A dollar fetches 35 shots. Younger kids may find this more frustrating than fun.

✔ **Splash Mountain:** If I had to pick one ride as the Kingdom's most popular, Splash Mountain would be it (that should properly prepare you for the lines you'll most definitely experience, which are sometimes longer than two hours). It's on par with SeaWorld's Journey to Atlantis (see Chapter 20), though half a click below Jurassic Park River Adventure at Islands of Adventure (see Chapter 19). Still, it has a flair that only Disney can deliver. Splash Mountain is a nifty voyage through the world of Disney's classic film *Song of the South,* past 26 colorful and delightful scenes that include backwoods swamps, bayous, spooky caves, and waterfalls. You ride in a hollow log flume as Brer Fox and Brer Bear chase the ever-wily Brer Rabbit, and finish with a 52-foot, 45-degree, 40-mph drop, with an impressively high splash factor (around 200 megatons worth of wet) that can thoroughly soak you and anyone remotely close by (but may at times be hit or miss for riders). If you're lucky enough to have some real heavyweights in the front seat, be prepared for an explosive ride on the five-story downhill. FASTPASS is available, but this is one that runs out early.

In summer, this ride can provide sweet relief from the heat and humidity, but in cool weather, parents may want to protect their kids (and themselves) from a chill. Splash Mountain is recommended for ages 8 and older. If your kids are unsure whether they want to ride, let them watch from the bridge for a few minutes — they'll make up their minds after they see one or two logs make the drop. *Riders must be at least 40 inches tall.*

On warmer days, the ride shoots out a spray of water onto the viewing bridge in front of the big drop. If you want to catch your friends unaware for a good soaking, count the log drops: Every third one emits a good spray.

✔ **Tom Sawyer Island:** Board Huck Finn's raft for a two-minute float across a river to this densely forested island, where kids can explore **Injun Joe's Cave** (complete with such scary sound effects as whistling wind), navigate a swinging bridge, and investigate an old wooden fort. Narrow, winding dirt paths lined with oaks, pines, and sycamores create an authentic backwoods atmosphere. It's easy to get briefly lost and stumble upon some unexpected adventure. It's a great place for kids to use up a little excess energy and for moms and dads to relax and maybe indulge in a snack at **Aunt Polly's,** which overlooks the river.

"It's fun just being able to run around, not wait in all the lines." "The caves and the bridges were really cool but so was the whole island." Nicolas (11) and Hailey (9) weren't the only ones who gave it great reviews — even the older kids (ages 13 and 15) concurred (though Davis, age 7, preferred to avoid exploring the darkened caves — which can be frightening and somewhat disorienting at times).

✔ **Woody's Cowboy Camp:** Headed up by Woody, Jesse, and Bullseye, this party is a rootin' tootin' good time. After being rounded up and roped in, kids (along with a few parents) join in on the foot-stompin' fun as they giddy-up on wooden horses to maneuver their way through the cacti, mountain, and mineshaft-filled obstacle course with Bullseye leading the way. For *Toy Story* fans and kiddie-cowboys (or -girls), this one's a must!

Adventureland

Adventureland is a left turn at the end of Main Street. Kids can engage in swashbuckling behavior while walking through dense tropical foliage (complete with vines) or marauding through bamboo and thatch-roofed huts. The architecture is a combination of the Caribbean, Southeast Asia, and Polynesia. Walt Disney wanted this section of the park to exude romance, mystery, and (duh!) adventure. Plenty of the latter is here, especially for kids, though you may have more trouble finding the first two. Here are some of the popular attractions in Adventureland:

✔ **The Enchanted Tiki Room:** Upgraded over the years, the show's newest cast member is Iago of *Aladdin* fame. This attraction is set in a Polynesian-style building with thatch roof, bamboo beams, and tapa-bark murals. Other players include 250 tropical birds, chanting totem poles, and singing flowers that whistle, tweet, and warble. The show runs continuously throughout the day. Young children are most likely to appreciate this one, but so will nostalgic adults. (Children younger than 2 may be frightened by the loud noises.) Otherwise, consider this only as a respite from the heat.

✔ **Jungle Cruise:** Give Disney ten minutes, and it gives you four famous rivers on three different continents. This narrated voyage on the Congo, Amazon, Mekong, and Nile rivers offers glimpses of animatronic animals, tropical and subtropical foliage (most of it real), a Temple of Doom–type camp, and lots of surprises. The ride passes animatronic pythons, elephants, rhinos, gorillas, and hippos that pop threateningly out of the water and blow snot — well, it could've been snot if they weren't robots — on you. This exhibit is about 30 years old, which means it's pretty hokey at times, but it's still a nice way to relax if the lines don't stretch too long (though the waiting area for this ride does offer some amusing moments — check out the prop menus on the walls).

✔ **The Magic Carpets of Aladdin:** The first major ride added in Adventureland since 1971 delights wee ones and even some older kids. Its 16 four-passenger carpets circle the giant genie's bottle, while camels spit water at unsuspecting riders in much the same way riders are spritzed at One Fish, Two Fish, Red Fish, Blue Fish at Islands of Adventure (see Chapter 19). As the fiberglass carpets spin, you can move them up, down, forward, and back.

If the lines are too long at Dumbo (see the "Fantasyland" section, earlier in this chapter), this is a good alternative; the rides are similar but the lines here aren't nearly as sluggish.

✔ **Pirates of the Caribbean:** This oldie-but-goodie is another cult favorite (a Disney archivist confessed to me that it's still his favorite, which should be no great surprise given that this is another ride that Walt Disney had a hand in creating). After walking through a long, somewhat eerie grotto, you board a boat headed into a dark cave where you are warned that "Dead men tell no tales." Therein, elaborate scenery and hundreds of incredibly detailed animatronic figures (some of Disney's best) re-create an almost refreshingly non-PC Caribbean town overrun by buccaneers. To the sounds of cheerful yo-ho-ho music, rushing waterfalls, squawking seagulls, and screams of terror, passengers pass through the line of fire into a raging raid and panorama of almost fierce-looking pirates swigging rum, looting, and plundering. Recent refurbishments, impeccably timed with the release of *Pirates of the Caribbean: Dead Man's Chest* in 2006, have Jack Sparrow, Barbossa, and Davy Jones joining the marauding mayhem; the tweak and the twist in the story line and the enhanced special effects freshen up this old favorite. This ride, in addition to being one of the best in the park, is another great place to cool off on a hot day.

"The drop takes you by surprise, but it's short and not all that scary — it's really pretty cool. The pirates — especially Captain Jack and Davy Jones — look so real, it's almost like you're in the middle of the movie." Kids ages 5 and younger may find a pirate's life a bit too scary, especially with the small drop in the dark. Most kids 6 or older, though, will enjoy it. The recent films based on the ride have made it even more popular with the young and teen sets, who have fun spotting the scenes, and now famous faces, found in the movies.

Captain Jack Sparrow's Pirate Tutorial entertains nearby crowds as the great captain himself (and believe me, you'd be hard-pressed to tell the difference), along with his mate Mack, take on a pint-size crew of pirates-in-training, teaching them the art of swordplay and other silly swashbuckling fun. The young recruits are then sworn in as honorary members of Captain Jack's crew as they say the pirate's oath. All the kids (recruits and younger onlookers alike) receive certificates. The show takes place several times a day; see the *Times Guide and New Information* brochure or check the Entertainment board on Main Street for a schedule.

✔ **Swiss Family Treehouse:** The story of the shipwrecked Swiss Family Robinson (via the 1960 Disney film of the same name) comes alive in this attraction made for swinging, exploring, and crawling fun. The "tree," designed by Disney Imagineers, has 330,000 polyethylene leaves sprouting from a 90-foot span of branches; although it isn't real, it's draped with actual Spanish moss. It's simple and devoid of all that high-tech stuff that's popular in today's parks, but that's what makes it so neat.

Be prepared to stand in a slow-moving line on busy days — the only thing that moves on this one are your feet, so the experience is only as fast paced as the people ahead of you make it. Lines are shortest later in the day, though darkness makes maneuvering the stairs even more challenging. The attraction is also difficult to navigate for travelers with limited mobility. When my kids were younger (under 8), they thought it was neat enough, but were relatively unimpressed as they got older — the older ones simply bypassed it from the beginning, in search of bigger adventures.

Parades and fireworks

Disney excels at producing fanfare, and its parades, shows, and fireworks displays are among the best of their kind in the world. Note, however, that some productions are staged only on a limited basis or during certain times of the year. Grab a *Times Guide and New Information* brochure when you arrive. It includes an entertainment schedule that lists special goings-on for the day, including concerts, encounters with characters, holiday events, and other major happenings. If you want to know whether a specific parade or fireworks show will be staged when you're in town, consult the calendar at www.disneyworld.com or call ☎ 407-934-7639.

During fireworks and parades, Disney ropes off designated viewing spots for travelers with disabilities and their parties. Consult your park map or a park employee at least an hour before the parade, or you may have trouble making it through the crowds to get to the designated spots. Additionally, if there are two showings of a parade, the later one is usually less crowded.

If nobody in your party is a huge parade fan, these are the best times to ride some of the more popular attractions — while everyone else is lined up along the parade route. You can also use the Walt Disney World Railroad (mentioned earlier in the chapter) to navigate around the various areas of the park when the parade route has blocked off most major routes through the park.

Here are Disney's best parades and fireworks displays:

- **Wishes Nighttime Spectacular:** This explosive display debuted in fall 2003 and is touched off nightly at closing, except during the summer and on holidays, when extended park hours allow for the fireworks to be shown between two scheduled showings of the "SpectroMagic" Parade (see next in this list). Before the display, Tinker Bell flies magically from Cinderella Castle. Then as a cacophany of intricately choreographed fireworks fills the skies, and Jiminy Cricket narrates, images are projected onto the castle in time to the medley of Disney songs being broadcast parkwide. Suggested viewing areas include almost anywhere on the front side of Cinderella Castle, including the very front of Liberty Square and Adventureland. The back of Liberty Square, Frontierland, and Mickey's Toontown Fair offer views as well, though some of the spectacular effects get a bit lost from behind. Disney hotels near the park (the Grand Floridian, Polynesian, Contemporary, and Wilderness Lodge — all reviewed in Chapter 9) also offer views, as the fireworks display is rather large. This show can make even the most blasé fireworks watcher say, "Wow!"

- **"SpectroMagic" Parade:** This after-dark parade combines fiber optics, holographic images, clouds of liquid nitrogen, old-fashioned twinkling lights, and a soundtrack featuring classic Disney tunes. Mickey, dressed in an amber and purple grand magician's cape, makes an appearance in a confetti of light. You'll also see the SpectroMen atop the title float, and Chernabog, *Fantasia*'s monstrous demon, who unfolds his 38-foot wingspan. It takes the electrical equivalent of seven lightning bolts (enough to power a fleet of 2,000 trucks) to bring the show to life. For those who visited Disneyland back in the day, think electric parade, with a few high-tech effects thrown in for good measure.

  SpectroMagic plays only *on select nights,* when park closing extends past dusk (generally during busy periods and on weekends). When park hours are extended to 10 p.m. or later, there are often two chances to view the parade. Check your show schedule to determine availability.

- **Disney Dreams Come True Parade:** Known as Share a Dream Come True in a previous life, you'll find that not too much has really changed. Loads of characters — most atop floats (now sans the snow globes), others alongside — sing, dance, and march their way up Main Street (and into Frontierland) on a daily basis. It's one of the most popular parades in the park and takes place during the height of the day.

Index of Attractions by Land

Adventureland

Captain Jack Sparrow's Pirate Tutorial
The Enchanted Tiki Room
Jungle Cruise
The Magic Carpets of Aladdin
Pirates of the Caribbean
Swiss Family Treehouse

Fantasyland

Bibbidi Bobbidi Boutique
Cinderella Castle
Cinderella's Golden Carousel
Dream Along with Mickey
Dumbo The Flying Elephant
"it's a small world"
Mad Tea Party
The Many Adventures of Winnie the Pooh
Mickey's PhilharMagic
Peter Pan's Flight
Snow White's Scary Adventures

Frontierland

Big Thunder Mountain Railroad
Country Bear Jamboree
Frontierland Shootin' Arcade
Splash Mountain
Tom Sawyer Island
Walt Disney World Railroad
Woody's Cowboy Camp

Liberty Square

The Hall Of Presidents
The Haunted Mansion
Liberty Square Riverboat

Main Street U.S.A.

Harmony Barber Shop
Main Street Family Fun Day Parade
Walt Disney World Railroad

Mickey's Toontown Fair

The Barnstormer at Goofy's Wiseacre Farm
Donald's Boat
Mickey's Country House
Minnie's Country House
Toontown Hall Of Fame
Walt Disney World Railroad

Tomorrowland

Astro Orbiter
Buzz Lightyear's Space Ranger Spin
Monsters, Inc. Laugh Floor
Space Mountain
Stitch's Great Escape!
Tomorrowland Indy Speedway
Tomorrowland Transit Authority
Walt Disney's Carousel of Progress

Chapter 13

Epcot

- -

In This Chapter

▶ Highlighting Epcot basics
▶ Checking out Future World
▶ Touring the World Showcase

- -

Grab a big pot. Start with a theme-park foundation, stir in a heaping helping of technology, and add splashes of global architecture, street performers, and interactive exhibits. What do you have? Epcot, a science field trip combined with a whirlwind tour of the world — without the jet lag, although some say it's just as draining when you try to experience it in one day.

Walt Disney wanted his "Experimental Prototype Community of Tomorrow" to be a high-tech city. But when it opened 15 years after his death, it was a theme park, and the name was shortened to an acronym, Epcot, because, well, it looked good in the snazzy Disney brochures.

 Although the Magic Kingdom is every child's dream, Epcot isn't. It's techno and worldly, best suited for older children (8 and up) and adults with vivid imaginations or cravings to know how things work — or will work in the future. This makes it the least friendly of the Disney parks for those younger than 8. That said, Disney has made a concerted effort to attract and entertain its younger guests in recent years. But even with recent additions — and there are some biggies — there still remains less for tots and tykes at Epcot than at any of Disney's other three theme parks. If you have wee ones, or if all your kids are under the age of 6, I recommend skipping it this time around. If, on the other hand, you have school-age kids (or a mix of tots to teens), or simply an inquiring mind yourself, I suggest at least a two-day visit because it's so vast and varied. In the **World Showcase,** you get to experience exotic, far-flung lands without a passport. In **Future World,** you can jump into the third millennium as you explore cutting-edge technology and the latest and greatest thrill rides.

Discovering Epcot's Essentials

Before helping you dive into Epcot's attractions, I need to get a few more practical matters out of the way.

Buying tickets and making reservations

Tickets to Epcot cost $75 for a one-day adult admission, $63 for kids ages 3 to 9, *but prices frequently change.* See Chapter 11 for other admission options.

 Tickets aren't the only thing that will deplete your stash of cash. The prices of consumables are pretty much standard among Disney parks: $2 or more for a soda or milk, $1.25 to $2 for bottled water, $2.50 for an ice-cream bar, and $1.70 (and up) for a cup of coffee or cocoa.

You can make **Advanced Dining Reservations** (see Chapter 10) at Guest Relations in the Entrance Plaza area, though it's best to do so well ahead of time by calling ☎ **407-939-3463.**

Future World is usually open from 9 a.m. to 7 p.m. and sometimes as late as 10 p.m. World Showcase opens at 11 a.m. and generally closes at 9 p.m., sometimes later.

Locating special services and facilities

In case you forget to bring essential items, or if you need special assistance while at the park, this list of services and facilities may come in handy:

- ✔ **ATMs** accept cards from banks using the Cirrus, STAR, and PLUS networks. You can find them at the front of the park, in the American Pavilion (near the very back), and on the bridge between World Showcase and Future World.

- ✔ The **baby-changing facilities** for Epcot are located in the **Baby Care Center** near the Odyssey Center in Future World. It sells disposable diapers, formula, baby food, and pacifiers. Changing tables can be found in all women's and some men's restrooms.

- ✔ **Disposable cameras and film,** including a limited selection of digital supplies, are sold throughout the park. CD-burning and picture-printing services are available at Kodak Picture Kiosks and select stores in all four theme parks.

- ✔ The **First Aid Station,** staffed by registered nurses, is located near the Odyssey Center in Future World.

- ✔ **Lockers** are located west of Spaceship Earth in the Entrance Plaza, and at the International Gateway (Epcot's back entrance). The cost is $10 a day, including a $5 deposit.

- ✔ **Lost children** are usually taken to Odyssey Center or the Baby Care Center. *Children under 7 should wear name tags inside their clothing.*

- ✔ You can send purchases from any store in the park to **Package Pick-Up** at the gift shop in the Entrance Plaza, where you can pick them up all at once at the end of the day. (This service is free.) Allow three hours for delivery. A Package Pick-Up is also located in

Epcot

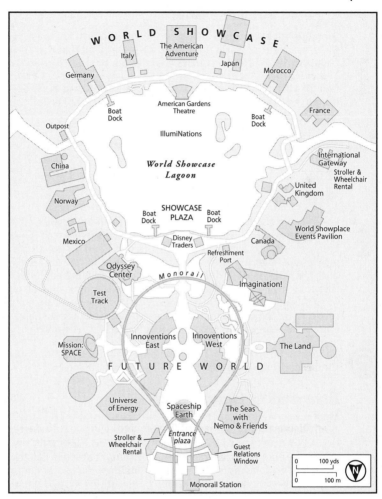

the World Traveler at the International Gateway entrance to the World Showcase. Disney resort guests can have their purchases sent directly to their hotels.

✔ **Pets,** except service animals, are prohibited in the parks, but you can board yours at the **Pet Care Kennels** outside Epcot's Entrance Plaza (☎ **407-824-6568**) for between $10 and $15 a day (depending on the type of pet and whether or not you are a Disney resort guest). Overnight stays are available at a cost of $13 to $20. Proof of vaccination is required. Four other kennels are available in the WDW complex.

> ✔ **Strollers** are available east of the Entrance Plaza and at World
> Showcase's International Gateway. The rental cost is $15 for a
> single and $31 for a double.
>
> ✔ **Wheelchairs** are available at the gift shop east of the Entrance
> Plaza and at World Showcase's International Gateway. The rental
> cost is $10. Electric chairs cost $45 a day plus a $5 deposit.

Call ☎ **407-934-7639** or visit `www.disneyworld.com` to obtain additional information about WDW properties.

Touring Epcot's Top Attractions

Epcot's 300 acres are vibrantly landscaped, so enjoy the scenery on your
way through its two very distinctive areas, Future World and World
Showcase.

Epcot is big enough that walking around it can be exhausting (the World
Showcase semicircle alone is 1.3 miles). That's why some people say
Epcot stands for "Every Person Comes Out Tired." If you don't spend
much time lingering in the World Showcase, you can see all of Epcot in
one day, but you'll need a vacation after you're finished. A boat launch
that runs from Future World to Germany or Morocco may be a great way
to get a sampling of World Showcase, unless you want the complete
world tour. The good news is that most of the attractions take a fair
amount of time, giving you a break between all that walking.

To locate the attractions I discuss in the following sections, check out
the "Epcot" map on p. 203.

Experiencing Future World

Most visitors enter Epcot through the main entrance at Future World
(unlike at any other park, there is also a back entrance, where guests of
the Beach Club, BoardWalk, Dolphin, Swan, and Yacht Club resorts have
access by boat). **Spaceship Earth,** that thing that looks like the giant
silver golf ball meant for a club to fit Paul Bunyan, centers Future World.
Major corporations such as Siemens, Hewlett-Packard, General Motors,
Nestlé, and Kodak sponsor Future World's nine themed areas. The
exhibits focus on discovery, scientific achievements, and technology in
areas spanning from energy to undersea exploration.

Innoventions: The Road to Tomorrow

The crescent-shaped buildings to your right and left, just beyond
Spaceship Earth, showcase cutting-edge technology and future products
in the Innoventions exhibit. The headliner in the building to the left
(Innoventions East) as you enter the park is **House of Innoventions,**
which offers a preview of tomorrow's smart house (including a refrigerator that can itemize and order groceries, plus a Jacuzzi with surround
sound). A recent addition is **Plastic Works,** where kids can build their

own robot and — bonus — they get to keep it for free. The **Test the Limits Lab** exhibit has six kiosks that let kids and fun-loving adults try out a variety of products. In one, you can pull a rope attached to a hammer that crashes into a TV screen to see whether it's shatter resistant. Other exhibits focus on communications, the Segway transport device, the Internet, and your business savvy. New additions include **Don't Waste It,** an area dedicated to garbage — the effect it has on our world and what we can do to reduce what we produce — and **Stormstruck,** where hurricanes, tornados, and other storms are showcased (as are the technologies being developed to reduce their devastating effects).

Across the way at Innoventions West, crowds flock to **Video Games of Tomorrow,** which has nearly three dozen game stations. **ThinkPlace presented by IBM** looks at various interactive software programs (including voice-recognition technology) and also features Internet postcards that allow you to take a picture and send it via e-mail to family and friends back home. **Where's the Fire?** is America's largest fire-safety display, where kids can get an up-close look at a life-size fire truck and follow a lighted path through a burning house to safety. Other diversions include a virtual-reality playground and a display highlighting advances in the life sciences at the **Great American Farm.** The latest addition to Innoventions, **Rockin' Robots,** has cyber-sonic cyborgs making music from items (some instrumental, others most definitely not) of your choosing.

 Epcot has an all-new spot (creatively titled the **Epcot Character Spot**) to meet and greet your favorite characters; even the great Mouse himself makes a daily appearance. This interactive venue, located in Innoventions West behind Club Cool, replaces the Character Connection. Hosting five themed areas (mirroring Future World's pavilions: energy, transportation, communication, the land, and space) are Mickey, Minnie, Goofy, Pluto, and Chip 'n' Dale, so shake hands, exchange hugs, and snap those photos.

Imagination! Pavilion

Even the fountains in front of this pavilion are magical — they shoot water snakes through the air. (The fountains are popular with kids, who like to try to catch the water snakes and, in the process, get a good soaking.)

The pavilion's main attraction is the 3-D **"Honey, I Shrunk The Audience"** ride, based on the Disney film *Honey, I Shrunk the Kids,* in which you're caught up in all the mayhem of another shrinking experiment gone awry. Inside, mice terrorize you and, after you're shrunk, a large cat adds to the trauma; then a giant 5-year-old gives you a good shaking. Vibrating seats and sensory effects enhance all the 3-D action. In the end, everyone is returned to proper size — but not the dog, who offers up one final surprise. Kids under 4 may be frightened by some of the special effects; most older kids will be utterly amused.

On **Journey Into Imagination With Figment,** things begin with an open house at the Imagination Institute, with Dr. Nigel Channing (played by

Monty Python's Eric Idle) taking you on a tour of the labs that demonstrate how the senses capture and control one's imagination. Figment
arrives at each of the areas to prove it's far, far better to set your imagination free. He invites you to his upside-down house, where a new perspective enhances your imagination. This ride is best for the younger
set; older kids will find it too tame.

After you disembark, head for the **Kodak "What If" Labs,** where your
kids can burn lots of energy while exercising their imaginations at a
number of interactive stations that allow them to conduct music, experiment with video, or transform themselves into animals. The lab can be
accessed from the outside as well, so older kids can experiment while
waiting for their younger siblings to ride along with Figment.

The Land Pavilion

The Land is Future World's largest pavilion (a whopping 6 acres) and
showcases the wonders of food and the environment. **Living with the
Land,** a 14-minute boat ride through a simulated rain forest, an African
desert, and the Great Plains, may be a tad too dry for visitors not interested in agriculture. New farming methods and experiments ranging
from hydroponics to plants growing in simulated Martian soil are showcased in real gardens.

A 45-minute **Behind the Seeds** walking tour for gardeners and others
who want a more detailed agricultural lesson is offered daily. It costs $14
for adults and $10 for kids 3 to 9. Sign up at the Green Thumb Emporium
to the right of the Sunshine Seasons food court.

Live footage and animation mix in **Circle of Life,** a 15-minute, 70mm
motion picture based on *The Lion King.* The story line has Timon and
Pumbaa building a monument to the good life called Hakuna Matata
Lakeside Village, but their project, as Simba points out, is damaging the
savanna for other animals. It's a fun, but pointed, environmental message.

The Land's newest attraction is **Soarin',** a ride borrowed from Disney's
California Adventure park. The experience combines cinematic artistry
and state-of-the-art motion technology as you're seated in mock-gliders
and lifted 40 feet inside a giant projection-screen dome. Completely surrounded with the beauty and wonder of the state of California, the elevated seats take you on a scenic tour over the Golden Gate Bridge, the
redwood forests, Napa Valley, and Yosemite, gliding and swooping over
the changing landscapes. You can even feel the sweeping winds and
smell fragrant orange blossoms and pine trees around you. The entire
experience is absolutely one of the best in all of Disney. It makes me
wonder if a version showcasing Florida's highlights may be next . . .
Epcot *is* in Florida, after all. *You must be 40 inches tall to ride.* This is definitely a good candidate for FASTPASS; the lines are lengthy, with wait
times of at least an hour, even during the slower seasons.

Water-cooler conversations

Many an ordinary item at Disney World has hidden entertainment value. Take a sip of water at the drinking fountain in Epcot's Innoventions Plaza (the one right next to the Mouse Gear shop close to Innoventions East) and it may beg you not to drink it dry. No, you haven't gotten too much sun — the fountain actually talks (much to the delight of kids and the surprise of unsuspecting adults). A few more talking fountains are scattered around Epcot.

The fountains aren't the only items at WDW that talk. I've kibitzed with a walking and talking garbage can (named PUSH) in Tomorrowland at the Magic Kingdom (he's been known to make appearances at Epcot as well). An assortment of sassy (if not mobile) garbage cans are also in place inside Cosmic Ray's Starlight Café at the Magic Kingdom. And a personable palm tree (who goes by Wes Palm) may strike up a conversation with you at Animal Kingdom. Ask a Disney employee to direct you if you want to meet any of these chatty contraptions.

Look for a second electronic information board to pop up near the entrance to the Land Pavilion sometime in upcoming months. What exactly will be displayed? No one knows. (Disney does, of course, but they're not telling.) It could be anything from FASTPASS information to wait times at the rides to show schedules or anything in between.

The Seas with Nemo & Friends Pavilion

This "reimagined" pavilion (formerly known as the Living Seas Pavilion), intent on keeping the kid set entertained, still contains its signature aquarium filled with 5.7 million gallons of saltwater, and coral reefs inhabited by some 4,000 sharks, barracudas, parrotfish, rays, dolphins, and other sea critters. Now, however, instead of exhibits tracing the history of undersea exploration and a seven-minute edu-flick, you pass through a serene undersea set (okay, it's really the queue) before picking up where the blockbuster hit *Finding Nemo* left off. "Clamobiles" slowly transport guests through the colorful coral reef in search of Nemo — who has once again wandered off from his class field trip with Mr. Ray. Kids will spot several familiar characters along the way, including Dory, Bruce, Marlin, Squirt, and Crush, who happily join in on the search and, thanks to new animation technology, swim right alongside the aquarium's live inhabitants. The ending is, of course, a happy one, and Nemo is safely reunited with his friends.

Turtle Talk with Crush, an interactive theater presentation, captivates kids' attention, as well as their hearts. In the theater (now slightly larger, thanks to a recent refit), adults sit on benches in the back, while children are asked to sit on the floor right in front of the screen (which initially looks like a giant underwater viewing area). After a brief introduction, Crush, a 152-year-old sea turtle from *Finding Nemo,* appears swimming around, chitchatting to himself and, before you know it, with the kids — and I mean really conversing. Thanks to some amazing technology and animation, the turtle can "see" the audience, pick out whose question he'd like to answer by describing the person's clothing, and actually respond to questions. Kids (and parents) love it.

Disney has also added a small play area where little ones can expend some of their extra energy. **Bruce's Shark World** features some larger-than-life (albeit animated) sharks to climb on, in, and around.

The two-level sea base still displays numerous exhibits dealing with various aspects of marine science and technology, and — most important of all — through acrylic windows, you get close-up views of real denizens of the deep as they swim amid a tremendous man-made coral reef. Both kids and adults enjoy visiting the rescued manatees (sea cows), which reside on the second level.

Epcot DiveQuest is a program that enables certified divers ages 10 and up to take part in a three-hour program that includes a 40-minute dive in the Seas with Nemo & Friends aquarium. (Divers between 10 and 16 are required to have an adult participate along with them.) The program costs $140. Call ☎ **407-939-8687** for details. Keep in mind, however, that you get more dolphins for your money at **Discovery Cove** (see Chapter 20).

Spaceship Earth Pavilion

Epcot's iconic, silvery geosphere houses an attraction of the same name, a slow-track journey back to the roots of communications. The 15-minute ride begins with Cro-Magnon cave painting and then advances to Egyptian hieroglyphs, the Phoenician and Greek alphabets, the Gutenberg printing press, and the Renaissance. Technologies develop at a rapid pace, through the telegraph, telephone, radio, movies, and TV. It's but a short step to the age of electronic communications. But that's not where it ends. In 2007, in partnership with Siemens, the icon underwent a lengthy and much-needed update. Included in the improvements: an all-new ending that allows riders a sneak peek into the future, thanks in part to the newly installed interactive touch screens aboard each "time machine"; enhancements and upgrades to the existing scenes and special effects throughout the attraction; the addition of new scenes; and a hands-on exhibit (located just beyond the exit) featuring games and displays that showcase a variety of innovative future technologies. The presentation isn't nearly as engaging as others in the park, but if it's a really hot day, you need time off your feet, or you have time to spare, then by all means, sit back, cool off, and enjoy.

Test Track Pavilion

Test Track is a $60-million marvel of a ride that combines General Motors (GM) engineering and Disney Imagineering. You can wait in line an hour or more during peak periods, so use FASTPASS. (See Chapter 11 for more information on beating the long lines.) During the last part of your wait, you snake through displays about corrosion, crash tests, and more. The five-minute ride follows what looks to be an actual highway. It includes braking tests, a hill climb, and tight S-curves in a six-passenger "convertible." The left-front seat offers the most thrills as the vehicle moves through the curves. There's also a 12-second burst of heart-pumping speed to the tune of 65 mph on the straightaway (with no traffic!). It's one of the best thrill rides in Epcot, and for those who can't stomach roller coasters, it offers a few thrills that you most likely can handle.

"The beginning is a lot of stopping and starting, but once you hit 60 it's a blast. The only part I didn't like was waiting in line." Fifteen-year-old Ryan loved it, and 11-year-old Nicolas went back for more, but it may be too intense for those younger than 10, and it has a *40-inch height minimum.* The single-rider line (which allows singles to fill in vacant spots in select cars) can speed up your wait time if you can't snag a FASTPASS — but you have to be willing to split up your party to use it. Also keep in mind that rain will shut down the ride, so head here early in the day if there's even the slightest chance of a sprinkle.

In 2007, **Fuel for Thought,** a high-tech interactive walk-through exhibit highlighting GM's latest automotive fuel technologies, was added. Touch-screen games and interactive kiosks offer a glimpse of fuel cells, hybrids, and GM's environmental efforts.

Mission: SPACE Pavilion

The headliner for the Mission: SPACE Pavilion is a motion simulator like those used by astronauts training for space. (Think G-forces and weight-lessness.) You assume the role of commander, pilot, navigator, or engineer, depending on where you sit, and must complete related jobs vital to a flight to the Red Planet. (Don't worry if you miss your cue — you won't crash.) The ride uses a combination of visuals, sound, and centrifugal force to create the illusion of a launch and trip to Mars. As the launch begins, your rocket rumbles under you, white clouds of steam billow around you, and you shoot into the galaxy. Of course, some unexpected twists and turns require you to react pronto in order to complete your mission successfully. Even veteran roller-coaster riders who tried the simulator said the sensation mimics a liftoff, as riders are pressed into their seats and the roar and vibration tricks the brain during the launch portion of the four-minute adventure.

In the pre-ride show, you go to the futuristic International Space Training Center and then proceed to the Ready Room, where you learn your role as commander, pilot, navigator, or engineer from CapCom (played by actor Gary Sinise, who costarred in *Apollo 13*).

Because this is probably one of the most physically intense rides in all of Mickeyville, Disney was prompted to create a less-intense version after numerous guests reportedly experienced various adverse effects. By removing the centrifuge from two of the four simulators, riders can now choose their experience: the original G-force generator, or a milder, mellower Mission. If you are prone to motion sickness from spinning, have a sinus infection, or experience severe claustrophobia (it's a pretty tight fit), the mellower Green Team version would definitely be the better choice. (There's a reason they put motion-sickness bags in each capsule and post all the warnings.) After the door of your pod closes, that's it — there's no escape. You're going to Mars whether you like it or not. If you choose the original (Orange Team) and the experience gets to be too much midtrip, a Disney Imagineer told me that focusing straight ahead can help minimize the effects, and he warned against closing your eyes as that actually *enhances* the ride's intensity.

Just so you know, if you're taller (or shorter, in the case of younger kids) than average, you may have difficulties seeing the screen from the optimum perspective or handling the controls from the optimum angle.

"It was awesome — the whole ride was intense, but awesome." Fifteen-year-old Ryan, who has an intense hatred for most roller coasters, survived and was even smiling after the (original) ride. My 11- and 13-year-olds concurred. After riding the original version, 11-year-old Nicolas was overheard saying, "It's sooooooooo cool — it's even better than the roller coasters" (this from a roller-coaster junkie), and before we knew it he was headed back for more. But be aware that this ride (in particular, the original) may be far too intense for those younger than 10 and it has a *44-inch height minimum.*

Universe of Energy

Sponsored by Exxon, Universe of Energy has a roof full of solar panels and a goal of bettering your understanding of America's energy problems and potential solutions. **Ellen's Energy Adventure,** the pavilion's 32-minute ride, features comedienne Ellen DeGeneres tutored by Bill Nye the Science Guy to be a *Jeopardy!* champ. An animated movie depicts the Earth's molten beginnings, its cooling process, and the formation of fossil fuels. You then move back 275 million years into an eerie, storm-wracked landscape of the Mesozoic era. Giant audio-animatronic dragon-flies, pterodactyls, dinosaurs, earthquakes, and streams of molten lava threaten before you enter a misty tunnel deep in the bowels of a volcano. When you emerge into a giant space that looks like a NASA control room, a 70mm film projected on a massive 210-foot wraparound screen depicts the challenges of the world's increasing energy demands and the emerging technologies that will help meet them. The show ends on an upbeat note — a vision of an energy-abundant future and Ellen as a new *Jeopardy!* champion. The ride itself is a bit slow moving (literally), but the bits featuring Ellen are funny, and it's a good place to escape the heat. Younger kids may find brief parts of the film a bit intense and the fleeting appearance of the dinosaurs a tad too lifelike.

Wonders of Life Pavilion

At press time, the Wonders of Life Pavilion remains closed. This has, in fact, been the case since 2004 — a good deal longer than most "seasonal" shutdowns generally last. This of course begs the question: Is a new attraction in the works? Disney's not commenting, but the omission of the pavilion from park maps reads loud and clear. It would seem that the fate of Wonders of Life may very well be a slow death.

Traveling through the World Showcase

The World Showcase is enjoyed mainly by adults or older kids with an appreciation of world history, architectural wonders, and cultural shows, though strategically placed Kidcot stations offer a minor diversion for the preschool set. The World Showcase's 11 miniature nations, each re-created with meticulous detail, open at 11 a.m. daily and surround the park's 40-acre lagoon. The countries have authentically indigenous architecture, landscaping, background music, restaurants, and shops. The nations' cultural facets are explored in art exhibits, song-and-dance performances, and innovative rides, films, and attractions. And all the employees at each of the pavilions are natives of the country represented.

 Most of these nations offer some kind of live entertainment throughout the day. You may see acrobats, bagpipers, mariachi bands, storytellers, belly dancers, and stilt walkers, among other unique and interesting acts. Characters regularly appear in the Showcase Plaza. When you enter the park, check your *Times Guide and New Information* brochure for showtimes. Schedules are also posted near the entrance to each country.

 Those with kids should grab a copy of the **Magic and Wonder for Kids 5 and Under Guide** at Guest Relations upon entering the park; it uses a harlequin mask to note **Kidcot Fun Stops** inside the World Showcase (and a few in Future World, too), whereas the regular map uses a white *K* in a red square as a marker. These play and learning stations are for the younger set and allow them to stop at various World Showcase countries (and Future World pavilions), do crafts, get autographs, have Kidcot passports stamped (these are available for purchase in most Epcot stores and make a great souvenir), and, in the World Showcase, chat with cast members native to those countries. Your kids will get the chance to learn about different countries and make a souvenir to bring home. For more information, stop at Guest Relations when you get into the park. The Kidcot Fun Stop stations in World Showcase open at 11 a.m. daily; stations in Future World open at 9 a.m. daily.

Finally, excellent shopping and dining opportunities are available at all the pavilions. For details on dining inside the World Showcase, see Chapter 10; you can find shopping information in Chapter 17.

The American Adventure Pavilion

This flagship pavilion occupies the central spot in the World Showcase. Its main building is a 108,000-square-foot Georgian mansion. Notable U.S. landmarks that inspired Disney's Imagineers in the design of the building include Independence Hall, Monticello, and Colonial Williamsburg. The action takes place in an elegant Colonial-style 1,024-seat theater loaded with Corinthian columns, chandeliers, and 12 marble statues symbolizing the 12 "Spirits of America." The flags you pass under as you enter the theater — 44 in all — include every one that has flown over the United States throughout its history.

The actual production, a 29-minute CliffsNotes version of U.S. history, utilizes a 72-foot rear-projection screen, rousing music, and a large cast of lifelike audio-animatronic figures, including narrators Mark Twain and Ben Franklin. You follow the voyage of the *Mayflower,* watch Jefferson writing the Declaration of Independence, and witness Matthew Brady photographing a family that the Civil War is about to divide. You can also witness Pearl Harbor and the *Eagle* going to the moon. Teddy Roosevelt discusses the need for national parks; Susan B. Anthony speaks out on women's rights; Frederick Douglass discusses slavery; and Chief Joseph talks about the plight of Native Americans. It's one of Disney's best historical productions.

Entertainment includes the **Spirit of America Fife & Drum Corps** and the **Voices of Liberty** a cappella group, which sings patriotic songs in the lobby of the main theater between shows. Large-scale outdoor productions are often staged in the **America Gardens Theatre,** a 1,800-seat outdoor venue across from the main pavilion building.

Canada Pavilion

The pavilion's highlight attraction is **O Canada!** — a dazzling, recently updated, 18-minute, 360-degree CircleVision film that shows Canada's scenic wonders, from sophisticated Montréal to the thundering flight of thousands of snow geese departing the St. Lawrence River.

The theater has no seats and you stand for the entire production (though there are lean rails).

The architecture and landscape in the Canada Pavilion include a mansard-roofed replica of Ottawa's 19th-century Château Laurier (here called the Hôtel du Canada) and a Native village complete with 30-foot replicas of Ojibwa totem poles. The Canadian wilderness is reflected by a rocky mountain (really made of concrete and chicken wire); a waterfall cascading into a white-water stream; and a mini forest of evergreens, stately cedars, maples, and birch trees. Don't miss the stunning floral display inspired by Victoria's world-renowned Butchart Gardens. **Off Kilter** entertains visitors with New Age Celtic music.

China Pavilion

You enter Epcot's version of China through a triple-arched ceremonial gate inspired by the Temple of Heaven in Beijing, a summer retreat for Chinese emperors. Passing through the gate, you'll see a half-size replica of this ornately embellished red-and-gold circular temple, built in 1420 during the Ming Dynasty. Gardens simulate those at Suzhou, with miniature waterfalls, lotus ponds, and bamboo groves.

Inside the temple, you can watch **Reflections of China,** a 20-minute, 360-degree CircleVision film that explores the culture and landscapes in and around seven Chinese cities. It visits Hong Kong, Beijing, Shanghai, and the Great Wall (begun 24 centuries ago!), among other places.

Like Canada, the theater here has no seats and you stand for the entire production (though there are lean rails).

Land of Many Faces is an exhibit that introduces China's ethnic peoples. Entertainment is provided daily by the amazing **Dragon Legend Acrobats.** Other entertainment includes the authentic instrumental sounds of **SI XIAN.**

France Pavilion

This pavilion focuses on France's Belle Epoque (Beautiful Age) — the period from 1870 to 1910 — when art, literature, and architecture ruled. You enter via a replica of the beautiful cast-iron Pont des Arts footbridge over the Seine and find yourself in a park with bleached sycamores, Bradford pear trees, flowering crape myrtle, and sculptured parterre flower gardens inspired by Seurat's painting *A Sunday Afternoon on the Island of La Grande Jatte.* The grounds also include a 1:10 scale model of the Eiffel Tower, which was built from Gustave Eiffel's original blueprints.

The premier attraction here is **Impressions de France.** Shown in the palatial Palais du Cinema, a sit-down theater a la Fontainebleau, this 18-minute film is a journey through diverse French landscapes projected on a vast, 200-degree wraparound screen. Outside, grab a French pastry and watch the antics of **Serveur Amusant,** a comedic waiter who delights the crowd with a balancing act like no other.

Germany Pavilion

Enclosed by castle walls, Germany offers 'wursts, oompah bands, and a rollicking atmosphere. The clock tower in the central *platz* (plaza) includes a glockenspiel that heralds each hour with quaint melodies. The **Biergarten Restaurant** was inspired by medieval Rothenberg, while 16th-century building facades replicate a merchant's hall in the Black Forest and the town hall in Frankfurt's Römerberg Square.

If you're a model-train fanatic or visiting with young kids, don't miss the exquisitely detailed version of a small Bavarian town, complete with working train station, located between Germany and Italy.

Italy Pavilion

Italy lures visitors over an arched stone footbridge to a replica of Venice's intricately ornamented pink-and-white Doge's Palace. Other architectural highlights include the 83-foot Campanile (bell tower) of St. Mark's Square, Venetian bridges, and a piazza enclosing a version of Bernini's Neptune Fountain. A garden wall suggests a backdrop of provincial countryside, and citrus, cypress, pine, and olive trees frame a formal garden. Gondolas are moored on the lagoon.

In the street entertainment department, **Sergio,** a mime juggler, fascinates visitors young and old daily. You can also see the hilarious **World Showcase Players,** who, at times, have been seen spoofing Shakespeare's Italian-set *Taming of the Shrew* or heading off on a quest for the Holy Grail.

Japan Pavilion

A flaming red *torii* (gate of honor) on the banks of the lagoon and the graceful blue-roofed Goju No To pagoda, inspired by an 8th-century shrine built at Nara, welcome you to the Japan Pavilion, which focuses on Japan's ancient culture. If you have some leisure time, enjoy the exquisitely cultivated Japanese garden — it's a haven of tranquility in a place that's anything but, and 90 percent of the plants you see are actually native to Japan. The Shishinden, inspired by the ceremonial and coronation hall found in the Imperial Palace grounds at Kyoto, is home to the **Mitsukoshi Department Store** (discussed in Chapter 17). The **Bijutsu-kan Gallery** offers rotating exhibits ranging from 18th-century Bunraki puppets to Japanese baseball to tin toys.

Make sure that you include a performance of traditional Taiko drumming by **Matsuriza,** which entertains guests daily. Japanese storytellers offer up native tales every now and then, and right before your eyes, **Miyuki** transforms ribbons of rice dough into intricate sculptures to save or savor — you decide.

Mexico Pavilion

Mariachi bands greet you at Mexico's festive showcase, fronted by a Mayan pyramid modeled on the Aztec temple of Quetzalcoatl (God of Life) and surrounded by dense Yucatán jungle landscaping. Just inside the pavilion's entrance, a museum exhibits rare Oaxacan wood sculptures. Also inside the pyramid, you'll find an open-air marketplace filled with artisans peddling their wares under the star-filled skies above (it's always nighttime here), behind which is the **Gran Fiesta Tour Starring the Three Caballeros** (replacing El Rio Del Tiempo). This eight-minute cruise along the Mexican countryside now features Donald Duck, José Carioca, and Panchito (from the 1944 Disney classic *The Three Caballeros*) as they reunite to perform in Mexico City. Donald, however, wanders off to see the sights, leaving José and Panchito to search for him. An animated overlay blends the Caballero characters in with the existing scenery. Along the river route, passengers get a close-up look at the Mayan pyramid and the erupting Popocatepetl volcano.

Mariachi Cobre, a 12-piece mariachi ensemble, often performs in the marketplace as well as out in front of the Mayan temple.

Morocco Pavilion

A replica of the world-famous Koutoubia Minaret, the prayer tower of a 12th-century mosque in Marrakesh, overlooks the very atmospheric pavilion of Morocco, featuring the architectural styles of several cities inside the North African kingdom. The exotic ambience is enhanced by geometrically patterned tile work, hand-painted wood ceilings, and brass lighting fixtures. The Medina (old city), entered via a replica of an arched gateway in Fez, leads to a traditional Moroccan home and the narrow, winding streets of the *souk,* a bustling marketplace where authentic handicrafts are on display. The Medina's courtyard centers on a replica of the ornately tiled Najjarine Fountain in Fez.

The **Gallery of Arts and History** contains ever-changing exhibits of Moroccan art. A guided tour of the pavilion, **Treasures of Morocco,** runs three times daily. (Check your *Times Guide and New Information* brochure for show schedules.) Speaking of shows, the band **Mo'Rockin'** kicks things up with Arabian rock music.

Norway Pavilion

The Norway Pavilion's stave church, located off a charming cobblestone plaza, and styled after the 13th-century Gol Church of Hallingdal, features changing exhibits focusing on Norwegian art and culture. A replica of Oslo's 14th-century Akershus Castle is the setting for the pavilion's restaurant, **Akershus Royal Banquet Hall** (see Chapter 10). Other buildings simulate the red-roofed cottages of Bergen and the timber-sided farm buildings of the Nordic woodlands.

Norway includes a two-part attraction. **Maelstrom,** a boat ride in a dragon-headed Viking vessel, travels Norway's fjords and mythical forests to the music of Peer Gynt. Along the way, you see polar bears prowling the shore and you are turned into frogs by trolls that cast a spell on your boat. The watercraft crashes through a narrow gorge (two small separate drops) and spins into the North Sea, where a storm is in progress. (Don't worry — this is a relatively calm ride, though some of the thunder elements may frighten the very young.) The storm abates, a princess's kiss turns you into a human again, and you disembark to a 10th-century Viking village to view the 70mm film *Norway,* highlighting history and culture (you can proceed through the theater to the exit if you don't want to watch the film).

To the left of the Stave Church stands a large wooden Viking ship (much to my disappointment, it now stands simply as a display — rather than the imaginative play area it once was). On the entertainment front, **SPELMANNS GLEDJE** plays lively Norwegian folk music.

United Kingdom Pavilion

The United Kingdom Pavilion evokes Merry Olde England through its **Britannia Square,** a London-style park complete with copper-roofed gazebo bandstand, a stereotypical red phone booth (it really works!), an old-fashioned pub, a thatch-roofed cottage, and a statue of the Bard. Four centuries of architecture — from the Tudor era all the way through the English Regency period — line cobblestone streets. In the horticulture department, there's a formal garden with low box hedges in geometric patterns, and the flagstone paths and a stone fountain replicate the landscaping of 16th- and 17th-century palaces.

Don't miss the **British Invasion,** a group that impersonates the Beatles; vivacious pub pianist **Pam Brody;** and **Jason Wethington,** a pub magician who offers up Disney magic of the sleight-of-hand variety.

Ending your day at Epcot

Epcot's end-of-day celebration, **IllumiNations: Reflections of Earth,** is a moving blend of fireworks, lasers, and fountains in a display that's signature Disney. The show is worth dealing with the crowds that flock to the parking lot when it's over.

You can find tons of good viewing points around the lagoon (one excellent spot is the terrace at the **Rose & Crown Dining Room** in the United Kingdom — see Chapter 10 for more on the place). That said, it's best to stake your claim at least a half-hour or so before showtime, which is listed in your *Times Guide and New Information* brochure.

Index of Attractions by Land

Future World

Imagination! Pavilion
Innoventions: The Road to Tomorrow
The Land Pavilion
Mission: SPACE Pavilion
The Seas with Nemo & Friends
Pavilion
Spaceship Earth Pavilion
Test Track Pavilion
Universe of Energy

World Showcase

Canada Pavilion
China Pavilion
France Pavilion
Germany Pavilion
Italy Pavilion
Japan Pavilion
Mexico Pavilion
Morocco Pavilion
Norway Pavilion
United Kingdom Pavilion
U.S.A. Pavilion

Chapter 14

Disney's Hollywood Studios

In This Chapter
- Discovering Disney's Hollywood Studios' extras and essentials
- Comparing Disney's Hollywood Studios and Universal Studios
- Reviewing Disney's Hollywood Studios' main attractions
- Catching the shows and parades

Disney touts Disney's Hollywood Studios (the park's name changed from Disney–MGM Studios in 2008) as "the Hollywood that never was and always will be." Its movie- and TV-themed shows and props set the stage, so to speak, but this little park is also home to two of the biggest thrill rides in Orlando: **Twilight Zone Tower of Terror** and **Rock 'n' Roller Coaster Starring Aerosmith.** Its neighborhoods include Hollywood and Sunset boulevards, where Art Deco movie sets evoke the Golden Age of Hollywood. **Streets of America** is lined with miniature renditions of the cityscapes of New York City and San Francisco, including re-creations of actual city streets and buildings. You'll find some high-quality street performances (including **High School Musical 2: School's Out!** and the **Block Party Bash**) and stage productions here. Its standing as a working movie and TV studio has been downgraded over time, though shows are still produced here occasionally. The **Lights, Motors, Action! Extreme Stunt Show** lets you experience the thrills of a high-speed chase and other dramatic movie stunts, and also gives you insight into how such effects are created, designed, and filmed for the movies. Slated to debut in early 2009 is the **American Idol Experience,** an all-new interactive show based on the hit television show *American Idol,* adding an incredibly exciting element to the existing lineup of spectacular show-style experiences found at Disney's Hollywood Studios. Park guests are invited to audition, perform, and compete live on a stage (with the help of backup singers and a band) in a stage show that practically mimics the original.

Unlike the Magic Kingdom and Epcot, you can pretty much see Disney's Hollywood Studios' 154 acres of attractions relatively easily in a single day — that is, if you arrive reasonably early and keep up a brisk pace. If you don't get a Disney's Hollywood Studio's Guidemap and *Times Guide and New Information* brochure as you enter the park, be sure to grab one at Guest Relations.

Disney's Hollywood Studios

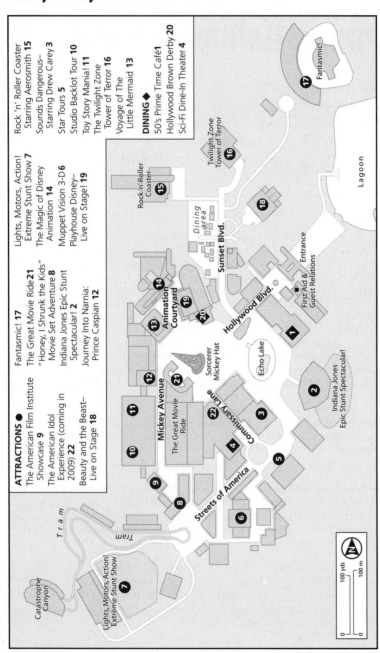

ATTRACTIONS ●
The American Film Institute Showcase **9**
The American Idol Experience (coming in 2009) **22**
Beauty and the Beast–Live on Stage **18**

Fantasmic! **17**
The Great Movie Ride **21**
"Honey, I Shrunk the Kids" Movie Set Adventure **8**
Indiana Jones Epic Stunt Spectacular! **5**
Journey Into Narnia: Prince Caspian **12**

Lights, Motors, Action! Extreme Stunt Show **7**
The Magic of Disney Animation **14**
Muppet Vision 3-D **6**
Playhouse Disney–Live on Stage! **19**

Rock 'n' Roller Coaster Starring Aerosmith **15**
Sounds Dangerous–Starring Drew Carey **3**
Star Tours **5**
Studio Backlot Tour **10**
Toy Story Mania! **11**
The Twilight Zone Tower of Terror **16**
Voyage of The Little Mermaid **13**

DINING ◆
50's Prime Time Café **1**
Hollywood Brown Derby **20**
Sci-Fi Dine-In Theater **4**

Check showtimes in the *Times Guide and New Information* brochure as soon as you arrive and come up with an entertainment schedule that works for you. Likewise, take a second to plan ahead for mealtimes and make your Advanced Dining Reservations immediately if you haven't already; many of the park's unique restaurants fill up quickly.

Acquainting Yourself with Disney's Hollywood Studios

Before I head off for a closer look at the park's rides and attractions, I must first deal with some mundane matters that you may very well appreciate after you're there.

Buying tickets and making reservations

Admission prices to Disney's Hollywood Studios are $75 for a one-day adult ticket, $63 for children ages 3 to 9. See Chapter 11 for other ticket options.

Tickets aren't the only thing you'll spend your hard-earned money on. The prices of consumables are pretty much standard among Disney parks. Disney's Hollywood Studios nails you to the tune of $2 or more for a soda or milk, $1.25 to $2.50 for bottled water, $2.50 for an ice-cream bar, and $1.70 (and up) for a cup of coffee.

If you haven't made **Advanced Dining Reservations** before you arrive by calling ☎ **407-939-3463** (the preferred course of action), do so the minute you enter the park if you care to eat a sit-down meal at one of the unique dining venues. (See Chapter 10 for details on Disney's Hollywood Studios' best restaurants.)

Park hours are generally from 9 a.m. to 6 or 7 p.m., with extended hours — sometimes as late as 10 p.m. — during holidays and summer.

Locating special services and facilities

In case you forget to bring essential items, or if you need special assistance while at the park, here's a list of services and facilities that may come in handy:

- ✔ **ATMs** accept cards from banks using the Cirrus, STAR, and PLUS networks. They're located to the right of the main entrance and next to Toy Story Pizza Planet, across from Muppet Vision 3-D.

- ✔ The **Baby Care Center** is to the left of the main entrance and includes places for nursing and changing. You can buy disposable diapers, formula, baby food, and pacifiers. Changing tables are also in all women's restrooms and some men's rooms.

- **Disposable cameras and film** are available throughout the park, although digital supplies like memory chips and batteries are limited.

- The **First Aid Station,** staffed by registered nurses, is in the Entrance Plaza adjoining Guest Relations.

- **Lockers** are located near Oscar's Classic Car Souvenirs, to the right of the entrance. They cost $10 a day, including a $5 refundable deposit.

- **Lost children** at Disney's Hollywood Studios are taken to Guest Relations. *Children younger than 7 should wear name tags inside their clothing.*

- Purchases can be sent to **Package Pick-Up** at Oscar's Super Service near the entrance — just remember to pick them up before you leave the park. Allow three hours for delivery. If you're staying at a Disney resort, packages can be sent directly to your resort, though it may take a day or two for them to get there. Both services are free.

- **Pets,** except service animals, are prohibited in the parks, but you can board yours at the **Pet Care Kennels** to the left and just outside the entrance (☎ **407-824-6568**). Day accommodations cost $10 to $15, depending on the type of pet and whether or not you are a Disney resort guest. Overnight stays run between $13 and $20. Proof of vaccinations is required, and walking and feeding your pet is your responsibility.

- **Strollers** are available at Oscar's Super Service, inside the main entrance. Rental costs are $15 for a single, $31 for a double.

- **Wheelchairs** are available at Oscar's Super Service inside the main entrance. The rental cost is $10 for a standard wheelchair; you can rent a battery-run chair for $45 plus a $5 deposit.

Call ☎ **407-824-4321** or visit Disney's Web site (www.disneyworld.com) to get more information on WDW properties.

Pitting Disney's Hollywood Studios against Universal Studios Florida

If you love the movies, Broadway-style productions, or the Golden Age of Hollywood, you'll enjoy wandering the streets, shops, and sets of Disney's Hollywood Studios. **Universal Studios Florida** (see Chapter 18) is aimed at tweens and teens, but caters to visitors with children more than in years past, thanks to Fievel's Playland and the other attractions in Woody Woodpecker's KidZone. But is this town big enough for two studios? Each offers its own flair and unique experiences, so if you can swing it, it's well worth your time to experience both. I genuinely feel for the visitor who has time to visit only one of these stellar parks.

Both have a variety of good shows (though most of Universal's border on a PG rating and are geared toward older audiences) and, alas, unavoidably long lines. Universal has an edge in the number and diversity of rides, but Disney's Hollywood Studios' **Twilight Zone Tower of Terror** is, arguably, the best thrill ride in either park (even with the addition of Universal's **Revenge of the Mummy the Ride**), and **Rock 'n' Roller Coaster Starring Aerosmith** is nothing to sneeze at either. Universal is larger, which means you wear out more shoe leather, but it isn't as congested.

Overall, Disney's Hollywood Studios has some great shows (most of which are geared to tinier tots) and uniquely themed rides, with standouts including **Toy Story Mania!** (which debuted in 2008), **Lights, Motors, Action! Extreme Stunt Show,** the **Indiana Jones Epic Stunt Spectacular!,** the **Twilight Zone Tower of Terror, Rock 'n' Roller Coaster Starring Aerosmith, Star Tours, Muppet Vision 3-D,** and the **Studio Backlot Tour,** but I give Universal, with its elaborate street sets, a very microscopic edge if only in the atmosphere department.

The following sections divide attractions in Disney's Hollywood Studios into two categories. Rides and shows rated G will assuredly entertain the youngest visitors and, in many cases, the older ones as well. PG-rated rides are those geared toward adults and teens (and may bore or frighten children). For a look at the park, turn to the "Disney's Hollywood Studios" map on p. 220.

Entertaining the Whole Family: G-Rated Attractions and Rides

Rides and attractions listed in this category are suitable for everyone, although a few may not appeal to teens or adults.

Beauty and the Beast—Live on Stage

A 1,500-seat covered amphitheater provides the stage for this 30-minute live production of *Beauty and the Beast,* adapted from the movie version. Musical highlights include the rousing "Be Our Guest" opening number and the poignant title song featured in a romantic waltz-scene finale. Sets and costumes are lavish, and the production numbers are spectacular. Arrive early to get a good seat. The park usually hosts four or five shows a day.

"Honey, 1 Shrunk the Kids" Movie Set Adventure

In this 11,000-square-foot playground, everything is larger than life. A thicket of grass is 30 feet tall, mushroom caps are three stories high, and a friendly ant makes a suitable seat. Play areas include a massive cream cookie, a 52-foot garden hose with leaks, cereal loops 9 feet wide and cushioned for jumping, and a waterfall cascading from a leaf to a dell of fern sprouts. (The sprouts form a musical stairway, activated when you step from sprout to sprout.) There's also a root maze with a flower-petal slide, a filmstrip slide in a giant film canister, and a huge spider web with 11 levels. This attraction is a great place for children ages 2 to 8 to work off their excess energy, while you regain some of your sanity.

Indiana Jones Epic Stunt Spectacular!

"Spectacular" barely begins to describe this 35-minute rock 'em, sock 'em extravaganza guaran-double-teed to keep you entertained and on the edge of your seat. The show is held in a big, open-air stadium and recruits a handful of adult volunteers to help out. It begins with Indy rappelling down from the rafters; the amazing special effects soon have him dodging spikes, falling into a pit of molten something-or-other, surviving two ax-wielding gargoyles, grabbing a priceless amulet, and then outrunning fire, steam, and a tremendous boulder that nearly flattens him — and that's only the first five minutes. The actors, special-effects folks, and director use the breaks to explain what you just saw or are about to see, including stunt secrets. In later scenes, Indy battles the evil Nazis in a Cairo marketplace and at an airport munitions dump. Shots are fired and flames are bursting all around the set.

The closer to the front of the theater you are, the more likely you are to feel the extreme heat from the explosions, so if you have young kids along, you may want to sit a few rows back.

"It looked just like the movie — how cool is that!" It's definitely an adrenaline booster, though loud noises and moments of violence (really quite mild when compared to today's movie standards) may make this show a little too intense for kids under 5. There are usually five or six shows a day.

Journey Into Narnia: Prince Caspian

Thanks to a recent refit, guests will no longer journey through the wardrobe to the wintry world of Narnia; instead they'll explore Aslan's Stone Table chamber. The basic premise however, is not unlike the attraction's predecessor, as scenes from the movie are shown against the backdrop (this time from *Prince Caspian*) and Prince Caspian (rather than the White Witch) makes an appearance (live), albeit momentarily, before you exit through the gallery housing elaborate costumes, storyboards, blueprints, props, creatures, and other movie memorabilia used in making the film. Although this small attraction doesn't make the top of my must-see list, fans will find it's worth the wait.

Lights, Motors, Action! Extreme Stunt Show

Inspired by the popular Stunt Show Spectacular at Disneyland Paris, this high-octane stunt show takes places on the set of a spy thriller in progress, with a quaint Mediterranean village as the backdrop. The show features specially designed stunt cars, motorcycles, and jet skis, plus some rather amazing special effects and even more spectacular driving — with an audience member pulled in for a bit of the fun. Much like the Indiana Jones Epic Stunt Spectacular!, insiders reveal industry secrets, detailing how stunts are created, designed, and filmed for the movies. Filmed images are shown on an oversize screen, illustrating how the use of different camera angles can add drama to filmed scenes.

Seating is in a large outdoor stadium with a degree of cover from the sun, but a late afternoon show may be the best way to avoid the direct rays and heat. The only bad seats in the house are the few rows in the center just above an entrance to the set used by some of the vehicles. Note that this one gets loud . . . Loud . . . LOUD! Children under 3 may not tolerate the revving engines and explosions well.

The Magic of Disney Animation

This tour opens with a live artist interacting with Mushu from Disney's *Mulan* and a cute video on the making of that film. Alas, Disney's real-life Florida animators were all laid off in 2004, so the inspection of their former working quarters strikes a somewhat sour chord. The tour ends on an up note, however, as visitors attempt their own Disney character drawings under the supervision of a working animator. Just before exiting, be sure to have the kids head to an animation station. The short computerized program photographs your children's faces and asks a few questions to determine which Disney character they're most like.

Muppet Vision 3-D

This must-see production stars Kermit and Miss Piggy in a delightful marriage of Jim Henson's puppets and Disney audio-animatronics, special-effects wizardry, 70mm film, and cutting-edge 3-D technology. The action takes place in a pretty-darn-accurate reproduction of the theater you probably grew up watching on TV. In the show, you encounter flying Muppets, cream pies, cannonballs, high winds, fiber-optic fireworks, bubble showers, and even an actual spray of water. Kermit is host, Miss Piggy sings "Dream a Little Dream of Me," Statler and Waldorf heckle the action from the balcony, and Nicki Napoleon and his Emperor Penguins (a full Muppet orchestra) provide music from the pit. Kids of all ages will enjoy this whimsical attraction; adults will be just as delighted. The 25-minute show (including a 12-minute video pre-show) runs continuously.

Playhouse Disney–Live on Stage!

Younger audiences (2–8 years old) will love this recently updated 20-minute show, with a whole new cast of characters that debuted in 2008, including favorites from *Mickey Mouse Clubhouse, Little Einsteins, Handy Manny,* and more. The show runs several times daily and encourages preschoolers to dance, sing, and play along with the cast. Check your *Times Guide and New Information* brochure for show schedules.

Sounds Dangerous–Starring Drew Carey

Drew Carey (on film) provides laughs while dual-audio technology provides some incredible hair-raising effects during a 12-minute mixture of movie and live action at ABC Sound Studios. You feel like you're right in the middle of the action of a TV pilot featuring undercover police work and plenty of amusing mishaps. Even when the picture disappears, you continue the chase via headphones that demonstrate "3-D" sound effects such as a roomful of angry bees, a herd of galloping elephants, and a deafening auto race.

Sound World, an interactive exhibit near the exit, lets you create your own video soundtracks and listen to more 3-D sounds through headsets in darkened booths. There's an outside entrance if you skipped the show.

Most of the show takes place in total darkness, and the sound and sensory effects may be frightening to younger ears, so think twice before bringing children under 8.

Toy Story Mania!

Making its debut in 2008, Toy Story Mania! is the newest family attraction to grace the stage at Disney's Hollywood Studios. This carnival-inspired ride has guests sporting 3-D glasses, shrinking to the size of a toy, and traveling along a *Toy Story*–themed midway — think "Honey, I Shrunk The Audience" meets Buzz Lightyear's Space Ranger Spin. Shooting at animated targets to earn points, you'll move from one game to the next with Woody, Buzz, Hamm, Bo Peep, and the Little Green Men cheering you on as you go. Hidden targets add extra points to your score, lead to different levels of play, and make for a different experience each time you ride. This one's a must for the entire family!

Voyage of The Little Mermaid

Hazy lighting helps paint a picture of an underwater world in a 17-minute show that combines live performances, movie clips, puppetry, and special effects. Sebastian sings "Under the Sea"; Ariel performs "Part of Your World"; and the evil Ursula, 12 feet tall and 10 feet wide, belts out "Poor Unfortunate Soul." The Voyage has some scary scenes, but most little kids don't mind because, just like the movie, they know the show has a happy ending. You get spritzed with water during the show, making this an especially good experience during hot days.

Exploring PG-Rated Attractions and Rides

Rides and attractions in this category appeal to older children and adults. In some cases, they have age, height, or health restrictions — most of them well deserved.

The American Film Institute Showcase

More of a shop than anything, the showcase includes an exhibit area where you can waltz through Hollywood history, learning about the folks behind the movies — editors, cinematographers, producers, and directors whose names roll by in the blur of credits. It also spotlights some of the institute's lifetime-achievement winners, including Bette Davis, Jack Nicholson, and Elizabeth Taylor. A special exhibit here, **Villains: Movie Characters You Love to Hate,** features the costumes and props of several notable bad guys, including Darth Vader.

The Great Movie Ride

Set inside a replica of Los Angeles's famous Grauman's Chinese Theatre, this 22-minute journey down Disney's Hollywood Studios' memory lane starts in the 1930s and moves forward from there, using lifelike audio-animatronic versions of famous actors to re-create some memorable movie moments. The line/waiting area features film clips from various classic films, and several cinematic artifacts to gawk at, including a set of Dorothy's ruby slippers from *The Wizard of Oz.* Then, you're off to watch Bogey say goodbye to Bergman, Tarzan (the Johnny Weismuller version) swing through the jungle, James Cagney act tough, and Gene Kelly dance — and sing — in the rain. A live outlaw enhances the action when he kidnaps you and your mates, but — revenge is so sweet, isn't it? — he goes the wrong way, hopping onto a set that has an uncanny resemblance to one in *Raiders of the Lost Ark.* After a narrow escape from the space thing from *Alien,* your bank-robbing buddy gets incinerated when he tries to steal the sphinx's jewel. You survive to follow the yellow brick road to Oz, where a remarkable likeness of the witch warns, "I'll get you my pretty, ahahahaha!"

Even though this ride was recently refurbished, the three oldest kids expressed zero interest, so we split up. They instead headed for the heart-pounding thrills down on Hollywood Boulevard while my two youngest (ages 7 and 9) and I enjoyed the slow-moving trip (with a brief moment or two of excitement thrown in for good measure) through Tinseltown. Movie buffs, nostalgic adults, and those in need of a rest will love it.

Rock 'n' Roller Coaster Starring Aerosmith

It takes a lot to really wow anyone anymore, but this ride is sure to do the trick. This inverted roller coaster is one of the best thrill rides that WDW has to offer.

Rock 'n' Roller Coaster is a fast-and-furious indoor ride that puts you in a 24-passenger stretch limo, outfitted with 120 speakers that blare Aerosmith at 32,000 watts! A flashing light warns you to "prepare to merge as you've never merged before," and faster than you can scream "Stop the music!" (around 2.8 seconds, actually), you shoot from 0 to 60 mph and into the first gut-tightening inversion at 5 Gs. The ride's beginning is a real test of your courage as you blast into a wild journey through a make-believe California freeway system. One inversion cuts through an *O* in the Hollywood sign, but you won't feel like you're going to be thrown out because the ride's too fast and too smooth for that. It's so fast, the Disney hype says, that it's similar to sitting atop an F-14 Tomcat. The ride lasts 3 minutes and 12 seconds, the running time of Aerosmith's hit, "Sweet Emotion," which is one of the tunes played in the limos. Similar to Space Mountain, the entire ride takes place indoors and in the dark, but this one packs far more of a punch.

This ride is definitely not for younger kids or anyone with neck or back problems, faint heart, a tendency toward motion sickness, or fear of the dark. *Riders must be at least 48 inches tall.* Plus-size guests with larger chests may not be able to pull the shoulder harness fully closed and, therefore, may not be able to ride. People with sensitive ears should probably wear earplugs.

"Wow — let's do it again!" screamed 11-year-old Nicolas while playing air guitar. Austin (age 13) screamed back in agreement and they were off. I wasn't sure if they were screaming from the excitement or as a result of the loud music being pumped from the speaker behind their heads on the ride. My oldest, who has a hatred for most coasters (especially those with loop-de-loops), was still spinning from the experience, hoping to head elsewhere as quickly as possible — in effect a backhanded endorsement of the thrill factor.

Star Tours

Star Tours is a virtual ride where you go nowhere, but you feel like you do. Your journey to a place far, far away begins with a pre-ride warning about high turbulence, sharp drops, and sudden turns, and then a winding walk (a line) through the woodlands, where you see an Ewok village in the trees overhead and a humungous Imperial Walker standing guard near the entry. The pre-ride has R2-D2 and C-3PO running a galactic travel agency of sorts. After boarding your StarSpeeder, the ride itself starts kind of slowly, but it finishes fast as you soar through space as the good-guy fighter, with R2-D2 and C-3PO helping you make passes through the canals of a Death Star. The special effects include hitting hyperspace speed (you feel like you're going up against a very small G-force) and falling. All things considered, this ride isn't quite up to modern rides here and at Orlando's other theme parks, including the Simpsons Ride (replacing Back to the Future) at Universal Studios Florida (see Chapter 18), but it's still highly enjoyable. Sit in the last row to best feel the motion. If you feel a twinge of motion sickness, there are plenty of stationary objects you can look at to get your bearings.

"That was so awesome!" Nicolas (11) and Davis (7), the latter a huge *Star Wars* fan, were definitely impressed. It's not nearly as threatening or active as the Rock 'n' Roller Coaster Starring Aerosmith, but Star Tours still carries a *40-inch height minimum.*

Studio Backlot Tour

This fun, 35-minute special-effects show starts on foot and finishes in a tram. You get a behind-the-scenes look at the vehicles, props, costumes, sets, and special effects used in some of your favorite movies and TV shows. On most days, you see costume makers at work in the wardrobe department (the largest of its kind, with around 2 million garments). But the real fun begins when the tram heads for Catastrophe Canyon, where an earthquake in the heart of oil country causes canyon walls to rumble. A raging oil fire, massive explosions, torrents of rain, and flash floods threaten you and other riders before you're taken behind the scenes to see how filmmakers use special effects to make such disasters.

Groans at the thought of enduring a tour of the backlot gave way to screams after Ryan (15), Austin (13), and Nicolas (11) experienced Catastrophe Canyon, where the "earthquake" shook the tram and a very large, *very wet* wave threw 70,000 gallons of water our way.

All in all, this ride is very similar in type to the ride portion of Disaster! at Universal Studios Florida (see Chapter 18). Sit on the left side of the tram if you want to get wet.

The Twilight Zone Tower of Terror

A truly stomach-lifting (and -dropping) ride, Disney continues to fine-tune the Tower of Terror to make it even better. That includes an upgrade that added random drop sequences, meaning you get a different fright every time you ride. Its legend says that during a violent storm on Halloween night 1939, lightning struck the Hollywood Tower Hotel, causing an entire wing and an elevator full of people to disappear. And you're about to meet them as you star in a special episode of *The Twilight Zone* (cue that television show's famously creepy music). En route to this formerly grand hotel, guests walk past overgrown landscaping and faded signs that once pointed the way to stables and tennis courts; the vines above the entrance trellis are dead, and the hotel is a crumbling ruin. Eerie corridors lead to a dimly lit library, where you can hear a storm raging outside. The detailing on this ride is some of the best around. After various ghostly apparitions, blasts of chilling air, and creepy experiences, your ride ends in a dramatic climax: a terrifying 13-story fall into *The Twilight Zone!* From there it's anyone's guess as to what happens next — not even the bellhops operating the elevator know what the ride is going to do. At 199 feet, it's the tallest WDW attraction, and it's a cut (or two or three) above its rival, Doctor Doom's Fear Fall at Universal's Islands of Adventure (see Chapter 19).

"Absolutely the coolest ride ever!" Austin (age 13) couldn't get enough, riding over and over again, but my 11- and 15-year-olds wouldn't get near it. I have no way of knowing whether it was from the screams coming from the building or the semi-green faces on a family that came out as we were about to get in line. They aren't alone, though: One of the

Disney Imagineers who helped design the attraction is too afraid to ride his own creation. Note, however, that there were plenty of other kids ready for more at the ride's end. This ride carries a *40-inch height minimum.*

Taking Time Out for Fantastic Parades and Fireworks

In addition to its assortment of rides, Disney's Hollywood Studios also offers its own daily parade and an exceptional evening fireworks display.

Fantasmic!

It's hard not to be in awe of the choreography, laser lights, and fireworks that are the core of this 25-minute extravaganza held once — sometimes twice — a night, weather permitting. Shooting comets, great balls of fire, and animated fountains are among the many special effects that entrance the audience. The cast includes 50 performers, a gigantic dragon, a huge king cobra, and 1 million gallons of water. The entire show represents Mickey's dream, filled with fanciful songs and fantastic visuals. The dream turns into a nightmare thanks to the mischievous magic of some of Disney's more infamous villains. Surprisingly, much of the show is rather dark, with foreboding music and frightening creatures, and Mickey taking on some evil villains. The Magical Mouse triumphs, of course, and the show ends on a festive note. Younger children may be frightened.

If you want to avoid a real traffic jam after the show, arrive up to 60 minutes early and sit on the right side of the amphitheater (the theater empties right to left). When there are two shows per night, especially during peak periods, finding a seat at the later show is usually easier.

At press time, Disney was offering preferred seating at the end-of-the-day spectacular, along with a fixed-price dinner at one of Disney's Hollywood Studios' sit-down restaurants. All you need to do is make **Advanced Dining Reservations** (☎ 407-939w3463) and request the *Fantasmic!* package for the **Hollywood Brown Derby** ($47 adults, $12 kids 3–11), **Mama Melrose's Ristorante Italiano** ($33 adults, $12 kids 3–11), or **Hollywood & Vine** ($25 adults, $12 kids 3–11). *Note:* You must tell the reservations agent you want the *Fantasmic!* package. At the restaurant, you'll get your line pass and instructions on getting to the special entrance to the preferred-seating area of the show. Be aware that these prices are for a fixed-price meal and don't include tax, tip, or alcoholic beverages; ordering off the menu costs you more. The prices also don't include a reserved seat at *Fantasmic!* — only a pass that gets you into the preferred-seating area. (You must arrive at least 30 minutes in advance — a much shorter wait than usual.)

Block Party Bash

This all-new interactive dance party parade in the streets debuted in 2008 (replacing Disney's Stars and Motor Cars Parade). The sound of retro tunes blasts through the streets, high-flying acrobatics amaze those watching from below, and fan-favorite Disney-Pixar characters from blockbuster hits like *Finding Nemo; Toy Story 2; Monsters, Inc.; The Incredibles;* and *A Bug's Life* (among others) join in the festive fun.

Index of Attractions and Rides

G-Rated

Beauty and the Beast–Live on Stage
"Honey, I Shrunk the Kids" Movie Set Adventure
Indiana Jones Epic Stunt Spectacular!
Journey Into Narnia: Prince Caspian
Lights, Motors, Action! Extreme Stunt Show
The Magic of Disney Animation
Muppet Vision 3-D
Playhouse Disney–Live on Stage!
Sounds Dangerous–Starring Drew Carey
Toy Story Mania!
Voyage of The Little Mermaid

PG-Rated

The American Film Institute Showcase
The Great Movie Ride
Rock 'n' Roller Coaster Starring Aerosmith
Star Tours
Studio Backlot Tour
The Twilight Zone Tower of Terror

Chapter 15

Disney's Animal Kingdom

• •

In This Chapter

▶ Acquainting yourself with Disney's Animal Kingdom

▶ Comparing Disney's Animal Kingdom to Busch Gardens

▶ Exploring the attractions in Disney's Animal Kingdom

• •

Disney's fourth major park combines exotic animals, elaborate land-scapes, and a handful of rides and shows to create yet another reason why many WDW resort-goers don't venture outside the World. The $800-million park opened in 1998; its most recent land, Asia, was fin-ished in 1999. Its first and long-awaited thrill ride, **Expedition Everest–Legend of the Forbidden Mountain,** debuted in 2006, featuring a high-speed, coaster-like train ride that travels through glaciers, waterfalls, and canyons, climaxing with an encounter with the Yeti. In 2007, Disney's most spectacular stage show to date opened — an entrancing, musically re-imagined version of the Disney-Pixar hit *Finding Nemo* (aptly named **Finding Nemo–The Musical**). Even with these and other smaller additions, and although the park offers some unique experiences, an expedition here requires only half (if you keep up a brisk pace) to three-quarters of a day, leaving some visitors to believe there isn't enough to justify the admis-sion charge.

But don't go canceling that safari vacation just yet. Animal Kingdom is a theme park, after all — even if the exotic wildlife can move out of your view. It's filled with some amazing experiences and some of the most remarkable landscaping and architectural re-creations in all of Disney (after Epcot's World Showcase pavilions, that is). In this chapter, I give you helpful information on Disney's Animal Kingdom and its marvels, as well as basic info for visiting the park.

Finding Helpful Services in Animal Kingdom

Before trekking through the jungle of attractions at Disney's Animal Kingdom, you need to know some basic information, key to your sur-vival when on safari around the park.

Disney's Animal Kingdom

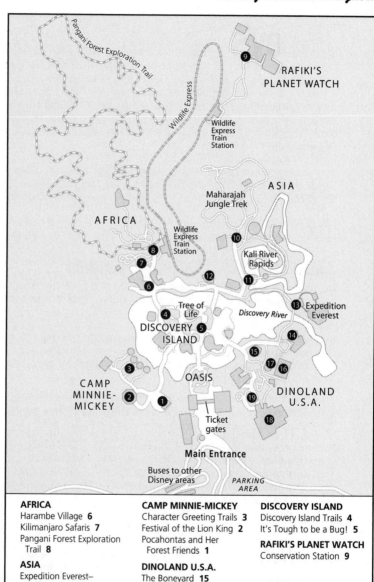

AFRICA
Harambe Village **6**
Kilimanjaro Safaris **7**
Pangani Forest Exploration
  Trail **8**

ASIA
Expedition Everest–
  Legend of the Forbidden
  Mountain **13**
Flights of Wonder **12**
Kali River Rapids **11**
Maharajah Jungle Trek **10**

CAMP MINNIE-MICKEY
Character Greeting Trails **3**
Festival of the Lion King **2**
Pocahontas and Her
  Forest Friends **1**

DINOLAND U.S.A.
The Boneyard **15**
DINOSAUR **18**
Dino-Sue **19**
Finding Nemo–The Musical **14**
Primeval Whirl **16**
TriceraTop Spin **17**

DISCOVERY ISLAND
Discovery Island Trails **4**
It's Tough to be a Bug! **5**

RAFIKI'S PLANET WATCH
Conservation Station **9**

Buying tickets and making reservations

A one-day ticket costs $75 for adults, $63 for children 3 to 9. See Chapter 11 for other ticket options.

Tickets aren't the only things to cut down on your cash. You'll pay the Disney park standard of $2 and up for a soda, $1.25 to $2.50 for bottled water, $2.60 for an ice-cream bar, and $1.70 (and up) for a cup of coffee. If you buy a soda, note that the park doesn't provide lids or straws with its fountain drinks. They're not trying to make it difficult for you to walk around with your soda — these items are banned because, in the hands of litterbugs, they can become deadly to the wildlife. Another no-no: chewing gum.

You can make **Advanced Dining Reservations** at Guest Relations just inside the entrance, though it's best to make them in advance by calling ☎ **407-939-3463.** See Chapter 10 for details on call-ahead dining.

Hours at Animal Kingdom are generally from 9 a.m. to 5 or 6 p.m., but they're sometimes extended to 8 a.m. to 7 or 8 p.m. (though that's rare).

Locating special services and facilities

In case you forget to bring essential items, or if you need special assistance while at the park, here's a list of services and facilities that may come in handy:

- ✔ **ATMs** are located near Garden Gate Gifts to the right of the park entrance and across from Chester and Hester's Dinosaur Treasures in DinoLand U.S.A. Cards from banks using the Cirrus, STAR, and PLUS systems are accepted.

- ✔ The **Baby Care Center** is located near Creature Comforts on the west side of the Tree of Life. As in the other Disney parks, you can also find changing tables in women's restrooms and some men's rooms. You can buy disposable diapers at Guest Relations.

- ✔ **Disposable cameras and film,** as well as a limited selection of digital supplies, are available throughout the park. CD-burning and picture-printing services are available at Kodak Picture Kiosks and select stores in all four Disney theme parks.

- ✔ The **First Aid Station,** which is staffed by registered nurses, is located near Creature Comforts near the Tree of Life.

- ✔ **Lockers** are located in Garden Gate Gifts to your right as you enter the park. You can also find them to the left, near Rainforest Café. You can rent lockers for $10 a day, including a $5 deposit.

- ✔ A **lost-children center** is located near Creature Comforts by the Tree of Life. This area is also the site of same-day lost and found. *Children younger than 7 should wear name tags inside their clothing.*

✔ Shop clerks can send your purchases to **Package Pick-Up** at Garden Gate Gifts near the park entrance. Allow three hours for delivery. If you're staying at a Disney resort, you can have your packages shipped there, though they may take a day or two to get to you. Both services are free.

✔ **Pets,** except service animals, are prohibited in the parks, but you can board yours at the **Pet Care Kennels** just inside the park entrance to the right (☎ 407-824-6568). Day accommodations cost $10 to $15 a day (depending on the type of pet and whether you are a Disney resort guest). Overnight stays are $13 to $20. Proof of vaccinations is required, and you are responsible for walking and feeding your pet.

✔ **Strollers** are available at Garden Gate Gifts, to the right as you enter the park. Rentals cost $15 for a single, $31 for a double.

✔ **Wheelchairs** are available at Garden Gate Gifts, to the right as you enter the park. Rentals cost $10 for a standard wheelchair, $45 (plus a $5 deposit) for electric chairs. Ask Disney employees about other locations in the park.

You can call ☎ 407-934-7639 or visit Disney's Web site (www.disney world.com) to find out more about WDW properties.

Deciding between Animal Kingdom and Busch Gardens

When Disney's fourth theme park opened, it raised two questions: Is it a first-rate park worthy of the same sticker shock as Orlando's other major parks, and when does the area have too many parks?

Well, when it comes to visitor volume and diversity of things to do, Disney's Animal Kingdom ranks as one of the top two animal parks in Florida. **Busch Gardens** ($68 per adult, $58 per child) in Tampa is the other. Although I discuss Busch Gardens in Chapter 23, I talk about it briefly here so that I can draw a few comparisons.

Disney's Animal Kingdom is as much a park for animals (a conservation venue) as it is an attraction. The short of it is that its creatures aren't as easy to see; the animals are given much more cover than they are at Busch Gardens, so when they want to avoid your probing eyes and the heat, they can. Even in high-profile areas, such as **Pangani Forest Exploration Trail,** Disney goes to great lengths to protect resident lowland gorillas, including a magnificent silverback, from prying eyes. The beautiful foliage used to create that cover also means that Disney's Animal Kingdom is a lot prettier than its Tampa rival.

Although I'm all for protecting wildlife, Disney's Animal Kingdom can do a much better job of providing shade for the only species that doesn't get much consideration in the park — the Homo sapiens who paid to get in. The amount of cover given to tourists waiting in line is decidedly unimpressive (a problem in all of Disney's parks, in my opinion). Arriving early at both parks, especially in summer, saves you the unpleasant experience of languishing under a blistering sun.

The best time to catch the animals out and about at Disney's Animal Kingdom is in the early morning just after the park opens — usually 8 or 9 a.m. (depending on the season) — or at closing as the day begins to cool. Most animals are on the prowl at those times, not at midday (especially during the summer). Busch's animals are far easier to see, regardless of the time of day, because they have far fewer places to take cover.

Disney's Animal Kingdom wins the battle of shows, with humdingers like **Finding Nemo–The Musical** and **Festival of the Lion King.** Although Animal Kingdom has four thrill rides (and I'm being kind in including two of them in the thrill category), Busch Gardens pulls ahead with five roller coasters, including **SheiKra,** an incredible floorless dive coaster, and **Gwazi,** a set of dueling wooden coasters.

Busch comes out ahead when it comes to rides and attractions, but it isn't nearly as impressive in the categories of landscaping or themed architecture. New additions aside, many criticize Disney's Animal Kingdom — fairly, in my opinion — for not offering enough to justify a ticket price comparable to Busch Gardens and the other Orlando theme parks. That said, I appreciate the park more now that I've learned to think of the surroundings, and not necessarily the attractions themselves, as the highlight. Geographically speaking, you may not have or want a choice between the two. Disney's Animal Kingdom is located right in the center of the Orlando action, where you can find a ton of other things to do. Busch Gardens, alas, is at least a 75-minute drive or shuttle trip from O-Town, and the Tampa Bay area simply doesn't have the draw of Orlando (though it does offer cultural centers, museums, aquariums, and sandy beaches). If you're considering a trip to the Tampa Bay area, *Florida For Dummies,* 5th Edition, by Lesley Abravanel, or *Frommer's Florida 2009,* by Lesley Abravanel and Laura Lea Miller (both published by Wiley Publishing, Inc.), both have a wealth of information about attractions, accommodations, and restaurants on the state's Suncoast.

Checking Out Animal Kingdom's Top Attractions

The overall conservation theme in this state-of-the-art park is simple but not subtle. Everywhere you turn, you find an environmental message, including on the park's signs and in the narratives of the tour guides on rides such as Kilimanjaro Safaris. It's this underlying theme that connects the park's rather diverse sections, where you'll encounter everything from a dinosaur-themed thrill ride to a kid-friendly character zone where Disney characters are plentiful.

Disney's Animal Kingdom, like WDW's Magic Kingdom, is set up on a hub-and-spoke format with the Tree of Life (in Discovery Island) as its hub and six other areas scattered around it. The following sections offer a closer look at the seven lands of Animal Kingdom. You can find all these attractions on the "Disney's Animal Kingdom" map on p. 232.

Oasis

The **Oasis Exhibits** is your introduction to Disney's Animal Kingdom, but a lot of folks, itching to get to the action, launch their way through it, overlooking the fact that this is one of the better places to see animals early in the day. The lush vegetation, streams, grottoes, and waterfalls on either side of the walkway are good places to spot wallabies, miniature deer, anteaters, sloths, iguanas, tree kangaroos, otters, and macaws. But a misty fog and the landscaping also give them room to escape your eyes whenever they choose.

Discovery Island

After you pass through Oasis, Discovery Island lies directly ahead, with the park's signature icon, the **Tree of Life,** in the center of it all. Although you'll find only three attractions in this land, they are among the park's most unique features.

Discovery Island Trails

Discovery Island Trails is another of the park's animal viewing areas, a leisurely path through the root system of the Tree of Life (Disney's Animal Kingdom's 145-foot man-made tree, described in detail later in this section) and a chance to see real critters such as axis deer, red kangaroos, otters, flamingos, lemurs, Galapagos tortoises, ducks, storks, and cockatoos.

The best viewing times are early or late in the day, though I'd save this one for later and head to the park's few thrill rides first.

It's Tough to be a Bug!

Take the walkway through the Tree of Life's 50-foot base, grab a pair of 3-D glasses, and settle into a sometimes creepy-crawly seat. Based on the Disney-Pixar film *A Bug's Life,* the special effects in this multimedia adventure are pretty impressive. Although it may not be a good choice for kids younger than 4 (it's dark and loud) or bug haters, the attraction offers a fun and sometimes-poignant look at life from a smaller perspective. After you put on your bug-eye glasses, all your senses are awakened by the stars, including ants, beetles, spiders, and — oh, no! — a stink bug.

More than one of my kids came out in tears, but for reasons you may not expect. The simple sensory effects, mostly because they occur unexpectedly and in the dark, terrorized even some of the older ones. The issue my youngest had was with the bugs — he *hates* them.

On the other hand, Katie (a cousin), thought the show was "really funny." Viewers experience some spritzes of water, blasts of air, and a foul smell when the stink bug gets its revenge. The show's finale, when the on-screen insects run amok, definitely leaves you buzzing.

The Tree of Life

Like **Cinderella Castle** at the **Magic Kingdom** (see Chapter 12 for details) and **Spaceship Earth** in **Epcot** (described in Chapter 13), the 14-story Tree of Life is a park icon. The man-made tree and its carved animals are the work of Disney artists, teams of which worked for more than a year on its free-form animal sculptures. It isn't as tall or imposing as those other icons, but it is certainly impressive. It has 8,000 limbs, 103,000 leaves, and 325 mammals, reptiles, amphibians, insects, birds, dinosaurs, and Mickeys carved into its trunk, limbs, and roots. Different animals appear or vanish depending on the angle from which you view the tree.

Although passing up a detailed inspection of the tree as you enter the park is hard to do (it is awesomely difficult to ignore), I recommend gawking only while standing in line for It's Tough to be a Bug! You'll have time for a more detailed look at the tree — if you so desire — on the way out.

Camp Minnie-Mickey

Youngsters love this place, though I don't share their enthusiasm. It's a favorite hangout for Disney characters from the forest and jungle, including Simba from *The Lion King* and Baloo from *The Jungle Book.* Mickey, Minnie, Goofy, Pluto, Donald, Daisy, and other stars also make appearances from time to time around this woodsy retreat, which was designed to resemble an Adirondack summer camp. The lines for the meet-and-greets are often excruciatingly long, and unless the kids insist on visiting, I recommend avoiding the wait to meet with Disney characters here.

In addition to the characters, this land is also home to Disney World's best stage show, **Festival of the Lion King,** an exhilarating and interactive extravaganza.

Camp Minnie-Mickey Greeting Trails

If you're traveling with children, this attraction is probably a must-do, but be prepared for a long wait. A variety of Disney characters from Timon and Winnie the Pooh to Pluto and Donald Duck shake your hand, give hugs, allow photos to be taken, and sign autographs. Mickey and Minnie, in recognition of their star status, get their own shaded pavilions.

Festival of the Lion King

This Broadway-style production at the Lion King Theater is one of the best in Disney's Animal Kingdom (coming in a close second behind Finding Nemo–The Musical) and one of the top three productions in all of Walt Disney World. The extravaganza celebrates nature's diversity with a talented, colorfully attired cast of singers, dancers, and life-size critters who lead you in an inspiring singalong. Based loosely on the animated movie, this stage show combines the pageantry of a parade with a tribal celebration. The action takes place on the center stage and even around the audience. Even though the pavilion has 1,000 seats, arrive at least 20 minutes early to ensure you get a spot. The show lasts just under a half-hour.

Pocahontas and Her Forest Friends

The wait to see Pocahontas and Her Forest Friends can be nightmarish, and the 15-minute show isn't remotely close to the caliber of its neighbor, Festival of the Lion King. In this presentation, Pocahontas and Grandmother Willow, with the help of some of the forest creatures (a raccoon, turkey, porcupine, rat, and more), bring to light the importance of treating nature with respect and protecting our forests. Young fans of the movie and of little creatures will be most appreciative of the performance. If you must go, go early. The theater has a mere 350 seats, but standing-room crowds are admitted.

Africa

Enter through the village of **Harambe,** which means "coming together" in Swahili. This area of Africa is a re-creation of an African coastal village poised on the edge of the 21st century. The impressive whitewashed structures, built of coral stone and thatched with reed brought from Africa, surround a beautifully landscaped central marketplace that's rich with local wares and colors. After passing through the town, the various trails lead you to Africa's other rides and attractions.

Kilimanjaro Safaris

This attraction is one of the few rides and the best animal viewing venue in Disney's Animal Kingdom. But remember: The animals are scarce during the middle of the day, especially in the heat of summer.

You can wait 45 minutes or more in line here. Yes, using FASTPASS (see Chapter 11) is an option, but it virtually eliminates the chance of riding during the best viewing times. My advice: Skip FASTPASS, get to the park a bit before its scheduled opening time, and make your way straight here. If you simply aren't a morning person, your next best shot is to get a FASTPASS that lets you ride as close to the park's closing as you can get. (Know ahead of time, you'll have to check back every so often to get a pass that doesn't have you returning midday!)

After you reach the end of the very long and winding line, you'll board a rather large truck specially made for such an expedition, and set off on a bouncy ride through the African landscape. Animals in the safari include black rhinos, hippos, antelopes, Nile crocodiles, zebras, wildebeests, and lions that, if your timing is right, may offer a half-hearted roar toward some gazelles that are safely out of reach. The animals roam freely, occasionally crossing the path of the truck and allowing a really up-close view, but again, that's far more likely to occur in the morning or evening hours. Predictably, the theme is conservation. There's even a little drama — this is, after all, a theme-park ride — as you and your mates help pursue some park poachers (though word has it that new scripts are being tested and a new story line will be in place by the time this book hits the shelves).

"The bumpy ride was really fun, and way better than having to walk around to see the animals. Looking over railings or into cages isn't nearly as neat. And they got so close, it was way cool." I agree with Nicolas (11), Hailey (9), and Davis (7) — several giraffes came nearly within arm's length. This one's fun for the whole family, but very small infants shouldn't ride because of the bumps.

Pangani Forest Exploration Trail

You can get a good look at hippos, mole rats, and African birds on the Pangani Falls Exploration Trail, but lowland gorillas are the main feature. The trail has two gorilla-related areas: One is home to a family composed of a 500-pound silverback, his ladies, and kids; the other has five bachelors. Most people tend to rush through the trails, missing out on the chance to see the giant apes, and the animals are not always cooperative, especially in hot weather, when they tend to spend most of the day in shady areas out of view. But visitors who have good timing or who make return visits are truly rewarded with up-close views (through Plexiglas) of these magnificent creatures.

Rafiki's Planet Watch

This land, located just above Africa, includes **Conservation Station**, which offers a behind-the-scenes look at how Disney cares for animals inside the park — you walk past a series of nurseries and veterinary stations. The problem is that these facilities need staff members present to make them interesting, and that isn't always the case. **Affection Section** gives you a chance to cuddle some friendly animals (including goats and potbellied pigs), while **Habitat Habit!** has a trail that's home to some smaller animals, such as cotton-topped tamarins. *Note:* Take heed of the signs in the Affection Section that instruct you to put all paper, including maps, away. Goats love paper and will cause a stampede in an attempt to snatch your paper products from you.

Asia

Disney's Imagineers outdid themselves in creating the mythical kingdom of Anandapur (place of delight) in the Asia section of Animal Kingdom, with an exotic atmosphere enhanced by the crumbling ruins of an ancient village, its temples, and even a maharajah's palace, all decorated with intricate carvings and artwork.

Expedition Everest–Legend of the Forbidden Mountain

After years of anticipation, Disney's Animal Kingdom's newest thrill ride made its debut in mid-2006. The journey begins in the mythical Himalayan village of Serka Zong, one of the best queues in all of Disney, where after winding around you'll board an old mountain railway bound for Mount Everest, which, at 200 feet, is one of Florida's highest peaks. Passing through bamboo forests, thundering waterfalls, and glacier fields, the train ascends higher and higher to the snow-capped peaks of the mountain. As you may expect, what starts as a relaxing tour turns into an exciting expedition when the train hits tracks that are mangled and twisted. The train races frantically through the icy canyons and caverns as you suddenly find yourself face to face with the Yeti (also known as the Abominable Snowman), guardian and protector of the mountain.

Touted as a family thrill ride, don't be fooled — it packs quite a punch. The feeling that you may plummet down the side of the mountain as you hit the tangled and severed tracks before suddenly thrusting backward into the darkness. . . . yikes! This ride is more intense than **Big Thunder Mountain Railroad** in the **Magic Kingdom** (see Chapter 12) but a step or two down from the twists, turns, loops, and inversions of the **Rock 'n' Roller Coaster Starring Aerosmith** at **Disney's Hollywood Studios** (see Chapter 14).

"Wow! We were staring straight down the mountain — for a second I thought we were really going to fall right off." Eleven-year-old Nicolas is coaster crazy, and this one's at the top of his list of favorites. My 15-year-old, however, said, "No way, you're not getting me on that!" after watching (and hearing the screams) from below.

A FASTPASS is the only way to avoid this ride's incredibly lengthy lines (though you'll miss much of the queue's spectacular detailing). Although touted as a family ride, children not tall enough to make the *44-inch height requirement* will have to wait this one out. Guests with head-, neck-, or back-related ailments should avoid the trek as well.

Flights of Wonder

This live-animal action show is a low-key break from the madness and offers a few laughs, including Groucho the African yellow nape, who entertains the audience with his op-*parrot*-ic a cappella solos, and the just-above-your-head soaring of a Harris hawk and a Eurasian eagle owl. Other feathered stars include an American bald eagle and a crowned crane.

Kali River Rapids

White-water fanatics may scoff, but for a theme-park raft ride, Kali River Rapids is pretty good. It's slightly better than **Congo River Rapids** at **Busch Gardens** (see Chapter 23), but not nearly as wild as **Popeye & Bluto's Bilge-Rat Barges** at **Islands of Adventure** (see Chapter 19) — though the theme is more alluring here. This ride's churning water mimics realistic rapids, and its optical illusions make you wonder whether you're headed over the falls. The ride begins with a peaceful tour of lush foliage, but soon you're dipping and dripping as your tiny raft tosses and turns through the jungles. You *will* get wet (but how wet depends on where you're seated). The lines are long, but keep your head up, and enjoy the marvelous art overhead and on the beautiful murals.

This ride has a *38-inch height minimum.*

Maharajah Jungle Trek

Disney keeps its promise to provide up-close views of animals with this exhibit, the setting of which is almost an attraction in its own right. Lush tropical foliage and bamboo grow amidst the ruins, architecture, and carvings of Nepal, India, Thailand, and Indonesia. It's some of Disney's best thematic work.

If you don't show up in the midday heat, you'll probably see Bengal tigers roaming an abandoned maharajah's palace through a thick glass barrier. Nothing but air separates you from dozens of giant fruit bats hanging in what appears to be a courtyard. Some of the bats have wingspans of 6 feet. (If you have a phobia, you can bypass this, but know that the bats are harmless.) Guides are on hand to answer questions, and you also get a brochure that lists the animals you may spot. You also have chances to see Komodo dragons, tapirs, playful gibbons, and acrobatic siamangs, whose calls have been likened to someone in the throes of pain or passion.

DinoLand U.S.A.

Located to the right, or east side, of Discovery Island as you enter, DinoLand U.S.A. is Disney's attempt to capitalize on the dinosaur craze inspired by *Jurassic Park* and (ugh) *Barney.* You enter beneath Olden Gate Bridge, a 40-foot-tall brachiosaurus reassembled from excavated fossils. Speaking of which, until late summer 1999, DinoLand had three paleontologists working on the very real skeleton of **Sue,** a monstrously big Tyrannosaurus rex unearthed in the Black Hills of South Dakota in 1990. The paleontologists patched and assembled the bones here, mainly because Disney helped pay for the project. Alas, Sue has moved to her permanent home at the Field Museum in Chicago, but a cast replica of her 67-million-year-old bones, called **Dino-Sue,** is on display.

The Boneyard

The Boneyard is a great place for parents to catch a second wind. Kids love the prehistoric playground, and there are plenty of activities to wear them down a bit. They can slide and climb over a paleontological dig site and squeeze through the fossils and skeletons of a triceratops and a brontosaurus. They can even search the sands for skeletal remains.

 You have to be vigilant about keeping track of your kids here. The Boneyard is a large area, and although Disney staff monitors them at both ends, kids play in a multilevel arena where tube slides can take them from one level to the next in a heartbeat.

DINOSAUR

This ride hurls you through darkness in a CTX Rover time machine, past an array of snarling audio-animatronic dinosaurs. Some kids may find the dinosaurs (and darkness) frightening; adults may find them a bit hokey. However, after Expedition Everest–Legend of the Forbidden Mountain, DINOSAUR is as close as Animal Kingdom comes to a thrill ride — a twisting, turning, and very jerky adventure in which you and 20 other passengers try to save the last Iguanadon on Earth from an asteroid. Evolution, nature's fragility, and potential catastrophe are the punch lines in this lip-biting, armrest-clenching ride against time. It features some very large lizards (such as a 33-ft. carnotaurus, named for its favorite food — meat).

 Plus-size riders may find the seats uncomfortably narrow, especially with the jerky motions of the ride. *Riders must be at least 40 inches tall.* DINOSAUR also has a list of warnings aimed at folks with neck and back ailments. If you've ever wondered what it feels like aboard a bucking bronco, this rough ride is probably pretty comparable.

 "You felt like you were really being thrown around," 15-year-old Ryan announced after he got off. Austin (age 13) called it "awesome!" — but added that it wasn't nearly as scary as he thought it would be.

Finding Nemo–The Musical

Making a splashy debut in 2007, **Finding Nemo–The Musical** is, in a word, enchanting. In this visually stunning undersea production ("re-imagined" as a musical), Nemo, Marlin, Dory, Crush, and Bruce (along with a few other finned film favorites) come to life before your eyes as live actors in spectacular puppet-like costumes re-create the adventure made popular by the Disney-Pixar film *Finding Nemo*. The story line, for those who don't already know it, has the ever-curious Nemo becoming separated from his overly protective father, who then goes to great lengths traveling through the big blue to be reunited with his son. Even the squirmiest toddler will sit mesmerized through this 30-minute show — it's a must-see for the entire family.

Primeval Whirl

Disney's Animal Kingdom jumped into the coaster craze with this ride. Primeval Whirl is a bit tame, and it doesn't have inversions, but it does have plenty of spinning action in carnival-style, rider-controlled cars that whirl by asteroids and hokey dinosaurs that pop up along the track. The ride has tight loops, short dips, and a final spin that sends you into the gaping jaws of a fossilized dinosaur.

Though Primeval Whirl was originally supposed to enlarge the park's appeal to the kid set, this ride has a *48-inch height minimum*.

TriceraTop Spin

The principle behind this kiddie favorite is pretty much the same as the **Magic Carpets of Aladdin** and **Dumbo The Flying Elephant** at the **Magic Kingdom** (see Chapter 12). Cartoonish dinosaurs take riders up, down, and all around. To the delight of the kids, a dinosaur occasionally pops its head in and out of the central hub. Most young children, especially those ages 2 to 6, love it. Parents loathe the long lines.

Index of Attractions by Land

Africa
Kilimanjaro Safaris
Pangani Forest Exploration Trail

Asia
Expedition Everest–Legend of the Forbidden Mountain
Flights of Wonder
Kali River Rapids
Maharajah Jungle Trek

Camp Minnie-Mickey
Camp Minnie-Mickey Greeting Trails
Festival of the Lion King
Pocahontas and Her Forest Friends

DinoLand U.S.A.
The Boneyard
DINOSAUR
Finding Nemo–The Musical
Primeval Whirl
TriceraTop Spin

Discovery Island
Discovery Island Trails
It's Tough to be a Bug!
The Tree of Life

Oasis
The Oasis Exhibits

Rafiki's Planet Watch
Affection Section
Conservation Station
Habitat Habit!

Chapter 16

Enjoying the Rest of Walt Disney World

In This Chapter

▶ Playing in an interactive adventure park

▶ Experiencing a sports fan's nirvana

▶ Speeding around the Disney NASCAR circuit

▶ Golfing, Disney style

▶ Splashing into the Disney water parks

▶ Enjoying holiday happenings

▶ Cruising with Disney

*I*n Chapters 12 through 15, I acquaint you with the major theme parks of Walt Disney World. But the House of Mouse is home to much, much more. In this chapter, I introduce you to the smaller, second-tier attractions, as well as a few holiday happenings and the Disney Cruise Line.

Playing It Up at DisneyQuest

The minute you step inside, you realize this is no ordinary arcade — the five levels offer some of the most cutting-edge games anywhere. Disney has taken the state-of-the-art technology of virtual reality, added a spirit of adventure, and shaken it up with some of that magical pixie dust for good measure. The result is the World's most interactive game complex. From kids just old enough to work the controls to teens, reactions to DisneyQuest are pretty much the same: "Awesome!" And although many adults enter the arcade thinking that they're only going to find kids' stuff, many bite the hook as hard as their offspring when they get a gander at the electronic wizardry — everything from old-fashioned pinball with a newfangled twist to virtual-reality adventure rides.

Here are just some of the entrees that you can find at DisneyQuest:

> ✔ **Aladdin's Magic Carpet Ride:** Straddling the magic carpet, you'll fly through the 3-D Cave of Wonders and the alleys and streets of

Agrabah in search of the magic lamp. This is definitely fun, but your head may get hot from the virtual-reality helmets.

✔ **Animation Academy:** If you need quiet time, sign up at Animation Academy for a mini course in Disney cartooning (but you'll have to pay extra to keep your artwork — shame on you, Disney!). The academy also has snack and food areas; a typical theme-park–style meal and drink runs from $12 to $15 per person.

✔ **CyberSpace Mountain:** If you have an inventive mind (and a steel stomach), stop in at CyberSpace Mountain, where Bill Nye the Science-Turned-Roller-Coaster Guy helps you create the ultimate loop-and-dipster, which you then can ride in a very real-feeling simulator. It's a major hit with the coaster-crazy crowd. Bring your own motion-sickness medicine (though you can choose slow, medium, or quick death). *There's a 51-inch height requirement.*

✔ **Mighty Ducks Pinball Slam:** In this interactive, life-size game, players ride platforms and use body English to try to score points. It's your opportunity to explore life as a pinball — from the ball's perspective. Just try to stop the quivering in your arms after this.

✔ **Pirates of the Caribbean–Battle for Buccaneer Gold:** You and up to three mates are outfitted in 3-D helmets so that you can battle pirate ships, virtual-reality style. One of you volunteers to be the captain, steering the ship, while the others assume positions behind cannons to blast the black hearts into oblivion — maybe. Each time you do, you're rewarded with some doubloons, but beware of sea monsters that can gobble up you *and* your treasure. In the game's final moments, you come face to face with the ghost of Davy Jones. *There's a 35-inch height requirement.*

Crowds really start building after lunch, when the heat of the day begins to truly kick in, and they're simply maddening after dark.

Although some rides and games are appropriate for a variety of ages, DisneyQuest is the most appealing to those over 8 or even 10 (remember also that some attractions have height requirements). If you have toddlers in tow, be aware that strollers are not allowed in the building.

See map p. 173. In Downtown Disney West Side (off Buena Vista Dr.). ☎ *407-828-4600.* www.disneyquest.com. *Admission: $40 adults, $34 kids 3–9 for unlimited play. Open: Sun–Thurs 11:30 a.m.–11 p.m., Fri–Sat 11:30 a.m. to midnight.*

Fielding the Fun at Disney's Wide World of Sports Complex

Disney's Wide World of Sports is a 220-acre mega-complex that has a 7,500-seat baseball stadium, 10 other baseball and softball fields,

6 basketball courts, 12 lighted tennis courts, a track-and-field complex, a golf driving range, and 6 sand volleyball courts. The Jostens Center, an all-new multipurpose auxiliary field house that debuted in 2008, houses 6 basketball courts, 12 volleyball courts, and 2 roller hockey rinks, doubling the complex's capacity to host indoor sporting events.

If you're a true sports fan, call for a package of information about the facilities and a calendar of events. You can also consult the facility's Web site. Here's a sampling of the options available:

✔ The **Atlanta Braves** play spring-training games during a one-month season that begins in March. Tickets cost $14 to $24; call **Ticketmaster** (☎ **407-839-3900**). The facility also hosts training camp for the NFL's **Tampa Bay Buccaneers** in July and August.

✔ The **Multi-Sports Experience,** which is included in Wide World's general admission price, is open on select days. It challenges guests with activities covering many sports: football, baseball, basketball, hockey, soccer, and volleyball.

✔ The **NBA, NCAA, PGA,** and **Harlem Globetrotters** also stage events, sometimes annually and sometimes more frequently, here.

See map p. 173. On Victory Way, just north of U.S. 192 (west of I-4). ☎ **407-828-3267** *or 407-939-4263; 407-939-1500 for sports information.* www.disneysports.com. *Admission: $11 adults, $8 kids 3–9 (tax included). Open: Daily 10 a.m.–5 p.m., but hours may vary by venue.*

Gearing Up at the Richard Petty Driving Experience

Compared to the Richard Petty Driving Experience at the **Walt Disney World Speedway,** Epcot's thriller Test Track is for sissies. This is your chance to race like a pro in a 600-horsepower NASCAR race car.

How real is it? You must sign a waiver with words such as *Dangerous, Calculated Risk,* and *Update Your Will!* before getting into a car.

At one end of the spectrum, you can ride shotgun for a couple of laps at 145 mph ($116). At the other end, you can spend from three hours to two days learning how to drive the car yourself and racing other daredevils in 8 to 30 laps of excitement (for a cool $425–$1,330, including tax). You must be 18 or older to ride in the car.

See map p. 173. At Walt Disney World Speedway, on World Dr. at Vista Blvd. just off U.S. 192, south of the Magic Kingdom. ☎ **800-237-3889.** www.1800bepetty.com. *Admission varies by seasons and hours, so call ahead. Open: Tues and Thurs 9 a.m.–4 p.m., though hours may vary.*

Preparing for the PGA at Disney Golf

The Magic Mickey offers **99 holes of golf:** five 18-hole, par-72 courses and a 9-hole, par-36 walking course. All WDW courses are open to the public and offer pro shops, equipment rentals, and instruction. For tee times and information, call ☎ **407-939-4653** up to 60 days in advance. (Disney resort guests can reserve up to 90 days in advance.) Golf packages are also available, with select packages available only seven days in advance. (Call ☎ **407-934-7639** to make reservations.)

Greens fees for Disney hotel guests can range from $89 to $159 per 18-hole round (it's $10 more if you're not a resort guest), though rates are subject to change at any time and do vary by course, season, and time of day (in the case of twilight specials). Here's a rundown of the courses:

- ✔ **Disney's Eagle Pines (18 holes):** Expansive traps and sloping fairways follow the natural lay of the land. Rough pine straw and sand welcome wayward shots, and 16 holes feature water hazards.

- ✔ **Disney's Lake Buena Vista (18 holes):** This course has a classic country-club style, with many pines spread across a residential area. Well-bunkered, it's also a challenge that demands accuracy. This course has played host to PGA, LPGA, and USGA events.

- ✔ **Disney's Magnolia (18 holes):** The longest course on Disney property is designed in classic PGA style. Wide fairways are deceiving; you have to hunker down and whack the ball, but take care: Eleven holes have water hazards, and 97 bunkers are on the course. The 6th hole has a special hazard — a Mickey Mouse–shaped sand trap.

- ✔ **Disney's Oak Trail (9 holes):** If you can't go a day without getting in a few holes, but you don't have time for the 18-hole courses, this course is the place to spank the ball. This 9-hole walking course is designed for families or for a quick golf fix.

- ✔ **Disney's Osprey Ridge (18 holes):** This Tom Fazio–designed course combines rolling fairways cut through forests of scrub oak, pine, palmetto, cypress, and bay trees. *Golf Digest* ranks the course as one of the best in Florida.

- ✔ **Disney's Palm (18 holes):** Disney's toughest course, the Palm is set among natural Florida woodlands. Its elevated greens, water, and sand traps offer more hazards than Interstate 4. Good luck with the 18th; it's rated among the toughest holes on the PGA Tour.

Disney occasionally offers discounted twilight tee times — often during the summer and fall seasons. To find out whether a discount is available during your visit, call ☎ **407-939-4653** up to seven days in advance or consult www.disneygolf.com.

If you want more golfing options or want to get out of Disney for a bit, two excellent sources of information and tee-time reservations are

Golfpac (☎ **888-848-8941** or 407-260-2288; www.golfpacinc.com) and
Tee Times USA (☎ **888-465-3356**; www.teetimesusa.com).

Puttering Around at Disney Miniature Golf

Those too timid to tee off at Disney's majors — or whose big games
aren't yet up to par — can try out the World's miniature-golf courses.
Thanks to four whimsically themed courses, everyone, from novices to
master minigolfers, should find at least one course to their liking.

Disney's Winter Summerland Miniature Golf Course

Santa Claus and his elves supply the theme at Winter Summerland, a
well-designed miniature-golf spread that has two 18-hole courses. The
winter course takes you from an ice castle to a snowman to the North
Pole. The **summer course** is pure Florida, from sand castles to surfboards to a visit with Santa on the Winternet.

See map p. 173. East off Buena Vista Dr., across from Blizzard Beach. ☎ *407-
560-3000.* www.disneyworld.com. *Admission: $13 adults, $10 kids 3–9 (tax
included). Open: Daily 10 a.m.–11 p.m.*

Fantasia Gardens Miniature Golf Course

Fantasia Gardens, across from Disney's Hollywood Studios, offers two
18-hole courses drawing inspiration from the classic cartoon of the same
name. On the **Fantasia Gardens course,** hippos, ostriches, and gators
appear, and the Sorcerer's Apprentice presides over the final hole. This
is a good course for beginners and kids. Seasoned minigolfers will prefer
the tougher **Fantasia Fairways,** a scaled-down golf course complete with
sand traps, water hazards, tricky putting greens, and holes ranging from
40 to 75 feet — but only those kids who can actually golf may find the
Fairways any fun.

See map p. 173. On Buena Vista Dr., just east of World Dr. ☎ *407-560-4582.*
www.disneyworld.com. *Admission: $11 adults, $9 kids 3–9 (tax included). Open:
Daily 10 a.m.–11 p.m.*

Making a Splash at Disney's Water Parks

Disney's two water parks are great places to chill out for all or part of a
day. Here are a few things to keep in mind:

  ✔ **Go in the afternoon — about 2 p.m., even in summer — if you
    can stand the heat that long and want to avoid crowds.** The early
    birds are usually gone by then, and lines are far shorter.

  ✔ **If you hold a ticket with the Water Park Fun & More Option and
    are staying at a Disney resort, beat the heat and the lines by**

> heading to the water parks an hour earlier than anyone else.
> During peak seasons, Disney's water parks (usually one, sometimes both) open an hour early for **Extra Magic Hours.**
>
> ✔ **Choose an early weekday.** Early in the week, most weeklong guests are filling the lines at the theme parks.
>
> ✔ **Keep in mind that kids can get lost just as easily at a water park as they can at a theme park, and the consequences can be worse.** All Disney parks have lifeguards, usually wearing bright-red suits, but to be safe, ask how to identify an on-duty lifeguard, and keep an eye on your little ones. Life jackets are available, at no charge, for an added measure of safety, but they're limited in availability and are in no way a substitute for adult supervision.
>
> ✔ **If you're a woman and modesty is your policy, bring a one-piece bathing suit for the more daring slides.** All bathers should remember the wedgie factor on the more extreme rides, such as Summit Plummet. You may enter the park wearing baggies, but, thanks to high-speed water pressure, find yourself in a thong.

Blizzard Beach

The youngest of Disney's water parks is also tops in the country in attendance. Blizzard Beach is a 66-acre "ski resort" set in the midst of a tropical lagoon beneath 90-foot — uh-oh — Mount Gushmore. The base of Mount Gushmore has a sand beach and several other attractions, including a wave pool and a smaller kids' version of the mountain.

Here are brief descriptions of other Blizzard Beach attractions:

✔ **Cross Country Creek** is a 2,900-foot tube ride around the park and through a cave where you get splashed with melting ice.

✔ **Melt-Away Bay** is a relatively calm, 1-acre wave pool.

✔ **Runoff Rapids** offers a choice of three twisting-and-turning runs, one of which plunges you and your tube into darkness.

✔ **Ski Patrol Training Camp** is designed for preteens. It features a rope swing; an airborne water drop from a T-bar; slides; and a challenging ice-floe walk along slippery floating icebergs.

✔ **Slush Gusher** is a speed slide that shoots you along a snow-banked gully. It packs a *48-inch minimum height requirement.*

✔ **Snow Stormers** has three flumes that descend from Mount Gushmore on a switchback course through ski-type slalom gates.

 ✔ **Summit Plummet** is wild! Read *every* speed, motion, vertical-dip, wedgie, and hold-onto-your-breastplate warning in this guide. Then test your bravado in a bull ring, a space shuttle, or dozens of other death-defying hobbies as a warm-up. This one starts out slow, with a lift ride to the 120-foot summit. At the top, kiss any kids or religious medal you may carry with you because, if you board, you will be on *the world's fastest body slide*. It's a test of your courage and your swimsuit as you head virtually straight down, moving, sans vehicle, at 60 mph by the time you reach the catch pool. A veteran thrill-seeker has described the experience as "15 seconds of paralyzing fear." *Minimum height requirement is 48 inches.*

✔ **Teamboat Springs,** the World's longest white-water raft ride, twists down a 1,200-foot series of rushing waterfalls.

✔ **Tike's Peak** is a mini version of Blizzard Beach for mini visitors. It offers short slides, a squirting ice pool, a fountain play area, and a snow castle.

✔ **Toboggan Racers** is an eight-lane slide that sends you racing, head first, over exhilarating dips into a "snowy" slope.

See map p. 173. On World Dr., north of Disney's All-Star Resorts and across from Winter Summerland. ☎ *407-560-3400.* www.disneyworld.com. *Admission: $40 adults, $34 kids 3–9. Open: Daily 10 a.m.–5 p.m., with extended hours during peak times, such as summer.*

Typhoon Lagoon

Typhoon Lagoon is the ultimate in water theme parks. Its fantasy setting is a palm-fringed island village of ramshackle shacks, the entire area strewn with cargo, surfboards, and other marine wreckage left by the great typhoon. The storm-stranded fishing boat (the *Miss Tilly*) dangles precariously atop the 95-foot Mount Mayday, the steep setting for several rides. Every 30 minutes, *Tilly's* stack blows, shooting a 50-foot geyser even higher into the air.

Here are some other Typhoon Lagoon highlights:

✔ **Castaway Creek** is a 2,100-foot lazy river that circles most of the park. Hop onto a raft or an inner tube and meander through a misty rain forest and then past caves and secluded grottoes. At Water Works, jets of water spew from shipwrecked boats and a Rube Goldberg assemblage of broken bamboo pipes and buckets soaks you. Tubes are included in the admission.

✔ **Crush 'n' Gusher** is the newest addition. Coaster crazies will appreciate its gravity-defying drops between which powerful jets of water propel riders back uphill, through twists and turns, only to drop them again. The Banana Blaster, Coconut Crusher, and Pineapple Plunger offer an out-of-control experience, each sending riders careening on a different route through the remains of a ramshackle fruit-exporting plant. Roughly the same length (410–420 ft. long), the three spillways feature varying degrees of slopes and turns to keep you coming back for more.

✔ **Humunga Kowabunga** consists of three 214-foot Mount Mayday slides that propel you down the mountain on a serpentine route through waterfalls and bat caves at up to 30 mph before depositing you into a bubbling catch pool; each slide offers slightly different thrills. Seating is available for non-Kowabunga folks whose kids have commissioned them to "watch me." Women should wear a one-piece on the slides. This attraction has a *48-inch height minimum.*

✔ **Ketchakiddee Creek** is designed exclusively for the kiddie set (2–5 years). An innovative water playground, it has bubbling fountains; mini waterslides; a pint-size white-water tubing run; spouting whales and squirting seals; rubbery crocodiles on which to climb; and waterfalls under which to loll.

✔ **Typhoon Lagoon** is the park's main swimming area. This large and lovely lagoon (one of the world's largest inland wave pools) is the size of two football fields and is surrounded by a white sandy beach. Large waves hit the shore every 90 seconds. A foghorn sounds to warn you when a wave is coming. Young children can wade in the lagoon's more peaceful tidal pools — Blustery Bay and Whitecap Cove.

You can catch a wave at popular **early-bird surfing sessions** that take place on select mornings before the park officially opens. For those not brave enough to learn in the ocean, this controlled environment may be a good alternative. For more information on the surfing program, see Chapter 27.

✔ **White-Water Rides,** found in Mount Mayday, is the setting for three rafting adventures — **Keelhaul Falls, Mayday Falls,** and **Gang Plank Falls.** Keelhaul Falls has the most spiraling route, Mayday Falls has the steepest drops and fastest water, and the slightly tamer Gang Plank Falls uses large tubes so that the whole family can pile on.

See map on p. 173. Located off Buena Vista Dr., between Downtown Disney Marketplace and Disney's Hollywood Studios. ☎ *407-560-4141.* www.disney world.com. *Admission: $40 adults, $34 kids 3–9. Open: Daily 10 a.m.–5 p.m., with extended hours during some holiday periods and summer.*

Enjoying the Holiday Season at Disney

Disney uses extra pixie dust during the holidays, when the parks and resorts are decked out more spectacularly than you can even imagine. Lights, trees, caroling, and special activities begin around Thanksgiving and last until the first of the new year. For more information on all the events in this section, call ☎ 407-934-7639 or check out www. disneyworld.com.

Three of the best yuletide attractions include the following:

✔ **Mickey's Very Merry Christmas Party,** an after-dark ticketed event (7 p.m. to midnight), takes place on select nights at the **Magic**

Kingdom and offers a traditional Christmas parade and a breath-taking fireworks display. Tickets purchased in advance run $49 for adults and $43 for kids ages 3 to 9; on the day of the event, they'll cost an extra $6 per person. A ticket includes cookies, cocoa, and a souvenir photo. The best part? Shorter lines for the rides that are open.

✔ **Holidays Around The World** at **Epcot** features a **Candlelight Processional** with hundreds of carolers, a celebrity narrator telling a Christmas story, a 450-voice choir, and a 50-piece orchestra. Held on select nights, this moving event features several celebrities during its five-week run. Normal theme-park admission ($71 adults, $60 kids 3–9) is charged.

✔ **The Osborne Family Spectacle of Lights** came to **Disney's Hollywood Studios** in 1995, when an Arkansas family ran into trouble with local authorities over their multimillion-light display. Their Christmas-light collection of 2-million-plus blinkers, twinklers, and strands was so bright that their neighbors complained. After the flow of faithful spectators in cars caused mile-long backups, the neighbors, finally seeing the light, went to court. Disney came to the rescue and moved the whole thing to Orlando, adding a million or so bulbs and a bit of Disney magic. You can see it all for the normal park admission.

The other Orlando parks and many of the WDW resorts hold their own holiday festivities featuring special activities, spectacular decorations, holiday-themed parades, and more. Be sure to ask in advance or check with your concierge or at Guest Services when you arrive.

Sailing the Seas with Disney

It took them a while to catch on, which is unusual for the Disney folks, but they finally discovered another place to expand their empire — the high seas. **Disney Cruise Line** launched the *Disney Magic* and the *Disney Wonder* in 1998 and 1999, respectively.

The two ships have but small differences. The *Magic* is Art Deco, with a giant Mickey in its three-level lobby and a *Beauty and the Beast* mural in its top restaurant, Lumiere's. The *Wonder* is Art Nouveau, Ariel commands its lobby, and its featured eatery, Triton's, sports a mural from *The Little Mermaid.* Both ships have recently been refurbished.

In 2007, Disney announced plans to add two new ships to the existing Disney Cruise Line, doubling the size of its existing fleet. The ships, yet unnamed, are slated to launch in 2011 and 2012. Specifics, including design plans and itineraries, are still being developed, but I do know that the new ships will dwarf the existing *Magic* and *Wonder* by at least two decks. This begs the question: Will European and Mexican Riviera itineraries become permanent ports of call? Will an Alaskan cruise be next on Disney's list?

The restaurants, nightlife, shows, and other onboard activities on both vessels are very family oriented. One of the ships' unique features is a dine-around option that lets you move among main restaurants (each ship has four) from night to night while keeping the same servers. Disney also offers **Castaway Cay,** its own private Bahamian island, featuring watersports and other activities.

The *Disney Magic* sails seven-day eastern Caribbean (St. Thomas, St. Maarten, and Castaway Cay) and seven-day western Caribbean (Key West, Grand Cayman, Cozumel, and Castaway Cay) itineraries on an alternating basis year-round. In 2009, eastern cruises will, for the first time, include a choice of stops in either St. Croix or the British Virgin Island of Tortola. The *Disney Wonder* offers shorter three- and four-day Bahamas cruises that are often (though not necessarily) sold as part of seven-day vacation packages, combining the sailings with a **Walt Disney World** land experience. Subtle differences aside, these two ships are nearly identical twins. Both are 83,000 tons with 12 decks, 875 extra-large cabins, and room for up to 1,755 guests. (When each ship's children's berths are filled to capacity, that total can reach as high as 3,325.) The ships have some adults-only areas but no casinos.

Beginning in the summer of 2007, the *Disney Magic* set sail on the high seas starting from two very different ports of call. The first — Barcelona, Spain — marked the second time that Disney included a European itinerary in its lineup. In 2008, departures from Los Angeles featured seven-day itineraries to the Mexican Rivera and included stops in Puerto Vallarta, Mazatlan, Cabo San Lucas, Acapulco, and Aruba, with 15-day cruises to the Panama Canal, and prices ranging from $849 to $7,099. The popularity of these unique itineraries makes me wonder if they might become permanent ports of call. For more information, sail over to www.disneycruise.com or call ☎ **888-325-2500.**

Recently updated, the line's free kids' programs are some of the best at sea. Just as at Disney World, costumed Disney characters are available at scheduled times during the voyage, so passengers can line up for hugs and photos. The children's program is divided into five age groups: the **Flounder's Reef Nursery** for ages 3 months to 3 years, **Disney's Oceaneer Club** for ages 3 to 7, **Disney's Oceaneer Lab** for ages 8 to 12, **Ocean Quest** for ages 10 to 14, and **The Stack** or **Aloft** for ages 13 to 17. Each program offers numerous activities and diversions.

Especially important to parents with young kids, Disney has expanded its Flounder's Reef Nursery on both ships to hold as many as 30 children, with a child/counselor ratio of four to one. Extended hours are featured on seven-night cruises so that parents can dine alone, try a spa treatment, or sneak off for a shore excursion. Best of all, unlike other cruise lines, the nursery welcomes infants from as young as 12 weeks old to 3-year-old toddlers. The space has cribs, and counselors do change diapers (though you must supply them). The hourly price is $6 per child for the first child, $5 per each additional child, with a one-hour minimum (and a ten-hour maximum).

You can get discounted fares if you book well in advance and go during non-peak periods. The line also offers special fares for kids 3 to 12 traveling as a third, fourth, or fifth passenger and sharing a cabin with two adults.

Florida-based cruises depart from Port Canaveral, about an hour east of Orlando by car. If you buy a **Land & Sea package,** transportation to and from Orlando is included. For more information, call Disney Cruise Line or check out its very informative Web site, which also allows you to plan and reserve shore excursions before you go.

Hwy. 528 at Exit A1A, Cape Canaveral. ☎ *800-951-3532.* www.disneycruise.com. *7-day Land & Sea packages (3 or 4 days afloat, with the rest of the week at a WDW resort): $939–$5,399 adults, $399–$2,199 kids 3–12, and $189 kids younger than 3, depending on your choice of resort and stateroom. Some packages include round-trip air and unlimited admission to Disney parks, as well as other Disney attractions. 3-night cruises: $429–$2,999 adults, $229–$1,099 kids 3–12, and $149 kids younger than 3. 4-night cruises: $499–$3,999 adults, $329–$1,199 kids 3–12, and $149 kids younger than 3. 7-night cruises: $849–$5,399 adults, $399–$2,199 kids3–12, and $189 kids younger than 3.*

Chapter 17

Shopping in Walt Disney World

*P*art of the fun of going on vacation is stocking up on souvenirs. A trip to Walt Disney World shouldn't be any different — unless you want to arrive home with money in your wallet. In this chapter, I fill you in on the ins and outs of shopping for Walt Disney World mementos.

Money-Saving Tips for Top-Notch Take-Homes

The kids are tugging at your shirt, begging you for 14-carat Mouse ears and the biggest stuffed Mickey on the planet, your mother just has to have a pair of Goofy slippers, and you've always wanted a crystal Cinderella clock for the den. Then you see the price tags. *Gasp!* Are they kidding? No, unfortunately, they are not.

When you're at Disney, you're an emotional and physical captive of a commercial enterprise sprinkled with feel-good pixie dust. Now I'm just guessing and don't know this for sure, but I think Disney uses a simple formula for setting prices: Start with reasonable retail and then multiply . . . by *three.* Don't panic just yet: Not everything is completely out of reach, and if you keep reading I'll point you in the right direction.

But no matter how much I warn you, you probably won't escape without a sizable contribution to the stockholders' fund, especially if it's your first trip to Walt Disney World or if you have kids in tow. So before you start spending, here are a few things to think about:

> ✔ If there's a **Disney Store** near your hometown, items at least similar to some of what's sold in the Disney parks are likely sold there as well. You can also choose from a fairly large selection at www. disneystore.com. So there's no need to rush into a purchase.

(Notable exceptions, however, are goods sold in the World Showcase pavilions at Epcot, as well as Walt Disney World logo merchandise sold throughout the parks.)

✔ At the other end of the spectrum, many WDW shops sell products themed to their particular area of the park (such as the shops found at the exit of many rides or the kiosks found throughout the different lands), and finding an identical item elsewhere in the parks (let alone outside the parks) may be difficult at best.

✔ Don't be fooled by the discount stores offering you a "bargain." You usually won't find bargains or discounts on true or authentic WDW merchandise anywhere. If someone offers you one (especially outside the parks), beware. The bargain or discount may be a cheap imitation or knockoff — or worse, "hot."

✔ Don't forget to account for the 6.5 percent sales tax on purchases.

Loading Up Your Cart at Walt Disney World

In general, you'll find three categories of merchandise in the WDW parks. **Souvenirs** that scream "Disney!" are the most common. (The number of choices — from Ariel to Winnie the Pooh and beyond — can, and will, fog your brain.) **Collectibles,** including some not related to Disney, are another. You find these items in some of the **Main Street** shops in the **Magic Kingdom,** as well as around the **World Showcase** in **Epcot** and at the **Downtown Disney Marketplace.** The last category, merchandise native to the 11 countries featured in Epcot's World Showcase, and completely unrelated to Disney whatsoever, is aptly considered a **World Showcase** specialty.

Why lug all your bulky purchases around? You can send your purchases from any store to designated areas near the entrance, where you can pick them up as you leave the park that day. In the **Magic Kingdom,** you can pick up packages at Package Pick-Up next to City Hall in the entrance area. In **Epcot,** you can send your packages to Package Pick-Up at the gift shop in the Entrance Plaza or the World Traveler at the International Gateway in World Showcase. Shop clerks at **Disney's Hollywood Studios** will send your goodies to the Package Pick-Up next to Oscar's Super Service near the park entrance. And you can pick up your **Disney's Animal Kingdom** purchases at Garden Gate Gifts near the Entrance Plaza. (Allow at least three hours for delivery.) If you're a Disney resort guest, you can have your packages delivered to your resort (more specifically, the resort gift shop) for free. Packages may not arrive until the next afternoon if purchased prior to 7 p.m.; if purchased after 7 p.m. they'll arrive the *second* afternoon after your purchase was made.

Disney bargains: A well-kept secret

From a pink Cadillac to a 4-foot beer stein, tons of wacky treasures are regularly put on the auction block at Walt Disney World.

In addition to castoffs from the theme parks and WDW resorts, there are more routine items available, from over-the-hill lawn maintenance gear to never-been-used stainless-steel pots and pans. If you're looking for a unique piece of Disney, the auctions are held six times a year. Some of the more unusual items sold in the past include furniture from Miss Piggy's dressing room and a motorized surfboard. The auction takes place on Disney's back lots. Call property control (☎ 407/824-6878) for information, dates, and directions.

Bigger yet are trinkets sold by gavel at www.disneyauctions.com. Mainstream items, including artwork, figurines, cookie jars, pins, and snow globes are available on a regular basis (and sold at a set price). But when movie props, costumes, and theme park artifacts go on the block, prices can soar. A dress Glenn Close wore as Cruella De Vil in 102 Dalmatians sold for $5,000.

Magic Kingdom

The **Emporium** along **Main Street U.S.A.** has a large selection of Disneyana, including pricey collectibles such as Minnie Mouse cookie jars and vintage Mickey Mouse wristwatches, as well as apparel, toys, and trinkets. The **Fantasy Faire** inside **Cinderella Castle** sells family crests, tapestries, suits of armor, and miniature carousels.

In **Adventureland,** the **Pirates Bazaar** peddles hats, Captain Hook T-shirts, ships in bottles, toy muskets, and loads of other yo-ho-ho buccaneer booty, in addition to jewelry and a small selection of resort wear. It's outside the Pirates of the Caribbean ride.

In **Fantasyland, Pooh's Thotful Shop** is dedicated to Hundred-Acre Gang merchandise, including plenty of Pooh and Tigger items. Wares at **Tinker Bell's Treasures** include Peter Pan merchandise, costumes (Tinker Bell, Snow White, Cinderella, Pocahontas, and others), and collector dolls. At the exit of **Mickey's PhilharMagic** is a collection of trinkets, toys, and T-shirts that feature Donald Duck.

In **Frontierland,** the **Frontier Trading Post** hawks cowboy hats, Western shirts, coonskin caps, turquoise jewelry, belts, and toy rifles.

In **Liberty Square,** the **Yankee Trader** is a charming country store that sells cookie jars, Disney cookie cutters, and fancy food items.

In **Mickey's Toontown Fair,** the **Toontown Hall of Fame** carries a large array of toys, T-shirts, candy, and other Disney-themed trinkets.

In **Tomorrowland,** both **Mickey's Star Traders** and **Merchants of Venus** have Disney collectibles along with just about anything else Disney. The spaceship-shaped kiosk outside **Buzz Lightyear's Space Ranger Spin** has enough *Toy Story* toys to fill any kid's toy chest.

Epcot

Future World has only a few shops to call its own, and most are ride related. The most notable is **Mouse Gear,** filled top to bottom with everything Disney, from T-shirts to trinkets and everything in between. The **Art of Disney** has a small but impressive selection of original art-work, lithographs, cels, and various posters available for purchase.

World Showcase pavilions carry unique and unusual items that repre-sent their respective pavilion's country. Following are some of the shop-ping highlights.

In the **American Adventure Pavilion, Heritage Manor Gifts** sells auto-graphed presidential photographs, needlepoint samplers, quilts, can-dles, Davy Crockett hats, books on U.S. history, dolls, classic political campaign buttons, and vintage newspapers with banner headlines such as "NIXON RESIGNS!" You can also buy Disney art and character merchan-dise, as well as popular Disney pins.

In the **Canada Pavilion,** the **Northwest Mercantile** carries sandstone and soapstone carvings, fringed leather vests, duck decoys, moccasins, an array of stuffed animals, Native dolls and spirit stones, rabbit-skin caps, knitted sweaters, and, of course, maple syrup.

In the **China Pavilion,** the bustling **Yong Feng Shangdian Department Store** has an array of merchandise, including silk robes, brocade paja-mas, lacquer and inlaid mother-of-pearl furniture, jade figures, cloisonné vases, tea sets, silk rugs and embroideries, dolls, fans, wind chimes, and clothing. Artisans demonstrate calligraphy here, too.

In the **France Pavilion,** the covered shopping area called **Emporia** is filled with art, cookbooks, wines (there's a tasting counter), Madeline and Babar books and dolls, perfumes, and original letters written by famous Frenchmen, such as Napoleon. This is one of only two locations in the entire world to feature signature Guerlain fragrances.

In the **Germany Pavilion,** shops feature Hummel figurines (one of only eight worldwide locations to carry a complete collection), crystal, glass-ware, cuckoo clocks, cowbells, Alpine hats, foods and wines (there's a tasting counter), books, and toys (German Disneyana, teddy bears, dolls, and puppets). An artisan sometimes demonstrates molding and painting Hummel figures; another paints detailed scenes on eggs.

In the **Italy Pavilion, La Cucina Italiana** and **Il Bel Cristallo** stock cameos and delicate filigree jewelry, fine leather goods, cookware, wines and foods, Murano and other Venetian glass, alabaster figurines, inlaid wooden music boxes, and festive Carnivale masks.

In the **Japan Pavilion,** the **Mitsukoshi Department Store** stocks lacquerware, kimonos, fans, dolls, origami books, samurai swords, Japanese Disneyana, bonsai trees, foods, Netsuke carvings, pottery, and electronics. Artisans demonstrate the ancient arts of *anesaiku* (shaping brownrice candy into dragons, unicorns, and dolphins), *sumi-e* (calligraphy), and *origami* (paper folding). Kids interested in the Hello Kitty gang or anime cartoons will find plenty to ask you to buy.

Given Tokyo's notorious astronomical prices, this store may be one of the few places in WDW where you can actually score a relative bargain.

In the **Mexico Pavilion,** shops in and around the **Plaza de Los Amigos** (a Mexican *mercado* with a tiered fountain and street lamps) display an array of leather goods, baskets, sombreros, piñatas, pottery, embroidered blouses, maracas, jewelry, papier-mâché birds, and blown-glass objects. (An artisan gives glass-blowing demonstrations.)

In the **Morocco Pavilion,** the streets lead to the ***souk,*** a bustling marketplace where handcrafted pottery, brassware, hand-knotted Berber carpets, ornate silver and camel-bone boxes, straw baskets, and prayer rugs are sold. You can also catch weaving demonstrations here.

In the **Norway Pavilion,** the shops sell hand-knitted wool hats and sweaters (including a collection by Dale of Norway), toys (there's a LEGO table where kids can play), trolls, woodcarvings, foods, pewterware, Christmas items, body creams, and candles.

In the **United Kingdom Pavilion,** shops on **High Street** and **Tudor Lane** display a broad sampling of British merchandise, including toy soldiers, Paddington bears, Thomas the Tank Engine wooden train sets, personalized coats of arms, Scottish clothing (cashmere and Shetland sweaters, tams, knits, and tartans), Wimbledon sportswear, fine china, Waterford crystal, and pub items such as tankards and dartboards. A tea shop occupies a replica of Anne Hathaway's thatch-roofed, 16th-century cottage in Stratford-upon-Avon.

Disney's Hollywood Studios

The **Animation Gallery** carries collectible animation cels, books about animation, arts-and-crafts kits for future animators, and collector figurines. **Sid Cahuenga's One-of-a-Kind** sells autographed photos of the stars, original movie posters, and other memorabilia. Over at the **Darkroom/Cover Story,** you can have your photograph put on the cover of your favorite magazine. **Celebrity 5 & 10,** modeled after a 1940s Woolworth's, is filled with unique Disney-esque housewares, Disney's Hollywood Studios T-shirts, trinkets, and movie posters.

Great things to buy at Epcot

Epcot's World Showcase shines in the shopping department. Although the selections here change from time to time and may not necessarily represent bargains, they are the kind of unique and unusual items you may not find anywhere else.

- ✔ If you're into **silver jewelry,** don't miss the **Mexico Pavilion.** You can find trinkets ranging from simple flowered hair clips to stone-and-silver bracelets.

- ✔ The shops in the **Norway Pavilion** have great **sweaters** and **Scandinavian trolls** that are so ugly you're likely to fall in love with them.

- ✔ In the **China Pavilion,** browse through **jade teardrop earrings, Disney art,** and more. Its merchandise is among the most expensive and most fetching in Epcot.

- ✔ The **Italy Pavilion** has **silk scarves and ties** that come in several patterns.

- ✔ Style-conscious teenagers may love a **Taquia knit cap,** something of a colorful fezlike chapeau, that's available in the **Morocco Pavilion.** You can also find beautifully painted **pottery.**

- ✔ **Wimbledon shirts, shorts, and skirts** are among the hard-to-find items in the **United Kingdom Pavilion,** which also has an assortment of tea accessories, sweaters, and Beatles memorabilia.

Many of the park's major attractions also have shops or kiosks filled with items such as *Indiana Jones* accessories, *Little Mermaid* stuffed characters, *Star Wars* light sabers, *Star Wars* LEGO sets, and so on.

Disney's Animal Kingdom

In the **Oasis,** the **Outpost Shop** deals in T-shirts, sweatshirts, hats, toys, and other souvenir items.

In **Discovery Island,** the **Beastly Bazaar** has a wide selection of items related to the Tree of Life and the show It's Tough to be a Bug!, along with chocolates, candies, and home-décor items. **Creature Comforts,** mostly geared for kids, sells clothing, stuffed animals, and toys. **Island Mercantile** offers theme merchandise that represents the park's lands. It also has a hair-braiding service and a pin-trading location.

In **Africa,** stop at **Mombasa Marketplace/Ziwani Traders** for Kilimanjaro Safaris apparel and gifts, as well as realistic animal items, including beautiful wood carvings, and other authentic African gifts.

In **Asia, Serka Zong** offers stuffed Yetis, T-shirts, and everything Expedition Everest. **Mandala Gifts** carries Asian-themed items such as ornate wind chimes, colorful kites, and stuffed tigers.

In **DinoLand U.S.A.,** look for wild and wacky dinosaur souvenirs at **Chester & Hester's Dinosaur Treasures,** which also carries T-shirts and tons of toys and trinkets (many under $5).

Disney Shopping outside the Theme Parks

Don't think that the enticement to spend money magically disappears when you step outside the theme parks. Walt Disney World also encompasses some shopping districts that house a multitude of shops — some of which carry merchandise you can't get anywhere else — that offer you the chance to blow your budget.

Disney's West Side

Disney's West Side has many unique specialty stores where you can find plenty of unusual gifts and souvenirs.

Hoypoloi is a New Age store offering artsy glass, sculptures, and other decorative doodads. **Magnetron Magnetz** is, well, wow! Can there be a market for this many refrigerator magnets? **Magic Masters,** a re-creation of Harry Houdini's private library, is the place for magic tricks and illusions. Smoking may be on the way to sayonara-ville, but **Sosa Family Cigars** beckons with sweet smells and a tradition reaching back to yesterday's Cuba. Over at **Starabilias,** the main events are jukeboxes, Coke machines, and other nostalgic treasures. **Pop Gallery,** named for the colorful artwork that seemingly "pops" out at passersby, features limited-edition paintings, sculptures, and gifts.

Disney's West Side (☎ 407-828-3800; www.disneyworld.com) is on Buena Vista Drive. From I-4, exit on Highway 536 or Highway 535 and follow the signs. Some shop hours vary, but the complex is open daily from 9:30 a.m. to 11 p.m.

Downtown Disney Marketplace

Basin has a cornucopia of fresh-made bath products, including wonderful bath bombs. The **Art of Disney** is filled with animation cels, original artwork, limited editions, lithographs, and fine art. **Arribas Brothers** has products that crystal and metal artists make before your eyes. **Summer Sands** features hip designer duds (think skate and surf) as well as a selection of swimwear. If you prefer a sportier look, try **Team Mickey Athletic Club,** with its sports-minded character clothing and NASCAR and ESPN merchandise. **Once Upon A Toy**, one of my favorite toy stores of all time, shelves popular games (including Disney-themed versions of Mr. Potato Head, Clue, and Monopoly) and touts a build-your-own-lightsaber station.

Getting your fill

The neatest way to buy toys at several Downtown Disney stores (especially Once Upon a Toy) is in bulk . . . sort of. Toys such as Lincoln Logs and Mr. Potato Head, as well as a few others, can be purchased by the piece. Here's how it works: You pick out a box (often with two sizes to choose from), and fill it up with as many (or few) pieces as you can fit inside. The only stipulation — you have to be able to close the lid properly. No matter how many pieces you've stuffed inside, the price of the box remains the same. If you've got good space-saving skills, buying your toys this way may net you a very good deal. (Here's a hint to get you started — Mr. Potato Head has a hole in his back, so fill it up and you'll fit more pieces in your box.)

The **LEGO Imagination Center** is one of the best shops around, a fabulous spot for parents to relax while their young whippersnappers unwind in a free LEGO play area beside the store. The 50,000-square-foot **World of Disney** is the largest store in Downtown Disney and comes with the (don't-hold-it-to-them) promise that if it exists, and it's Disney, it's on their shelves. Within the walls of World of Disney you'll also find two very unique rooms: the **Adventure Room,** where pint-size pirates can set sail for the high seas and try their hand at Disney's latest video games; and the **Princess Room,** where little girls can play and pretend in royal fashion. The **Bibbidi Bobbidi Boutique,** a salon of sorts, is where little princesses can get the royal treatment.

Downtown Disney Marketplace (☎ 407-828-3800; www.disneyworld.com) is on Buena Vista Drive at Hotel Plaza Boulevard. From I-4, exit on Highway 536 or Highway 535 and follow the signs. It's open daily from 9:30 a.m. to 11 p.m.

Pleasure Island

While few stores currently operate on the island, **Curl by Sammy Duvall,** an all-new high-end skate-and-surf shop, is a standout, featuring the hottest clothes, accessories, gear, and boards.

As the newly reimagined island (no longer filled with nightclubs) begins to takes shape in upcoming months, look for several new upscale shops (not to mention restaurants and attractions) to pop up.

Pleasure Island (☎ 407-828-3800; www.disneyworld.com) is on Buena Vista Drive. From I-4, exit on Highway 536 or Highway 535 and follow the signs. Some shop hours vary, but the complex is open daily from 9:30 a.m. to 11 p.m.

Part V
Exploring the Rest of Orlando

The 5th Wave   By Rich Tennant

"Since we lost the dolphins, business hasn't been quite the same."

In this part . . .

Mickey may be the toughest mouse around, but he doesn't own Orlando anymore. Yes, this is still the town that Disney built, but the fact is, half of the nine big-league attractions in Orlando don't belong to Disney.

This part of the book explores the rest of Orlando, including the exciting attractions at Universal Orlando, as well as what you find at SeaWorld, Discovery Cove, Aquatica, some of the smaller attractions, and some of the best shopping venues outside the parks. It also includes information on great day trips to two of the most popular attractions outside the immediate Orlando area: Busch Gardens and the Kennedy Space Center.

Chapter 18

Universal Studios Florida

* *

In This Chapter

▶ Discovering helpful Universal facts
▶ Seeing the best things at Universal Studios Florida
▶ Eating at Universal Studios Florida
▶ Shopping for souvenirs

* *

*W*ith two studios in Orlando, you soon get the picture, literally and figuratively, about which studio produces what films. Both **Universal Studios** and **Disney's Hollywood Studios** (see Chapter 14) have plenty to offer, and both spend plenty of money plugging their movies and characters. At Universal, that investment means you'll encounter *The Mummy, Twister, Terminator, Jaws, Shrek, E.T., Barney, The Simpsons,* and many more. You'll find plenty of grown-up, cutting-edge, hurl-'em-and-twirl-'em rides, such as **Revenge of the Mummy the Ride, Men in Black Alien Attack, Disaster!–A Major Motion Picture Ride . . . Starring YOU,** and **Hollywood Rip, Ride, Rockit** (the park's newest multisensory mega-coaster, slated to debut in 2009). Universal has recently made great strides to appeal to younger kids as well, especially with **Woody Woodpecker's KidZone** and its pint-size rides, shows, and play areas.

As a plus, Universal is a working television and movie studio, so occasionally some live filming is done at the various sound stages in the park. You can also see reel history displayed in the form of actual sets exhibited along Hollywood Boulevard and Rodeo Drive. A talented troupe of actors portraying Universal stars, such as the Blues Brothers, or a wide range of not-so-recognizable characters often wanders the park chatting with guests. And park shows, such as **Terminator 2: 3D Battle Across Time, Fear Factor Live,** and **Blue Man Group** (a separately ticketed show), deliver heart-pumping excitement.

In this chapter, I give you helpful hints and basic information about visiting Universal Studios Florida and experiencing its attractions.

Finding Out Important Park Information

Before I get to the good stuff of USF, I need to get the logistical bits out of the way; believe me, you'll appreciate it when you get there.

Buying tickets and making reservations

You can choose from several ticket options and tours:

- ✔ A **one-day ticket** costs $75 (plus 6.5 percent sales tax) for adults, $63 for children 3 to 9.

- ✔ A **two-day, two-park admission ticket** is $120 for adults and $110 for kids. These passes enable you to move between Universal Studios Florida and Islands of Adventure (see Chapter 19) whenever you like. Two-day tickets also give you free access at night to select CityWalk clubs (see Chapter 25).

  For a limited time, Universal is offering online tickets at substantial savings at www.universalorlando.com. For example, a two-park unlimited-admission ticket, good for entrance to both Universal Studios and Islands of Adventure for seven consecutive days, costs $100 (kids and adults alike).

- ✔ **Annual passes** (the **Premier Annual Pass,** the **Preferred Annual Pass,** and the **Power Pass**) allow entry to the park for an entire year (some blackout dates apply to the Power Pass; there are no blackout dates with the Premier or Preferred Annual Pass — but there are plenty of perks). The costs are $280, $200, and $140, respectively. For more details, check out www.universalorlando.com.

- ✔ The **FlexTicket** multiday, multipark option is the most economical way to see the various "other-than-Disney" parks. You pay one price to visit any and all of the participating parks during a 14-day period. The Orlando FlexTicket to Universal Studios Florida, Islands of Adventure, Wet 'n Wild, SeaWorld, and Aquatica is $235 for adults and $195 for children ages 3 to 9. The Orlando FlexTicket Plus, which adds Busch Gardens in Tampa, is $280 for adults and $234 for kids. You can order the FlexTicket by calling ☎ 407-363-8000 or by going to www.universalorlando.com.

- ✔ Universal Studios Florida offers five-hour guided **VIP Tours** for $100 to $120 per person; a two-park, seven-hour tour that also includes Islands of Adventure runs $125 to $150 per person. Guided tours include line-cutting privileges and preferred seating at several attractions; they start at 10 a.m. and noon daily. For more information on the tours, call ☎ **407-363-8295.** *Note:* The price of the VIP Tour includes neither the 6.5 percent sales tax *nor admission to the park!*

Theme-park prices are not the only things that will lighten your wallet. Expect to spend up to $3 for a soda, $2 (and up) for a cup of coffee, about $5 (and up) for a beer, $2.80 for popcorn ($4.50 in a souvenir bucket), and $2.50 for bottled water. However, you can save 10 percent on your purchases at any gift shop or on a meal by showing your **AAA card.** This discount isn't available at food or merchandise carts. Likewise, tobacco, candy, film, collectibles, and sundry items aren't included in discounts.

For information about new travel packages and other theme-park information, call ☎ **877-801-9720,** 800-711-0080, 800-224-4233, or 407-363-8000; write to Guest Services at Universal Studios Florida, 1000 Universal Studios Plaza, Orlando, FL 32819-7601; or go to www.universalorlando.com. After you're at the park, just head over to Guest Services.

Universal Orlando is located about half a mile north of I-4's Kirkman Road/Highway 435 exit. You may find construction in the area, so keep an eye out for the road signs directing you to Universal Orlando.

The park is open 365 days a year. Park hours generally are from 9 a.m. to 6 or 7 p.m., though they vary seasonally and the park may close as late as 10 p.m. during the summer and on holidays. Call or check online for exact times before you go.

Locating special services and facilities

In case you forget to bring essential items, or if you need special assistance while at the park, here's a list of services and facilities that may come in handy:

- ✔ **ATMs** accepting cards from banks using the Cirrus, STAR, and PLUS systems are on the outside near Guest Services and just inside Universal's entrance, as well as in San Francisco/Amity near Lombard's Seafood Grille.

- ✔ **Baby-changing tables** are located in all men's and women's restrooms; **nursing facilities** are at **Family Services,** just inside the main entrance and to the right. (Family Services doesn't sell any diapers or infant supplies, so be sure to bring your own.)

- ✔ **Disposable cameras and film** (and limited digital supplies) are available at the **On Location** shop in the Front Lot, just inside the main entrance. One-hour photo developing is available, but I don't recommend paying park prices. Cheaper one-hour or overnight places are all around town, including many near tourist-area hotels.

- ✔ Universal has its own version of Disney's FASTPASS, called **Universal Express Plus Pass.** Unfortunately, at Universal, the *Plus* means having to pay for your park tickets *plus* the Express Pass. Passes are available for purchase online or at the park, but be aware that they (like the freebies at Disney) run out, often by midday, sometimes earlier, during peak seasons. The pass allows

Universal Studios Florida

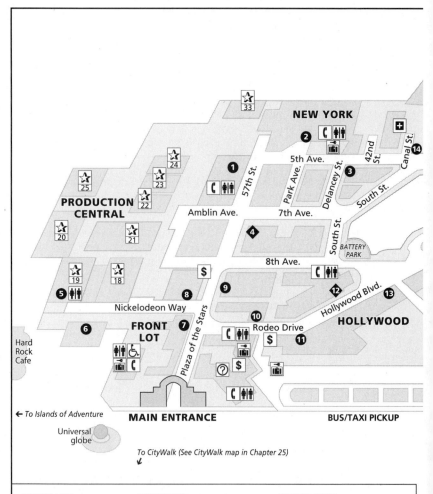

FRONT LOT
Universal Studios Store **7**

PRODUCTION CENTRAL
Blue Man Group (Sharp
  AQUOS Theatre) **5**
Hollywood Rip, Ride, Rockit
  (coming in 2009) **6**
Jimmy Neutron's
  Nicktoon Blast **8**
Shrek 4-D **9**

NEW YORK
The Blues Brothers **3**
Revenge of the Mummy
  the Ride **2**
TWISTER…Ride It Out **1**

SAN FRANCISCO/AMITY
Beetlejuice's Graveyard Revue **14**
Disaster!–A Major Motion Picture
  Ride…Starring YOU **15**
Fear Factor Live **18**
JAWS **17**

WORLD EXPO
Men in Black Alien Attack **19**
The Simpsons Ride **20**

WOODY WOODPECKER'S KIDZONE
Animal Actors on Location! **22**
Curious George Goes To Town **26**
A Day in the Park with Barney **27**
E.T. Adventure **23**
Fievel's Playland **24**
Woody Woodpecker's
  Nuthouse Coaster **25**

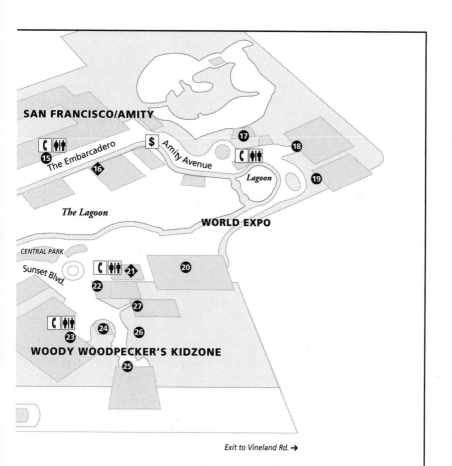

Exit to Vineland Rd. →

Film & TV Production Stage

$ Banking

First Aid

Lockers

Restrooms

C Telephones

? Guest Services

Wheelchair & Stroller Rental

HOLLYWOOD
Lucy–A Tribute **10**
Terminator 2: 3D Battle
Across Time **11**
Universal Horror
Make-Up Show **13**

DINING◆
Classic Monsters Cafe **4**
International Food and Film
Festival **21**
Lombard's Seafood Grille **16**
Mel's Drive-In **12**

access to the Express line at each and every attraction that accepts the Universal Express Pass without having to continually obtain separate passes or wait for any time limits to expire before heading to the Express line at the next attraction. The downside is that you can use it only once at each of the attractions. The price varies and can run between $20 and $56 per ticket, depending on whether it's good for one or both Universal parks and what date the pass is valid for. Visit www.universalorlando.com for all the details.

Universal offers a separate line-beating option as a perk for guests staying at its resorts. Guests of the **Hard Rock Hotel, Portofino Bay Hotel,** and **Royal Pacific Resort** (see Chapter 9) just have to show their room keys to get unlimited Express-line access to the rides and front-of-the-line access to most of the restaurants.

✔ You can find **First Aid Stations** between New York and San Francisco/Amity, next to Louie's Italian Restaurant, and just inside the main entrance next to Guest Services.

✔ **Lockers** cost $8 to $10 a day. Be sure to read the instructions carefully when using the newer electronic lockers — otherwise you'll spend valuable time tracking down a park attendant to help retrieve your gear instead of riding the rides.

✔ Report **lost children** to any staff member and then go to Guest Services near the main entrance or Security (behind Louie's Italian Restaurant, between New York and San Francisco/Amity). *Children under 7 should wear name tags inside their clothing.*

✔ **Package delivery** is available for purchases made at park stores (though not at the kiosks and carts). You can have your purchases sent to It's A Wrap, at the Universal Studios Store near the entrance, to be picked up on your way out. If you're a guest at one of the three Universal hotels, you can have your purchases delivered to your room (though delivery will be the following day, so don't try this if it's your last day).

If you find you have arrived home without that essential USF T-shirt or all-important blaster gun, you can call ☎ **407-224-5800** and the **Universal Mail Order Department** will help. Just let them know what the item is and where it's located, and they can arrange to have it shipped to your home (for a fee, of course).

✔ When **parking** in multilevel garages, write down your location (character, level, row, and space number) so that you can find your car later. Parking costs $12 for cars and trucks. Valet parking is available for $20. If you arrive after 6 p.m., parking is free. Universal's garages are connected to its parks by walkways and a series of moving sidewalks, but reaching the gates can take a while.

If you need **car assistance,** including battery jumps, raise the hood and tell any parking attendant your location, or use the call boxes located throughout the parking garage to call for security.

✔ **Pet care** for small animals is available at the Studio Kennel in the parking garages for $10 a day (no overnight stays), but you'll have to feed and walk your pet yourself. Ask the parking attendant to direct you to the kennel. (Note that the kennels may be a bit small for larger pets.)

✔ **Strollers** are available on Amity Avenue in San Francisco and at Guest Services, just inside the entrance to the right. The rental cost is $13 for a single and $21 for a double, tax included.

✔ **Wheelchairs** are available in the Rotunda area of the parking garage and at Guest Services just inside the main gate. The rental cost is $12 per day for a regular wheelchair, $45 per day for an electric wheelchair. Both require a $50 deposit and a signed rental agreement. Prices include taxes.

Exploring the Top Attractions at Universal Studios Florida

Universal matches Disney stride for stride, and in some cases is a half-step ahead, when it comes to cutting-edge rides. Real and virtual thrills, terrific special effects, mammoth screens, and 3-D action are all part of its successful mix.

The rides and shows at Universal are located in six distinctive sets: **Hollywood, New York, Production Central, San Francisco/Amity, Woody Woodpecker's KidZone,** and **World Expo.** The Front Lot serves as the park's main entrance. Universal is much better than Disney at keeping you occupied while you're standing in line. Elaborate surroundings and entertaining preshows, some just as amusing or interesting as the main event, make the wait more bearable. Most lines are under cover from the sun, with the occasional water spritzer or drinking fountain nearby. Although these extras may not initially seem like a big deal, it makes your time in line far more tolerable.

The "Universal Studios Florida" map, found on p. 268, will help you visualize the layout of the park.

Hollywood

Hollywood is to the right of the Front Lot, and its main streets include Rodeo Drive, Hollywood Boulevard, and Sunset Boulevard, all lined with ornate buildings in soft hues, much like you would have found in Hollywood's heyday so many years ago. Here's a list of the best that Hollywood has to offer:

✔ **Lucy–A Tribute:** This show is a remembrance of America's queen of comedy, Lucille Ball. If you love Lucy, it's a must, with a really neat interactive trivia game and lots of memorabilia. If you're pressed for time or have smaller kids along, it's skippable.

✔ **Terminator 2: 3D Battle Across Time:** This attraction is billed as "the quintessential sight and sound experience for the 21st century!" and the park has little need to be modest about its claim. The movie's director, Jim Cameron, supervised this $60-million production, which combines 3-D film, live action, and sensory effects into a seamless winner. After a slower start (the preshow sets up a pre-*Terminator* story line), it builds to one of the best action shows in town. Live actors and six giant cyborgs interact with the Governator himself, who appears on three huge screens. The crisp 3-D effects are among the best in Orlando. (When liquid mercury falls from the screen, cold water really hits your legs.)

"All the action was so cool — just like the movie, the motorcycle and all the special effects were wild. I thought for sure the hand that came out into the audience was going to grab me," says 13-year-old Austin. The show, however, is rated **PG-13,** Universal's way of saying violence and loud noises may make it unsuitable for preteens. Younger children may find the crashing and flying 3-D effects (in conjunction with a few of the sensory effects) too intense.

✔ **Universal Horror Make-Up Show:** This show, loaded with corny humor, gives you a behind-the-scenes look at the wizardry behind Hollywood's monster makeup. It also takes an up-close look at some cinematic makeup masterpieces, including the transformation scenes from such movies as *The Fly* and *The Exorcist.* It's rated **PG-13,** mostly due to the scary on-screen characters.

Keep your eyes and ears open as you make your way along Hollywood Boulevard — you may be in for a treat. Lucy and Ricky liven things up while singing and dancing through the studio streets and entertaining the crowds as their seven-piece band plays traditional Cuban rhythms.

New York

New York is near the back of the park and includes rides and shows set among mock-ups of 42nd and 57th streets, Park Avenue, and Delancey Street. The premier attractions in this section are the following:

✔ **The Blues Brothers:** This foot-stomping revue takes to Delancey Street five times a day. Clap along as Jake and Elwood, the "bad boys of the blues," belt out a medley of their greatest hits.

✔ **Revenge of the Mummy the Ride:** Billed as a "psychological thrill ride," this indoor roller coaster relies on a combination of speed, pyrotechnics, and a cast of creepy creatures (animatronic, of course) to induce the screams often heard as you make your way through the dimly lit queue. Once aboard, riders are hurtled through elaborate Egyptian sets, passageways, and tombs moving both forward and backward — at times in complete darkness. This five-minute adventure may seem like a lifetime to some as it truly preys on your deepest and darkest phobias with overhead flames, pitch-dark blackness, insects, and skeletal warriors that hop aboard your car, combining to create the most frightening experience in the park. If you have severe phobias or if you have medical conditions, pay close attention to the posted warnings, and don't even think about getting on board. Coaster crazies that meet the *48-inch height requirement,* however, will likely make this one tops on their list — mine sure did!

Austin (age 13), a coaster crazy and fan of the movie, couldn't stop talking about it (or riding it): "It was so cool and so creepy . . . You never knew what was going to happen next — first you went one way, then another, and then the skeleton jumped right down on us from out of nowhere. . . . And the ride was soooooo smooth — it was unbelievable!"

✔ **TWISTER . . . Ride It Out:** This windy incarnation of **Earthquake–The Big One** (see "San Francisco/Amity," later in this chapter) packs quite a wallop. Based on the hit film, the curtain rises on the movie town of Wakita, where Universal engineers have created a five-story funnel cloud by injecting 2 million cubic feet of air per minute. (That's enough to fill four full-size blimps.) The sensory elements are pretty incredible. Power lines spark and fall, an oak tree splits, and the storm rumbles at rock-concert level as cars, trucks, and a cow fly about while the audience watches from only 20 feet away. In the finale, the floor begins to buckle at your feet. The only downside is that you tend to get way too much water whipped at your face (it is a tornado, after all).

"You don't really ride anything as much as walk through it, but it was pretty wild," 11-year-old Nicolas offered. It's similar to **Backdraft,** an attraction at **Universal Studios Hollywood** that once drew a lengthy queue (before it was destroyed by fire in 2008), though the California attraction was (sacrilege!) a step or two better than this one. TWISTER doesn't have a minimum height, but it carries the park's **PG-13** rating, so it may be too intense for younger children.

Production Central

Production Central is directly behind and to the left of the Front Lot. Its main thoroughfares are Nickelodeon Way, Plaza of the Stars, and 7th and 8th avenues. Here are some of the area's highlights:

✔ **Jimmy Neutron's Nicktoon Blast:** This ride is based on the movie *Jimmy Neutron: Boy Genius.* You climb aboard a Mark IV rocket, and motion-simulator technology and sophisticated computer graphics send you on a spinning, careening adventure that includes a battle against Yokians — evil, egg-shaped aliens. The attraction also features characters from several popular cartoons, including *Rugrats* and *Fairly OddParents.* If you feel any twinge of motion sickness, simply look at any stationary object in the large theater.

Quiet on the set!

The comedy, music, and multimedia theatrics of **Blue Man Group** have a new home. This dynamic group of wild and, at times, wacky performers is now wowing audiences at Universal Studios in the newly refurbished 1,000-seat Sharp AQUOS Theatre (previously Nickelodeon Studios), accessible from both Universal Studios and CityWalk. Park admission is not required for this separately ticketed show (which features two daily performances). Tickets (show only) run $64 to $74 for adults, $54 to $64 for children ages 3 to 9. Combination tickets (including theme-park admission and a single show — at a discounted price) are also available ($126–$155 adults, $116–$155 children ages 3–9). Pricing varies with showtimes and the type of park ticket chosen; options currently include a one-day, two-park pass or a two-park unlimited-admission ticket.

"It was cool, just like being part of the TV show. The Chicken Dance was pretty funny, too," said Nicolas (age 11). His younger sister, Hailey (age 9), and younger brother, Davis (age 7), were equally impressed with this very kid-friendly ride filled with familiar favorites. That said, kids do *need to be at least 40 inches tall to ride.* There is a small area near the front for those who want to skip the moving spaceships.

✔ **Shrek 4-D:** This 4-D fractured fairytale is based on the hit movie *Shrek.* You can see, hear, feel, and smell this 15-minute show, thanks to 3-D film, motion simulators, OgreVision glasses, and other special effects, including water spritzers. The attraction picks up where the movie leaves off — you join Shrek and Princess Fiona on their honeymoon (which, predictably, gets interrupted by the evil Lord Farquaad). Fractured or not, you know this one will have a happy ending, and it's similar in style to Disney's **It's Tough to be a Bug!** (see Chapter 15) and **"Honey, I Shrunk the Kids"** (see Chapter 14). But, as with all Universal rides, it's a bit edgier all around. The preshow is one of the funniest in the park and is as good as the show itself. The line can stretch for miles (made worse with the release of *Shrek the Third*), but thankfully you can use Express passes; if you didn't shell out the extra cash, at least you'll wait under cover from the sun.

"Awesome! Except for the spiders — they totally freaked me out," 11-year-old Nicolas giggled. Kids not into sensory effects may get freaked out as well. This ride can also be rather bumpy, but the front row has stationary seats for those who need them.

San Francisco/Amity

San Francisco/Amity faces the waterfront, and its attractions line the Embarcadero and Amity Avenue.

✔ **Beetlejuice's Graveyard Revue:** Dracula, Wolfman, the Phantom of the Opera, Frankenstein and his bride, and Beetlejuice show up to scare you silly. This funky rock musical has pyrotechnic special effects and MTV-style choreography. It's most popular with young teens but loud and lively enough to aggravate some older adults and scare small children. It carries Universal's **PG-13** rating.

✔ **Disaster!–A Major Motion Picture Ride . . . Starring YOU:** Replacing the popular (albeit dated) Earthquake–The Big One, Disaster! still rocks the Richter scale. While the ride itself remains almost identical to its predecessor, tweaks to the story line (placing you smack in the middle of filming of *Mutha Nature,* a fictitious action-adventure flick) and all-new high-tech special effects add an interactive element to the recently revamped experience. That said, sparks still fly shortly after you board the underground train, a massive quake — a whopping 8.3 on the Richter scale! — hits, leaving you trapped as vast slabs of concrete collapse around you, a propane truck bursts into flames, a runaway train comes hurtling at you, and the station floods, with 65,000 gallons of water cascading down the steps.

✔ **Fear Factor Live:** Based on the NBC reality-TV show, this relatively new show takes center stage. Contestants (who are actual Universal Studios guests ages 18 and older and who meet certain height, weight, and health restrictions) face some of their greatest fears in front of thousands of people. They'll go head to head with other competitors, each trying to outdo the other in order to be proclaimed the winner. The wild stunts, similar to what you've seen on the television show, test both their physical and emotional limits — not to mention their stomachs. Leave it to Universal to be the first to transform a blockbuster reality-TV show into one of the hottest attractions around. Note that although this show is officially part of San Francisco, it's actually located directly to the left of Men in Black Alien Attack, near the World Expo area of the park.

Austin (age 13), and once a fan of being grossed out by the TV show, looked over and whispered "Gross! I'm *sooooooo* glad I didn't volunteer . . . Bet they didn't expect they would have to actually drink that stuff (referring to a lumpy, gray, slimy "beverage") when *they* did!"

✔ **JAWS:** As your boat heads into a 7-acre, 5-million-gallon lagoon, an ominous dorsal fin appears on the horizon (and the blockbuster film's famous score starts to run through your brain). What follows is a series of attacks by a somewhat hokey looking, 3-ton, 32-foot-long, mechanical great white shark (which, after catching a rerun of the famous flick on TV, actually looks more lifelike than the on-screen version) that tries to sink its urethane teeth into your hide — or at least into your boat's hide. A 30-foot wall of flame caused by burning fuel surrounds your ride, and you'll truly feel the heat at this $45-million attraction.

The effects of this ride are definitely more startling after dark; during the day, it's too easy to see the shark coming. Though the attraction doesn't have any height limitations, you may want to think twice before bringing along the 5-and-younger crowd.

Woody Woodpecker's KidZone

Woody Woodpecker's KidZone contains rides and attractions sure to please the littlest members of your party. If you're traveling with young children, plan to spend plenty of time here. Highlights include the following:

- ✔ **A Day in the Park with Barney:** This musical is Universal's sadistic answer to Disney's **"it's a small world,"** one of those attractions that eats the brains and ignites the nerves of anyone but 2- to 6-year-olds and their loving parents. Set in a parklike theater-in-the-round, this 25-minute musical stars the Purple One, Baby Bop, and BJ. It uses song, dance, and interactive play to deliver an environmental message. This show can be the highlight of your youngster's day. The playground next door has chimes to ring, treehouses to explore, and more.

- ✔ **E.T. Adventure:** You soar with E.T., who is on a mission to save his ailing planet, through the forest and into space aboard a star-bound bicycle. You also meet some new characters that Steven Spielberg created for the ride, including Botanicus, Tickli Moot Moot, Horn Flowers, and Tympani Tremblies. It's a family-friendly charmer. A cool wooded forest serves to create one of the most pleasant waits for any ride in Central Florida, although you have to endure two lines before you actually make it onto the ride.

- ✔ **Woody Woodpecker's Nuthouse Coaster:** This ride is the top attraction in the KidZone, an 8-acre concession Universal Studios made after being criticized for having too little for young visitors. Sure, it's a kiddie coaster, but the Nuthouse Coaster will thrill some moms and dads, too. Although it's only 30 feet at its peak, this ride offers quick, banked turns while you sit in a miniature steam train. It's very much like the **Barnstormer at Goofy's Wiseacre Farm** in the **Magic Kingdom** (see Chapter 12).

The ride lasts only 55 seconds, and you can wait as long as 40 minutes in line, but your children probably won't let you skip it if they see it. It has a *36-inch height minimum,* and *kids have to be 48 inches or taller to ride without an adult.*

There's even more to do in Woody Woodpecker's KidZone. **Fievel's Playland** is a wet, Western-themed playground with a house to climb and a small water slide. **Curious George Goes To Town** has water- and ball-shooting cannons, plus a huge water tower that empties (after an alarm), drenching anyone who doesn't run for cover. And kids of all ages will laugh at the on-stage (and on-screen) antics of **Animal Actors on Location!**

World Expo

The smallest zone in Universal Studios Florida packs a bunch of punch. World Expo is on Exposition Boulevard, between San Francisco/Amity and KidZone. The top attractions here are the following:

✔ **Men in Black Alien Attack:** You and your mates have to blast the bug eyes, or the end of the world may be at hand. You buzz the streets of New York in six-passenger cruisers, using your "zapper" to splatter up to 120 bug-eyed targets. You have to contend with return fire and distractions (noise, clouds of liquid nitrogen, and such), any of which can send you spinning out of control. Your laser-tag–style gun fires infrared bullets. Earn a bonus by hitting Frank the Pug (to the right, just past the alien shipwreck). The four-minute ride relies on 360-degree spins and some scary-looking insects rather than speed for its thrill factor. Near the end, you're swallowed by a giant roach (it's 30 ft. tall with 8-ft. fangs and 20-ft. claws) that explodes — dousing you with bug guts (actually warm water) — as you blast your way to safety and into the pest-control hall of fame. After you survive unscathed (well, maybe a trifle wet), Will Smith rates you anywhere from a galaxy defender to bug bait. (There are 38 possible scores.)

Men in Black often has a *much* shorter line for single riders. If you're not alone but you're willing to be split up, get in this line — you'll usually be able to hop right on a vehicle that has fewer than six passengers.

"I hate bugs! But blasting those gigantic creepy crawlies into a million pieces was way cool, and the spinning made it even more fun." Eleven-year-old Nicolas clearly didn't end up as bug bait. Even 9-year-old Hailey thought blasting her way through this one was tons of fun. This $70-million ride-through video game has a *42-inch height minimum.*

✔ **Universal 360–A Cinesphere Spectacular:** Universal has lagged behind Disney in the evening entertainment department — that is, until this show debuted in 2006. Spread across the park's central lagoon, lasers project colorful scenes from some of Universal's biggest blockbuster movies onto two tremendous four-story-high spheres (hence, the term *cinesphere* in the show's title). Flashing lights, pyrotechnic effects, and an original musical score blasting from 300 outdoor speakers all add to the experience. On occasion, variations of the sound-and-light spectacular have been known to be "projected" during Halloween Horror Nights, as well as through-out the winter holidays, even though it's really a summertime show.

The Simpsons have moved in

Alas, in 2007, Back to the Future The Ride became part of Universal Studios past. Even though this wild ride through time was one of the park's best, it was removed to make way for a more updated attraction based on the ever-popular (and longest-running) TV sitcom *The Simpsons*.

The Simpsons Ride (similar in nature to Back to the Future The Ride) has sitcom sensations Bart, Homer, Marge, Maggie, and Lisa Simpson taking off on a wildly amusing adventure — and you're right smack in the middle of it. Riders are rocketed off through Springfield (though a side that's never before been seen) as they explore and experience a Krusty the Clown–created amusement park. An over-the-top exterior gives way to the signature Universal queue hidden inside — an appropriate prelude of what's to come, filled with oversized attraction posters, video screens, and animated elements hinting at its predecessor. Krusty himself makes an appearance, taunting guests before they enter the Fun House (okay, it's really just the small waiting area that opens to the ride). From here, it becomes a bit more familiar as you board one of several elevated cars, each facing the gargantuan screen — though instead of time travel, you're off on a wild ride through Krustyland. While a tweak to the motion simulator's mechanics has smoothed out the ride, expect to be bounced around just the same — the special effects, however, are enough to make you hold on for dear life. This hysterical high-speed adventure, like its predecessor, carries more warnings than a centipede has legs.

This is, of course, not the first time that Universal has replaced a popular attraction, claiming that its relevance has long since passed (but remind me again, what years did *Earthquake, E.T.,* and even *The Terminator* come out?), rather than expand its offerings (there seems to be plenty of room — Production Central has gotten pretty sparse, as has the World Expo). What once made this movie-studio theme park so inviting (other than its amazing streetscapes) was its wide range of offerings — spanning from the early days of movie making to present day. I must, however, still be a bit put off by the mysterious disappearance of classics such as Alfred Hitchcock, the Psycho House that once stood off in the distance, the Star Trek Studio (okay, that one was pretty hokey, but it was still fun), the Wild West Show, Kongfrontation, and now Back to the Future The Ride.

Grabbing a Bite to Eat

Universal Studios Florida has more than a dozen places to eat, with offerings that range from lobster to corn dogs. Quality-wise, things inside the park are on the same level (though some are a step above) as those found in the Disney parks (see Chapters 11–15), meaning that they're generally overpriced and oversized. Here are my favorites by category:

> ✔ **Best Sit-Down Meal: Lombard's Seafood Grille,** across from Disaster!–A Major Motion Picture Ride . . . Starring YOU, has a hearty fried-shrimp basket, rich chowder, and a selection of seafood, pasta, salads, and sandwiches ($11–$18).

✔ **Best Counter Service: Universal Studios' Classic Monsters Cafe** serves up salads, pizza, pasta, and rotisserie chicken with a side of classic and creepy creatures ($7–$9). It's off 7th Avenue near Shrek 4-D.

✔ **Best Place for Hungry Families:** Similar to a mall food court, the **International Food and Film Festival** offers a variety of choices in one location. Options range from stir-fry to fried chicken to Mediterranean tuna salad. This is a place where a family can split up and still eat under one roof. It's far from gourmet, but it's a cut above regular fast food ($7–$10). It's located behind Animal Actors on Location!

✔ **Best Places for Snacks:** Grab a malt ($4) and enjoy the classic atmosphere of **Mel's Drive-In,** located across from the Universal Horror Make-Up Show. The **San Francisco Pastry Co.,** located across from Disaster! – A Major Motion Picture Ride . . . Starring YOU, has a glass case full of sweet treats, including a large and decadent chocolate brownie. **Boardwalk Snacks,** in San Francisco, and **Schwab's Pharmacy,** about halfway along Hollywood Boulevard, both offer plenty of ice-cream treats to cool you off on a hot day.

See Chapter 10 for the best places to eat at **Universal's CityWalk.**

Shopping at Universal Studios Florida

If Disney can do it, Universal can, too. Most major attractions at Universal have a theme store attached. Just as at Disney, the prices are high when you consider you're just buying a T-shirt or trinket.

More than 25 other shops in the park sell souvenirs ranging from *I Love Lucy* collectibles to *Men in Black* souvenirs. Be warned, however, that, unlike WDW, these shops are even more specific to individual attractions — if you see something you like, buy it. You probably won't see it in another store even throughout the park itself. Here's a sampling of the more unusual gifts available at some of the Universal stores:

✔ **E.T.'s Toy Closet and Photo Spot:** This is the place for plush stuffed animals, including a replica of the alien namesake.

✔ **MIB Gear:** Clothes, T-shirts, and everything else the well-dressed alien should own — oh, and the cool shades that are the staple of the *Men in Black* uniform.

✔ **Quint's Surf Shack:** This is the place to go if you plan on hanging ten in the future. It's got all the latest in beach apparel.

✔ **Silver Screen Collectibles:** Fans of *I Love Lucy* will adore the small variety of collector dolls. There's also a Betty Boop line. And how can you pass up a Bates Motel shower curtain?

✔ **Universal Studios Store:** This store, near the entrance, sells just about everything when it comes to Universal apparel. It's also the spot to pick up your packages if you've had them delivered from another store.

Index of Attractions by Area

Front Lot
Blue Man Group (Sharp AQUOS Theatre)

Hollywood
Lucy–A Tribute
Terminator 2: 3D Battle Across Time
Universal Horror Make-Up Show

New York
The Blues Brothers
Revenge of the Mummy the Ride
TWISTER . . . Ride It Out

Production Central
Hollywood Rip, Ride, Rockit (coming in 2009)
Jimmy Neutron's Nicktoon Blast
Shrek 4-D

San Francisco/Amity
Beetlejuice's Graveyard Revue
Disaster!–A Major Motion Picture Ride . . . Starring YOU
Fear Factor Live
JAWS

Woody Woodpecker's KidZone
Animal Actors on Location!
Curious George Goes To Town
A Day in the Park with Barney
E.T. Adventure
Fievel's Playland
Woody Woodpecker's Nuthouse Coaster

World Expo
Men in Black Alien Attack
The Simpsons Ride
Universal 360–A Cinesphere Spectacular

Chapter 19

Islands of Adventure

* *

In This Chapter

▶ Getting the lowdown on Islands of Adventure
▶ Exploring the islands
▶ Tasting the native cuisine
▶ Taking home souvenirs

* *

*U*niversal's second theme park opened in 1999 with a vibrant, cleverly themed collection of edgy, fast, and fun rides. Heart-pounding roller coasters thunder above (and, in one case, dive below) pedestrian walkways, water rides careen through the center of the park, and themed restaurants are camouflaged to match their surroundings, adding to your overall immersion in the various "islands" in this adventure.

From the wobbly angles and day-glo colors of Seuss Landing to the lush foliage and distant rumblings of gigantic beasts in Jurassic Park, Universal does an incredible job of differentiating between the various islands. Navigation is far easier than at its sister park (Universal Studios Florida), where the studio's sets often blend together, making it difficult to tell when you've left New York and entered San Francisco, and side streets are overlooked. At Islands of Adventure (IOA), almost the entire park, save the Port of Entry, surrounds the central sea. Between islands, a simple walkway creates a bridge from one island to the next.

This billion-dollar park is currently divided into six islands (with a seventh on its way in 2009). Beginning with the **Port of Entry,** you find a marketplace filled with shops, bazaars, and eateries occupying a street designed to recall ancient lands and exotic ports of call. The surrounding islands include: **Seuss Landing,** where you feel as if you've jumped into the pages of the good doctor's whimsical classic tales; the **Lost Continent,** which combines mythical and mystical enchantments; **Jurassic Park,** where you're surrounded by towering dense foliage and can hear the rumblings of gigantic prehistoric beasts; **Toon Lagoon,** which takes you on an amusing stroll through the classic Sunday comics of the past; and **Marvel Super Hero Island,** where super heroes and their arch nemeses jump off the pages of comic books to entertain with their super powers. Slated to debut in late 2009 is the **Wizarding World of Harry Potter,** a multimillion-dollar 20-acre park-within-a-park filled with interactive attractions, immersive experiences, and themed shops and restaurants — including meticulous re-creations of Hogwarts Castle, Hogsmeade, and even the Forbidden Forest. Each of the existing islands is covered in further detail throughout this chapter.

Islands of Adventure boasts an incredible collection of thrill rides and coasters, with a more modest selection of play areas and somewhat tamer rides for younger adventurers. It's unquestionably the best park in town for tweens, teens, and adrenaline junkies. The trade-off is that the park features only a few shows and stage productions.

Knowing Essential Park Information

Before you embark on your journey through the park's rides and attractions, here are some mundane matters that you may need to know.

Buying tickets and making reservations

You can choose from several ticket options and tours:

✔ A **one-day ticket** costs $75 (plus 6.5 percent sales tax) for adults, $63 for children 3 to 9.

✔ A **two-day/two-park pass** is $120 for adults and $110 for children; kids younger than 3 are admitted free. These passes enable you to move between Islands of Adventure and Universal Studios Florida (see Chapter 18) throughout the day, so you can go back and forth whenever you like. Multiday passes also give you free access at night to select CityWalk clubs (see Chapter 25).

For a limited time, Universal is offering online tickets at substantial savings at www.universalorlando.com. For example, a two-park unlimited-admission ticket, good for admission to both Universal Studios and Islands of Adventure for seven consecutive days, costs $100 (kids and adults alike).

✔ **Annual passes** (the **Premier Annual Pass,** the **Preferred Annual Pass,** and the **Power Pass**) allow entry to the park for an entire year (some blackout dates apply to the Power Pass; there are no blackout dates with the Premier or Preferred Annual Pass — but there are plenty of perks). The costs are $280, $200, and $140, respectively. For more details, check out www.universalorlando.com.

✔ The **FlexTicket** multiday, multipark option is the most economical way to see the various "other-than-Disney" parks. You pay one price to visit any and all of the participating parks during a 14-day period. The Orlando FlexTicket to Islands of Adventure, Universal Studios Florida, Wet 'n Wild, SeaWorld, and Aquatica is $235 for adults and $195 for children ages 3 to 9. The Orlando FlexTicket Plus, which adds Busch Gardens in Tampa, is $280 for adults and $234 for kids. You can order the FlexTicket by calling ☎ **407-363-8000** or by going to www.universalorlando.

Islands of Adventure

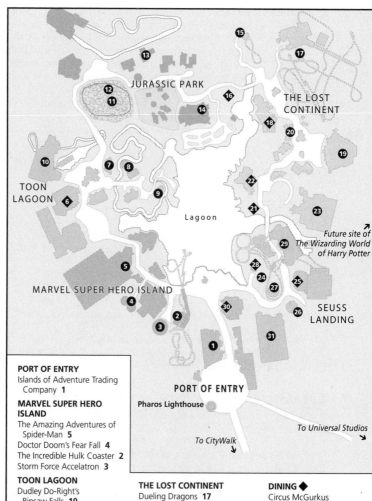

JURASSIC PARK

THE LOST CONTINENT

TOON LAGOON

Lagoon

Future site of
*The Wizarding World
of Harry Potter*

MARVEL SUPER HERO ISLAND

SEUSS LANDING

PORT OF ENTRY
Pharos Lighthouse

To Universal Studios

To CityWalk

PORT OF ENTRY
Islands of Adventure Trading
  Company **1**

**MARVEL SUPER HERO
ISLAND**
The Amazing Adventures of
  Spider-Man **5**
Doctor Doom's Fear Fall **4**
The Incredible Hulk Coaster **2**
Storm Force Accelatron **3**

TOON LAGOON
Dudley Do-Right's
  Ripsaw Falls **10**
King's Row &
  Comic Strips Lane **7**
Me Ship, The Olive **9**
Popeye & Bluto's
  Bilge-Rat Barges **8**

JURASSIC PARK
Camp Jurassic **12**
Jurassic Park Discovery
  Center **14**
Jurassic Park River
  Adventure **13**
Pteranodon Flyers **11**

THE LOST CONTINENT
Dueling Dragons **17**
The Eighth Voyage of Sindbad **19**
The Flying Unicorn **15**
The Mystic Fountain **20**
Poseidon's Fury **23**

SEUSS LANDING
Caro-Seuss-el **27**
The Cat in the Hat **31**
The High in the Sky Seuss Trolley
  Train Ride! **29**
If I Ran the Zoo **24**
One Fish, Two Fish,
  Red Fish, Blue Fish **26**

DINING ◆
Circus McGurkus
  Cafe Stoo-pendous **25**
Comic Strip Cafe **6**
Confisco Grille **30**
Enchanted Oak Tavern
  and Alchemy Bar **18**
Fire Eater's Grill **21**
Green Eggs and Ham
  Cafe **28**
Mythos Restaurant **22**
Thunder Falls Terrace **16**

✔ Islands of Adventure offers five-hour guided **VIP Tours** for $100 to $120 per person for just Islands of Adventure, $125 to $150 per person for a two-park, seven-hour tour that also includes Universal Studios Florida. Guided tours include line-cutting privileges and preferred seating at several attractions; they start at 10 a.m. and noon daily. For more information on the tours, call ☎ **407-363-8295.** Note that the price of the VIP Tour includes neither the 6.5 percent sales tax *nor admission to the park!*

Theme-park prices aren't the only things gnawing a hole in your wallet. Expect to spend upwards of $3 for a soda, $2 for a cup of coffee, $5 for a beer, $2.60 for popcorn, and $2.50 for bottled water. However, you can save 10 percent on your purchases at any gift shop or on a meal by showing your **AAA card.** This discount isn't available at food or merchandise carts. Likewise, tobacco, candy, film, collectibles, and sundry items aren't included in discounts.

For information about new travel packages and theme-park information, call ☎ **800-711-0080** or 800-224-4233; write to Guest Services at Universal Studios Florida, 1000 Universal Studios Plaza, Orlando, FL 32819-7601; or go to www.universalorlndo.com. After you're at the park, just head over to Guest Services.

Universal Orlando's Islands of Adventure is about half a mile north of I-4's Kirkman Road/Highway 435 exit. You may find construction in the area, so watch for the road signs directing you to Universal Orlando.

Islands of Adventure is open daily, generally from at least 9 a.m. to 6 or 7 p.m. Closing hours vary seasonally and holiday hours extend later into the evening; special activities often extend the hours as well.

Locating special services and facilities
If you forget to bring essential items, or if you need special assistance while at the park, this list of services and facilities may come in handy:

✔ **ATMs** accepting cards from banks using the Cirrus, STAR, and PLUS systems are outside and to the right of the park's entrance and in the Lost Continent near Mythos Restaurant, as well as near the bridge to Jurassic Park. In Marvel Super Hero Island, you'll find an ATM near the Amazing Adventures of Spider-Man.

✔ **Baby-changing tables** are located in all men's and women's restrooms. You can find nursing facilities at **Family Services,** in the Guest Services building at the Port of Entry. (It doesn't sell any diapers or infant supplies, so be sure to bring your own.)

✔ **Disposable cameras and film** (and limited digital supplies) are available at **De Foto's Expedition Photography,** inside the main entrance to the right.

✔ Universal has its own version of Disney's FASTPASS, called **Universal Express Plus Pass.** Unfortunately, the *Plus* means having to pay for your park tickets *plus* the Express Pass. Passes are available online or at the park, but be aware that they (like the freebies at Disney) run out, often by midday, sometimes earlier, during peak seasons. The pass allows access to the Express line at every attraction that accepts the Universal Express Pass without having to continually obtain separate passes or wait for any time limits to expire before heading to the Express line at the next attraction. The downside is that you can use it only once at each of the attractions. The price ranges from $20 to $56 per ticket, depending on whether it's good for one or both Universal parks and what date the pass is valid for. Visit www.universalorlando.com for details. The all-new one-day, two-park VIP Express Pass allows you to bypass the lines as many times as you want — for a price ($150 for adults, $140 for kids 3–9). Visit www.universalorlando.com for all the details.

Universal offers a separate line-beating option as a perk for guests staying at its resorts. Guests of the **Hard Rock Hotel, Portofino Bay Hotel,** and **Royal Pacific Resort** (see Chapter 9) just have to show their room keys to get unlimited Express-line access to the rides and front-of-the-line access to most of the restaurants.

✔ You can find **First Aid Stations** just inside and to the right of the main entrance in the Port of Entry as well as in the Lost Continent, across from Oasis Coolers.

✔ **Lockers** are a smart place to keep valuables that you may lose on the wilder rides, and there are even lockers near the entrances to the **Incredible Hulk Coaster, Dueling Dragons,** and **Jurassic Park River Adventure;** the first 45 minutes are free and every hour thereafter is $2 (with a $14 maximum). Be sure to read the instructions when using the newer electronic lockers — otherwise you'll spend valuable time tracking down a park attendant to help retrieve your gear instead of riding the rides.

✔ Report **lost children** to any staff member, who will direct you to the "found children" area, usually at Guest Services or Security. *Children under 7 should wear name tags inside their clothing.*

✔ When **parking** in the multilevel garages, be sure to write down your location (level, character, row, and space number) so that you can find your car later. Parking costs $12 for cars and trucks. Valet parking is available for $20. If you arrive after 6 p.m., parking is free. Universal's garages are connected to its parks by walkways and moving sidewalks, but reaching the gates can take a while.

If you need **car assistance,** including battery jumps, raise the hood and tell any parking attendant your location, or use the call boxes located throughout the garage to call for security.

✔ **Pet care** is available at the Studio Kennel in the parking garages for $10 a day (no overnight stays), but you'll have to feed and walk your pet yourself. Ask the parking attendant to direct you to the kennel. (Note that the kennels may be a bit small for larger pets.)

✔ For **strollers,** look to the left as you enter the park. Rentals cost $13 for a single, $21 for a double, tax included.

✔ **Wheelchairs** are available in the parking garage concourse. The rental cost is $12 per day for a regular wheelchair, $45 per day for an electric wheelchair. Both require a $50 deposit and a signed rental agreement. Prices include taxes.

Practical Advice for Island Adventurers

If you want to get the most out of your adventure, keep the following tips in mind when you're exploring Islands of Adventure:

✔ **Of the 14 major rides at Islands of Adventure, 13 of them have minimum-height restrictions between *40 and 54 inches.*** You can find a child-swap service at all major attractions, enabling you or your partner to ride while the other watches over your tykes, but sitting in a waiting room isn't much fun for them. Take your child's height into consideration before visiting the park, or consider splitting up for part of the day. Islands actually has a few fun play areas that will keep younger kids entertained while older kids and parents ride some of the wilder rides.

In recent years, Universal added three notable attractions to its lineup to answer criticism that Islands of Adventure had too little for young guests. The **High in The Sky Seuss Trolley Train Ride!** is a slow-moving car ride that takes riders past Seussian scenery along tracks set high above ground. The **Flying Unicorn** is a small roller coaster that travels through a mythical forest; it's comparable to the **Barnstormer at Goofy's Wiseacre Farm** in Disney's **Magic Kingdom** (see Chapter 12) and **Woody Woodpecker's Nuthouse Coaster** at **Universal Studios Florida** (see Chapter 18), though it still has plenty of zip. **Storm Force Accelatron** is a spinning attraction in which guests help the X-Men's Storm harness the weather to fight her archenemy, Magneto. It's a bit wilder and edgier in its theme than the **Mad Tea Party** at **Magic Kingdom** (see Chapter 12), but the idea's the same.

✔ **See the preceding note about short visitors and add the warning that height isn't the only limiting factor.** If you're pregnant, prone to dizziness or motion sickness, or have heart, back, or other health problems, this may not be the best choice of parks for you. Consider heading to a tamer park, like the **Magic Kingdom** (see Chapter 12), **Disney's Animal Kingdom** (see Chapter 15), **Epcot** (see Chapter 13), **Disney's Hollywood Studios** (see Chapter 14), **SeaWorld** (see Chapter 20), or even **Universal Studios Florida** (see Chapter 18).

✔ **If you hauled your stroller on vacation, bring it to the park.** The walk from your car is a long one, through the parking garage and the **CityWalk** entertainment district. Carrying a young child and all that paraphernalia can make a long trek seem even longer.

✔ **Beat the heat.** Several rides have lengthy pathways outside that offer little cover from the sizzling Florida sun. Bring some bottled water with you for the long waits (a bottle that costs $2.50 here is less than $1 in the outside world) or take a sip from fountains placed in the waiting areas. Alcohol is more readily available at this park than at Disney, so remember that liquor, roller coasters, and sweltering heat can make for a *very* messy mix.

Exploring the Top Attractions at Islands of Adventure

Islands of Adventure features more than 20 rides and attractions, as well as a number of uniquely themed restaurants and shops, all surrounding its central sea. (It's similar in layout to the **World Showcase** at **Epcot** [see Chapter 13].)

See the "Islands of Adventure" map on p. 283 to locate all the attractions in the sections that follow.

Port of Entry

Beyond the gigantic, crumbling-stone archway, you'll find the Port's numerous souvenir shops, bazaars, and eateries lining the exotic streetscape. Save this area for last (unless you're in need of nourishment to start you on your way), spending only a few minutes now to take in your surroundings — the architecture and attention to detail are striking.

I suggest you begin your adventure just beyond the second stone archway by heading to either **Seuss Landing** (to the right) or **Marvel Super Hero Island** (to the left). Your direction will likely be determined by the age of your children, or whether you're willing to start out by riding one of the most intense rides in the entire park.

Seuss Landing

Within these 10 fanciful acres, you step onto the pages of Dr. Seuss's classic tales, complete with whimsical architecture and a cast of classic characters. The main attractions are aimed at the younger set.

✔ **Caro-Seuss-el:** This not-so-ordinary carousel replaces the traditional wooden horses with seven whimsical Seussian characters (a total of 54 mounts), including Cowfish, the elephant birds from *Horton Hatches the Egg,* and Mulligatawnies. Pull the reins to make their eyes blink or heads bob.

This ride has a rocking-chariot platform and a wheelchair loading system that makes it a fun attraction for guests with disabilities.

✔ **The Cat in the Hat:** All aboard the couch! In this case, the couches are six-passenger futons that steer you through 18 silly scenes, retelling the tale of a day gone terribly south. The highlight is a revolving 24-foot tunnel that alters your perceptions and leaves you feeling a bit woozy. While a bit herky-jerky at times, that's all part of the fun. The audio is somewhat muffled, making it difficult to hear the story as it's broadcast throughout the ride.

"Are you kidding? That's not a ride — it's not fast, there's no loop-de-loops — and besides, *The Cat in the Hat* is a little-kids' story," was 13-year-old Austin's verdict. Nine-year-old Hailey and 7-year-old Davis, however, thought otherwise. The Cat in the Hat is one of the signature "young" experiences of Islands of Adventure, thus your older children may find it a bit tame. Small children may be slightly unsettled by the pop-up characters, although most kids ages 4 to 7 will find it a winner.

✔ **The High in The Sky Seuss Trolley Train Ride!:** The mini-monorail hanging high over Seuss Landing is once again taking guests of all ages on a whimsical journey through several classic Seussian stories and way up high in the sky over Seuss Landing.

✔ **If I Ran the Zoo:** This small interactive play area is filled with 19 play stations that include slides, wheels to spin, caves to explore, and other things geared to burning off some of the excited energy of tinier tots. Just plan on them getting wet — that's half the fun!

✔ **One Fish, Two Fish, Red Fish, Blue Fish:** You move "up, up, up" and "down, down, down" on this attraction, where you ride in a funky flying fish whose controls enable you to ascend or descend 15 feet as you spin around on an arm attached to a hub (much like the **Magic Carpets of Aladdin** in the **Magic Kingdom** [see Chapter 12]). Watch out for squirt posts, which spray unsuspecting riders who don't follow along with the ride's little rhyme (and sometimes even the ones who *do* follow it).

Marvel Super Hero Island

Thrill-ride junkies love the twisting, turning, stomach-churning rides on this island. The streets are filled with giant-size murals of Marvel Super Heroes, making you feel as if you've stepped onto the pages of a gigantic comic book. The hard-rockin' music here is loud — definitely a reflection of the island's overall personality.

✔ **The Amazing Adventures of Spider-Man:** This primo ride combines moving vehicles, 3-D action, and an array of special effects. The script: While you're on a ho-hum tour of the *Daily Bugle* newspaper — *yikes!* — the boys in black hats (Doc Oc, Hobgoblin, and the rest of the Sinister Syndicate) filch the Statue of Liberty. You have to help Spidey get it back. Unlike the many roller coasters and stationary motion simulators in Orlando, this ride offers a unique experience. Passengers squeal as real and computer-generated objects fly toward their 12-person cars. A simulated 400-foot drop feels an awful lot like the real thing.

Expectant mothers or those with heart, neck, or back problems shouldn't ride. For the rest of you, know that lines here can get ridiculously long. If you hold a Universal Express Plus Pass, use it; otherwise, if you don't mind splitting up your party, use the faster single-rider line when it's available.

"This was the coolest ride ever!" exclaimed Austin (age 13). Ryan (15) added, "You gotta do this one a couple times at least!" Nicolas (11) and Hailey (9) agreed wholeheartedly. A number of Universal employees rate this the best ride in the park. Dark scenes, the motion of the car, the in-your-face 3-D effects, and the simulated motion make this ride unsuitable for extremely young kids and even some preteens (though Hailey and Davis had a blast). Keep in mind that you can close your eyes if a scene is too intense, as the motion of the car, without the combined effects, isn't overwhelming by itself. There's a *40-inch height minimum.*

✔ **Doctor Doom's Fear Fall:** Look! Up in the sky! It's a bird, it's a plane . . . uh, it's you falling 200 feet if you're courageous enough to climb aboard. The plot: You're touring a lab when — are you sensing a theme here? — something goes horribly wrong as supervillain Doctor Doom tries to drain you of fear in order to power his latest evil scheme. You're fired to the top of the towering metal skeleton (pulling 4 Gs in the process), and then you're dropped in intervals, leaving your stomach at several levels.

If you're an expectant mother or you experience heart, neck, or back problems, you shouldn't ride. Make sure all items are secured well — or give them to someone not riding for safekeeping. *Minimum height is 52 inches.* Though it's less nightmarish than **Twilight Zone Tower of Terror** (see Chapter 14), I recommend kids be a minimum of 10 years old before attempting this one.

After Austin (age 13) regrouped and got his legs back, he said, "Well . . . it's pretty good . . . but not at all as cool and creepy as the Tower of Terror at Disney." He also noted that he didn't like sitting in an outside seat. I couldn't believe that Ryan (age 15), who's not a fan of heights, even got on — and neither could he (a mistake he won't make twice).

✔ **The Incredible Hulk Coaster:** Bruce Banner is working in his lab when — yes, again — something goes wrong. This coaster rockets from a dark tunnel into the sunlight, while accelerating from 0 to 40 mph in 2 seconds. Although it's only two-thirds the speed of the **Rock 'n' Roller Coaster Starring Aerosmith** at **Disney's Hollywood Studios,** this ride is in broad daylight, and you can *see* the asphalt! After you're launched, you spin upside down 128 feet from the ground and careen through the center of the park over the heads of other visitors. If you're a coaster lover, you'll be pleased to know that this ride, which lasts 2 minutes and 15 seconds, includes seven rollovers and two deep drops. The ride is surprisingly smooth, making it much more comfortable than coasters that are far less intense.

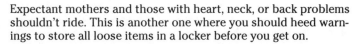

Expectant mothers and those with heart, neck, or back problems shouldn't ride. This is another one where you should heed warnings to store all loose items in a locker before you get on.

Mixed reviews for this "monster" of a coaster from my reviewers. "No way. Uh-uh, you go upside down — you won't even get me on it," were 15-year-old Ryan's final words on the subject.

Nicolas (age 11) and Austin (age 13), both coaster crazies, agreed that it was "the most amazing roller coaster ever — you think you're going to hit the pavement, but then you don't." This is another ride that I think is best for riders 10 to 12 years and older. *Riders must be at least 54 inches tall.*

✔ **Storm Force Accelatron:** This ride is a 22nd-century version of the **Mad Tea Party** in the **Magic Kingdom.** You and the X-Men's Storm try to defeat the evil Magneto by spinning faster and faster to give the mistress of weather a little boost in the energy department. In addition to some upset stomachs, your motion creates a thunderstorm of sound and light. Some young kids (5 and under) may find the characters, lights, and sounds a bit too intense. Davis, however, gave it a "thumbs up" when he was only 4.

This ride is closed during some off-peak periods.

Toon Lagoon

More than 150 life-size sculpted cartoon images — from Betty Boop to Flash Gordon — let you know you've entered an island dedicated to your favorites from the Sunday funnies.

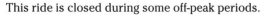

✔ **Dudley Do-Right's Ripsaw Falls:** This adrenaline-pumping flume ride drops 75 feet at 50 mph. The boats take you around a 400,000-gallon lagoon and plunge you 15 feet below the water's surface, but this is mainly hype — the water is contained on either side of you. That said, you *will* get very wet anyway. Though it beats **Splash Mountain** (see Chapter 12) in the adrenaline department, the latter offers better effects and a nicer atmosphere.

Expectant mothers and people with heart, neck, or back problems shouldn't ride this attraction. It has a *44-inch height minimum.* Tall folks should note that the boats on this ride offer legroom on par with that in an airline's coach section.

✔ **King's Row & Comic Strip Lane:** Here you'll find Beetle Bailey, Dudley, and plenty of other classic comic characters out and about.

✔ **Me Ship, The Olive:** This three-story boat offers dozens of interactive activities. Kids can toot whistles, clang bells, or play the organ. **Sweet Pea's Playpen** is a favorite of younger guests. Kids 6 and older love **Cargo Crane,** where they can use water cannons to drench riders on **Popeye & Bluto's Bilge-Rat Barges** (see the following bullet).

✔ **Popeye & Bluto's Bilge-Rat Barges:** Here's a churning, turning, twisting, listing raft ride with the same kind of vehicle as **Kali River Rapids** at **Disney's Animal Kingdom** (see Chapter 15), but this one's a bit faster and bouncier (though not nearly as scenic). You'll get wet from mechanical devices and from the water cannons fired by guests at **Me Ship, The Olive** (see the preceding bullet). The 12-passenger rafts bump and dip along a course lined with villains, including Bluto and Sea Hag.

"That water is freezing cold, but it really feels good when it's so hot, and I loved all the bouncing up and down." Eleven-year-old Nic's right; the water is *c-c-cold,* which is a blessing on hot summer days but less so in January, and trust me — you can get completely soaked. *Riders must be at least 42 inches tall.*

Jurassic Park

All the basics from Steven Spielberg's wildly successful films, and some of the high-tech wizardry, are incorporated into this lush locale, which includes one of the best themed attractions in the park.

✔ **Camp Jurassic:** This amazingly entertaining play area, designed along the same lines as the **Boneyard** in **Disney's Animal Kingdom** (see Chapter 15), has everything from lava pits to a tropical rain forest where you can hear dinosaurs off in the distance. Watch out for spitters that lurk in the caves. The multilevel area offers plenty of places for kids to climb, crawl, explore, and wear down their batteries (eventually).

Nicolas (11), Hailey (9), and Davis (7) all had to be dragged out under protest (even after more than an hour of exploration).

Although there's only one way in and out, keep a close eye on young children — it's easy to get lost inside the caves.

✔ **Jurassic Park Discovery Center:** Inside this air-conditioned spot, you can relax while your kids discover something new. The center has life-size dinosaur replicas; interactive games, including a sequencer that lets you combine your DNA with a dinosaur's; and the **Beasaur** exhibit, where you can see and hear as the dinosaurs did. You can also play the game show **You Bet Jurassic** (bet you wouldn't see an attraction name like this at Disney), watch a tiny Velociraptor "hatch," and turn your voice into a dinosaur screech.

Nicolas (11), Hailey (9), and Davis (7) all give this one high marks, but because there are a limited number of interactive stations, this attraction can consume a lot of time on busy days.

✔ **Jurassic Park River Adventure:** Your adventure cruise throws you into a world of jungle plants and stormy skies, where you literally come face-to-face with five-story "breathing" inhabitants of Jurassic Park. To escape, you take a breathtaking 85-foot plunge in a flume that's steep and quick enough to lift your fanny from the seat. (When Spielberg rode it, he made them stop the ride and let him out before the plunge.) Oh, yeah — you'll get soaked. If you can stomach the thought of getting on only one flume ride at Islands, make it this one — both the atmosphere and comfort level far exceed that of **Dudley Do-Right's Ripsaw Falls.**

"That was amazing — the dinosaurs looked so real and the water-fall at the end was wild!" Austin (age 13) could have gone back for more, though people with height issues may not be as happy.

Ryan (age 15) said, "The drop at the end was definitely too long and way, *way* too steep." *Riders must be at least 42 inches tall.*

✔ **Pteranodon Flyers:** For an 80-second ride, neat as it may be, you'll often wait up to an hour or more. This high-flying ride swings from side to side and, unlike traditional gondolas in sky rides, on this one your feet dangle free. Now that I've scared you, this is a kiddie ride — *single passengers must be between 36 and 56 inches;* adults can ride *only* when accompanying someone that size. For what it's worth, I wouldn't put my young squirmers on it even if the wait weren't so long.

The Lost Continent

Universal has created a foreboding mood in this section of the park, the entrance of which is marked by menacing stone griffins and fire-lit torches. This uniquely themed area combines various mythical and mystical elements, including ancient Greek gods, crumbling ruins, medieval magicians, and a magical forest.

✔ **Dueling Dragons:** This ride has a scream factor of 11 on a 10-point scale. True coaster crazies love this intertwined set of leg-dangling racers that climb to 125 feet, invert five times, and, on three occa-sions, come within only 12 inches of each other as the two dragons battle it out; you prove your bravery by tagging along. The **Fire Dragon** can reach speeds of up to 60 mph, while the **Ice Dragon** makes it to only 55 mph. It, of course, comes with the usual health warnings. You shouldn't ride this one if you're an expectant mother or if you have heart, neck, or back problems.

For the best ride, try to get one of the two outside seats in each row. Also, pay attention — the lines for both coasters split near the loading dock so that daredevils can claim the very first row, which many hard-core thrill junkies claim offers the city's ultimate adrena-line rush. And, yes, that line is even longer!

"That was so scary — but so, so cool." Austin (age 13) barely took time to give his review as he headed back for another battle. After riding it several times, he added, "The best seat is the front seat on Ice." The other coaster crazy (an adult) found this one a bit too sharp and abrupt, though still worthy of a thumbs-up rating. *Riders must be at least 54 inches tall.*

✔ **The Eighth Voyage of Sindbad:** The mythical sailor Sindbad is the star of a stunt demonstration with 6 water explosions and 50 pyrotechnic effects, including a 10-foot circle of flames. It doesn't, however, come close to the quality of the **Indiana Jones Epic Stunt Spectacular!** at **Disney's Hollywood Studios** (see Chapter 14), and some of the characters are far scarier for young kids.

✔ **The Flying Unicorn:** This small roller coaster is similar to **Woody Woodpecker's Nuthouse Coaster** at **Universal Studios Florida** (see Chapter 18) and the **Barnstormer at Goofy's Wiseacre Farm** in **Magic Kingdom** (see Chapter 12). That means a fast, corkscrew run sure to earn squeals, but probably not at the risk of someone losing his lunch. Younger kids love it, but *riders must be at least 36 inches tall.* I'd have them watch for a few minutes before they commit to getting on.

✔ **The Mystic Fountain:** This interactive smart fountain delights 3- to 8-year-olds. It can see, hear, and spit water, leading to plenty of kibitzing with those who stand before the stone fountain. (A staff member viewing the action through cameras is at the helm, which makes for a personable experience.)

✔ **Poseidon's Fury:** Poseidon's Fury is the park's best show, but that may be a backhanded compliment because it's one of the park's *only* shows. It exposes you to fire and water in the same manner that **Disaster!–A Major Motion Picture Ride . . . Starring YOU** does at **Universal Studios Florida.** You pass through a 42-foot vortex — where 17,500 gallons of water swirl around you, barrel-style — and then get a front-row seat at a battle royale, where Zeus and Poseidon hurl 25-foot fireballs at each other. Some of the special effects are not up to the usual Universal standards. If the line is short, check it out; otherwise it's not worth waiting for.

Children younger than 7 may find the flaming fireballs, explosive sounds, and rushing water a little too intense. Also, if you wear eyeglasses, take them off before you walk through the water vortex or they'll fog up completely and you won't see much of anything.

Dining at Islands of Adventure

You can get a quick bite at a number of stands in the park, as well as a handful of full-service restaurants — any and all of which are well above the standards at most other theme-park eateries. The park's creators have taken some extra care to tie in restaurant offerings with the theme of the island they're in. For example, the **Green Eggs and Ham Cafe,** in Seuss Landing, may be one of the few places on Earth where you're willing to eat tinted *huevos.* (They're sold in the form of an egg-and-ham sandwich for about $8.)

- ✔ **Best Sit-Down Meal:** At the upscale **Mythos Restaurant,** in the Lost Continent, diners are transported to a mythical underwater world. Selections range from wood-fired oven pizzas and burgers to elaborate entrees of fish, seafood, and steaks. You can dine here without a park ticket, but there's a time limit and you need to leave a credit card number at the gate. If you're running late, the restaurant can call the gate to let them know so that you won't be charged. This restaurant is best suited for adults, although older kids may be okay. Entrees range from $11 to $18. Open daily from 11:30 a.m. to 3:30 p.m. and from 5 p.m. until park closing.

- ✔ **Best Atmosphere for Adults:** In the Lost Continent, the **Enchanted Oak Tavern** and the **Alchemy Bar** look like a mammoth tree from the outside. The tables and chairs are thick planks, and the servers are clad like wenches. Try the chicken/rib combo with waffle fries for $16. You can also choose from 45 brands of beer.

- ✔ **Best Atmosphere for Kids:** The fun never stops under the big top at **Circus McGurkus Cafe Stoo-pendous,** in Seuss Landing, where animated trapeze artists swing from the ceiling. Kids' meals are $6 to $8. The adult menu features fried chicken, chicken sandwiches, cheeseburgers, spaghetti, and pizza. Try the fried-chicken platter for just under $9 or the spaghetti for just under $8.

- ✔ **Best Diversity:** In Toon Lagoon, **Comic Strip Cafe** is a four-in-one, counter-service–style eatery offering burgers, pizza, pasta, chicken, fish, and even Chinese ($7–$9).

You can also find several restaurants (see Chapter 10) and clubs (see Chapter 25) just a short walk from Islands of Adventure at the **CityWalk** entertainment complex. If you get your hand stamped, you can leave the park and return after eating.

Shopping at Islands of Adventure

The park's 20-something shops have plenty of theme merchandise. You may want to check out **Cats, Hats & Things** and **All the Books You Can Read** for special Seussian material. **Jurassic Outfitters** offers an array of stuffed and plastic dinos, plus safari-style clothing. If you're a superhero fan, check out the **Marvel Alterniverse Store.**

Remember that you may find theme- or character-specific merchandise in only one store in the park. For example, the **Betty Boop Store** in Toon Lagoon has everything imaginable with the character's famous mug on it, while the **Spider-Man Shop** specializes in its namesake's paraphernalia, including red Spidey caps covered with black webs.

Index of Attractions by Area

Jurassic Park

Camp Jurassic
Jurassic Park Discovery Center
Jurassic Park River Adventure
Pteranodon Flyers

The Lost Continent

Dueling Dragons
The Eighth Voyage of Sindbad
The Flying Unicorn
The Mystic Fountain
Poseidon's Fury

Marvel Super Hero Island

The Amazing Adventures of
Spider-Man
Doctor Doom's Fear Fall
The Incredible Hulk Coaster
Storm Force Accelatron

Seuss Landing

Caro-Seuss-el
The Cat in the Hat
The High in The Sky Seuss Trolley
Train Ride!
If I Ran the Zoo
One Fish, Two Fish, Red Fish,
Blue Fish

Toon Lagoon

Dudley Do-Right's Ripsaw Falls
King's Row & Comic Strip Lane
Me Ship, The Olive
Popeye & Bluto's Bilge-Rat Barges

Chapter 20

SeaWorld and Discovery Cove

. . . .

In This Chapter

▶ Understanding the basics
▶ Checking out attractions at SeaWorld
▶ Exploring Discovery Cove
▶ Deciding where to eat and shop

. . . .

*A*lthough I've always included **SeaWorld** on my must-see list of parks, not everyone gives it the chance it deserves. This modern marine-adventure park focuses more on discovery than on thrill rides, but it offers its share of excitement with **Journey to Atlantis,** a steep flume-like ride; the thundering **Kraken,** a floorless roller coaster; and **Manta,** an innovative flying coaster slated to debut in summer 2009. SeaWorld's more than 200 acres of educational fun features stars such as Shamu and his expanding family of performing killer whales, polar bears Klondike and Snow, and a supporting cast of seals, sea lions, manatees, penguins, dolphins, walruses, and more. You can also feed some nonperforming critters and feel the crushed-velvet texture of a gentle ray in various pools throughout the park — something Disney and Universal just don't offer.

SeaWorld's sister park, **Discovery Cove,** opened in summer 2000. It lets guests swim with a dolphin in an adventure that, at $269 to $289 per person (plus 6.5 percent sales tax) ages 6 and up, goes off the price chart; you can also just swim with the fishes for a lower, though still stiff, ticket price of $169 to $189. The payoff is that you only have to share the park with 999 other people, not the tens of thousands you find at the other parks. A day here offers a tranquil and relaxing experience where you can sit in the sand or swim with the sea life — a refreshing way to spend the day in Orlando.

Aquatica, SeaWorld's newest sibling, made its debut in spring 2008. The eco-themed water park takes guests on an undersea adventure like no other — and one that only SeaWorld could create. An inviting and whimsical South Seas atmosphere mixes with uniquely thrilling water rides

SeaWorld

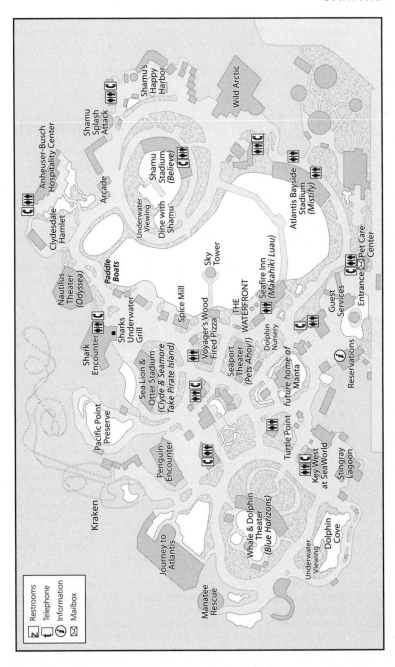

Shamu's Happy Harbor

Wild Arctic

Shamu Splash Attack

Anheuser-Busch Hospitality Center

Shamu Stadium (*Believe*)

Arcade

Atlantis Bayside Stadium (*Mistify*)

Clydesdale Hamlet

Underwater Viewing
Dine with Shamu

Pet Care Center

Sky Tower

Nautilus Theater (*Odyssey*)

Paddle Boats

Spice Mill

Seafire Inn (*Makahiki Luau*)

Entrance

Guest Services

Shark Encounter

Sharks Underwater Grill

THE WATERFRONT

Voyager's Wood Fired Pizza

Dolphin Nursery

Reservations

Sea Lion & Otter Stadium (*Clyde & Seamore Take Pirate Island*)

Pacific Point Preserve

Seaport Theater (*Pets Ahoy!*)

future home of Manta

Penguin Encounter

Turtle Point

Key West at SeaWorld

Stingray Lagoon

Kraken

Whale & Dolphin Theater (*Blue Horizons*)

Journey to Atlantis

Dolphin Cove

Underwater Viewing

Manatee Rescue

Restrooms
Telephone
Information
Mailbox

(some of which will have you splashing and sliding through undersea habitats filled with dolphins and colorful fish), lush lagoons, and white sandy beaches — adding yet another dimension to the immersive undersea experiences available at SeaWorld's oceanic adventure parks. For the lowdown on Aquatica, check out Chapter 21.

In this chapter, I tell you all you need to know to make the most out of SeaWorld and Discovery Cove.

Gathering Important SeaWorld Information

Before I start wading through the park's attractions and shows, here are some helpful matters that you may find helpful to know.

Buying tickets and making reservations

You have a couple different ticket options at SeaWorld. A one-day ticket costs $70 for adults, $60 for kids 3 to 9 (plus 6.5 percent sales tax). Buy your tickets online to avoid long lines and save 10 percent off the regular price. SeaWorld often offers online specials, sometimes including a second day free, other times combining tickets with partnering parks (including Aquatica, Discovery Cove, Universal Orlando's two theme parks, and Busch Gardens Tampa Bay).

If you're planning to see a number of non-Disney parks during your stay, consider the **FlexTicket.** This multiday, multipark pass enables you to pay one price to visit any of the participating parks during a 14-day period. The Orlando FlexTicket, which includes admission to SeaWorld, Aquatica, Universal Studios Florida, Islands of Adventure, and Wet 'n Wild, is $235 for adults and $195 for children 3 to 9. The Orlando FlexTicket Plus, which adds Busch Gardens in Tampa, is $280 for adults and $234 for kids. You can order the FlexTicket through SeaWorld by calling ☎ **407-351-3600** or heading to www.seaworld.com.

SeaWorld's Adventure Express Tour ($95 for adults, $80 for kids 3–9, plus park admission fees) is a six-hour guided excursion that includes front-of-the-line access to Kraken, Journey to Atlantis, and Wild Arctic; reserved seating at two animal shows; lunch; and a chance to touch or feed penguins, dolphins, stingrays, and sea lions. It's the only way to dodge park lines. SeaWorld doesn't have an equivalent to FASTPASS or Universal Express, although its lines aren't nearly as long as the ones at Disney and Universal parks. Advance reservations are recommended and can be made by calling ☎ **800-406-2244.**

Additionally, you have three one-hour tour options: **Polar Expedition Tour** (touch a penguin), **Predators Tour** (touch a shark), and **Saving a Species** (see manatees and sea turtles). Each tour costs $12 to $18 for adults and $8 to $12 for kids 3 to 9 (plus park admission fees); you have to sign up for them at the Information Center just inside the park's entrance. Call ☎ **800-406-2244** or 407-351-3600 for information.

To gather park information before you leave home, write to SeaWorld Guest Services at 7007 SeaWorld Dr., Orlando, FL 32801; call ☎ 407-351-3600; or visit www.seaworld.com. Once inside the park, head for the Information Center, which is on your left as you enter the park.

If you're arriving on I-4, just look for the signs pointing the way to the SeaWorld exit. You also can reach it via International Drive (it's located on the southern third of I-Drive).

The park is usually open from 9 a.m. to 6 p.m., 365 days a year, and later during summer and holidays.

Locating special services and facilities

In case you forget to bring essential items, or if you need special assistance while at the park, here's a list of services and facilities that may come in handy:

- ✔ **ATMs** that accept cards from banks using the Cirrus, STAR, and PLUS systems are available at the front of the park, near Atlantis Bayside Stadium, and across from the Sea Lion & Otter Stadium near the Friends of the Wild gift shop.

- ✔ **Baby-changing tables** are available in or near most women's restrooms and at the men's restroom at the front entrance near Shamu's Emporium. You can buy diapers in machines located near all changing areas and at Shamu's Emporium. **Nursing stations** are located near the women's restroom at Friends of the Wild gift shop, near the center of the park, near the restrooms in Shamu's Happy Harbor, and near the first-aid center behind Stingray Lagoon.

- ✔ **Disposable cameras and film** (and limited digital supplies) are available at stores throughout SeaWorld.

- ✔ **First-aid centers,** staffed by registered nurses, are located behind Stingray Lagoon and near Shamu's Happy Harbor.

- ✔ **Lockers** cost $6 to $8 per day, depending on size. Short-term lockers are currently located near Journey to Atlantis and Kraken. The cost is 50¢.

- ✔ **Lost children** are taken to the Information Center, where a parkwide paging system helps reunite them with their families. *Children under 7 should wear name tags inside their clothing.*

- ✔ **Parking** costs $10 for cars, pickups, and vans; preferred spaces cost extra ($15). The parking lots aren't huge, so most people can walk to the park, but trams also run most times. Remember to note the location of your car. SeaWorld characters mark sections, but forgetting where you parked is still easy after a long day.

- ✔ **Pet care** is available at the kennel between the parking lot and the main gate. The cost is $6 per day (no overnight stays). Proof of vaccinations is required.

> ✔ **Strollers** are available at the Information Center near the entrance. The dolphin-shaped strollers cost $10 for a single, $17 for a double.
>
> ✔ **Wheelchairs** are available at the Information Center. The rental cost is $10 for a regular wheelchair, $38 for an electric wheelchair. No deposits are required.

 SeaWorld and **Busch Gardens** in Tampa (see Chapter 23), both owned by Anheuser-Busch, have a shuttle service that costs $10 round-trip to get you from Orlando to Tampa and back. The 1½- to 2-hour one-way shuttle runs daily and has five pickup locations in Orlando, including one at Universal and one on I-Drive (☎ **800-221-1339**). The schedule allows for about a seven-hour stay at Busch Gardens. The service is free if you have an Orlando FlexTicket Plus.

Exploring the Top Attractions at SeaWorld

SeaWorld explores the mysteries of the deep in a theme-park format that combines wildlife-conservation awareness and education with simple laid-back fun. Up-close encounters with a montage of marine life are the major draws here, but you can also find plenty of amusing shows, plus a handful of thrill rides added to the mix.

To get a good look at the park's layout, check out the "SeaWorld" map on p. 297.

Believe

 Believe, the park's newest killer-whale show (replacing the Shamu Adventure, though still taking place at the Shamu Stadium), made its debut in 2006. Spectacular ballet-like choreography, a new three-story-high set design (featuring a gigantic whale tail, fountains, and video screens), and an exciting musical score combine to create an impressive and splashy show. And don't worry: Shamu remains in the starring role.

Adjoining the exhibit is an underwater viewing area that lets you get a close-up view of the killer whales — you may even get to see a mother with her big baby.

 Summers bring extended hours — and extended hours bring nighttime entertainment. Among the lineup: **Shamu Rocks,** an all-new nighttime killer-whale show set to a rock 'n' roll remix of the hottest hits on the airwaves from the likes of Jennifer Lopez, Savage Garden, and Shakira; and **Mistify,** a spectacular combination of fireworks and fountains on the lagoon (and if you're dining at the Spice Mill, you can enjoy dinner and a show). Even **Blue Horizons** and **Clyde and Seamore** (in Clyde and Seamore Present Sea Lions Tonight) spiff up their shows after nightfall. Alas, SeaWorld stages these shows only seasonally.

Blue Horizons

Blue Horizons, one of SeaWorld's most spectacular shows to date, made its debut in 2005. It combines the grace and power of SeaWorld's most famous inhabitants, the dolphins and false killer whales, with the pageantry of a Broadway production. The show transports you into the dreams of a young girl whose wish is to fly like the birds and swim like the dolphins. Bringing the story to life, aerialists twirl high in the air, while dolphins, whales, and bungee jumpers perform acrobatics in the water. Adding to the drama are brightly colored birds that fly over the audience. The entire show is set to an original score performed by the Seattle Symphony Orchestra. This is by far the most unique show that SeaWorld has created and one that certainly shouldn't be missed.

Clyde and Seamore Take Pirate Island

A lovable and amusing sea-lion-and-otter duet, with a supporting cast of walruses and harbor seals, stars in this fish-breathed comedy that comes with swashbuckling stunts. The show, staged inside the aptly named Sea Lion & Otter Stadium, is corny, but don't hold that against the animal actors, who are predictably adorable. The performance is a welcome change from the high-tech rides and shows at the other theme parks. Be sure to arrive early enough to catch the mime — he pokes fun at the guests who arrive a bit late, much to the amusement of the audience.

Clydesdale Hamlet

Twice a day except Fridays, eight of the tremendous Clydesdale horses are hitched to the big red wagon for a parade through the park, beginning and ending at their stables, where visitors can also watch the parade tack going on and off. Daily petting sessions are scheduled — they're a great time to get a snapshot of you with one of the horses. In late winter and spring, you may get to see a mare and foal that aren't part of the Clydesdale team.

Journey to Atlantis

Taking a cue from Disney's Imagineers, SeaWorld created a part-flume, part-coaster ride that carries the customary surgeon general's warning about heart problems, neck or back ailments, pregnancy, dizziness, and claustrophobia. The story line involves a fisherman, Hermes (the Greek god), and wicked Sirens in a fierce battle between good and evil, but what really matters is the drop — a wild 60-foot plunge, with a bunch of luge-like twists and turns, and a shorter drop thrown in for good measure. There's no hidden lesson here, just a splashy thrill when you least expect it. Oh, and you will get *totally* soaked.

Key West at SeaWorld

Although not quite the way Hemingway saw Key West, this 5-acre, tree- and flower-lined, Caribbean-style village has food, street vendors, and entertainers. It has three animal habitats: **Stingray Lagoon,** where you get a hands-on encounter with harmless southern diamond and cownose rays, an absolute favorite for younger kids; **Dolphin Cove,** a habitat for bottlenose dolphins where you can sometimes feed or pet them as they pass by; and **Turtle Point,** home to endangered and threatened species. Shortly after this area opened, the dolphins often teased visitors by swimming just out of arm's reach. But they soon discovered the advantages to human interaction — namely smelt.

Speaking of smelt, it's real easy to be melted by the dolphins' begging, and you can quickly burn $20 buying trays of their favorite snack to feed to your newfound aquatic friends. I once spent half a park admission feeding them before coming to my senses, so set a limit to your spending (and feeding) ahead of time.

Kraken

Launched in 2000, this coaster is SeaWorld's deepest foray into the world of thrill-ride battles. Kraken is named for a mythological underwater beast that Poseidon kept caged. This 21st-century monster has floorless and open-sided 32-passenger trains that plant you on a pedestal high above the track. When the coaster breaks loose, you climb 151 feet, fall 144 feet, hit speeds of 65 mph, go underground three times (spraying bystanders with water), and make seven loops over a 4,177-foot course. This ride may be the longest 3 minutes, 39 seconds of your life. According to a coaster-fanatic friend who lives for adrenaline, this is the best coaster in Central Florida. (Take that, Disney and Universal!)

Kraken carries a *54-inch height minimum.* This is not a coaster for beginners or youngsters — even if they meet the height requirement.

Manatee Rescue

This exhibit is as close as most people get to endangered West Indian manatees. Underwater viewing stations, innovative cinema techniques, and interactive displays combine for a tribute to these gentle marine mammals. It's a nicer and roomier (for the manatees) exhibit than the tight quarters their cousins have at the **Seas with Nemo & Friends** in **Epcot** (see Chapter 13). Kids especially like the more-natural outdoor viewing area near the entrance to the exhibit.

Marine Mammal Keeper Experience

Expect to invest a sizable chunk of your day and budget in this nine-hour program (it runs 6:30 a.m.–3:30 p.m., so you'll also need to be an early riser). You get to work side by side with a trainer, preparing meals and feeding the animals, learning basic training techniques, and sharing lunch. It costs $399, which includes seven days of consecutive admission to SeaWorld, lunch, a career book, and a T-shirt. The program is limited to three people per day, so make reservations far in advance. You must be 13 or older, *at least 52 inches tall,* able to climb, and able to lift and carry 15 pounds of vittles. Call ☎ **800-327-2424** for more information.

Odyssea

Inside the Nautilus Theater, a cast of acrobats, mimes, dancers, musicians, and comics puts on this undersea show that, at times, is artistic and funny (and always entertaining). The sets and costumes focus on a whimsical underwater world. It's similar in style to the **Cirque du Soleil** production at **Downtown Disney** (see Chapter 25), but on a much smaller scale. It's also a great spot to give your feet a break and to cool off, making it a good stop in the afternoon.

Penguin Encounter

The Penguin Encounter transports you via a 120-foot-long moving sidewalk through Antarctic Tuxedoville. The stars of the show — four different species of penguins — are on the other side of a Plexiglas shield. You get a quick look at them as they preen, socialize, and swim at bullet speed in a 30°F habitat.

Though you get a nice view of the penguins (and they're always a hit with the kids), the viewing-area surroundings leave a bit to be desired.

Pets Ahoy!

A menagerie of cats, dogs, pot-bellied pigs, skunks, and a horse are joined by birds and rats (nearly 100 animals in all) to perform comic relief in a 25-minute show held several times a day inside the SeaWorld Theater. Almost all the performers were rescued from animal shelters.

Stick around after the show and your kids can have an up-close encounter with a couple of the featured animal stars.

Shamu's Happy Harbor

This 4-acre play area has a four-story net tower with a 35-foot crow's-nest lookout, water cannons, remote-controlled vehicles, a life-size ship, and a water maze. It's one of the most extensive play areas at any park. Recent additions include the **Shamu Express,** a kid-friendly coaster with Shamu seats; **Jazzy Jellies,** a ride that lifts and spins kids in jellyfish-like seats; **Swishy Fishies,** a Mad Tea Party–style ride; **Ocean Commotion,** a swinging tug boat that gently rocks back and forth and whirls from side to side; the **Flying Fiddler,** a red fiddler crab that gently lifts its 12 passengers up into the air, and then, in a series of very short drops, begins his descent; and **Sea Carousel,** a whimsical ride with an ocean full of colorful sea creatures including dolphins, fishes, sharks, otters, and sea lions gently going 'round and 'round, up and down, to the sounds of the sea.

Bring extra clothes for the tots (or for yourself) — much of Shamu's Happy Harbor isn't designed to keep you dry. Also, because of the size of the Harbor, smaller kids can easily get lost — and while there's only one escape, it's still possible for them to get out to other areas of the park if you're not paying very close attention.

Shark Encounter

This attraction has been expanded to include 220 species of aquatic predators. Pools out front have small sharks and rays. (Feeding isn't allowed.) Eerie background music sets the mood for viewing big eels, beautiful lionfish, hauntingly still barracudas, and the fat, bug-eyed pufferfish in large indoor aquariums.

This attraction isn't for the claustrophobic: You walk through a Plexiglas tube beneath hundreds of millions of gallons of water. Very small children may find the swimming sharks a bit too much to handle.

Sharks Deep Dive offers limited, hands-off contact with over 50 sharks, including a nearly 9-foot sand tiger, in the Shark Encounter area. Two at a time, guests don wetsuits and underwater helmets (allowing you to breathe and communicate without the need for scuba gear) for a close-up encounter inside an actual shark cage that rides a 125-foot track. Part of the cage is above water, but participants can dive up to 8 feet underwater for a closer look at the inhabitants. The cost is $150; you must be a minimum of 10 years old to participate. The price includes a souvenir booklet, T-shirt, and snorkel gear, but does not include the required park admission fee. Additional up-close animal encounters are available as well. For reservations, call ☎ 800-406-2424.

Wild Arctic

Wild Arctic combines a high-definition adventure film with flight-simulator technology to envelop guests in the beauty, exhilaration, and danger of a polar expedition. After a hazardous simulated helicopter flight over the frozen north, visitors emerge at a remote research base, home to star residents and polar-bear twins Klondike and Snow, seals, walruses, and white beluga whales. A separate walk-through line is available for those who want to skip the bumpy simulator ride.

More SeaWorld fun

Other SeaWorld attractions include **Pacific Point Preserve,** a 2½-acre natural setting that duplicates the rocky northern Pacific Coast home of California sea lions and harbor seals. (Yes, there are smelt opportunities here!)

The **Anheuser-Busch Hospitality Center,** next to the Clydesdale Hamlet, has a deli and offers free samples of Anheuser-Busch beers. At the **Budweiser Beer School,** guests 21 and over can learn how Anheuser-Busch brews the world's top-selling beer.

SeaWorld's **Waterfront** area, which debuted in 2003, added a 5-acre seaport-themed village to the park's landscape. On High Street, look for a blend of shops and the **Seafire Inn** restaurant, where lunch includes a lively and comical musical performance of dueling pianists in **Sizzlin' Pianos.** At Harbor Square, the funny **Groove Chefs orchestra** has chefs making music with pots and pans. The park has also added street performers, including a crusty old sea captain, who tells fish tales and makes music with bottles and brandy glasses. Other eateries include **Voyager's Wood Fired Pizza** and the **Spice Mill.**

In addition to its regular productions, SeaWorld stages a few seasonal shows such as **Mistify,** a nighttime spectacular that takes place out on the lagoon and combines stunning fireworks, fountains, and lighting effects. In summer, guests are treated to the special-effects extravaganza nightly. Those dining at the Spice Mill (located along the Waterfront) can turn an ordinary dinner (if timed right) into dinner and a show.

Dining and Shopping at SeaWorld

For details on SeaWorld's **Makahiki Luau,** a full-scale dinner show featuring South Seas food (mahimahi, chicken, and pork) and entertainment, see Chapter 24. For the lowdown on **Sharks Underwater Grill,** see the nearby "Eating with the fish" sidebar.

SeaWorld has several counter-style eateries offering the usual burgers, fajitas, salads, and so on. Most fast-food meals cost about $8 to $10 per person; drinks will set you back another $2.50 or so.

The Waterfront is home to a number of full-service dining options with decent cuisine, including the following:

- ✔ **Seafire Inn:** Choose from a number of burgers (about $8–$10), stir-fries, sandwiches, and assorted salads, or try a jumbo baked potato served with several toppings for around $8.

- ✔ **The Spice Mill:** This eatery specializes in the spices of famous seaport cities. Try the jambalaya, the jerk-grilled chicken sandwiches, or an array of other more distinctive offerings. Disappointingly, the food isn't nearly as spicy as the restaurant's name implies. An entree will set you back about $12.

- ✔ **Voyager's Wood Fired Pizza:** The pizza-and-parmesan-fries combo platter here offers good value at $8, with seafood, pasta, chicken, sandwiches, and assorted salads and a kids' menu with a huge selection to choose from as well.

SeaWorld doesn't have nearly as many shops as the other major theme parks, but the stores do stock plenty of cuddly sea creatures. You can buy a stuffed manatee at **Manatee Cove.** The **Friends of the Wild** gift shop near **Penguin Encounter** is also nice, as is the shop attached to **Wild Arctic.** Because of the Anheuser-Busch connection, the gift shop outside the park entrance offers a staggering array of Budweiser- and Busch-related items. A handful of unique boutiques at the **Waterfront** feature items from garden art to unique toys and T-shirts.

Eating with the fish

SeaWorld is diving deeper into the restaurant game with **Dine with Shamu** (☎ **800-327-2420** or 407-351-3600; www.seaworldorlando.com), a reservations-only poolside dining experience with Shamu as special guest. While eating, guests can talk to SeaWorld trainers. The menu includes seafood Creole, pasta primavera, beef stew, pasta shrimp Alfredo, sides, salads, rolls, and desserts (plus a buffet of kid-friendly favorites). The cost is $39 for adults and $19 for kids 3 to 9, in addition to park admission.

Other dining experiences include a character breakfast called **Breakfast with Elmo and Friends** ($17 adults, $15 kids 3–9); a **4th of July Picnic** ($14 adults, $8 kids); **Backstage at Believe Buffet,** a behind-the-scenes poolside buffet where the secrets behind the making of Believe are revealed ($25 adults, $10 kids); and the poolside **Shamu Rocks Dinner Buffet,** which includes preferred seating at Shamu Rocks, the park's newest nighttime show ($32 adults, $17 kids).

At **Sharks Underwater Grill** (☎ **407-363-2559**), diners can dig into Floridian and Caribbean treats while watching denizens swim by in the Shark Encounter exhibit — almost the entire back wall of the restaurant serves as a gigantic viewing area. Menu prices are $22 to $28 for adults and $6 to $12 for kids 3 to 9 (pasta, hot dogs, chicken breast, steak, and popcorn shrimp); theme-park admission is required.

Checking Out Discovery Cove

SeaWorld's second theme park opened in 2000. Its $100-million construction cost may be one-tenth the sticker price of Islands of Adventure, but Discovery Cove's admission price is four times higher. The options: $269 to $289 per person (plus 6.5 percent sales tax) if you want to swim with a dolphin (minimum age 6), or $169 to $189 if you can simply settle for the fishes. The prices vary seasonally, so check when you make your reservations (which are required for this park).

A perk of the higher price tag is that it includes a seven-day consecutive pass to either **SeaWorld, Aquatica,** or **Busch Gardens** (see Chapter 23). You can upgrade this feature to a 14-day consecutive pass for two parks for an additional $30, or all three parks for an additional $50. If you plan on visiting all four parks, that's actually a pretty good deal.

Almost everyone who does the **Dolphin Swim** finds it exciting — just the kind of thing that makes for a most memorable vacation. If, however, your kids are younger than age 6, or you decide to skip the Dolphin Swim, it's hard to imagine that you'll get your $169 worth. The atmosphere here isn't tailored to toddlers and is, instead, meant to be a relaxing oasis, quiet and serene. I can't really recommend this park for anyone with very young children in tow.

The park has more than two dozen dolphins, and each works from two to four hours a day. They're pretty incredible animals, and, although their size may be a bit intimidating to some, they're very people-friendly. Many of them are mature critters that have spent their lives in captivity, around people. Most of them love getting their bellies, backs, and flukes rubbed. They also have an impressive bag of tricks. Given the proper hand signals, they can mimic the sound of a human passing gas, chatter in dolphin talk, and do seemingly effortless 1½ gainers in 12 feet of water. They also take guests for piggyback rides.

The Dolphin Swim lasts 90 minutes, about 35 to 40 minutes of which is actually spent in the lagoon. Trainers use the rest of the time to teach visitors about these remarkable mammals.

The rest of your day won't be nearly as exciting, but it is wonderfully relaxing. Discovery Cove doesn't deliver thrill rides, water slides, or acrobatic animal shows; that's what SeaWorld, Disney, and Universal are for. This is where you come to get away from all that!

Discovery Cove is an all-inclusive park, so in addition to the dolphin experience — and seven days of unlimited admission to SeaWorld or Busch Gardens in Tampa — your fee tosses in the following:

- ✔ **Elbow room:** There's a limit of 1,000 guests per day. (To give you an idea of how little that is, the normal daily attendance at Disney's Magic Kingdom is 41,000.) This ensures that your experience will be more relaxing and private, which is essentially what you're paying for.

- ✔ **Food:** The continental breakfast includes fruit, danishes, muffins, juice, and coffee. Lunch, with entrees such as fajitas, salmon, stir-fry, and pesto chicken, is included as well. Snacks are available throughout the day at either of the park's beach bars.

- ✔ **Supplies and gear:** You get a towel, sunscreen, snorkeling gear, a flotation vest, and a souvenir photo.

- ✔ **Parking:** Free self-parking is included.

- ✔ **Activities:** They include the following:

  - Swimming near (but on the other side of Plexiglas from) barracudas and black-tip sharks

  - Snorkeling around a huge pool containing a coral reef with colorful tropical fish and another area with gentle rays

  - Touching and feeding 300 exotic birds in an aviary hidden under a waterfall

  - Cooling off under foaming waterfalls

  - Soaking up the sun on the beaches

  - Enjoying the soothing waters of the park's pools and rivers (both freshwater and saltwater)

Reservations are required far in advance, but you have at least a chance of getting in as a walk-up guest — the park reserves a small number of tickets daily for folks whose earlier dolphin sessions were canceled due to bad weather. Your best chance for last-minute tickets comes during any extended period of good weather.

To get to Discovery Cove, follow the directions to SeaWorld given in the "Gathering Important SeaWorld Information" section, earlier in this chapter.

For up-to-the-minute information about this park, call ☎ 877-434-7268 or go to www.discoverycove.com.

Index of SeaWorld Main Attractions

Believe

Blue Horizons

Clyde and Seamore Take Pirate Island

Clydesdale Hamlet

Journey to Atlantis

Key West at SeaWorld

Kraken

Manatee Rescue

Marine Mammal Keeper Experience

Mistify

Odyssea

Pacific Point Preserve

Penguin Encounter

Pets Ahoy!

Shamu's Happy Harbor

Shark Encounter

The Waterfront

Wild Arctic

Chapter 21

Discovering Orlando's Other Attractions

. . . .

In This Chapter

▶ Exploring Orlando's best smaller attractions
▶ Getting wet outside Walt's World

. . . .

*I*n Chapters 11 through 20, I cover the major theme parks in and around Orlando. But you're probably wondering if there's *anything* that's more relaxed, a little — and I do mean little — cheaper, and still offers a memorable experience.

The answer is yes.

In this chapter, I explore the city's best alternatives to the mega-parks. To further help you out, I divide them into two categories: those in which you stay dry and those in which you get wet — the latter are very popular options in the midst of Orlando's summer heat and humidity. (For more about the weather, see Chapter 3.)

 Most of the attractions listed in this chapter offer coupons online (different from their online-only promotional pricing) that you can print out at home and redeem when you purchase your admission tickets (at the attraction). When you tally up the savings for an average family of four, even using a $1 or $2 coupon (per ticket) for a handful of attractions can add up to a fistful of cash.

Checking Out the City's Best Attractions

 For a list of bargain-basement–priced attractions, even easier on your wallet than the ones I mention here, see Chapter 26.

Gatorland
North of Kissimmee

It's hard to miss the gigantic green jaws — a perfect vacation photo-op, by the way — marking this park's location. Founded in 1949, with just a handful of alligators living in huts and pens, Gatorland, still privately owned and operated, now houses thousands of alligators (including a rare blue one) and crocodiles on its 110-acre grounds that do dual duty as a wildlife preserve and theme park. Gatorland has survived the arrival of Disney, Universal, and SeaWorld in part because of its old-Florida charm and its resistance to becoming overly commercialized (though it hasn't escaped entirely). Breeding pens, nurseries, and rearing ponds are scattered throughout the densely landscaped property, which also displays monkeys, snakes, birds, Florida turtles, and a Galapagos tortoise. Its 2,000-foot boardwalk winds through a cypress swamp and breeding marsh with an observation tower for those who prefer an overhead view. The park's shows include **Gator Wrestlin',** where, at the same time wrestlers are wrangling the reptilians, they're educating the audience about their opponents and how they live; **Gator Jumparoo,** which features the giant reptiles lunging 4 to 5 feet up out of the water to snatch a dead chicken right from a trainer's hand; and **Upclose Encounters,** which showcases a variety of the park's wildlife, including some venomous snakes. There's an open-air restaurant where you can try smoked gator ribs and nuggets, though more-familiar favorites, such as burgers and hot dogs, are available as well, and a shop where you can buy gator-leather goods and souvenirs. (Gatorland also operates a breeding farm for meat and hides.) Younger guests will appreciate the park's water play area, petting zoo, and train ride. The atmosphere here is laid back. It's always been a huge hit with my family, and it serves up the best half-day experience in the area.

The **Gator Gully Splash Park,** a splashy $1-million expansion within the existing park, opened in 2007. This quarter-acre water-based (and loosely bayou-themed) play area is filled with plenty of wet and watery fun as gigantic gators (this kind won't bite), armed with water guns, stand (okay, sit) ready to squirt, enormous egrets spew streams of water from their beaks, and a bucket tree spills over onto anyone standing (or running) within reach.

Gatorland's **Trainer for a Day** program lets up to five guests get up close and personal with the gators for a day (or part of it, anyway). The two-hour, $125 experience puts you side by side with trainers and includes a chance to wrangle some alligators (minimum age 12). Advance reservations are required, and admission to the park is included; a 20 percent discount off a regular admission ticket is extended to up to six members of your party. A one-hour **Night Shine** tour is also available ($20 for all ages), taking you along the wooden walkways with only a flashlight and a guide. Advance reservations are required.

See map p. 311. 14501 S. Orange Blossom Trail/U.S. 441 (between Osceola Pkwy. and Hunter's Creek Blvd.). ☎ ***800-393-5297*** *or 407-855-5496.* www.gatorland.com. *Admission: $23 adults, $15 kids 3–12; advance online purchase price $19 adults, $12 kids 3–12. Parking: Free. Open: Daily 9 a.m.–6 p.m., sometimes later.*

Orlando Area Attractions

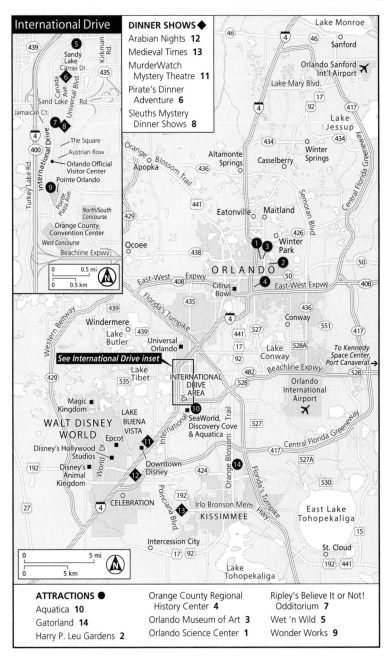

International Drive

DINNER SHOWS ◆
Arabian Nights **12**
Medieval Times **13**
MurderWatch
  Mystery Theatre **11**
Pirate's Dinner
  Adventure **6**
Sleuths Mystery
  Dinner Shows **8**

ATTRACTIONS ●
Aquatica **10**
Gatorland **14**
Harry P. Leu Gardens **2**

Orange County Regional
  History Center **4**
Orlando Museum of Art **3**
Orlando Science Center **1**

Ripley's Believe It or Not!
  Odditorium **7**
Wet 'n Wild **5**
Wonder Works **9**

Harry P. Leu Gardens
Near Winter Park

This serene, 50-acre botanical garden on the shores of Lake Rowena offers a delightful break from the theme-park razzle-dazzle. Meandering paths lead through camphors, oaks, and palms. The camellia collection is one of the world's largest, blooming October through March. The formal rose gardens are the largest in Florida, with 75 varieties. Italian fountains, statues, and a gazebo enhance the gardens. Other highlights include orchids, azaleas, desert plants, beds of colorful annuals and perennials, a butterfly garden, and a 50-foot floral clock.

Businessman Harry P. Leu, who donated his estate to the city in the 1960s, created the gardens. There are guided tours of his house, built in 1888, on the hour and half-hour (advance reservations suggested). The interior has Victorian, Chippendale, and Empire furnishings and fine-art pieces.

See map p. 311. 1920 N. Forest Ave. (between Nebraska St. and Corrine Dr.).
☎ *407-246-2620.* www.leugardens.org. *Admission: $7 adults, $2 children grades K–12. Admission is free Mon 9 a.m. to noon. Parking: Free. Open: Gardens daily 9 a.m.–5 p.m., house daily 10a.m.–4 p.m., except Christmas. Leu House is closed July.*

Orange County Regional History Center
Downtown

Located within a beautifully restored and historic courthouse built back in 1927, the history center is filled with a multimedia experience that takes visitors on a tour of the Florida and Orlando of long ago, moving up to the thriving urban community it is today. The interactive and multisensory experience makes for a unique walk through history. Among the five stories of exhibits: a Florida back porch where the sights and sounds of Central Florida's natural environment surround you; a Paleo and Seminole Indian settlement; pioneer cabins; and Florida Crackers. There is also an old courtroom where Ted Bundy is said to have scratched his name into the defendants' table. For those who believe, it is said that ghosts have been known to roam the hallways, causing supernatural disturbances that have induced more than a few letters of resignation over the years. Guided tours are available on Saturdays at 11 a.m. Visiting shows change throughout the year, so check the Web site for current exhibits. Allow two hours.

See map p. 311. 65 E. Central Blvd. ☎ *407-836-8500.* www.thehistorycenter. org. *Admission: $9 adults, $7 students and seniors, $6 children5–12. Parking: Free at the Orlando Public Library. Open: Mon–Sat 10 a.m.–5 p.m., Sun noon to 5 p.m.*

Orlando Museum of Art
Downtown

This local heavyweight handles some of the most prestigious traveling exhibits in the nation. The museum, founded in 1924, hosts special exhibits throughout the year, but even if you miss one, it's worth a stop to see its rotating permanent collection of 19th- and 20th-century American art, pre-Columbian art dating from 1200 B.C. to A.D. 1500, and African art. Allow two to three hours.

See map p. 311. 2416 N. Mills Ave. (in Loch Haven Park). ☎ *407-896-4231.* www.omart.org. *Admission: $8 adults, $7 seniors, $5 children 6–18. Parking: Free. Open: Tues–Fri 10 a.m.–4 p.m., Sat–Sun noon to 4 p.m.*

Orlando Science Center
Downtown

This modern, four-story center — the largest of its kind in the Southeast — has ten halls in which visitors can explore everything from the swamps of Florida to the arid plains of Mars. One of the big attractions is the **Dr. Phillips CineDome,** a 310-seat theater that features films, planetarium shows, and laser-light presentations. In **KidsTown,** small fries wander in a mini version of the world around them. **DinoDigs,** located nearby, has a dig pit where pint-size paleontologists can unearth fossils, and **TechWorks** is filled with interactive activities — among them a simulated hurricane and hands-on experiments at Dr. Dare's Laboratory. This is just a small sample of what you can expect to find. This option is a great change of pace, especially if you're traveling with children. Allow three to four hours (more if you have an inquiring mind).

Strollers are available at no extra charge.

See map p. 311. 777 E. Princeton St. (between Orange and Mills aves. in Loch Haven Park). ☎ *407-514-2000 or 888-672-4386.* www.osc.org. *Admission (includes exhibits, CineDome film, and planetarium show): $23 adults, $18 kids 3–17, $21 seniors 55 and older and students with valid ID. Parking: $5 in a garage across the street. Open: Sun–Thurs 10 a.m.–6 p.m., Fri–Sat 10 a.m.–9 p.m.*

Ripley's Believe It or Not! Orlando Odditorium
International Drive

Do you crave weird science? If you're a fan of the truly bizarre, come here to see lots of oddities. Among the hundreds of exhibits in its 16 galleries: a shrunken head, a two-headed calf, a 1,069-pound man, a five-legged cow, a three-quarter-scale model of a 1907 Rolls-Royce made of 1 million matchsticks, a mosaic of the *Mona Lisa* created from toast, torture devices from the Spanish Inquisition, and a Tibetan flute made of human bones — you're getting the idea, right? You'll also find exhibits on Houdini, films of people swallowing coat hangers, and other human oddities. Visitors are greeted by a hologram of Robert Ripley himself. There are 27 Odditoriums throughout the world, and no two are alike. The tour makes for a fun rainy-afternoon or late-night activity. Allow two hours.

See map p. 311. 8201 International Dr. (1½ blocks south of Sand Lake Rd.). ☎ *407-363-4418.* www.ripleysorlando.com. *Admission: $19 adults, $12 children 4–12. Parking: Free. Open: Daily 9:30 a.m. to midnight.*

Go Orlando!

The **Go Orlando Card** is a great way to see the "best of the rest" that Orlando has to offer, with admission to attractions such as the **Orlando Science Center, Kennedy Space Center, Gatorland, Ripley's, Fun Spot Action Park, WonderWorks, Boggy Creek Airboat Rides, Cypress Gardens,** and numerous others throughout the greater Central Florida area, along with discounts at area restaurants and shops. Bonus attractions — including **Wet 'n Wild, Pirate's Dinner Adventure,** and the **Arabian Nights** dinner show — are often included with the purchase of three-, five-, or seven-day cards.

Here's how it works: You purchase the all-inclusive Go Orlando Card instead of individual tickets to each venue. You then have two weeks in which to use the card at any of the participating venues. They are available in two-, three-, five-, or seven-day increments; the card is activated with the first use and is good for up to 14 days after activation (for example, a two-day ticket can be used any two days during the two-week time frame).

When you purchase a card, you'll receive maps and a free guidebook with information on the included attractions. Depending on the number of attractions you plan to visit, the Go Orlando Card may very well save you some bucks. The cost of a one-day card is $60 for adults, $55 for kids ages 3 to 12; a two-day card is $100 for adults, $75 for kids; a three-day card costs $160 for adults, $140 for kids; a five-day card is $220 for adults, $180 for kids; and a seven-day card runs $260 for adults, $200 for kids. Sales on select passes are offered on occasion. For details, go to www.goorlandocard.com.

WonderWorks
International Drive

On an uncharted island somewhere in the Bermuda Triangle, a tornado was inadvertently created by scientists experimenting with some seriously weird science. In the midst of the storm, the gigantic building where they were working was swept up and carried off, dropping right in the middle of Orlando — amazingly, the building is fully intact, but it's now upside down. This attraction is educational and fun — just don't come expecting things to be as glitzy as they are in some of the major parks. Throughout the three levels, you'll feel the tremble of an earthquake, experience the rush of hurricane-force winds, create massive bubbles, lie on a bed of nails, walk across the bridge of fire — a hair-raising, electrical experience — and even ride the rails via a simulator on a create-your-own-coaster ride. You'll experience plenty of mind-boggling visual effects and learn dozens of fun and interesting facts. (Where are a cricket's ears? On its knees.) More than 100 exhibits are included, but if you're not a good shot, steer clear of the Lazer Tag game: It costs $4.95 above regular admission and can make for a frustrating few minutes — and while you're at it, skip the arcade extras as well.

WonderWorks also features a nightly combination of magic and comedy in the **Outta Control Magic Comedy Dinner Show.** The 90-minute show features magic and improvisational comedy, as well as unlimited pizza, popcorn, soft drinks, and beer. It's a fun time for the kids and not too bad for adults, either. Call to reserve a spot for the show.

 Combination tickets for discounted admission to WonderWorks, Lazer Tag, and the dinner show are a good buy. Discount coupons are also available on the attraction's Web site, so check it out before you arrive.

See map p. 311. 9067 International Dr. ☎ *407-351-8800.* www.wonderworks online.com. *Admission: $20 adults, $15 kids 4–12 and seniors 55 and older; combination ticket offering admission to WonderWorks, Lazer Tag, and Outta Control $40 adults, $30 kids 4–12 and seniors 55 and older; Outta Control alone is $25 adults, $17 kids 4–11 and seniors. Parking: $2 an hour next door at the Pointe Orlando parking garage. Open: Daily 9 a.m. to midnight; dinner show nightly at 6 and 8 p.m.*

Getting Wet at Orlando's Water Parks

For more aquatic fun, see Chapter 16 for information on **Disney World**'s pair of water parks: **Typhoon Lagoon** and **Blizzard Beach.**

Aquatica, SeaWorld's Water Park
International Drive

This whimsical one-of-a-kind water park, an innovative addition to the Anheuser-Busch-owned World of Discovery family of parks, combines the up-close encounters and eco-edutainment of SeaWorld and Discovery Cove with water rides ranging from serene to extreme. Across the beautifully landscaped grounds are 36 slides and rides (each quite unique), six winding rivers, hidden grottoes and lagoons, and stretches of white sandy beaches. Setting this park apart are its animal inhabitants — including Commerson's dolphins, giant anteaters, thousands of exotic fish, and brilliantly colored birds (among others). Aquatica's signature ride is **Dolphin Plunge,** which takes riders down through 250 feet of clear tubes, under the water, and right through the dolphin habitat (those not willing to take the plunge can sneak a peek at Dolphin Lookout). Other options include **Taumata Racer,** an eight-lane 300-foot slide that has riders flying in and out of tunnels and around a 360-degree turn before crossing the finish line; **HooRoo Run,** one of the wildest flume rides anywhere around with three, count 'em three, drops straight down; and **Tassie's Twisters,** a 129-foot flume that takes riders on single or double tubes, spinning and splashing their way down through a gigantic bowl before dropping them into **Loggerhead Lane** (a lazy river that offers not only a relaxing ride through the park, but also a great underwater view of the dolphins as well as thousands of exotic fish). **Whanau Way** is a five-story, 340-foot multilane slide that's filled with drops, unexpected curves, water curtains, and other thrills before dropping riders into the pool below. **Walhalla Wave,** a family raft ride, takes up to four riders down six stories of tunnels filled with twists and turns. You can catch a wave (or two or three) at **Big Surf Shores** (whose crashing waves are best for older kids and adults) or **Cutback Cove** (whose gentler rolling surf is more appropriate for kids), the world's only side-by-side wave pools. If you prefer to sit it out, you can zip through the waterfalls on **Roa's Rapids,** passing geysers as you go along 1,500 feet of rapids — and while it's similar to a lazy-river raft ride, there's nothing lazy about this one! The park also has a family play area, **Walkabout Waters,** which sports one of the world's largest interactive water play areas (including a 60-ft. rain fortress, family slides, water cannons, and plenty of fountains) as well as a children's area **(Kata's Kookaburra Cove)** for tinier tots with mini raft rides (Mom and Dad can ride along). If you enjoy the water, plan on spending a full day here. Keep in mind that most slides and rides carry height restrictions. See the Web site (www.aquaticabyseaworld.com) for details.

You can rent single strollers ($10), double strollers ($15), wheelchairs ($12), ECVs (electric convenience vehicles; $38), lockers ($8–$10), and beach towels ($4, with a $2 refundable deposit) at Aquatica. Life vests are available at no charge throughout the park. Private cabanas are $150 to $175 for up to four people, plus $30 for each additional person up to seven. A gift shop sells sportswear, beachwear, trinkets, toys, and sundries. Note that this is one of the few water parks open year-round, thanks to a constant water temperature of 84 degrees.

In addition to the admission prices below, Aquatica is part of the multiday, multipark **FlexTicket** package, which enables you to pay one price to visit any of the participating parks during a 14-day period. The Orlando FlexTicket includes admission to Aquatica, SeaWorld, Universal Studios Florida, Islands of Adventure, and Wet 'n Wild; it costs $235 for adults and $195 for children 3 to 9. The Orlando FlexTicket Plus, which adds Busch Gardens in Tampa (see Chapter 23), is $280 for adults and $234 for kids. You can order the FlexTicket through Aquatica by calling ☎ **407-351-3600** or heading to www.aquaticabyseaworld.com. Combination tickets that include admission to both Aquatica and SeaWorld are also available for $90 plus tax, regardless of age.

See map p. 311. 5800 Water Play Way (off International Dr., near the entrance to the Beachline Expwy.). ☎ 888-800-5447. www.aquaticabyseaworld.com. *Admission: $42 adults, $36 kids 3–9. Parking: $10. Open: Hours vary seasonally, but the park is usually open at least 10 a.m.–6 p.m. daily, often later, weather permitting. It's closed on select Mon–Tues in Nov–Dec.*

Wet 'n Wild
International Drive

This 25-acre Universal-owned water park is in the same league as **Typhoon Lagoon** and **Blizzard Beach** with regard to its rides (but not, in my opinion, with regard to atmosphere). In terms of popularity, it ranks third in the country, right behind the two Disney parks. It has several first-rate water rides, including the **Flyer,** a six-story, four-passenger toboggan ride packing 450 feet of banked curves; the **Surge,** which offers 600 feet of greased curves and is billed as the fastest tube ride in the Southeast; the **Black Hole,** in which two-person rafts shoot through 500 feet of twisting, sometimes dark passages; the **Bomb Bay,** where the floor drops right out from under you like a bomb being dropped from high in the sky, plunging down a 76-foot vertical (almost) slide; the all-new **Brain Wash,** a two- or four-person tube ride that sends you careening down a 53-foot vertical drop inside an enclosed tunnel — and if that doesn't make you lose your grip on reality, the 65-foot domed funnel you spiral down afterward might; and the **Disco H₂O,** which takes riders back in time on a four-person raft through an enclosed and rather wild flume ride. Riders eventually end up floating about in the **Aqua Club,** giving a whole new meaning to the phrase *Disco Duck.* Laser lights and disco balls flash as you move and groove to the sounds of the '70s. *All multiperson rides require that kids 36 to 48 inches tall have an adult with them.*

You can also ride **Mach 5,** which consists of a trio of twisting, turning flumes; the **Blast,** a tube ride that sends you winding along a ruptured pipeline; the **Storm,** where you drop from an elevated chute into a gigantic open bowl; the **Bubba Tube,** a family-sized tube ride down a six-story triple-dip slide; and **Der Stuka,** a six-story slide built for speed. The park also has a large kids' area with miniature versions of some of the grownup rides, a lazy river, and a surf lagoon. The **Knee Ski,** a cable-operated knee-boarding course *(56-in. height minimum);* the **Wild One,** a wild two-person tube ride across an open lake; and **Wakeboarding** (all open only in warm weather) are available at the **Wake Zone.** If you enjoy the water, plan on spending a full day here.

You can rent tubes ($4), towels ($2), and lockers ($5), or a combination of all three ($9); each rental requires a $2 to $4 refundable deposit. Life vests are free.

If you're considering visiting several of the non-Disney theme parks, the most economical way to see them is with a **FlexTicket,** which enables you to pay one price to visit any of the participating attractions during a 14-day period. The Orlando FlexTicket includes admission to Wet 'n Wild, Aquatica, SeaWorld, Universal Studios Florida, and Islands of Adventure; it costs $235 for adults and $195 for children 3 to 9. The Orlando FlexTicket Plus, which adds Tampa's Busch Gardens (see Chapter 23), is $280 for adults and $234 for kids. You can order the FlexTicket through Wet 'n Wild, Universal Orlando, or SeaWorld.

See map p. 311. 6200 International Dr. (at Universal Blvd.). ☎ *800-992-9453 or 407-351-9453.* www.wetnwild.com. *Admission: $42 adults, $36 kids 3–9. Parking: $7. Open: Hours vary seasonally, but the park is open at least 10 a.m.–5 p.m. daily, sometimes as late as 11 p.m., weather permitting.*

Chapter 22

Shopping in Orlando

* *

In This Chapter

▶ Getting acquainted with Orlando's shopping districts
▶ Checking out the malls, the outlets, and more
▶ Exploring the antiques district

* *

*I*n this chapter, I offer a rundown of some of the better spots outside the Disney district where you can shop to your heart's content. Because Walt Disney World is so expert at separating you from your money, you'll find the lowdown on shopping at Disney in Chapter 17 . . . yes, it actually requires its very own chapter.

Surveying the Scene

Orlando is a shopper's paradise, offering everything from antiques to souvenirs to one-of-a-kind boutiques. Bargains, however, are few and far between. Orlando hosts an array of indoor malls, many of them with upscale department stores and unique specialty stores. There are also a few factory outlets, but the bargains there are often not much better than the sale prices offered at many department stores. The city proper has an antiques district where it's lots of fun to window-shop, but unless you're a serious collector, the prices tend to be prohibitive. Most of Central Florida's tourist areas (Orlando, Kissimmee, and the surrounding territory included) are riddled with T-shirt shacks and souvenir stands promising bargains that don't (or rarely) exist.

The same is true of the theme parks. If you line up at the registers at Disney, Universal, and the other parks, you pay more than what the merchandise is worth. But if you must have those mouse ears, check out the Disney shopping options in Chapter 17; for merchandise related to the other major theme parks, check out Chapters 18, 19, and 20.

You can actually get cheaper authentic theme-park merchandise outside the parks than you can within them. Both Disney and Universal operate outlet stores in some of the city's most popular malls (though selections are often very limited). See "Checking Out the Big Names," later in this chapter, for more details on these rare opportunities.

Orlando Area Shopping

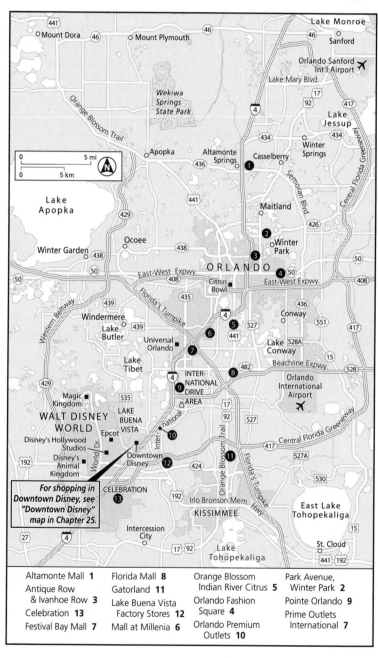

Altamonte Mall **1**	Florida Mall **8**	Orange Blossom	Park Avenue,
Antique Row	Gatorland **11**	Indian River Citrus **5**	Winter Park **2**
& Ivanhoe Row **3**	Lake Buena Vista	Orlando Fashion	Pointe Orlando **9**
Celebration **13**	Factory Stores **12**	Square **4**	Prime Outlets
Festival Bay Mall **7**	Mall at Millenia **6**	Orlando Premium	International **7**
		Outlets **10**	

Here are three shopping heads-ups before you get started:

- ✔ **Sales tax:** In Orange County, which includes the I-Drive area and most of the parks, sales tax is 6.5 percent. Kissimmee and the rest of Osceola County charge 7 percent sales tax.

- ✔ **Store hours:** Most stores in this chapter are open daily from 9 or 10 a.m. until 9 p.m. (6 p.m. on Sun). Small stores, including those in the antiques district, usually close around 5 or 6 p.m. and often close on Sunday. Call to check; the hours are subject to change.

- ✔ **Money:** Most stores accept major credit cards, traveler's checks, and, of course, cash (U.S. currency only). An ATM may not be handy in some areas, so be prepared before heading out.

All the places listed in this chapter can be found on the "Orlando Area Shopping" map on p. 319.

Because Orlando is geared toward travelers, many retailers offer to ship packages home for a few dollars more. So, if you're pondering an extra-large or fragile purchase that you don't want to drag home yourself, ask. If a retailer doesn't offer this service, check with your hotel. Many have a business center where you can mail it yourself, or they can arrange a pickup by UPS, the U.S. Postal Service, or another carrier to keep you from dragging a 6-foot stuffed Pluto into the friendly skies.

Exploring Great Shopping Neighborhoods

Orlando doesn't have a central shopping district. Instead, most shops are sprinkled throughout and around the tourist hotspots and in retail areas where locals shop, such as malls and so on. The following is a list of some of the more frequented shopping zones:

- ✔ **Celebration:** Think *Pleasantville* a la Disney. Created by Disney, the town of 25,000 is more of a charming diversion than a place to power-shop. The downtown has a dozen or so stores, a handful of art galleries, a grocer, and a parfumerie. The storefronts are filled with enticing displays, while inside they peddle interesting and, often, unique — though pricey — merchandise; but the real attraction is the mid-20th-century Main Street atmosphere. Those nostalgic for yesteryear, or in search of a quieter, more sophisticated afternoon out on the town, love it. From WDW, take U.S. 192 east 5 miles, past Interstate 4. The entrance to Celebration is on the right. Call ☎ 407-566-2200 for more information.

- ✔ **Kissimmee:** Southeast of the Disney parks, Kissimmee straddles U.S. 192/Irlo Bronson Memorial Highway — a sometimes tacky, too-often-under-construction stretch of highway lined with budget motels, smaller attractions, and a branch of every fast-food

restaurant in the known universe. Although Kissimmee has recently
begun to evolve and now includes more family-oriented attractions
and better hotels and eateries, the town's shopping merit remains
negligible unless you're looking for a cheap T-shirt, seashells not
sold by the seashore, or the like. That said, lovers of all things
cowboy might appreciate the area's Western shops, a sign that the
city is still mindful of its cowboy roots.

✔ **International Drive area:** This tourist magnet is east of, and
extends 7 to 10 miles north of, the Disney parks between Highway
535 and the Florida Turnpike. The southern end offers a little elbow
room, the midsection is somewhat upscale, and the northern part
is a tourist strip crowded with small-time attractions, fast food-
eries, and souvenir shacks. Its most redeeming shopping draws:
Pointe Orlando and the **Orlando Premium Outlets** (see "Checking
Out the Big Names," later in this chapter).

Locally, International Drive is better known as *I-Drive.*

✔ **Downtown Orlando:** Orlando's downtown is northeast of the
theme parks along I-4. The biggest draws here are the shops along
Antique Row (see "Antiquing Downtown," later in this chapter).

✔ **Winter Park:** Just north of downtown Orlando, Winter Park began
as a haven for wealthy Yankees escaping the cold Northeast. Today,
Winter Park's centerpiece is **Park Avenue,** a collection of upscale
shops, galleries, and restaurants. Ann Taylor, Restoration Hardware,
Bath & Body Works, Crabtree & Evelyn, and Williams-Sonoma are
among the dozens of specialty stores along its tree-lined cobblestone route. No matter which end of Park Avenue you start at, there
are more shops than most visitors can get through in a day, but
you're bound to find something here you won't find anywhere else.
For more information on Winter Park, call ☎ **407-644-8281.**

Checking Out the Big Names

Orlando's reputation wasn't built on shopping. In fact, it isn't even the
top shopping area in Florida, falling well short of Miami–Fort Lauderdale.
But Orlando has attracted some big names, including Neiman Marcus,
Nordstrom, Bloomingdale's, Macy's, and a very small Saks. Specialty
stores include Tiffany & Co. and Charles David, along with unique retailers like Ron Jon Surf Shop and Hilo Hattie. Orlando also has a growing
stable of discount centers.

Factory outlets

Shoppers can find plenty of name brands at the outlets, but not always
big bargains. Although many of the stores claim savings of 50 percent
to 75 percent, a discount on a heavily marked-up or overpriced item
doesn't always mean you're getting a deal. You will find, however, a

decent selection of designer and name-brand merchandise at slightly lower prices than you would normally pay at the malls.

If you're a smart outlet shopper, you know the suggested retail prices for items before you hit the stores. Therefore, you'll know just what is — and what *isn't* — a bargain.

Here's a list of outlet stores and centers in and around Orlando:

- ✔ **Lake Buena Vista Factory Stores:** The three dozen or so outlets here include Aeropostale, Big Dogs Sportswear, Carter's, Casuals (Ralph Lauren and Tommy Hilfiger), Converse, Dressbarn, Ecko Unlimited, Eddie Bauer, Gap, Fossil, Liz Claiborne, Nike, Nine West, OshKosh, Reebok, Samsonite, Tommy Hilfiger, and the only Old Navy outlet in the area. There's also a food court, a salon, and a small children's play area. Savings are modest, but the plaza itself is quiet and inviting. It's at 15591 S. Apopka-Vineland Rd. (☎ 407-238-9301; www.lbvfs.com).

- ✔ **Orlando Premium Outlets:** This is my favorite outlet mall in Orlando, and it's also the only truly upscale outlet mall close to Disney. The center's 110 tenants include AG Adriano Goldschmied, Armani, Barneys New York, BCBG, Brooks Brothers, Burberry, Calvin Klein, Coach, Cole Haan, Diesel, DKNY, Etro, Fendi, Ferragamo, Frette, Hugo Boss, J. Crew, Joe's Jeans, Kenneth Cole, Lacoste, La Perla, Miss Sixty, Nautica, Nike, Oilily, Puma, Ralph Lauren, Theory, Timberland, Tommy Hilfiger, Wolford, and Zegna. Some of the best buys here are at Banana Republic. In contrast to most of the outlet centers in the city, its character is more of an open-air outdoor mall with a Mediterranean flair. A major expansion (which began in 2008) will add several more designer outlets to the already impressive lineup of stores. In addition, the center now offers a "Personal Stylist Service" package — but at a price tag of between $500 and $750, this one's for serious shoppers only. It's at 8200 Vineland Ave., just off the southern third of I-Drive (☎ 407-238-7787; www.premiumoutlets.com), next to Dolly's Dixie Stampede.

- ✔ **Prime Outlets International** (formerly Belz Factory Outlet World): This is the granddaddy of all Orlando outlets, with hundreds of stores laid out in an outdoor Mediterranean-style center. The mall offers more than a dozen shoe stores (including Vans, Cole Haan, and Nine West), housewares stores, and more clothing and accessories shops than you can count (Aeropostale, BCBG, Coach, Columbia Sportswear, DKNY, Ecko Unlimited, Esprit, Guess, Hugo Boss, J. Crew, Juicy Couture, Kate Spade, Kenneth Cole, Nautica, OshKosh, PacSun, Perry Ellis, Polo, and others). You'll also find music, electronics, sporting goods, health and beauty aids, jewelry, toys, gifts, lingerie, and so on. The mall is at 5401 W. Oak Ridge Rd., at the north end of International Drive (☎ 407-352-9600; www.primeoutlets.com).

Malls

The Orlando area is home to several traditional shopping malls. As in malls throughout the country, good buys are often elusive. Arguably, a mall's best bargain is the people-watching, which is free. Here's a list of Orlando's malls:

- ✔ **Altamonte Mall:** Built in the 1970s, this is the area's second largest mall, behind the Florida Mall (see later in this list). Tenants include JCPenney, Macy's, and Sears, plus 175 specialty shops. Renovations have added a food court; a play area for younger kids; rides for toddlers; and an 18-screen AMC movie theater. It's at 451 E. Altamonte Dr., about 15 miles north of downtown Orlando (☎ **407-830-4422;** www.altamontemall.com).

- ✔ **Festival Bay Mall:** One of the newest additions to the shopping scene, Festival Bay's tenants include Bass Pro Shops, Hilo Hattie, Ron Jon Surf Shop, and other specialty stores. Restaurants include fast-food eateries as well as Bergamo's Italian Restaurant, Cricketers Arms British Pub & Eatery, Dixie Crossroads, Fuddruckers, and Monkey Joe's, with a Cold Stone Creamery to top off your meal. Some of the area's more unique recreational venues can be found here as well, including Vans (indoor) Skatepark; the Putting Edge for glow-in-the-dark miniature golf; and a 20-screen Cinemark Theater. The Ron Jon Surf Park splashed onto the scene in 2007. This mall is at 5250 International Dr. (☎ **407-351-7718;** www.shopfestivalbaymall.com), at the far north end of I-Drive across from Prime Outlets International.

- ✔ **Florida Mall:** Anchors include Dillard's, JCPenney, Macy's, Nordstrom, Saks, and Sears to go along with the Florida Hotel and more than 250 shops (such as Abercrombie & Fitch, Club Libby Lu, and Coach), restaurants (including Buca di Beppo, California Pizza Kitchen, and Le Jardin), and entertainment venues. It's at 8001 S. Orange Blossom Trail, at Sand Lake Road, 4 miles east of I-Drive (☎ **407-851-6255;** www.shopsimon.com).

- ✔ **Mall at Millenia:** This 1.3-million-square-foot center debuted in 2002 with Bloomingdale's, Macy's, and Neiman Marcus as its anchors. In addition to the heavyweights, Millenia offers 200 specialty stores that include Burberry, Chanel, Charles David, Gucci, Juicy Couture, and Tiffany & Co. Restaurants include Brio Tuscan Grille, Cheesecake Factory, McCormick & Schmick's Seafood, Panera Bread, and P. F. Chang's China Bistro. The Blue Martini, an upscale bar featuring a tapas menu and 29 designer martinis, is a good place to celebrity-watch. The mall is 5 miles from downtown Orlando at 4200 Conroy Rd., at I-4 near Universal Orlando (☎ **407-363-3555;** www.mallatmillenia.com).

- ✔ **Orlando Fashion Square:** This city-side mall is home to Macy's, JCPenney, Sears, 165 specialty shops (such as American Eagle Outfitters, Express, Hot Topic, Nine West, Sunglass Hut, and

Homegrown souvenirs

Given Orlando's history as a major citrus producer, oranges, grapefruit, and other citrus products rank high on the list of local products. **Orange Blossom Indian River Citrus,** 5151 S. Orange Blossom Trail (☎ **800-624-8835** or 407-855-2837; www.orange-blossom.com), is one of the top sellers during the late-fall to late-spring season. It makes a great place to shop for anyone left in charge of your pets, house, or other such duties while you're off vacationing in the Sunshine State.

And if you have a love affair with leather, alligator-skin leather goods are a specialty of the gift shop at **Gatorland,** 14501 S. Orange Blossom Trail (☎ **407-855-5496;** www.gatorland.com). For details on this classic Florida theme park, see Chapter 21.

Victoria's Secret), and an extensive food court. The mall is 5 miles from downtown Orlando at 3201 E. Colonial Dr. (☎ **407-896-1132;** www.orlandofashionsquare.com).

✔ **Pointe Orlando:** Pointe Orlando's two levels of stores, restaurants, and 21-screen IMAX theater are set in an inviting open-air complex with brick walkways, courtyards, gardens, fountains, and flowering foliage. Headliners among the 40 shops include Bath & Body Works, Boardwalk Surf & Sport, Chico's, Everything But Water, Foot Locker, Hollister, Kiehl's, Life is good, L'Occitane, Tommy Bahama, and Victoria's Secret (with more big-name shops on their way). For some of the dining options at the Pointe, see Chapter 10. Parking is $5 in the garage, but most restaurants, nightclubs, and the movie theater will validate with a purchase. It's at 9101 International Dr. (☎ **407-248-2838;** www.pointeorlando.com).

Antiquing Downtown

If you can think of nothing better than a relaxing afternoon of sifting through yesterday's treasures, check out **Antique Row** and **Ivanhoe Row,** on North Orange Avenue in downtown Orlando.

Flo's Attic (☎ **407-895-1800**) and **A. J. Lillun** (☎ **407-895-6111**) feature traditional antiques. **Fredlund Wildlife Gallery** (☎ **407-898-4544;** www.fredlundwildlife.com) sells pricey, original works of art. And the **Fly Fisherman** (☎ **407-898-1989;** www.flyfishermaninc.com) sells — no surprise here — fly-fishing gear. You can often watch people taking lessons in the park across the street.

The stores are spread over 3 miles along Orange Avenue. The heaviest concentration is between Princeton Street and New Hampshire Avenue, although a few are scattered between New Hampshire and Virginia avenues. The more upscale shops extend a few blocks beyond Virginia Avenue. To reach the area from the theme parks, take I-4 east to Princeton Street (Exit 43); turn right on Orange Avenue. Parking is limited, so stop wherever you find a space.

Most of the stores are open from 9 or 10 a.m. to 5 p.m., Monday through Saturday. (Hours can vary; call before you head out. A small number of shops are open Sun, but it isn't worth the trip from the resorts.)

If you decide to do your antiquing on a Sunday, you can also shop for fresh produce, plants, baked goods, and crafts every Sunday beginning at 9 a.m. at downtown's **Sunday Eola Market.** It's located at the intersection of North Magnolia Avenue and East Central Boulevard. Get more information at www.downtownorlando.com.

Chapter 23

Going Beyond Orlando: Two Day Trips

- -

In This Chapter

▶ Going on safari at Busch Gardens
▶ Lifting off at the Kennedy Space Center

- -

*E*ven with all that Orlando has to offer (and if you've read Chapters 12–22, you know there's plenty), you may want to drive to the coast for a day to enjoy a change of pace, some sugary sand beaches, and warm waters. In addition to Florida's spectacular beaches, two places are worth going out of your way to visit: **Busch Gardens** in Tampa Bay and the **Kennedy Space Center** at Cape Canaveral. The first is a combination of SeaWorld's lush landscaping, relaxing atmosphere, and eco-educational themes (see Chapter 20); Disney's Animal Kingdom's array of African wildlife (see Chapter 15); and Universal's Islands of Adventure's heart-pounding thrill rides (see Chapter 19). Kennedy Space Center is a unique experience that you just can't get in Orlando (unless Disney starts developing a space-shuttle program, which would be a stretch, even for them).

Trekking to Busch Gardens

When this Tampa theme park grew out of a brewery in the '60s, the main (and only) attractions were a bird show and free beer. Both are alive and well, but Busch Gardens has grown into one of Florida's top theme parks, filled with coasters that can out-thrill even Universal Orlando, as well as wildlife, eco-educational themes, and landscaping that all give the park a unique and fascinating allure.

Getting there

If you're driving from Orlando, head west on I-4 to I-75. Go north on I-75 to Exit 265 (Fowler Ave./University of South Florida). Bear left on the exit ramp, and it will lead you directly onto Fowler Avenue. Proceed west on Fowler to McKinley Avenue (the first light past the main entrance to the university). Turn left on McKinley and proceed south to the parking lot and the main entrance to the park. Parking costs $10. The drive should take a little more than an hour, depending on traffic.

SeaWorld (see Chapter 20) and Busch Gardens, both owned by Anheuser-Busch, have a shuttle service that offers $10 round-trip tickets to get you from Orlando to Tampa and back. The 1½- to 2-hour one-way shuttle runs daily and has five pickup locations in Orlando, including at Universal Orlando and on I-Drive (call ☎ **800-221-1339** for schedules, reservations, and pickup locations). The schedule allows about seven hours at Busch Gardens. The service is free if you have an Orlando FlexTicket Plus. For more about the FlexTicket, see "Admission options," later in this chapter.

Most Orlando shuttle services will also take you to Busch Gardens. See Chapter 8 for details on the city's shuttle companies.

Visitor information

You can get information in advance of your visit by calling ☎ **888-800-5447** or 813-987-5283, or heading online to www.buschgardens.com. After you're inside the park, you can obtain information from several visitor centers or the Expedition Africa Gift Shop. Be sure to grab a guide map of the park when you enter.

Busch Gardens is open daily, generally from 10 a.m. to 6 p.m. (though hours can range from 9 a.m.–9 p.m. during peak season). The park's hours change seasonally, so be sure to call or check the Web site for the latest information before you depart.

 You can save a few bucks and avoid waiting in line by buying your tickets to Busch Gardens at the privately owned **Tampa Bay Visitor Information Center,** opposite the park at 3601 E. Busch Blvd., at North Ednam Place (☎ **813-985-3601;** www.hometown.aol.com/tpabay infoctr). Owner Jim Boggs worked for Busch Gardens for 13 years and gives expert advice on visiting the park.

Admission options

Busch Gardens has a number of admission schemes, though your options are usually limited to two as a day visitor:

- ✔ **One-day regular park admission** costs $68 for adults, $58 for kids 3 to 9; children younger than 3 are admitted free. Prices do not include the 7 percent sales tax.

 ✔ The **FlexTicket Plus** is a multiday, multipark option that may work for you if you plan on visiting Universal Orlando or SeaWorld while in Orlando. The most economical way to see the various "other-than-Disney" parks, you pay one price to visit any of the participating parks during a 14-day period. A pass to **Universal Studios Florida, Islands of Adventure, Wet 'n Wild, Aquatica, SeaWorld,** and **Busch Gardens** is $280 for adults and $234 for kids. You can order the FlexTicket by calling ☎ **888-800-5447** or by going to www.buschgardens.com. (For more about the other FlexTicket parks, see Chapters 18 through 21.)

Busch Gardens occasionally runs other discount admissions specials and offers a host of other multiday and annual-pass selections. For details on these options, call ☎ **888-800-5447** or 813-987-5283, or check the Web site at www.buschgardens.com.

Seeing the park

Busch Gardens is older than Disney World but has aged quite well. This park has eight distinctive areas, each with its own theme, animals, live entertainment, rides, dining, and shopping. A Skyride cable car offers a bird's-eye view of it all. Two things set Busch Gardens apart from its nearest rival (Disney's Animal Kingdom): its vast array of thrill rides (some of the best in the country) and the accessibility of its wildlife.

Chasing thrills

Busch Gardens has five — count 'em, *five!* — wild roller coasters (and that doesn't include the flume and rapids rides) to keep your adrenaline pumping and stomach jumping.

The recently reintroduced **SheiKra** is the first of its kind in the Americas. This dive coaster hurtles you 90 degrees straight down at speeds reaching 70 mph. Then it's on to a rolling loop and a second 90-degree drop, plummeting you 138 feet through an underground tunnel. *There is a height restriction of 54 inches to ride this one.*

Gwazi is a wooden wonder named for a fabled African lion with a tiger's head. This $10-million ride slowly climbs to 90 feet before turning, twisting, diving, and *va-rrroommming* to speeds of 50 mph — enough to give you air time (also known as weightlessness). These twin coasters, the **Lion** and the **Tiger,** provide 2 minutes and 20 seconds of thrills and chills, steep-banked curves, and bobsled maneuvers. At six points on the ride, you're certain you're going to slam the other coaster.

There's a *48-inch minimum height* for Gwazi, and the 15-inch seat is smaller than an airline seat, so it's a tight squeeze for thin folks and the next best thing to misery for larger models.

Busch's other big coasters are made of steel. **Kumba** *(54-in. height minimum)* is a 143-foot-high number that covers 4,000 feet of track at 60 mph and jerks you with sudden turns. **Montu** *(54-in. height minimum)* musses your hair at speeds exceeding 60 mph while the G-force keeps you plastered to your seat. **Scorpion** *(42-in. height minimum)* offers a high-speed 60-foot drop and 360-degree loop.

The park's water rides are a welcome relief from the summer heat. **Tanganyika Tidal Wave** *(48-in. height minimum)* is a steep flume, while **Congo River Rapids** *(42-in. height minimum)* is similar to **Kali River Rapids** in **Disney's Animal Kingdom** (see Chapter 15).

Meeting animals and seeing shows

Busch Gardens has thousands of animals living in very naturalistic environments that continue the park's African theme. Most authentic is the 80-acre **Serengeti Plain,** reminiscent of the real Serengeti of Tanzania and Kenya. Unlike the animals on the real Serengeti, however, these grazing zebras and giraffes have nothing to fear from lions, hyenas, and other predators, which are confined to enclosures. Busch's critters have fewer places to hide and, therefore, are much easier to see than those at Disney's Animal Kingdom (see Chapter 15).

Twenty-six acres of the Serengeti Plain are devoted to free-roaming white rhinos. **Rhino Rally,** a Land Rover tour, takes up to 16 passengers on a very bumpy, seven-minute journey where the white rhinos, Asian elephants, cape buffaloes, alligators, and antelopes roam. If you can handle the bumps, it's a pretty good ride, and one of the few that's appropriate for almost all ages.

Nairobi's **Myombe Reserve** is home to gorillas; this area also has a baby-animal nursery, petting zoo, turtle and reptile displays, and an elephant exhibit.

In addition to the animals, your children will love the slides, treehouse, and rides at **Land of Dragons;** the sandy dig site at **King Tut's Tomb;** and the friendly lorikeets of **Lory Landing.** Another favorite is **Pirates 4-D,** a 15-minute high-seas comedic adventure that combines sensory effects and 3-D film. At the Marrakesh Theater, the **Rock A Doo Wop** entertains with a lively 1950s- and '60s-style musical revue.

Jungala, a 4-acre park-within-a-park, made its debut in spring 2008 in the existing Congo. Orangutans, tigers, white gibbons, and flying foxes are just some of the exotic inhabitants here. A multi-story play area with climbing nets, bridges, tubes, and a water play area will keep even the most active kids busy, while thrill seekers will appreciate **Jungle Flyers,** a multi-level zipline ride, and the **Wild Surge,** a four-story freefall-style ride that shoots out from the top of a waterfall. Restaurants, shops, and live entertainment cap off the entire experience.

And did I mention the **free beer** if you're 21 or older? This is an Anheuser-Busch park, you know. You can sample their products at the Hospitality House.

Special tours and options

Although you can get close to Busch Garden's animals in their glass-walled enclosures with regular admission, the only way to mingle *with* the grazers is on a guided tour. Here are the best the park offers (*children must be at least 5 years old* to participate in any of them):

> ✔ For an extra $34 over the admission price, you can go on the 30-minute **Serengeti Safari,** which features an extra-close look at — and a chance to feed — giraffes, gazelles, and more (from the back

of a flatbed truck). If you're eager for a hands-on wildlife experience, the safari tour is worth the extra money. You can make reservations for the first tour of the day at the Expedition Africa Gift Shop or by calling ☎ 813-984-4043, but the midday and afternoon tours are first-come, first-served.

✔ The five-hour **Guided Adventure Tour** gives you the safari, lunch, and front-of-the-line access at the shows and rides for $95 ($85 kids 3–9) above park admission. The **Elite Adventure Tour** includes everything the Guided Adventure Tour does, plus free parking (normally $10), free bottled water on the tour, merchandise discounts, VIP seating at shows, and lunch, for $200 per person plus park admission. Reserve in advance by calling ☎ 813-984-4043 or going to www.buschgardens.com.

Blasting Off to John F. Kennedy Space Center

Each time a space shuttle blasts into the heavens, people all over the world wish they could be astronauts. Heck — maybe you're one of them. You can live out your childhood fantasies at the Kennedy Space Center, located on the Space Coast at Cape Canaveral.

Getting there

Though shuttles run from Orlando to Cape Canaveral, this area really demands a car in order to be seen properly. The center is an easy hour's drive from Orlando via the Beachline Expressway (Hwy. 528, a toll road). Take the S.R. 407 exit going to Kennedy Space Center (KSC) and Titusville, and continue on S.R. 407 until it dead-ends into S.R. 405. Turn right (east) onto S.R. 405 and follow the signs for Kennedy Space Center. You'll travel approximately 9 miles on S.R. 405. The KSC Visitor Complex will be on your right. Parking is free.

Visitor information

For information before you leave home, call ☎ 321-449-4444 or check out www.kennedyspacecenter.com. For general information on the Space Coast, call the **Florida Space Coast Office of Tourism/Brevard County Tourist Development Council** at ☎ 877-572-3224 or 321-868-1126, or go to www.space-coast.com.

The **Visitor Complex** is open daily from 9 a.m. to 6 p.m., and the **Astronaut Hall of Fame** is open daily from 10 a.m. to 7 p.m. (except Christmas and select launch days). Always call to confirm these hours before you set out for Cape Canaveral.

Admission options

Kennedy Space Center admission is $38 for adults and $28 for kids 3 to 11. Included in this price is admittance to the center, several IMAX films, access to exhibits and shows, entrance to the Astronaut Hall of Fame, and a chance to ride in an interactive space simulator.

You can also purchase Astronaut Hall of Fame admission only, for $17 per adult, $13 per child. A 12-month pass runs $50 per adult, $40 per child. The ATX, or Astronaut Training Experience (see "Special tours and options," later in this chapter), costs $250.

You can purchase admission tickets, guided tours, and other programs online at www.kennedyspacecenter.com.

Touring the center

Whether you're a space buff or not, you'll appreciate the sheer grandeur of the facilities and technological achievements displayed at NASA's primary space-launch facility. Highlights include trips down memory lane and glances into the future of space exploration. You also explore the history of manned flight, beginning with the wild ride of the late Alan Shepard in 1961 and Neil Armstrong's 1969 moonwalk. The center has dual 5½-story, 3-D IMAX theaters that reverberate with special effects. You'll need at least a full day to see everything here.

Begin your visit at the **Kennedy Space Center Visitor Complex,** which has real NASA rockets and the actual Mercury Mission Control Room from the 1960s. You'll find several hands-on activities for kids, including a chance to meet (even dine with) a real astronaut, as well as several dining venues and a shop selling a variety of space memorabilia and souvenirs. Because this privately operated complex has been undergoing an ambitious $130-million renovation and expansion, check to see whether it has changed its tours and exhibits before visiting.

Bus tours of the complex (included with your admission) run continuously every 15 minutes beginning at 10 a.m. Plan to take the tour early in your visit and be sure to hit the restrooms before boarding the bus — there's only one out on the tour. You can get off at the **LC-39 Observation Gantry,** which has a 360-degree view of shuttle launch pads; the **International Space Station Center,** where scientists and engineers prepare additions to the space station now in orbit; and the **Apollo/Saturn V Center,** which includes artifacts, photos, interactive exhibits, and the 363-foot-tall Saturn V rocket.

Don't miss the **Astronaut Memorial,** a moving black-granite monument that has the names of the U.S. astronauts who have died on missions or while in training. The 60-ton structure rotates on a track that follows the movement of the sun (on clear days, of course), causing the names to stand out above a brilliant reflection of the sky.

The **Astronaut Hall of Fame,** a separate attraction at the Kennedy Space Center Visitor Complex, includes displays, exhibits, and tributes to the heroes of the Mercury, Gemini, and Apollo space programs. There's also a collection of spacecraft, including an Apollo 14 command module. And in the **G-Force Trainer** (in the **Astronaut Adventure Room**), guests can experience the pressure of four times the force of gravity, ride a rover across Mars, and land a space shuttle.

In 2007, the **Shuttle Launch Experience,** a $60-million space launch simulator, began duplicating the sights, sounds, and sensations of launching into space; thanks to sophisticated motion technology, special-effects seats, and high-fidelity audiovisuals, astronauts-in-training will get the chance to experience the sensation of a real launch into space. Watch out, Disney — this one's the real deal (almost)!

On launch days, the center is closed at least part of the day. Although launch days aren't good times to see the center, they're great occasions to observe history in the making. Schedules for launch tickets, entitling you to admission to the center for the shortened operating hours, plus at least a two-hour excursion to NASA Parkway to see the liftoff, are available by calling ☎ 321-449-4444. You must pick up tickets, available five days prior to the launch, on-site.

Special tours and options

The Kennedy Space Center offers a number of special programs and tours to visitors. Here are a few that will delight wannabe astronauts:

- ✔ The ultrapopular **Lunch with an Astronaut** is available every day during lunch hours. Past participants have included John Glenn, Jim Lovell, and Wally Schirra. Seating is limited, so reserve well in advance by calling ☎ 321-449-4400 or going to www.kennedy spacecenter.com. The program costs $23 for adults and $16 for kids 3 to 11, plus admission to the center.

- ✔ The **Cape Canaveral: Then and Now** tour includes a visit to the first launch sites, the Air Force Museum, and the Missile Museum. The tour costs an extra $21 for adults and $15 for kids 3 to 11.

- ✔ On the 90-minute **NASA Up Close** tour, you'll be guided through the intricacies of the space shuttle program and get an up-close look at the launch pads. The tour almost always sells out, so reserve in advance by calling ☎ 321-449-4400 or going online to www.kennedyspacecenter.com. The tour costs $21 for adults and $15 for kids 3 to 11, plus the cost of admission to the center.

- ✔ For future space explorers, the **Astronaut Training Experience (ATX)** is a day-long interactive program including an orientation, mission briefing, and simulator training exercises. The day ends with a team shuttle mission from launch to landing in a full-scale space shuttle mock-up. A T-shirt, a class photo with a real astronaut, lunch, and a graduation ceremony are all part of the deal. Advance reservations are required. You must be at least 14 to participate; those under 18 must be accompanied by a paying adult. The price is $250 and includes ATX gear and lunch. A family experience (including an overnight stay at a select resort in Cocoa Beach) is also available. For details and up-to-date pricing, head to www.kennedyspacecenter.com.

Part VI

Living It Up After Dark: Orlando Nightlife

"Actually, they started out as just bickering pianos."

In this part . . .

Orlando's action used to literally rise and set with the sun, but that's hardly the case now. I tip my hat to you if you still have the energy for a nighttime adventure after a day in the parks. Whether you prefer rocking the night away, slow dancing until dawn, or dining while you watch pirates battle for treasure, you can liven up your evenings in Orlando, and this part of the book shows you how.

Chapter 24

Taking In the Dinner Shows

● ●

In This Chapter

▶ Seeing Orlando's best dinner shows
▶ Getting tickets for everything else

● ●

*I*f a day at the theme parks isn't enough to satisfy your appetite for entertainment, Orlando's dinner theaters serve up a rather diverse menu of amusements to keep you entertained as you dine. In this chapter, I tell you about dinner shows where you can solve a "murder," follow the nonstop action on a pirate ship, or cheer on a knight at a medieval joust.

Getting the Inside Scoop on Orlando Dinner Theater

Orlando's busy dinner-show scene is far different from those you find in high-flying cultural centers such as New York and London. Walt Disney World and Orlando feature family-oriented fun and fanfare rather than critically acclaimed dramatic performances. Most shows focus on entertaining the city's top VIPs: the kids. Expect action, adventure, and corny humor, all generally performed in a very loud stadium setting where the kids can scream to their hearts' content.

Did you ever notice that you never see dinner shows listed in the restaurant section? Ever wonder why? It's not the dinner you're going for. Eating adds its own ingredient of adventure to Orlando's dinner-theater experience. The fare is generally right off the rubber-chicken circuit. The meals usually consist of a choice of two or three generic entrees (often overcooked) and school-lunch–caliber side dishes. This may very well explain why some theaters serve free wine and beer after you've been seated — to dull your palate before dinner is served.

The prices of the shows that I list in this section include your meal and the aforementioned wine and beer (soda is available, too), but not tax or tips, unless otherwise noted.

You can often find discount coupons to the dinner shows in the tourist magazines distributed at information centers, hotel lobbies, gas stations, and sometimes on the listed Web sites. A good place to look for discounted tickets for dinner theaters is the **Orlando/Orange County Convention & Visitors Bureau** Web site at www.orlandoinfo.com.

For all dinner shows, advance reservations are strongly recommended. And when it comes to **Walt Disney World** dinner shows, always, always, *always,* make an **Advanced Dining Reservation** (☎ **407-939-3463**). (See Chapter 10 for more about Advanced Dining Reservations.) Disney's shows fill up fast, often months in advance for weekend performances and during peak vacation seasons and holidays. I've actually spent several days trying to make reservations (for the Hoop-Dee-Doo Musical Revue), calling the very minute the phone lines opened (usually around 7 a.m.) about a year in advance, and it took four days to finally get a reservation — and I didn't even get the day or the time I would have preferred.

Arabian Nights
Kissimmee

If you're a horse fan, this show is a winner. It stars many of the most popular breeds, from chiseled Arabians to beefcake Belgians. They giddy-up through performances that include trick riding, chariot races, a little slapstick comedy, and bareback daredevils. The premise of the show is the elaborate wedding of the prince and princess — what wedding would be complete without an uninvited guest? — and so begins the adventure. Locals rate it number one among Orlando dinner shows. On most nights, the performance opens with a ground trainer working one-on-one with a black stallion. The dinner, served during the two-hour show, includes salad; a choice of New York strip steak, chopped steak, grilled chicken, chicken tenders, or primavera penne pasta; a garden salad; and wedding cake for dessert. Special diets can be accommodated with advance notice. Unlimited beer, wine, or soda pop comes with the meal.

The Web site usually offers a discount on tickets purchased online.

See map p. 311. 6225 W. Irlo Bronson Memorial Hwy. (U.S. 192, east of I-4 at Exit 25A). ☎ *800-553-6116 or 407-239-9223.* www.arabian-nights.com. *Reservations recommended. Shows held daily; times vary. Admission: $46–$57 adults, $20–$31 kids 3–11. AE, DISC, MC, V. Stadium-style seating. Parking: Free.*

Disney's Spirit of Aloha Show
Walt Disney World

Although not quite as much in demand as the Hoop-Dee-Doo Musical Revue, **Disney's Polynesian Resort** (see Chapter 9) presents a delightful two-hour show that comes across like a big neighborhood party with island flair. The luau features Tahitian, Samoan, Hawaiian, and Polynesian singers, drummers, and dancers who entertain you while you feast on a menu that includes Lanai-roasted chicken, pork ribs, sliced pineapple,

Polynesian wild rice, Polynesian-style bread, South Seas vegetables, dessert, wine, beer, and other beverages. Kids can eat mac 'n' cheese, hot dogs, chicken nuggets, or PB&J if they prefer. The show takes place five nights a week in an open-air theater (dress for nighttime weather) with candlelit tables, red-flame lanterns, and tapa-cloth paintings on the walls.

 Reserve at least 60 to 90 days ahead (you can make reservations up to 180 days in advance), especially during peak periods such as summer and holidays. Payment must be made in full at the time of the reservation, but you can cancel up to 48 hours prior to your show for a full refund.

 As with the Hoop-Dee-Doo Musical Revue, ticket prices for Disney's Spirit of Aloha Show are now based on seating — the closer you sit to the action on stage, the higher the price you'll pay.

See map p. 344. 1600 Seven Seas Dr. (at Disney's Polynesian Resort). ☎ **407-939-3463.** www.disneyworld.com. *Reservations required. Shows: Tues–Sat 5:15 and 8 p.m. Admission: Adults $59, $55, and $51; kids 3–9 $31, $27, and $26; prices include tax and tip. AE, DISC, MC, V. Table seating. Parking: Free.*

 ### Hoop-Dee-Doo Musical Revue
Walt Disney World

This show at **Disney's Fort Wilderness Resort & Campground** (see Chapter 9) is Disney's most popular, so make Advanced Dining Reservations as early as possible. The reward: You feast on a down-home, all-you-can-eat barbecue (fried chicken, smoked ribs, salad, corn on the cob, baked beans, bread, salad, strawberry shortcake, and your choice of coffee, tea, beer, wine, sangria, or soda), all served up family style in tin buckets. While you stuff yourself silly in Pioneer Hall, performers in 1890s garb lead you in a foot-stomping, hand-clapping, high-energy show that includes plenty of jokes that you haven't heard since elementary school, but somehow seem just as funny now. The audience is quickly caught up in all the hoopla, and even the most skeptical find themselves having plenty of fun. Although the songs and skits are a bit corny, the talent is absolutely stellar. Audience participation is heavily encouraged, and the cast is more than happy to help you single out your friends.

If you catch one of the early shows, consider sticking around for the Electrical Water Pageant at 9:45 p.m., viewed from the Fort Wilderness Beach.

 Upon arriving at Fort Wilderness, you'll need to park in the guest lot and take the resort's internal bus system to Pioneer Hall, where the show is held. Add at least an extra half-hour to your traveling time because of this.

 You can make reservations up to 180 days in advance. Your travel dates will determine how far in advance to call; during holidays, spring break, and summer, make your reservations as early as possible. You have to pay the entire bill when making the reservation, but if you have to cancel, you'll be refunded your entire payment as long as you call at least 48 hours prior to the day of your scheduled show.

A new tiered pricing system is now in place — the closer you sit to the action, the higher the price you'll pay. Seating in tier 1 is located on the first floor nearest the stage; seating in tier 2 is in the back half of the first floor and in the center of the balcony; seating in tier 3 is to the right and left sides on the balcony level. To be honest, though, there's really not a bad seat in the house.

See map p. 344. 3520 N. Fort Wilderness Trail (at Disney's Fort Wilderness Resort & Campground). ☎ *407-939-3463.* www.disneyworld.com. *Reservations required. Shows: 5, 7:15, and 9:30 p.m. Admission: Adults $59, $55, and $51; kids 3–9 $31, $27, and $26; prices include tax and tip. AE, DISC, MC, V. Table seating. Parking: Free.*

Makahiki Luau
SeaWorld

SeaWorld's entry on the Orlando dinner circuit starts with the arrival of the tribal chief via boat, with a ceremonial progression leading the audience into a theater located in the **Seafire Inn,** in the park's Waterfront district (see Chapter 20 for more about SeaWorld). You'll experience ancient customs, rhythmic music and dance, authentic costumes, and family-style dining on Polynesian-influenced cuisine that includes tropical fruit, mahimahi, sweet-and-sour pork, Hawaiian chicken, island vegetables, fried rice, dessert, and beverages, including one free cocktail. My only complaint is that the ventilation in the theater isn't adequate for all the smoke used during the show. At one point, sitting at one of the front tables, I couldn't see anything, not even my food.

See map p. 297. 7007 SeaWorld Dr. (inside the Waterfront at SeaWorld). ☎ *800-327-2420.* www.seaworld.com. *Reservations required. Park admission not required. Shows: 5:30 and 8:15 p.m. Admission: $46 adults, $29 kids 3–9. AE, DISC, MC, V. Table seating. Parking: $10.*

Medieval Times
Kissimmee

Orlando has one of eight Medieval Times shows in the United States and Canada. Inside, guests gorge themselves on garlic bread, barbecued spare ribs, herb-roasted chicken, vegetable soup, appetizers, roasted potatoes, a pastry dessert, and beverages, including beer. But because this show is set in the 11th century, you eat with your fingers from metal plates while knights mounted on Andalusian horses run around the arena, jousting and clanging to please the fair maidens. Arrive 30 minutes early to allow time to tour the Medieval Village, a re-created Middle Ages settlement. There are plenty of opportunities to part with your cash, including photos and toys, so set your limits ahead of time.

See map p. 311. 4510 W. Irlo Bronson Memorial Hwy. (U.S. Hwy. 192, 11 miles east of the main WDW entrance, next to Wal-Mart). ☎ *800-229-8300 or 407-396-1518.* www.medievaltimes.com. *Reservations recommended. Shows nightly; times vary. Admission: $57 adults, $36 kids 3–11. AE, DISC, MC, VISA. Stadium-style seating. Parking: Free.*

MurderWatch Mystery Theatre
Lake Buena Vista

Mystery lovers, rejoice! The game's afoot every Saturday night at this all-you-can-eat buffet, which offers beef, chicken, fish, and a separate children's buffet while diners try to solve a mystery. The proceedings take place in the LakeView restaurant at the Regal Sun Resort. This somewhat sophisticated offering is one of the city's best.

See map p. 311. 1850 Hotel Plaza Blvd. (at the Regal Sun Resort). Turn west off Hwy. 535 onto Hotel Plaza Blvd.; it's close to Downtown Disney Marketplace. ☎ ***800-624-4109*** *or 407-827-6534.* www.murderwatch.com. *Reservations recommended. Shows: Sat 6 p.m. Admission: $40 adults, $11 kids 3–9. AE, DISC, MC, V. Table seating. Parking: Free.*

Pirate's Dinner Adventure
International Drive Area

The special-effects show at this theater includes a full-size ship in a 300,000-gallon lagoon, circus-style aerial acts, a lot of music, and swordfights by swashbuckling pirates. Dinner includes an appetizer buffet with the preshow, followed by a choice of roast chicken, roast pork, or garlic lobster with shrimp, plus rice, vegetables, dessert, and coffee. After the show, you're invited to the Buccaneer Bash dance party, where you can mingle with cast members. This show gets somewhat mixed reviews; the more favorable come from kids with an affinity for pirates and swordfights. The arena is smaller than some of the others in the area, which makes it a slightly friendlier experience overall.

See map p. 311. 6400 Carrier Dr. (from Disney, take I-4 to Sand Lake Rd., go east to International Dr., and then north to Carrier). ☎ ***800-866-2469*** *or 407-248-0590.* www.orlandopirates.com. *Reservations recommended. Showtimes vary. Admission: $58–$62 adults, $36–$41 kids 3–11; prices include tax. AE, DC, DISC, MC, V. Stadium-style seating. Parking: Free.*

Sleuths Mystery Dinner Shows
International Drive Area

While catering more to an adult crowd (though two afternoon versions for kids are available), the mysteries solved here are absolutely hilarious whodunits. In an intimate theater, guests are seated around small tables. After some of the characters serve hot and cold hors d'oeuvres, the show begins. Dinner is served between acts and includes a choice of Cornish game hen, herb stuffing, baked potato, vegetables, and cranberry sauce; prime rib (for an additional $3) with baked potato and vegetables; or four-cheese lasagna (with or without meat), vegetables, and garlic bread. You also get dessert and unlimited beer, wine, and soft drinks. Guests are encouraged to discuss the clues to solve the murder. The more the audience participates (which often seems directly related to the amount of alcohol they consume), the more amusing the show can be. Eleven unique mysteries keep guests coming back for more.

Discounts are often available online, as well as in many of the tourist publications.

See map p. 311. 8267 International Dr. (take I-4 East to Exit 75A; turn right at the light onto Universal Blvd.; Sleuth's is 1 mile down on the right in the Gooding's Plaza). ☎ *800-393-1985 or 407-363-1985.* www.sleuths.com. *Reservations recommended. Showtimes vary, with between 1 and 4 shows offered daily. Admission: $49 adults, $24 kids. AE, DISC, MC, V. Table seating. Parking: Free.*

Getting Information and Tickets for Other Events

Dozens of rock, rap, jazz, pop, country, blues, and folk stars are in town during any given week in Orlando. You can find schedules in the *Orlando Sentinel*'s Friday Calendar section, available online at www.orlandosentinel.com. The *Orlando Weekly*'s Calendar section (www.orlandoweekly.com) is also a good source for live-music events, including club schedules. **Metromix** (www.orlando.metromix.com) is yet another that features up-to-date information on area nightlife.

Ticketmaster is the key reservations player for most major events in Orlando, including concerts, shows, and professional sports. If you know of an event that's happening while you're in town, check first with your hometown Ticketmaster outlet to find out whether it sells tickets for the event. (If you live as close as Miami or Atlanta, it probably does.) Otherwise, call the Ticketmaster outlet in Orlando at ☎ **877-803-7073** or 407-839-3900, or go to its Web site at www.ticketmaster.com.

You can get additional event information — and often order tickets as well — from the **Orlando/Orange County Convention & Visitors Bureau** (☎ **407-363-5872;** www.orlandoinfo.com).

Chapter 25

Hitting the Clubs and Bars

• •

In This Chapter

▶ Rockin' the night away at Walt Disney World
▶ Cruising the clubs at Universal's CityWalk
▶ Exploring hotspots inside Orlando's hotels
▶ Finding a few more places to party

• •

*A*lthough Orlando has a reputation as a daylight destination, its nighttime offerings continue to grow as fun-seekers aren't ready to call it quits after a day at the parks.

Clubs such as **Rix Lounge** at Disney's Coronado Springs Resort and the **House of Blues** on **Disney's West Side** rock well into the wee hours. Universal Orlando's **CityWalk** entertainment district features nightspots such as **the groove, Rising Star,** and the **Red Coconut Club.**

A few of the clubs that I list in this chapter are open to anyone 18 or older, but remember that the minimum drinking age in Florida is 21, and the clubs will check your ID.

No More Guilty Pleasures at Pleasure Island

In a past life, this 6-acre warehouse-themed entertainment district claimed ownership to several nightclubs, bars, shops, and eateries. However, as of September 2008, the various clubs and bars stand quiet, their doors closed for good. While rumors had begun surfacing over the past several months, each pointing to an impending overhaul, Disney only confirmed plans to renovate the island as this guide went to press. Replacing the clubs will be a slew of upscale restaurants, trendy shops, and immersive attractions that include, among others, a gigantic tethered balloon. Enhancements and upgrades to existing restaurants (including the transformation of the Portobello Yacht Club into the Tuscan Country Trattoria, the addition of T-Rex, and updates to Fulton's Crab House) as well as construction of an all-new Marketplace Stage are included in the plans. Upon completion, the reimagined island will fall more in line with the existing Marketplace and West Side, widening its appeal to more than just the 21-and-over club crowd. Reopening in stages (beginning in late 2009), the island is scheduled to be complete by 2010. In the meantime, shops (including the all-new **Curl by Sammy Duvall, Orlando Harley-Davidson,** and **Fuego by Sosa Cigars**) and eateries (including **Raglan Road,** among others) will remain operational throughout the reconstruction. Self-parking is free. For information, call ☎ **407-939-2648** or check out Disney's Web site at www.disneyworld.com.

Exploring Downtown Disney's West Side

Immediately adjacent to Pleasure Island, Disney's West Side is a district where you'll find clubs, restaurants, and **DisneyQuest** (see Chapter 16).

Singer Gloria Estefan and her husband, Emilio, created **Bongos Cuban Café** (☎ **407-828-0999;** www.bongoscubancafe.com), an eatery/nightspot where a Desi Arnaz look-alike may show up to croon a few tunes. The upbeat salsa music makes this place noisy, so flee to the patio or upstairs if you want privacy. All in all, this isn't one of Florida's better Cuban restaurants, so you're better off coming for the atmosphere rather than the food (which will run you from $10–$26). Bongos is open daily from 11 a.m. to 2 a.m. and doesn't take reservations. You can find plenty of free self-parking.

Cirque du Soleil isn't your ordinary circus. It doesn't have any lions, tigers, or bears — but you won't feel cheated. This "Circus of the Sun" is nonstop energy. The eye-popping *La Nouba* (derived from the French for "to live it up"), set in a custom-built, state-of-the-art theater, is a Fellini-style amalgam of live music, dance, theater, and acrobatics that will have your jaw dropping in no time at all. Highlights include a cyclist who does things with a bicycle that would make an X-Gamer jealous, a spectacular coordinated trampoline performance, and a pint-size troupe of Chinese acrobats who do tricks with *diabolos* (Chinese yo-yos) that bring the house down. I rank this one just beneath Las Vegas's *Mystère,* though the comedic interludes in this production are the best of all the permanent Cirque shows. Though *La Nouba* is a ton of fun, it's also one of the priciest shows in town, so you need to decide if your budget can take the hit. Ticket prices vary according to location (don't feel you must spend extra for the expensive seats — nearly every spot in the theater offers a good view) and range from $65 to $114 for adults, $52 to $91 for children ages 3 to 9 (plus 6.5 percent sales tax). Shows are usually at 6 p.m. and 9 p.m. Tuesdays through Saturdays, though the show is dark six weeks each year. Occasional matinees are on offer, so call ahead (☎ **407-939-7600**) or check the show's Web site (www.cirquedusoleil.com) for information and tickets.

Downtown Disney

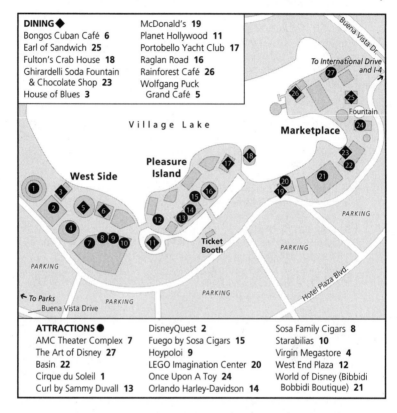

DINING◆

Bongos Cuban Café **6**
Earl of Sandwich **25**
Fulton's Crab House **18**
Ghirardelli Soda Fountain
  & Chocolate Shop **23**
House of Blues **3**

McDonald's **19**
Planet Hollywood **11**
Portobello Yacht Club **17**
Raglan Road **16**
Rainforest Café **26**
Wolfgang Puck
  Grand Café **5**

Village Lake

Marketplace

Pleasure
Island

West Side

Fountain

To International Drive
and I-4

Buena Vista Dr.

Ticket
Booth

PARKING

PARKING

PARKING

PARKING

PARKING

↖ To Parks
Buena Vista Drive

Hotel Plaza Blvd.

ATTRACTIONS●

AMC Theater Complex **7**
The Art of Disney **27**
Basin **22**
Cirque du Soleil **1**
Curl by Sammy Duvall **13**

DisneyQuest **2**
Fuego by Sosa Cigars **15**
Hoypoloi **9**
LEGO Imagination Center **20**
Once Upon A Toy **24**
Orlando Harley-Davidson **14**

Sosa Family Cigars **8**
Starabilias **10**
Virgin Megastore **4**
West End Plaza **12**
World of Disney (Bibbidi
  Bobbidi Boutique) **21**

Plus-size guests may find the seating at the Cirque du Soleil show a bit narrow — you can request a folding chair upon arrival.

The rafters in the **House of Blues** literally shake with rhythm and blues. The House is decorated with folk art, buttons, and bottle caps, and the patio has a view of the bay. If you like spicy food, offerings such as gumbo and jambalaya ($6–$19) are respectable. Sunday's **Gospel Brunch** ($33 adults, $16 kids 3–12) has foot-stomping music served with decent food (omelets, prime rib, smoked catfish, cheese grits, and chicken jambalaya, among other assorted items). Brunch is the only time you can make reservations. Guests who dine before attending a show that night are often eligible for early admission, which is handy for the general-admission shows. Ask your server for details, call ☎ **407-934-2583,** or go to www.hob.com. House of Blues is open daily from 11 a.m. to 2 a.m. and offers free self-parking.

Walt Disney World Nightlife

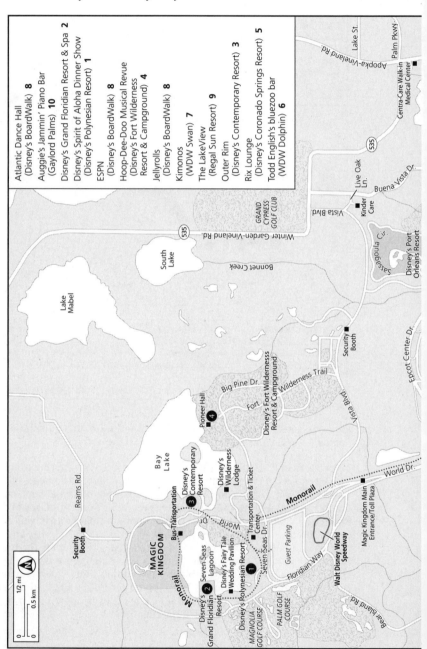

Atlantic Dance Hall
(Disney's BoardWalk) **8**

Auggie's Jammin' Piano Bar
(Gaylord Palms) **10**

Disney's Grand Floridian Resort & Spa **2**

Disney's Spirit of Aloha Dinner Show
(Disney's Polynesian Resort) **1**

ESPN
(Disney's BoardWalk) **8**

Hoop-Dee-Doo Musical Revue
(Disney's Fort Wilderness
Resort & Campground) **4**

Jellyrolls
(Disney's BoardWalk) **8**

Kimonos
(WDW Swan) **7**

The LakeView
(Regal Sun Resort) **9**

Outer Rim
(Disney's Contemporary Resort) **3**

Rix Lounge
(Disney's Coronado Springs Resort) **5**

Todd English's bluezoo bar
(WDW Dolphin) **6**

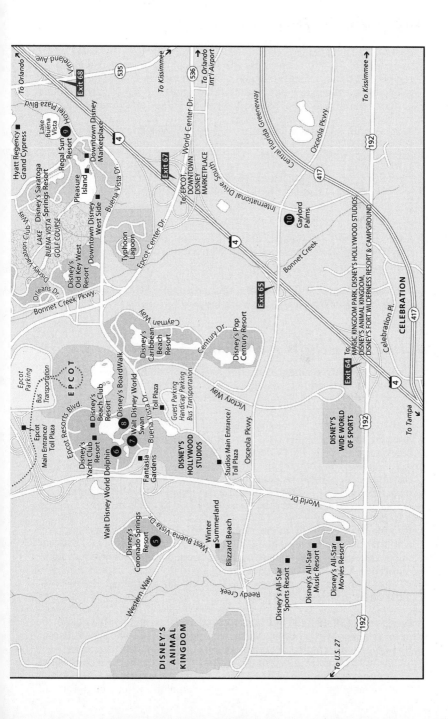

Strolling Along Disney's BoardWalk

Part of the same-named resort (see Chapter 9), the BoardWalk is home to several clubs and restaurants and is a great place for strolling and people-watching. Street performers sing, dance, juggle, and make a little magic most evenings. It has something of a midway atmosphere reminiscent of Atlantic City's heyday. Following are three standout options here:

- ✔ **Atlantic Dance Hall** features Top 40 and '80s dance hits Tuesdays through Saturdays. It's open to everyone 21 and older from 9 p.m. to 2 a.m. There's no cover.

- ✔ If you need a game fix, **ESPN Club** has 100 TV screens (there are even a few inside the bathrooms!), a full-service bar, food, and a small arcade, all without a cover charge. It's *the* sports mecca in town.

- ✔ The rustic, saloon-style **Jellyrolls** offers dueling pianos. Strictly for the over-21 set, it's open daily from 7 p.m. to 2 a.m. There's a $10 cover.

You can get information on all the spots listed here by calling ☎ 407-939-3463 or going to www.disneyworld.com.

Dancing the Night Away at CityWalk

Universal's entertainment district is a two-level collection of clubs and restaurants located between its two theme parks (Universal Studios Florida and Islands of Adventure). **CityWalk** (☎ 407-363-8000; www.universalorlando.com or www.citywalk.com) is open from 11 a.m. to 2 a.m. daily. Although no admission is charged, several clubs have cover charges after 5 or 6 p.m. and sometimes as late as 8 or 9 p.m. CityWalk also offers **Party Passes.** A pass to all clubs is $12 plus tax; for $15 plus tax, you get a movie at **Universal Cineplex** (☎ 407-354-5998). Universal also offers free club access to those who buy multiday theme-park tickets (see Chapters 18–19). Daytime parking in the Universal Orlando garages costs $12, but parking is free after 6 p.m.

Bob Marley–A Tribute to Freedom (☎ 407-224-3663) has architecture said to replicate Marley's home in Kingston, Jamaica. Local and national reggae bands perform frequently. Light Jamaican fare is served under umbrellas. The club is open daily from 4 p.m. to 2 a.m. There's a cover of $7 after 8 p.m., a price that goes up for concerts on special nights. You must be 21 or older after 9 p.m.

the groove (☎ 407-363-8000) has a loud sound system and a dance floor gleaming with chrome. Music-wise, it features hip-hop, jazz fusion, techno, and alternative. A DJ plays tunes on nights when recording artists aren't booked. Each of the club's three color-themed lounges has a bar and a specialty drink to fit its ambience. You must be at least 21 to enter (except on the occasional all-ages teen night, when you'll want to

CityWalk

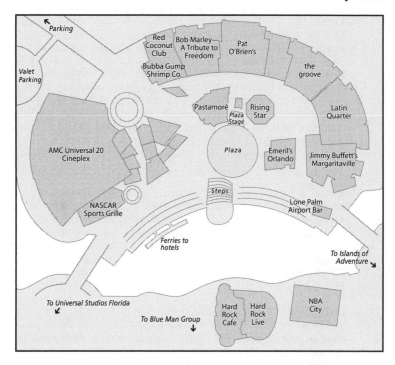

stay as far away from the place as possible). The club is open from 9 p.m. to 2 a.m., sometimes later. There's a cover of $7.

CityWalk's **Hard Rock Cafe** is the largest in the world, and the adjoining **Hard Rock Live** (☎ 407-351-5483; www.hardrock.com) is the first concert hall bearing the name. The cafe also has a free exhibit area, where you can browse displays of rock memorabilia, including the platform heels and leather jumpsuits of KISS. Concert prices vary by act, and MTV often films concert specials here. It's open daily from 11 a.m. to midnight.

Flip-flops and flowered shirts equal **Jimmy Buffett's Margaritaville** (☎ 407-224-2155; www.margaritavilleorlando.com). Tunes are piped through the building during the day, with a Jimmy sound-alike strumming on the back porch around dusk. Inside, there's nightly live entertainment, though nothing extraordinary. Bar-wise, you have three options: The Volcano erupts (I'm not kidding) killer margaritas; the Land Shark has fins swimming around the ceiling; and the 12 Volt is, well, a little electrifying. The menu screams "Key West!" — which means Cheeseburgers in Paradise, mahimahi, and Key lime pie. (See Chapter 10 for more information on the food front.) Margaritaville is open from 11:30 a.m. to 2 a.m. There's a $7 cover after 10 p.m.

The two-level **Latin Quarter** (☎ 407-224-3663) restaurant/club offers you a chance to absorb the salsa-and-samba culture and cuisine of 21 Latin nations. It's filled with the music of the merengue and the mambo, with a little Latin rock thrown in for good measure. The sound system is loud enough to blow you into the next county. It's open daily from 4 to 10 p.m.

Head over to the **Red Coconut Club** (☎ 407-224-3663), CityWalk's new two-story cocktail lounge, where you can sip martinis under the stars. An outdoor balcony offers the perfect spot to sit and sip exotic concoctions, while indoors offers a more intimate (though somewhat louder) setting. Martinis, an extensive wine list, and gourmet appetizers will keep you going all night long. Live music and DJs crank the tunes out daily. The Red Coconut is open Sunday through Thursday from 8 p.m. to 2 a.m., Friday and Saturday from 6 p.m. to 2 a.m. There's a $7 cover after 9 p.m.

Guessing the focus of a place that has a one-page food menu and a booklet filled with drinks doesn't take a genius. Just like the French Quarter's version, drinking is the highlight at **Pat O'Brien's** (☎ 407-363-8000). You can enjoy dueling pianos and a flame-throwing fountain while you suck down the signature drink — the Hurricane. Pat O'Brien's offers a limited menu of sandwiches, snacks, and treats like jambalaya and shrimp Creole ($8–$10). Hours are 4 p.m. to 2 a.m. No one younger than 21 is permitted after 9 p.m.

Rising Star (☎ 407-224-3663), replacing CityJazz, is CityWalk's latest addition to date. This all-new karaoke club features a live band, backup singers, and a host to get things going every Tuesday through Saturday; on Sundays and Mondays, the music's recorded, but the backup singers and host are live. There's a cover of $7 (no charge to sing). You must be 21 or older to enter, except on Thursdays, when you must be 18 or older.

Locating the Best Hotel Lounges

Some of Orlando's best nightlife is located in its hotels. Even the locals head to the resort areas for fun after dark. If you're staying at one of the places listed here, you can do an evening on the town without ever getting behind the wheel. None of the following charges a cover.

Rix, at Disney's Coronado Springs Resort (☎ 407-939-3806; www.rix-lounge.com), is a surprisingly sophisticated un-Disney-like lounge. It tempts guests with gourmet appetizers and signature drinks in a chic and trendy Mediterranean-inspired atmosphere.

At **Disney's Grand Floridian Resort & Spa** (☎ 407-824-3000), a pianist and band alternate playing time from 3 to 9:45 p.m. in the lobby. Meanwhile, **Outer Rim,** at Disney's Contemporary Resort (☎ 407-824-1000), is a trendy nightspot and close to the monorail.

Todd English's bluezoo bar, at the Walt Disney World Dolphin (☎ 407-934-1111; www.thebluezoo.com), serves up classic cocktails in a hip

Downtown Orlando

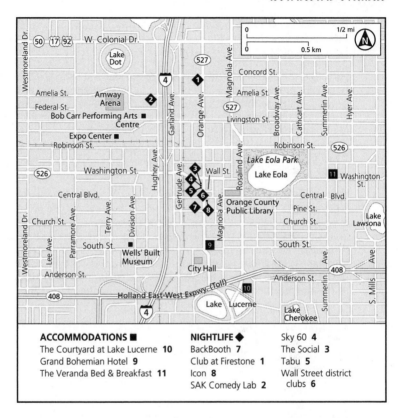

ACCOMMODATIONS ■	NIGHTLIFE ◆	
The Courtyard at Lake Lucerne **10**	BackBooth **7**	Sky 60 **4**
Grand Bohemian Hotel **9**	Club at Firestone **1**	The Social **3**
The Veranda Bed & Breakfast **11**	Icon **8**	Tabu **5**
	SAK Comedy Lab **2**	Wall Street district clubs **6**

and chic atmosphere. Over at the Walt Disney World Swan, **Kimonos** (☎ **407-934-3000**) offers karaoke after 8:30 p.m. to accompany its sushi.

The entertainment is purely visual at **Mist Sushi & Spirits,** at the Renaissance Orlando Resort at SeaWorld (☎ **407-351-5555**), which sits beneath the huge atrium overlooking the all-new trendy interior.

The **LakeView,** at the Regal Sun Resort (☎ **407-827-6534**), offers a solve-it-yourself mystery dinner show called **MurderWatch Mystery Theatre,** on Saturdays at 6 p.m. ($40 adults, $11 kids 3–9). (See Chapter 24 for details.)

Auggie's Jammin' Piano Bar, at the Gaylord Palms (☎ **407-586-0000**), offers dueling pianos at 9 p.m. nightly. Sit back and relax (in velvet chairs, I might add) at the **Velvet Lounge,** at the Hard Rock Hotel (☎ **407-503-3700**), where you can down cocktails while surrounded by rock-'n'-roll memorabilia and music.

Exploring Orlando's Other Hotspots

Downtown Orlando is home to a number of clubs and bars offering a vibrant nightlife. Here's my list of favorites:

- ✔ **Club at Firestone,** 578 N. Orange Ave. (☎ **407-872-0066;** www. clubfirestone.com), is home to a revolving list of parties that take place each day of the week. It continuously books some of the best DJs on the dance-music scene, especially on Saturday nights. The cover is $5, sometimes higher depending on the event. It's open daily from 8 p.m. to 2 a.m.

- ✔ **Icon,** 20 E. Central Blvd. (☎ **407-649-6496**), is a chic and trendy downtown hotspot where the first-level dance floor is always packed. The second-level balcony is the perfect perch for celebrity-spotting. DJs spin electronica, techno, and house sounds. It's open Tuesday through Saturday from 10 p.m. to 2 a.m.

- ✔ Locals perform at the 200-seat **SAK Comedy Lab,** 380 W. Amelia St. (☎ **407-648-0001;** www.sak.com), which offers several perform-ances weekly. Favorite acts include **Duel of Fools,** where two teams face off in improvised scenes based on suggestions from the audi-ence, and **Lab Rats,** where students play in improv formats. Admission costs $5 to $13. Shows usually take place Tuesday and Wednesday at 9 p.m., Thursday at 8 p.m., Friday at 8 and 10 p.m., and Saturday at 6, 8, and 10 p.m.

- ✔ **The Social,** 54 N. Orange Ave. (☎ **407-246-1419;** www.thesocial. org), the best spot in town for live music, offers an eclectic mix that changes dramatically from night to night. You're just as likely to hear an urban groove as the next big punk band on the airwaves. A $5 to $10 cover is charged for those 18 and older; covers for national acts vary. It's open daily from 8 p.m. to 2 a.m. Other nearby options include the **BackBooth** (☎ **407-999-2570;** www.backbooth.com), where jeans and a T-shirt are the norm as the atmosphere is far more laid back than most, and **Sky 60** (☎ **407-246-1599;** www.sky60.com), with its outdoor rooftop bar and upscale South Beach style (think hip, casual-chic dress code).

- ✔ **Tabu,** 46 N. Orange Ave. (☎ **407-648-8363;** www.tabunightclub. com), is one of the city's hottest see-and-be-seen spots. The Art Deco club boasts three dance floors and something of an attitude. DJs spin hip-hop records; live bands provide additional music. The club also hosts theme nights. A private lounge for VIPs means you may see a famous face or two. Leave the denim at home, though — the club's upscale dress code is strictly enforced. Cover is $5 to $12 on most nights. It's open Tuesday through Sunday from 10 p.m. to 2 a.m.

- ✔ Several downtown hotspots are clustered in the Wall Street district. **Chillers, Big Belly Brewery,** and **Latitudes** (☎ **407-939-4270;** www.churchstreetbars.com) offer three very different experi-ences, all in a single building. The trio of clubs is geared to the young-adult crowd with an atmosphere that's very casual. **Wall St. Plaza** (www.wallstplaza.net) is home to a wide variety of clubs, including the **Globe** (☎ 407-849-9904), a European patio cafe; **Slingapour's** (☎ 407-849-9904), a dance club with an indoor and outdoor patio for relaxing; **Waitiki** (☎ 407-849-0471), a retro Tiki lounge and restaurant; and the **Monkey Bar** (☎ 407-849-0471), a hip martini lounge and cocktail bar. Hours and cover charges vary, so call ahead.

In addition to the above recommendations, you can find out more about Orlando's nightlife by checking out **Metromix** (www.orlando.metro mix.com) — it's a great source for the latest information on the area's hottest clubs.

Part VII
The Part of Tens

The 5th Wave   By Rich Tennant

Tell them we work at one of the theme parks, and maybe they won't ask too many questions.

In this part . . .

*A*h, tradition. The Part of Tens chapters are to *For Dummies* books what noisemakers and silly hats are to New Year's Eve — an integral part of the experience. In this part of the book, I feed you plenty of useful and fun information that I think is especially handy, such as budget attractions that can stretch your dollars and fun ways to keep active when you're not at the theme parks.

Chapter 26

(Not Quite) Ten Cheap Alternatives to the Theme Parks

● ●

In This Chapter

▶ Spending some time at a museum
▶ Strolling through a real park
▶ Taking a leisurely boat tour

● ●

*I*t may shock you to learn that there are things to see and do in this city beyond Mickey, Shamu, and Shrek. I discuss some of the city's smaller but still-popular attractions in Chapter 21, but here are some hidden gems where you can dodge the enormous crowds, save a few dollars, and still have a great time while others are waiting in line or emptying their wallets at the big parks.

Audubon Center for Birds of Prey

This bird sanctuary — one of the largest rehabilitation centers in the Southeast — has treated more than 8,000 raptors and released more than 3,500 of them back into the wild since opening in 1979. It flies under the radar of most tourists, making it a great place to get to know the winged wonders (eagles, owls, hawks, and other raptors) that earn their keep by entertaining those who do visit. It's a wonderful place for nature lovers and kids who love getting up close with the feathered residents.

The center is at 1101 Audubon Way, Maitland. (Take I-4 to Lee Rd./Exit 46 and exit right; turn left at the first light [Wymore Rd.], and turn right at the next light [Kennedy Blvd.]. Continue a half-mile to East Avenue, turn left, and go to the stop sign at Audubon Way. Turn left, and the center is on the right.) For more information, call ☎ 407-644-0190 or visit www.audubonofflorida.org/who_centers_CBOP.html. The center accepts donations: $5 for adults, $4 for children 3 to 12. Visitor hours are Tuesday through Sunday from 10 a.m. to 3 p.m.

Central Florida Zoo

The animal collection at the Central Florida Zoo includes a number of endangered species, including beautiful clouded leopards and cheetahs. In addition to a lovable hippopotamus named Geraldine, you can meet black howler monkeys, siamangs, American crocodiles, a Gila monster, hyacinth macaws, bald eagles, and dozens of other species. The latest additions to the park include a puma enclosure, a rare king vulture exhibit, and an Australian exhibit featuring kangaroos and emus.

The park is located 20 to 30 minutes from Orlando at 3755 N. U.S. 17/92 in Sanford. (Take I-4 Exit 104, and follow the signs to the zoo.) For more information, call ☎ 407-323-4450 or visit www.centralfloridazoo.org. Admission is $10 for adults, $8 for seniors 60 and older, and $6 for kids 3 to 12 (children younger than 3 get in free). Strollers are available for rent at a cost of $3 or $6, depending on the type. The park is open daily from 9 a.m. to 5 p.m. and closes only on Thanksgiving and Christmas.

Charles Hosmer Morse Museum of American Art

Louis Comfort Tiffany is in the spotlight at the Charles Hosmer Morse Museum of American Art, and if you're a fan of the artist, a stop here is a must. This museum, founded in 1942, has 40 vibrantly colored windows and 21 paintings by the master artist. In addition, there are non-Tiffany windows ranging from creations by Frank Lloyd Wright to the works of 15th-century German masters. Also look for leaded lamps by Tiffany and Emile Gallé; paintings by John Singer Sargent and Maxfield Parrish; jewelry designed by Tiffany, Lalique, and Fabergé; and Art Nouveau furnishings.

The museum is at 445 Park Ave. N., in Winter Park. (Take the I-4 Fairbanks Ave. exit east to Park Ave., and then go left and through four traffic lights.) For more details, call ☎ 407-645-5311 or 407-645-5324 (a telephone recording), or check online at www.morsemuseum.org. Admission is $3 for adults, $1 for students 12 to 17; kids younger than 12 are free. The museum is open Tuesday through Saturday from 9:30 a.m. to 4 p.m., Sunday from 1 to 4 p.m. Between November and April, the museum remains open until 8 p.m. on Fridays, with free admission after 4 p.m.

Cornell Fine Arts Museum

This showplace has 6,000 works on display (European and American paintings, sculpture, and decorative art), making it one of Florida's most distinguished and comprehensive art collections. The museum also conducts lectures and gallery talks.

The museum is located at the east end of Holt Avenue on the Rollins College campus in Winter Park. (Take I-4 Exit 45/Fairbanks Ave. east to Park; turn right, and then left on Holt.) Admission is $5 for adults; free for students with current ID. The museum is open Tuesday through Saturday from 10 a.m. to 5 p.m., Sunday from 1 to 5 p.m. Parking is free with validation. Call ☎ 407-646-2526 or visit www.rollins.edu/cfam for more information.

Eatonville and the Zora Neale Hurston National Museum of Fine Arts

America's oldest black municipality is located just north of Orlando. Eatonville is the birthplace of Zora Neale Hurston — a too-little heralded African-American author. The best time to visit is in January, during the city's annual festival honoring her and her work. A small on-site gallery displays periodically changing exhibits of art and other work, and you can grab a map for a walking tour of the community, established in 1887.

The museum is at 227 E. Kennedy Blvd., Eatonville. (Take I-4 to Exit 46 and make a quick left onto Lee Rd., then left on Wymore, and then right on Kennedy. It's a quarter-mile down the road on the left.) Call ☎ 800-972-3310 or 407-647-3307, or visit www.zoranealehurstonfestival.com for more information. The museum accepts donations and is open Monday through Friday from 9 a.m. to 4 p.m.

Lake Eola Park

This quiet hideaway in downtown Orlando offers the city's skyline as a backdrop. The 43-acre park has a walking and jogging path, a playground, and swan-shaped paddleboats for rent if you want to take a quiet ride across the 23-acre lake. You can relax and feed the swans, birds, and fish (in certain areas only). There's also a small cafe. A variety of performances takes place throughout the year, most of which are free. The **Orlando Shakespeare Theater** (Apr to early May) costs $10 to $30 nightly. Call ☎ 407-447-1700 or head online to www.orlandoshakes.org for more information about the festival.

The park is located at Washington Street and Rosalind Avenue, Orlando. (Take I-4 to Anderson St., exit right, and turn left at the fourth light [Rosalind]. The amphitheater is on the right.) Call ☎ 407-246-2827 or check online at www.ci.orlando.fl.us/cys/recreation/lake_eola.htm for more information about the park and details on scheduled performances. The park is open daily during daylight hours, sometimes later. Admission is free.

Lakeridge Winery and Vineyards

Lakeridge Winery & Vineyards produces some of Florida's more note-worthy vintages. Tours include a look behind the scenes at the working vineyard and winery, a video presentation, and, of course, tastings.

The winery is at 19239 U.S. 27, Clermont. (Take U.S. 192 west of the WDW parks to U.S. 27, turn right, and go 25 miles north.) Call ☎ **800-768-9463** or visit www.lakeridgewinery.com for more information. Tours and tastings are offered from 10 a.m. to 5 p.m. Monday through Saturday, and from 11 a.m. to 5 p.m. on Sunday. Admission is free. Special and seasonal events are offered throughout the year. Admission is free for most events; select events cost $2.

The Peabody Ducks

One of the best shows in town is short, but sweet — and free. The posh Peabody Orlando hotel's five mallards march into the lobby each morn-ing, accompanied by John Philip Sousa's "King Cotton March" and their own red-coated duck master. They get to spend the day splashing in a marble fountain. Then, in the afternoon, they march back to the elevator and up to their fourth-floor "penthouse."

The hotel is at 9801 International Dr. (btw. the Beachline Expwy. and Sand Lake Rd.). Call ☎ **800-732-2639** or 407-352-4000 for more informa-tion, or go online to www.peabodyorlando.com. Admission is free. The ducks march daily at 11 a.m. and 5 p.m.

Winter Park Scenic Boat Tour

This peaceful water voyage has been operating since 1938. The narrated one-hour cruises showcase the area's beautiful lakes and canals, Rollins College, Kraft Azalea Gardens, and a number of historic mansions. Native wildlife, including cranes and alligators, may also make an appearance.

The boat tour launches from 312 E. Morse Blvd., Winter Park. Call ☎ **407-644-4056** or check out www.scenicboattours.com for addi-tional information. Admission is $10 for adults and $5 for children ages 2 to 11; kids younger than 2 are free. Weather permitting, the tours run daily, except Christmas, every hour from 10 a.m. to 4 p.m.

Chapter 27

Ten Recreational Activities in Orlando

● ●

In This Chapter

▶ Enjoying water-related activities
▶ Getting land-based exercise

● ●

*W*ant some exercise other than pounding theme-park pavement? Disney World and the surrounding areas offer plenty of recreational jaunts to keep even the most active people busy. The majority of these activities are most convenient for guests of Disney's resorts and official hotels, but many of the area's other resorts offer comprehensive facilities as well. The facilities I describe in this chapter are open to the public, regardless of where you're staying. For further information, call ☎ **407-939-7529** or visit www.disneyworld.com, hover over "More Magic," and then click "Other Recreation."

Biking

Bike rentals (single- and multispeed bikes, tandems, surreys, and children's bikes) are available from the **Bike Barn** (☎ **407-824-2742**) at **Disney's Fort Wilderness Resort & Campground,** which also has extensive bike trails. Rates run $8 per hour, $22 per day. You can also rent bicycles with training wheels and baby seats.

Boating

Cap'n Jack's (☎ **407-828-2204**) at **Downtown Disney** rents Sea Raycers by Sea Ray, Boston Whaler Montauks, and Sun Tracker Pontoons ($32–$48 per half-hour).

The **Bike Barn** at **Disney's Fort Wilderness Resort & Campground** (☎ **407-824-2742**) rents canoes and paddleboats ($6.50 per half-hour), canopy boats ($27 per half-hour), Sea Raycers ($32 per half-hour), pedal boats ($7 per half-hour), small sailboats ($20 per hour), and pontoon boats ($48 per half-hour).

Fishing

Disney offers a variety of fishing excursions (catch and release only) on various Disney lakes, including Bay Lake and Seven Seas Lagoon. The lakes are stocked, so you may catch something, but true anglers probably won't find it much of a challenge. You can arrange **B.A.S.S.** (Bass Anglers Sportsman Society) excursions 24 hours to 14 days in advance by calling ☎ **407-939-2277.** A license isn't required. The fee is $225 to $250 for up to five people for two hours, $435 for up to five people for four hours, including refreshments, gear, guide, and tax. Kids can get in on the action as well: Tours are available for children 6 to 12 at a cost of $28 for a one-hour excursion.

Here's a less expensive alternative: Rent fishing poles at the **Bike Barn** (☎ **407-824-2742;** $6 per hour or $10 per day, bait $3.50–$3.65) to fish in **Disney's Fort Wilderness** canals. A license isn't necessary.

Golf

Disney operates five 18-hole, par-72 golf courses and one 9-hole, par-36 walking course. All are open to the public and offer pro shops, equipment rentals, and instruction. The rates are $99 to $169 per 18-hole round for resort guests ($10 more if you're not staying at a WDW property). Rates depend on the course, the season, and the time of day you play. Twilight specials are often available. For tee times and information, call ☎ **407-939-4653** up to 60 days in advance (up to 90 days for Disney-resort and official-property guests). Call ☎ **407-934-7639** for information about golf packages. (For more details about each of the Disney courses, see Chapter 16.)

Beyond Mickey's shadow, **Celebration Golf Club** (☎ **888-275-2918** or 407-566-4653; www.celebrationgolf.com) has an 18-hole regulation course (greens fees are $69–$129, depending on the day and season) and a 3-hole junior course for 5- to 9-year-olds. Florida residents play for lower fees. **ChampionsGate Golf Club** (☎ **407-787-4653;** www.champions gategolf.com) offers 36 holes designed by Greg Norman; greens fees will set you back from $55 to $175.

Golf magazine recognized the 45 holes designed by Jack Nicklaus at the **Villas of Grand Cypress** as among the best in the nation. Tee times begin at 8 a.m. daily. Special rates are available for children under 18. For information, call ☎ **407-239-1909** or go to www.grandcypress.com. Greens fees run $120 to $175 for guests, $180 to $250 for nonguests. Lessons are available for $135 to $175 per hour.

Relative newcomers worth noting include **Shingle Creek Golf Club** and the **Brad Brewer Golf Academy** (☎ **866-966-9933** or 407-966-9933; www.shinglecreekgolf.com), both located at the Rosen Shingle Creek Resort; the **Legacy, Independence,** and **Tradition** golf courses, as well as the **ANNIKA Academy,** all at the Reunion Resort & Club (☎ 888-418-9610 or 407-662-1000); and the **Ritz-Carlton Golf Club** (☎ 407-393-4906) and **Grande Pines Golf Club** (☎ 407-239-6909), both located at the **Grande Lakes Orlando** and offering the only golf caddie concierge program around, to make your game all it can be.

Golfpac (☎ 800-486-0948 or 407-260-8989; www.golfpacorlando.com) packages golf vacations with accommodations and other features; it pre-arranges tee times at more than 40 area courses. The earlier you call (months, if possible), the better your options. **Tee Times USA** (☎ 888-465-3356; www.teetimesusa.com) and **Florida Golfing** (☎ 866-833-2663; www.floridagolfing.com) also offer a reservations service.

Horseback Riding

Disney's Fort Wilderness Resort & Campground offers guided 45-minute trail rides six times a day. The cost is $42 per person. Children must be at least 9 years old; the maximum weight limit is 250 pounds. For reservations up to 30 days in advance, call ☎ 407-824-2832.

At the **Villas of Grand Cypress** equestrian center, you can go on a 45-minute, walk-trot trail ride (four times daily) for $45 (group) to $85 (private). A 30-minute private lesson is $55. Call ☎ 800-835-7377 or 407-239-1938, or surf over to www.grandcypress.com.

Jogging

Many Disney resorts have scenic jogging trails. For example, the **Yacht Club** and **Beach Club** resorts share a 2-mile trail; the **Caribbean Beach Resort** has a 1.4-mile promenade around a lake; the **Port Orleans Resort** has a 1.7-mile riverfront trail; and **Fort Wilderness**'s tree-shaded 2.3-mile jogging path has exercise stations about every quarter-mile. Pick up a trail map at any Disney hotel's Guest Relations desk.

Surfing

Learn how to catch a wave at **Typhoon Lagoon.** (See Chapter 16 for the park listing.) Instructors from the **Ron Jon Surf School** (☎ 407-939-7529) show up for an early-bird session — before the park opens to the public — in the namesake lagoon. It's limited to 14 people; the minimum age is 8. The $140 cost doesn't include park admission, which you must pay if you want to hang around after the lesson.

 If you're staying at WDW and don't have a rental car, note that you can't use the Disney Transportation system to get to the park for the 7:30 a.m. start time of the lessons; the buses don't operate that early.

Ron Jon Surfpark, scheduled to open in mid-2009 at the Festival Bay mall, at the northern end of International Drive, promises to be the coolest place to catch a wave inland. Three separate pools ensure everyone can hang ten here. Surf over to www.ronjons.com for the most up-to-date information.

Swimming

Orlando is home to an amazing number and variety of swimming pools. Whiling away the heat of the afternoon at a pool is a great way to cool off after a morning of pounding the pavement at the parks. Keep in mind, however, that you won't be the only one with this bright idea — at times, the pools can seem as crowded as the parks.

Tennis

Twenty-six lighted tennis courts are scattered throughout the Disney properties (including ten at **Disney's Wide World of Sports Complex**). Most are free and available to resort guests on a first-come, first-served basis. The courts at Disney's Grand Floridian Resort & Spa are the exception, requiring reservations. Court fees run just under $11 an hour, while private lessons are $80 per hour, $15 for a group clinic. Call ☎ 407-939-7529 to make reservations.

Water-Skiing, Wakeboarding, and other Watersports

You can wakeboard and water-ski at **Sammy Duvall's Watersports Centre,** at Disney's Contemporary Resort (☎ 407-939-0754; www.sammyduvall.com), for $155 per hour. Parasailing costs $95 for a single rider, $160 for a tandem.

Snorkeling is available at **Typhoon Lagoon** (see Chapter 16). You can scuba-dive at Epcot's **DiveQuest,** at the Seas with Nemo & Friends Pavilion (see Chapter 13).

The **Orlando Watersports Complex,** 8615 Florida Rock Rd. (☎ 407-251-3100; www.orlandowatersports.com), has lights for nighttime thrill-seekers. Prices for skiing begin at about $22 an hour for a cable and $50 for a half-hour behind a boat. Check the Web site for specials.

Buena Vista Watersports, 13245 Lake Bryan Dr. (☎ 407-239-6939; www.bvwatersports.com), has a more inviting setting and a location closer to all the action. You can rent a Sea-Doo ($50 per half-hour), water-ski, wakeboard, and go tube-riding.

Appendix

Quick Concierge

Fast Facts

AAA

AAA members can get general information, maps, and optimum driving directions, as well as book vacation packages, by calling ☎ 800-222-1134 or going to www.aaa.com.

Area Codes

The main area code for Orlando is **407**, although calls to the **321** area code are often considered local as well. *Note:* When calling within Orlando, you must always dial the full ten-digit phone number (including the area code), even if you're trying to get the store right across the street.

ATMs

Machines honoring the Cirrus (☎ 800-424-7787; www.mastercard.com), PLUS (☎ 800-843-7587; www.visa.com), and STAR (www.star.com) ATM networks are common in all of Orlando's theme parks. (See Chapters 12–15 and 18–20 for locations.) They're also found in most banks and at some shopping centers and convenience stores. (See Chapter 4 for more details on using an ATM in Orlando.)

Baby Sitters

Many Orlando hotels, including all Disney resorts, offer baby-sitting services, usually from an outside service such as Kid's Nite Out (☎ 800-696-8105 or 407-828-0920; www.kidsniteout.com) or All About Kids (☎ 800-728-6506 or 407-812-9300; www.all-about-kids.com).
Child-care rates usually run somewhere between $10 and $15 per hour for the first child and $2 to $3 per additional child, per hour, with an additional transportation fee of $10. Several of Walt Disney World's more expensive resorts also have child-care centers that cater to kids ages 4 to 12. If you'd like to take advantage of the kids' programs and enjoy a few hours off, advance reservations are a must; call ☎ 407-939-3463. All three Universal Orlando resorts offer similar services.

Business Hours

Theme-park operating hours vary depending on the time of year and the day of the week. Although most open at 8 or 9 a.m. and close at 6 or 7 p.m., you should call or check a park's Web site for its most current schedule before arriving. Other businesses are generally open from 9 a.m. to 5 p.m. Monday through Friday. Bars are usually open until 2 a.m., with some after-hours clubs staying open into the wee hours of the morning (though the alcohol stops flowing at 2 a.m.).

Camera Repair

All Disney theme parks have a photo shop where you can get minor camera repairs or pick up an extra battery (check for locations in the park guide map you get upon entering). For more serious repair work, try Southern Photo Technical Service, 606 Virginia Dr. (☎ 407-896-0322; www.spts-orlando.com).

Convention Center

Orlando's Orange County Convention Center is located at 9800 International Dr.

(☎ 800-345-9845 or 407-685-9800; www.occc.net).

Credit Cards

Call the following emergency numbers if you lose your card or your wallet is stolen: American Express, ☎ 800-221-7282; MasterCard, ☎ 800-307-7309 or 636-722-7111; Visa, ☎ 800-847-2911 or 410-581-9994. For other credit cards, call the toll-free number directory at ☎ 800-555-1212.

Doctors and Dentists

For minor problems that occur during a theme-park visit (blisters, allergic reactions), visit the park's first-aid center; these are noted on the park map you pick up when you enter. Disney offers in-room medical service 24 hours a day by calling ☎ 407-238-2000. Doctors On Call Service (☎ 407-399-3627) makes house and room calls in most of the Orlando area. Centra-Care has several walk-in clinics listed in the Yellow Pages, including ones on Vineland Road near Universal Orlando (☎ 407-351-6682), at Lake Buena Vista near Disney (☎ 407-934-2273), and in Kissimmee near Disney (☎ 407-397-7032). The Medical Concierge (☎ 407-648-5252) offers a variety of services, ranging from hotel house calls to emergency dental appointments to medical equipment rentals. There's also a 24-hour, toll-free number for the Poison Control Center (☎ 800-282-3171). To find a dentist, call Dental Referral Service (☎ 800-235-4111; www.dentalreferral.com); its phones are staffed Monday through Friday from 10 a.m. to 7 p.m. Check the Yellow Pages for 24-hour emergency services.

Emergencies

Florida uses ☎ **911** as the emergency number for police, fire departments, ambulances, and other critical needs. If you have a cellphone and need urgent help, dial ☎ *FHP for the Florida Highway Patrol.

For less-urgent requests, call ☎ 800-647-9284, a hot line sponsored by the Florida Tourism Industry Marketing Corporation, the state tourism promotion board. With operators speaking more than 100 languages, this service can provide general directions and help with lost travel papers and credit cards, medical emergencies, accidents, money transfers, airline confirmation, and much more.

Hospitals

Sand Lake Hospital, 9400 Turkey Lake Rd. (☎ 407-351-8550), is about 2 miles south of Sand Lake Road. From the WDW area, take I-4 to the Sand Lake Road exit, turn left off the exit ramp onto Sand Lake Road, and make a left on Turkey Lake Road. The hospital is 2 miles on your right. The Florida Hospital, 400 Celebration Place (☎ 407-764-4000), is located near the tourist area of Kissimmee just off U.S. 192, not far from Disney. Take U.S. 192 East and turn right onto Celebration Place; the hospital is about a half-mile up on your left.

Information

To get local telephone information, call ☎ 411.

For local tourism information, see the "Where to Get More Information" section at the end of this appendix.

Internet Access and Cybercafes

Orlando doesn't have too many cybercafes (you're supposed to be having fun in the theme parks!), and the ones it does have are generally far from the tourist zones. At Walt Disney World, there is an Internet cafe inside DisneyQuest (see Chapter 16), and you can also send e-mail at Innoventions in Epcot (see Chapter 13), though you have to pay the park admission fees to use the Web terminals. Pay phones with touch-screen displays offering Internet access have been installed at locations throughout WDW; you can access your e-mail for 25¢ a minute with a four-minute minimum.

If you're traveling with your laptop, you'll be glad to know that most Orlando hotels offer in-room dataports, and many offer high-speed Internet access (ask about access fees when booking your room), with an increasing number offering Wi-Fi in public areas. Only a select number of resorts offer in-room Wi-Fi (again, be sure to ask about access fees). Disney offers high-speed Internet access to guests at all its resorts, with limited Wi-Fi access at select resorts. All Universal Orlando resorts offer high-speed Internet access. Check with your hotel for the most up-to-date details on what type of service it currently offers and what it charges to use the service.

Liquor Laws

Florida's liquor laws are pretty straightforward. You must be 21 to buy or consume alcohol. Alcohol is sold in supermarkets and liquor stores daily from 9 a.m. to 2 a.m. It's served at bars and restaurants from 11 a.m. to 2 a.m. Some places that serve liquor allow you to enter if you're younger than 21, but most won't let you sit at the bar.

Note: No liquor is served in the Magic Kingdom at Walt Disney World. Alcoholic drinks are available, however, at the other Disney parks and are quite evident at Universal Orlando's parks (even more so at its seasonal celebrations).

Maps

AAA (see "AAA," earlier in this Quick Concierge) and other auto clubs generally provide good maps (to members), as do many Orlando rental-car agencies. The Orlando/Orange County Convention & Visitors Bureau, VISIT FLORIDA (Florida's official tourist bureau), and the Kissimmee Visitors Bureau all offer an array of area maps (which can be sent via U.S. mail upon request or picked up locally).

Pharmacies

There are 24-hour Walgreens stores at 8050 International Dr. (☎ 407-352-7071) and 5935 W. Irlo Bronson Memorial Hwy./U.S. 192 (☎ 407-396-1006). Many other locations near tourist areas can be found by checking the local phone directory or logging on to www.walgreens.com.

Post Office

The post office most convenient to Disney and Universal is at 10450 Turkey Lake Rd. (☎ 800-275-8777). It's open Monday through Friday from 8 a.m. to 7 p.m., Saturday from 9 a.m. to 5 p.m. There is also a post office located at 12133 Apopka-Vineland Rd. (☎ 800-275-8777 or 407-238-0223), close to Downtown Disney.

Restrooms

You won't find any public restrooms on the streets in Orlando, but you can usually find one in a bar, restaurant, hotel, museum, department store, convenience store, attraction, fast-food eatery, or service station — and it'll probably be clean. (You may have to purchase something to gain entrance, because many of these places reserve their restrooms for patrons only.) All the major theme parks have an abundance of clean restrooms, many of which also have baby-changing facilities (all are clearly marked on the guide map you get upon entering the park).

Safety

Don't let the aura of Mickey Mouse allow you to lower your guard. Orlando has a crime rate that's comparable to other major U.S. cities. Stay alert and remain aware of your immediate surroundings. Keeping your valuables in your in-room safe or your hotel front desk's safe-deposit box is a good idea. Keep a close eye on your valuables when you're in a public place, such as a restaurant, theater, or airport terminal. Renting a locker is always preferable to leaving your valuables in the trunk of your car, even in the theme-park lots. Be cautious and avoid carrying large amounts of cash, especially if you're carrying a backpack or fanny pack, which thieves can easily access while you're standing in line for a ride or show. If you're renting a car, carefully read the safety instructions that the rental company provides. Never stop in a dark or unpopulated area. Remember that children should never ride in the front seat of a car equipped with air bags; those ages 3 and younger must be in a child safety seat; and those ages 4 and 5 must either be in a safety seat or booster seat or be wearing a seat belt.

Smoking

Restaurant space and hotel rooms for smokers are evaporating in Orlando. Disney doesn't sell tobacco, and there are precious few "you can smoke here" areas scattered about their hotels (which are now smoke free) and theme parks. And don't expect to light up over dinner: Florida bans smoking in public workplaces, including restaurants and bars that serve food. Stand-alone bars that serve virtually no food and designated smoking rooms in hotels are exempt.

Taxes

Expect to add 11 percent or 12.5 percent to room rates, up to 25 percent on rental cars, and 6.5 percent to 7 percent (the rate depends on the county you happen to be in) on most everything else — except groceries and health supplies or medical services.

Taxis

Yellow Cab (☎ 407-422-2222) and Ace Metro (☎ 407-855-1111) are among the cab companies serving the area. Rates run as high as $3.25 for the first mile, $1.75 per mile or higher thereafter.

Time Zone

Orlando is on eastern standard time from late fall until mid-spring, and on eastern daylight saving time (one hour later) the rest of the year. That means that when both of Mickey's gloved hands are on 12 noon in Orlando, it's 7 a.m. in Honolulu, 8 a.m. in Anchorage, 9 a.m. in Vancouver and Los Angeles, 11 a.m. in Winnipeg and New Orleans, and 5 p.m. in London.

Transit Info

LYNX (☎ 407-841-5969; www.golynx.com) bus stops are marked with a paw print. The buses serve Disney, Universal, and International Drive ($1.75 for adults, 85¢ for seniors and kids enrolled in K–12 with valid school ID), but they're not particularly tourist-friendly. The International Drive area has the I-Ride Trolley (☎ 407-248-9590; www.iride trolley.com). The Main Line and Green Line stops include most of I-Drive, from SeaWorld on the south end to Prime Outlets International on the north. Trolleys run about every 20 minutes with 77 stops along the Main Line, and about every 30 minutes with 26 stops along the Green Line. The I-Ride Trolley runs from 8 a.m. to 10:30 p.m.; the fare is $1 for adults, 25¢ for seniors, free for kids younger than 12 with a paying adult (one-day and multiday passes are also available; exact change is required). It's a good way to avoid I-Drive's dreadfully heavy traffic.

Weather

Call ☎ 321-255-0212 to get forecasts from the National Weather Service. When the phone picks up, punch in 412 from a touch-tone phone, and you'll get the Orlando forecast. Also check the Weather Channel if you have cable television or go to its Web site at www.weather.com.

Toll-Free Numbers and Web Sites

Airlines

Air Canada
☎ 888-247-2262
www.aircanada.ca

AirTran Airways
☎ 800-247-8726
www.airtran.com

Alaska Airlines
☎ 800-426-0333
www.alaskaair.com

American Airlines
☎ 800-433-7300
www.aa.com

America West Airlines
☎ 800-428-4322
www.usairways.com

Continental Airlines
☎ 800-525-0280
www.continental.com

Delta Air Lines
☎ 800-221-1212
www.delta.com

Frontier Airlines
☎ 800-432-1359
www.frontierairlines.com

Hawaiian Airlines
☎ 800-367-5320
www.hawaiianair.com

JetBlue Airlines
☎ 800-538-2583
www.jetblue.com

Northwest Airlines
☎ 800-225-2525
www.nwa.com

Southwest Airlines
☎ 800-435-9792
www.southwest.com

Spirit Airlines
☎ 800-772-7117
www.spiritair.com

United Airlines
☎ 800-241-6522
www.ual.com

US Airways
☎ 800-428-4322
www.usairways.com

Major car rental agencies

Alamo
☎ 800-327-9633
www.alamo.com

Avis
☎ 800-331-1212 in the continental
United States
☎ 800-879-3847 in Canada
www.avis.com

Budget
☎ 800-527-0700
www.budget.com

Dollar
☎ 800-800-4000
www.dollar.com

Enterprise
☎ 800-325-8007
www.enterprise.com

Hertz
☎ 800-654-3131
www.hertz.com

National
☎ 800-227-7368
www.nationalcar.com

Payless
☎ 800-729-5377
www.paylesscarrental.com

Thrifty
☎ 800-367-2277
www.thrifty.com

Major hotel and motel chains

AmeriSuites
☎ 800-833-1516
www.amerisuites.com

Baymont Inn & Suites
☎ 877-229-6668
www.baymontinns.com

Best Western International
☎ 800-780-7234
www.bestwestern.com

Clarion
☎ 877-424-6423
www.choicehotels.com

Comfort Inn
☎ 877-424-6423
www.choicehotels.com

Courtyard by Marriott
☎ 888-236-2427
www.courtyard.com

Days Inn
☎ 800-329-7466
www.daysinn.com

Doubletree
☎ 800-222-8733
www.doubletree.com

Econo Lodge
☎ 877-424-6423
www.choicehotels.com

Embassy Suites
☎ 800-362-2779
www.embassy-suites.com

Fairfield Inn by Marriott
☎ 888-236-2427
www.fairfieldinn.com

Hampton Inn & Suites
☎ 800-426-7866
www.hamptoninn.com

Hilton Hotels
☎ 800-445-8667
www.hilton.com

Holiday Inn
☎ 888-465-4329
www.holidayinn.com

Howard Johnson
☎ 800-446-4656
www.hojo.com

Hyatt Hotels & Resorts
☎ 888-591-1234
www.hyatt.com

La Quinta Inns & Suites
☎ 800-753-3757
www.lq.com

Loews Hotels
☎ 866-563-9792
www.loewshotels.com

Marriott Hotels & Resorts
☎ 888-236-2427
www.marriott.com

Motel 6
☎ 800-466-8356
www.motel6.com

Quality Inn
☎ 877-424-6423
www.choicehotels.com

Radisson Hotels & Resorts
☎ 800-201-1718
www.radisson.com

Ramada
☎ 800-272-6232
www.ramada.com

Red Roof Inn
☎ 800-733-7663
www.redroof.com

Renaissance Hotels & Resorts
☎ 888-236-2427
www.renaissancehotels.com

Residence Inn by Marriott
☎ 800-331-3131
www.residenceinn.com

Sheraton Hotels & Resorts
☎ 800-325-3535
www.sheraton.com

Super 8 Motels
☎ 800-800-8000
www.super8.com

Sleep Inn
☎ 877-424-6423
www.choicehotels.com

Travelodge
☎ 800-578-7878
www.travelodge.com

SpringHill Suites
☎ 888-287-9400
www.marriott.com

Westin Hotels & Resorts
☎ 800-937-8461
www.westin.com

Staybridge Suites
☎ 877-238-8889
www.staybridge.com

Wyndham Hotels & Resorts
☎ 877-999-3223
www.wyndham.com

Where to Get More Information

If you want additional information on attractions, accommodations, or just about anything else that's in Orlando, the city has some excellent sources for tourist information, discounts, maps, and more.

Orlando tourist information offices

The **Orlando/Orange County Convention & Visitors Bureau** can answer your questions regarding area attractions, dining, and accommodations, as well as send you maps and brochures. You should receive your info packet in about three weeks; it includes the **Magicard,** which is good for hundreds of dollars in discounts on accommodations, car rentals, attractions, and more. **Orlando's Official Visitor Center** is located at 8723 International Dr., Ste. 101, Orlando, FL 32819. For information, call ☎ 407-363-5872 (voice — you can talk to a real person!), 800-643-9492, or 800-551-0181 (automated). Or go online to www.orlandoinfo.com.

Get your info straight from the Mouse's mouth. Contact **Walt Disney World,** Box 10000, Lake Buena Vista, FL 32830-1000 (☎ 407-934-7639; www.disneyworld.com), to order vacation brochures and DVDs and get information on all the theme parks, attractions, dining, accommodations, and more.

For information on **Universal Studios Florida, Islands of Adventure,** and **CityWalk,** contact **Universal Orlando,** 1000 Universal Studios Plaza, Orlando, FL 32819 (☎ 407-363-8000; www.universalorlando.com). You can order vacation brochures, including information on restaurants and accommodations.

SeaWorld offers vacation brochures with information on the park, its restaurants, its hotel partners, Discovery Cove (where you can swim with dolphins), and Aquatica, SeaWorld's new eco-themed water park. Write to 7007 SeaWorld Dr., Orlando, FL 32801; call ☎ 407-351-3600; or surf over to www.seaworld.com. For information on **Discovery Cove,** call ☎ 877-434-7268 or head to www.discoverycove.com. For information on **Aquatica,** call ☎ 866-787-4307 or surf over to www.aquatica byseaworld.com.

Get in touch with the **Kissimmee Convention and Visitors Bureau,** 1925 E. Irlo Bronson Hwy./U.S. 192, Kissimmee, FL 34744 (☎ 800-327-9159 or 407-847-5000; www.floridakiss.com), for maps, brochures, coupon books, and a guide to local accommodations and attractions.

Newspapers and magazines

Check out the Sunday travel section in your hometown paper for the latest bargains, ideas, and tips. After you land in O-Town, pick up a copy of the *Orlando Sentinel* (www.orlandosentinel.com) to find out about current events and deals. **Destination Orlando** (www.orlando sentinel.com/travel/destinations/orlando) is the *Sentinel's* online section dedicated to visitors. The paper's CityBeat section (http://orlandocitybeat.metromix.com) is a gold mine for current information on the area's accommodations, restaurants, nightclubs, and attractions, as is the *Orlando Weekly* (www.orlandoweekly.com).

Other sources of information

✔ **Travel Insights Group** (www.travel-insights.com) is a great source of information for families traveling with children. If you're headed to Walt Disney World, Universal Orlando, SeaWorld, or even the coastal areas of Central Florida, the insider travel and theme-park touring tips, hotel and restaurant reviews, and other helpful hints are invaluable for families hoping to survive their vacation and still have fun.

✔ **The local ABC affiliate (WFTV)** offers a Web site (www.icflorida.com) full of information about dining, clubs, performances, theme parks, sports, and special events.

✔ **All Ears Net: Deb's Unofficial Walt Disney World Information Guide** (www.allearsnet.com) is an excellent information source and arguably the best unofficial Disney guide on the Internet. Though Disney doesn't own it, it's run and written by true-blue fans of Mickey, so although it's not entirely objective (and you should take that into consideration when looking at the tips it offers), the information is extremely detailed and up to date. There are also sections aimed at travelers with special needs that include good tips for touring the Disney parks if you're physically challenged or elderly, or if you have kids in tow.

✔ *Frommer's Walt Disney World & Orlando with Kids,* by Laura Lea Miller, has lots of tips and advice for those traveling with children ages 2 to 16, while *Frommer's Irreverent Guide to Walt Disney World,* by Chris Mohney, is a fun-filled guide aimed at singles and couples. (Both books are published by Wiley Publishing, Inc.)

Index

• *T* •

• Y •

• Z •

BUSINESS, CAREERS & PERSONAL FINANCE

Accounting For Dummies, 4th Edition*
978-0-470-24600-9

Bookkeeping Workbook For Dummies†
978-0-470-16983-4

Commodities For Dummies
978-0-470-04928-0

Doing Business in China For Dummies
978-0-470-04929-7

E-Mail Marketing For Dummies
978-0-470-19087-6

Job Interviews For Dummies, 3rd Edition*†
978-0-470-17748-8

Personal Finance Workbook For Dummies*†
978-0-470-09933-9

Real Estate License Exams For Dummies
978-0-7645-7623-2

Six Sigma For Dummies
978-0-7645-6798-8

Small Business Kit For Dummies, 2nd Edition*†
978-0-7645-5984-6

Telephone Sales For Dummies
978-0-470-16836-3

BUSINESS PRODUCTIVITY & MICROSOFT OFFICE

Access 2007 For Dummies
978-0-470-03649-5

Excel 2007 For Dummies
978-0-470-03737-9

Office 2007 For Dummies
978-0-470-00923-9

Outlook 2007 For Dummies
978-0-470-03830-7

PowerPoint 2007 For Dummies
978-0-470-04059-1

Project 2007 For Dummies
978-0-470-03651-8

QuickBooks 2008 For Dummies
978-0-470-18470-7

Quicken 2008 For Dummies
978-0-470-17473-9

Salesforce.com For Dummies, 2nd Edition
978-0-470-04893-1

Word 2007 For Dummies
978-0-470-03658-7

EDUCATION, HISTORY, REFERENCE & TEST PREPARATION

African American History For Dummies
978-0-7645-5469-8

Algebra For Dummies
978-0-7645-5325-7

Algebra Workbook For Dummies
978-0-7645-8467-1

Art History For Dummies
978-0-470-09910-0

ASVAB For Dummies, 2nd Edition
978-0-470-10671-6

British Military History For Dummies
978-0-470-03213-8

Calculus For Dummies
978-0-7645-2498-1

Canadian History For Dummies, 2nd Edition
978-0-470-83656-9

Geometry Workbook For Dummies
978-0-471-79940-5

The SAT I For Dummies, 6th Edition
978-0-7645-7193-0

Series 7 Exam For Dummies
978-0-470-09932-2

World History For Dummies
978-0-7645-5242-7

FOOD, GARDEN, HOBBIES & HOME

Bridge For Dummies, 2nd Edition
978-0-471-92426-5

Coin Collecting For Dummies, 2nd Edition
978-0-470-22275-1

Cooking Basics For Dummies, 3rd Edition
978-0-7645-7206-7

Drawing For Dummies
978-0-7645-5476-6

Etiquette For Dummies, 2nd Edition
978-0-470-10672-3

Gardening Basics For Dummies*†
978-0-470-03749-2

Knitting Patterns For Dummies
978-0-470-04556-5

Living Gluten-Free For Dummies†
978-0-471-77383-2

Painting Do-It-Yourself For Dummies
978-0-470-17533-0

HEALTH, SELF HELP, PARENTING & PETS

Anger Management For Dummies
978-0-470-03715-7

Anxiety & Depression Workbook For Dummies
978-0-7645-9793-0

Dieting For Dummies, 2nd Edition
978-0-7645-4149-0

Dog Training For Dummies, 2nd Edition
978-0-7645-8418-3

Horseback Riding For Dummies
978-0-470-09719-9

Infertility For Dummies†
978-0-470-11518-3

Meditation For Dummies with CD-ROM, 2nd Edition
978-0-471-77774-8

Post-Traumatic Stress Disorder For Dummies
978-0-470-04922-8

Puppies For Dummies, 2nd Edition
978-0-470-03717-1

Thyroid For Dummies, 2nd Edition†
978-0-471-78755-6

Type 1 Diabetes For Dummies*†
978-0-470-17811-9

---

* Separate Canadian edition also available
† Separate U.K. edition also available

INTERNET & DIGITAL MEDIA

AdWords For Dummies
978-0-470-15252-2

Blogging For Dummies, 2nd Edition
978-0-470-23017-6

**Digital Photography All-in-One
Desk Reference For Dummies, 3rd Edition**
978-0-470-03743-0

Digital Photography For Dummies, 5th Edition
978-0-7645-9802-9

**Digital SLR Cameras & Photography
For Dummies, 2nd Edition**
978-0-470-14927-0

**eBay Business All-in-One Desk Reference
For Dummies**
978-0-7645-8438-1

eBay For Dummies, 5th Edition*
978-0-470-04529-9

eBay Listings That Sell For Dummies
978-0-471-78912-3

Facebook For Dummies
978-0-470-26273-3

The Internet For Dummies, 11th Edition
978-0-470-12174-0

Investing Online For Dummies, 5th Edition
978-0-7645-8456-5

iPod & iTunes For Dummies, 5th Edition
978-0-470-17474-6

MySpace For Dummies
978-0-470-09529-4

Podcasting For Dummies
978-0-471-74898-4

**Search Engine Optimization
For Dummies, 2nd Edition**
978-0-471-97998-2

Second Life For Dummies
978-0-470-18025-9

**Starting an eBay Business For Dummies,
3rd Edition†**
978-0-470-14924-9

GRAPHICS, DESIGN & WEB DEVELOPMENT

**Adobe Creative Suite 3 Design Premium
All-in-One Desk Reference For Dummies**
978-0-470-11724-8

**Adobe Web Suite CS3 All-in-One Desk
Reference For Dummies**
978-0-470-12099-6

AutoCAD 2008 For Dummies
978-0-470-11650-0

**Building a Web Site For Dummies,
3rd Edition**
978-0-470-14928-7

**Creating Web Pages All-in-One Desk
Reference For Dummies, 3rd Edition**
978-0-470-09629-1

**Creating Web Pages For Dummies,
8th Edition**
978-0-470-08030-6

Dreamweaver CS3 For Dummies
978-0-470-11490-2

Flash CS3 For Dummies
978-0-470-12100-9

Google SketchUp For Dummies
978-0-470-13744-4

InDesign CS3 For Dummies
978-0-470-11865-8

**Photoshop CS3 All-in-One
Desk Reference For Dummies**
978-0-470-11195-6

Photoshop CS3 For Dummies
978-0-470-11193-2

Photoshop Elements 5 For Dummies
978-0-470-09810-3

SolidWorks For Dummies
978-0-7645-9555-4

Visio 2007 For Dummies
978-0-470-08983-5

Web Design For Dummies, 2nd Edition
978-0-471-78117-2

Web Sites Do-It-Yourself For Dummies
978-0-470-16903-2

Web Stores Do-It-Yourself For Dummies
978-0-470-17443-2

LANGUAGES, RELIGION & SPIRITUALITY

Arabic For Dummies
978-0-471-77270-5

Chinese For Dummies, Audio Set
978-0-470-12766-7

French For Dummies
978-0-7645-5193-2

German For Dummies
978-0-7645-5195-6

Hebrew For Dummies
978-0-7645-5489-6

Ingles Para Dummies
978-0-7645-5427-8

Italian For Dummies, Audio Set
978-0-470-09586-7

Italian Verbs For Dummies
978-0-471-77389-4

Japanese For Dummies
978-0-7645-5429-2

Latin For Dummies
978-0-7645-5431-5

Portuguese For Dummies
978-0-471-78738-9

Russian For Dummies
978-0-471-78001-4

Spanish Phrases For Dummies
978-0-7645-7204-3

Spanish For Dummies
978-0-7645-5194-9

Spanish For Dummies, Audio Set
978-0-470-09585-0

The Bible For Dummies
978-0-7645-5296-0

Catholicism For Dummies
978-0-7645-5391-2

The Historical Jesus For Dummies
978-0-470-16785-4

Islam For Dummies
978-0-7645-5503-9

**Spirituality For Dummies,
2nd Edition**
978-0-470-19142-2

NETWORKING AND PROGRAMMING

ASP.NET 3.5 For Dummies
978-0-470-19592-5

C# 2008 For Dummies
978-0-470-19109-5

Hacking For Dummies, 2nd Edition
978-0-470-05235-8

Home Networking For Dummies, 4th Edition
978-0-470-11806-1

Java For Dummies, 4th Edition
978-0-470-08716-9

**Microsoft® SQL Server™ 2008 All-in-One
Desk Reference For Dummies**
978-0-470-17954-3

**Networking All-in-One Desk Reference
For Dummies, 2nd Edition**
978-0-7645-9939-2

**Networking For Dummies,
8th Edition**
978-0-470-05620-2

SharePoint 2007 For Dummies
978-0-470-09941-4

**Wireless Home Networking
For Dummies, 2nd Edition**
978-0-471-74940-0

FOR

DUMMIES®

The fun and easy way™ to travel!

U.S.A.

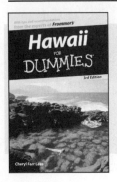

with tips and recommendations from the experts at Frommer's

Hawaii
FOR
DUMMIES
3rd Edition

Cheryl Farr Leas

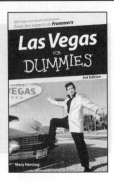

with tips and recommendations from the experts at Frommer's

Las Vegas
FOR
DUMMIES
3rd Edition

Mary Herczog

Also available:
Alaska For Dummies
Arizona For Dummies
Boston For Dummies
California For Dummies
Chicago For Dummies
Colorado & the Rockies For Dummies
Florida For Dummies
Los Angeles & Disneyland For Dummies
Maui For Dummies
National Parks of the American West For Dummies

New Orleans For Dummies
New York City For Dummies
San Francisco For Dummies
Seattle & the Olympic Peninsula For Dummies
Washington, D.C. For Dummies
RV Vacations For Dummies
Walt Disney World & Orlando For Dummies

EUROPE

With tips and recommendations from the experts at Frommer's

Italy
FOR
DUMMIES
3rd Edition

The fun and easy way™ to travel!
FREE daily eTips at dummies.com

France
FOR
DUMMIES
1st Edition

A Travel Guide for the Rest of Us!

Also available:
England For Dummies
Europe For Dummies
Germany For Dummies
Ireland For Dummies
London For Dummies

Paris For Dummies
Scotland For Dummies
Spain For Dummies

OTHER DESTINATIONS

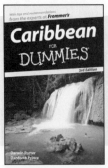

with tips and recommendations from the experts at Frommer's

Caribbean
FOR
DUMMIES
3rd Edition

Darwin Porter
Danforth Prince

with tips and recommendations from the experts at Frommer's

Cruise Vacations
FOR
DUMMIES
2005

Fran Wenograd Golden
& Jerry Brown

Also available:
Bahamas For Dummies
Cancun & the Yucatan For Dummies
Costa Rica For Dummies
Mexico's Beach Resorts For Dummies
Montreal & Quebec City For Dummies
Vancouver & Victoria For Dummies

Available wherever books are sold.
Go to www.dummies.com or call 1-877-762-2974 to order direct.

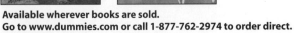

WILEY

Good for Grown-Ups

ACCOMMODATIONS

Buena Vista Palace Hotel & Spa (p. 100)
Celebration Hotel (p. 101)
Courtyard at Lake Lucerne (p. 103)
Crowne Plaza Orlando–Universal (p. 103)
Disney's Coronado Springs Resort (p. 107)
Disney's Grand Floridian Resort & Spa (p. 108)
Ginn Reunion Resort (p. 114)
Grand Bohemian Hotel (p. 115)
Hyatt Regency Grand Cypress (p. 117)
Orlando World Center Marriott (p. 120)
Peabody Orlando (p. 121)
Portofino Bay Hotel (p. 121)
Renaissance Orlando Resort at SeaWorld (p. 122)
Ritz-Carlton Orlando, Grande Lakes (p. 122)
Veranda Bed & Breakfast (p. 124)

RESTAURANTS

Bice Ristorante (p. 137)
California Grill (p. 139)
Christini's (p. 139)
Citricos (p. 140)
Dux (p. 142)
Emeril's Orlando (p. 144)
Emeril's Tchoup Chop (p. 144)
Hemingway's (p. 145)
Il Mulino New York Trattoria (p. 146)
Jimmy Buffett's Margaritaville (p. 147)
Manuel's on the 28th (p. 150)
Marrakesh (p. 150)
Samba Room (p. 155)
Todd English's bluezoo (p. 157)
Victoria & Albert's (p. 157)

THEME PARK ATTRACTIONS

Magic Kingdom
Hall of Presidents (p. 193)
SpectroMagic (p. 199)

Disney's Hollywood Studios
The Great Movie Ride (p. 225)
Indiana Jones Epic Stunt Spectacular! (p. 222)
Muppet Vision 3-D (p. 223)
Rock 'n' Roller Coaster (p. 225)
The Twilight Zone Tower of Terror (p. 227)

Animal Kingdom
Expedition Everest (p. 239)
Kilimanjaro Safaris (p. 237)
Maharajah Jungle Trek (p. 240)

Universal Studios Florida
Men in Black: Alien Attack (p. 277)
Revenge of the Mummy (p. 272)
Shrek 4-D (p. 274)
Terminator 2: 3-D Battle Across Time (p. 272)

SeaWorld
Believe (p. 300)
Journey to Atlantis (p. 301)
Kraken (p. 302)
Marine Mammal Keeper Experience (p. 302)

MISCELLANEOUS

Cirque du Soleil (p. 342)
CityWalk (p. 346)
Richard Petty Driving Experience (p. 245)

Some may find it hard to believe, but Orlando is the top honeymoon destination in the country. The city is exceptionally receptive to small fries, so finding some calm inside the kiddie storm can be quite the challenge. You can't really avoid kids here as a rule, but here's a handy checklist of hotels, restaurants, and selected attractions that offer special appeal to adults.

Tip: Of all the theme parks in the city, Disney's Epcot (Chapter 13), Universal's Islands of Adventure (Chapter 19), and SeaWorld's Discovery Cove (Chapter 20) are the best for adults.

Walt Disney World & Orlando For Dummies, 2009 Edition

Cheat Sheet

Hidden Mickey Checklist

Started as an inside joke among Disney Imagineers, Hidden Mickeys (a.k.a. HMs) are now a Disney tradition. Today, dozens of subtle Mickey images—usually silhouettes of his world-famous ears, profile, or full figure—are hidden (more or less) in attractions and resorts throughout the Walt Disney empire. Many are strictly in the eye of the beholder, but discover a new one that's accepted into the pantheon by HM watchers and you're a made mouse. Here's a quick checklist to start you off on your HM treasure hunt through the World.

In the Magic Kingdom

🔎 In the Haunted Mansion banquet scene, check out the arrangement of the plate and adjoining saucers on the table.

🔎 In the Africa scene of It's a Small World, note the purple flowers on a vine on the elephant's left side.

🔎 While riding Splash Mountain, look for Mickey lying on his back in the pink clouds to the right of the Zip-A-Dee Lady paddlewheeler.

🔎 Take a good look at the French horn on the right side of the stage at Mickey's PhilHarMagic.

★ ★ ★ ★ ★ ★ ★ ★ ★ ★ ★ ★ ★ ★ ★ ★ ★ ★

At Epcot

🔎 In Journey Into Imagination, check out the little girl's dress in the lobby film of Honey, I Shrunk the Audience, one of five HMs in this pavilion.

🔎 In The Land pavilion, don't miss the small stones in front of the Native American man on a horse and the baseball cap of the man driving a harvester in the Circle of Life film.

🔎 As you cruise through the Mexico pavilion on El Rio del Tiempo, notice the arrangement of three clay pots in the marketplace scene.

🔎 In Maelstrom in the Norway pavilion, a Viking wears Mickey ears in the wall mural facing the loading dock.

🔎 There are four HMs inside Spaceship Earth, one of them in the Renaissance scene, on the page of a book behind the sleeping monk. It's up to you to spot the other three.

★ ★ ★ ★ ★ ★ ★ ★ ★ ★ ★ ★ ★ ★ ★ ★ ★ ★

At Disney's Hollywood Studios

🔎 At Jim Henson's Muppet*Vision 3D, take a good look at the top of the sign listing five reasons for turning in your 3-D glasses, and note the balloons in the film's final scene.

🔎 In the Twilight Zone Tower of Terror, note the bell for the elevator behind Rod Serling in the film. There are more than 8 HMs in this attraction.

🔎 By the way, the park's least Hidden Mickey is...itself. Yep. That's right. When viewed from the sky, the entire park is one giant Hidden Mickey.

★ ★ ★ ★ ★ ★ ★ ★ ★ ★ ★ ★ ★ ★ ★ ★ ★ ★

In Animal Kingdom

🔎 Look at The Boneyard in DinoLand U.S.A., where a fan and two hard hats form an HM.

🔎 There are 25 Hidden Mickeys at Rafiki's Planet Watch, where Mickey lurks in the murals, tree trunks, and paintings of animals.

★ ★ ★ ★ ★ ★ ★ ★ ★ ★ ★ ★ ★ ★ ★ ★ ★ ★

In the Resort Areas

🔎 HMs are on the weather vane atop the Grand Floridian Resort & Spa's convention center and one forms a giant sand trap next to the green at the Magnolia Golf Course's 6th hole.

Found all of these HMs? Good for you. But these are just the tip of the mouse's tail. For more HMs—or to report your own brand-new sighting—check out www.hiddenmickeys.org.